CANADA
in the World

CANADA
in the World

Internationalism in Canadian Foreign Policy

Edited by **Heather A. Smith** and **Claire Turenne Sjolander**

OXFORD
UNIVERSITY PRESS

OXFORD
UNIVERSITY PRESS

Oxford University Press is a department of the University of Oxford.
It furthers the University's objective of excellence in research, scholarship,
and education by publishing worldwide. Oxford is a registered trade mark of
Oxford University Press in the UK and in certain other countries.

Published in Canada by
Oxford University Press
8 Sampson Mews, Suite 204,
Don Mills, Ontario M3C 0H5 Canada

www.oupcanada.com

Copyright © Oxford University Press Canada 2013

Library and Archives Canada Cataloguing in Publication

Canada in the world : internationalism in Canadian foreign
policy / edited by Heather A. Smith & Claire Turenne Sjolander.

Includes bibliographical references and index.
ISBN 978–0–19–544369–1

1. Canada—Foreign relations—1945–. 2. Canada—Foreign relations—
21st century. 3. Internationalism. I. Smith, Heather A. (Heather Ann), 1964–
II. Sjolander, Claire Dorothy Turenne, 1959–

FC242.C367 2012   327.71009'045   C2012-904757-0

Cover image: Mike Bentley/iStockphoto

Oxford University Press is committed to our environment.
This book is printed on Forest Stewardship Council® certified paper
and comes from responsible sources.

Printed and bound in Canada
1 2 3 4 — 16 15 14 13

To the children in our lives

Mark and Andrew

Alison and William

Maya, Henri, and Emily

Contents

PART II   INTERNATIONALISM FROM THE OUTSIDE

Acknowledgements

All writing projects are a journey, sometimes together and sometimes alone. The idea for this volume was first tested at the International Studies Association meeting in New York City in 2009 and then in four linked panels at the Canadian Political Science Association annual meeting in Ottawa in 2009. Since that time, we have discussed or worked on this volume in New Orleans, in Montreal, in Waterloo, in San Diego, in northern Denmark, in a lovely garden in Paris, and in the solitude of our respective homes in Prince George and Ottawa. Together with our chapter authors, we have created a volume of which we are very proud.

In 2006, Stephen Harper came to power as Canada's twenty-second prime minister. Almost as soon as he took the oath of office, public commentators began to question whether or not this new government would be faithful to Canada's foreign policy traditions—whether the much-vaunted Canadian "internationalism" would survive. In our wish to unpack this question, one of the challenges we set for ourselves in putting together this volume was to resist offering a definitive view on the meaning of internationalism. We encouraged authors to determine what internationalism meant to them. As a result of freeing the authors from an editorially prescribed definition, we have a volume that is testimony to the contested nature of the concept of internationalism—a concept so often taken as given.

To our authors, we owe our heartfelt thanks. Your continued support for this project has sustained us as editors. We cannot tell you how much we appreciate being part of a community of scholars, and indeed, a community of friends, who have lent their voices to this volume. The insights in the pages that follow are thanks to your hard work.

We would also like to thank Oxford University Press—and particularly Patricia Simoes—for its faith in and enthusiasm for this project. The comments from our reviewers and from the press challenged us to reflect on our analysis and ultimately enhanced the quality of the volume. We appreciate the time and effort taken by both Patricia and the three anonymous reviewers. Our copy editor, Judith Turnbull, was patient, precise, and a delight to work with. Thanks so very much, Judith!

Heather: I want to begin by acknowledging the financial support of the Social Sciences and Humanities Research Council and the University of Northern British Columbia, which meant that all the work for this book was not done solo, but rather at times in the company of my co-editor and the wonderful chapter authors. And while the life of an academic is often solitary, the support of my family and friends ensures that I never really travel alone. To the awesome women of RPGRG, the Wilson sisters, Deb, Kath, Gwennie, and a host of others, I say thank you. You kept me grounded in the midst of it all. Mom, Dad, Moe, Ross—there are not enough words of thanks to express my gratitude for your continued support. And Will and Ali—you teach me about joy. Finally, to my co-editor and dear friend, Claire: I'm happy to be the Oscar to your Felix anytime.

Claire: The University of Ottawa has always provided me with a rich intellectual environment and the support of wonderful colleagues, whether at the School of Political Studies, at the Institute of Women's Studies, or at the Faculty of Social Sciences. As this book project evolved and the manuscript came together, I was active in all three places within the university and have found a home in each. The Faculty of Social Sciences has always been generous to me in my various administrative roles and in supporting my research, and it deserves my appreciation and thanks. Ashley Bickerton has been my tireless research assistant for over two years, and both Heather and I are grateful for her assistance in taking care of the logistics of the manuscript preparation. Michael, Christine, Ivaylo, Miguel, and Caroline—my days are brighter for the time we spend together over coffees and lunches. To my family—especially to my parents—I owe thanks for unfailing support, not to mention the Sunday dinners that get me out of the house and away from my work. Mark and Andrew—you make me smile always, and that is a gift. Stefan—your support gives me strength in so many ways—thank you. Finally, to my co-editor and dear friend, Heather! I owe you a Cosmo—for everything.

Heather Smith, Prince George
Claire Turenne Sjolander, Ottawa
May 2012

Contributors

David R. Black is professor of Political Science and International Development Studies and director of the Centre for Foreign Policy Studies at Dalhousie University.

Jean-Christophe Boucher is assistant professor of Political Science at Dalhousie University.

Krystel Carrier is a Ph.D. student in the War Studies program at the Royal Military College of Canada. She is also a recipient of the SSHRC (Social Sciences and Humanities Research Council) Joseph-Armand Bombardier Canada Graduate Scholarship Doctoral Award.

Daryl Copeland is visiting professor at the University of East Anglia's London Academy of Diplomacy, and research associate at the Centre for International Policy Studies at the University of Ottawa. From 1981 to 2009, he served as a Canadian diplomat.

Paul Gecelovsky is assistant professor in the Department of Political Science at the University of Western Ontario.

Veronica M. Kitchen is associate professor of Political Science in the Balsillie School of International Affairs at the University of Waterloo.

Andrew Lui is assistant professor in the Department of Political Science at McMaster University.

Justin Massie is assistant professor at the Graduate School of Public and International Affairs at the University of Ottawa.

Kim Richard Nossal is Sir Edward Peacock Professor of International Relations and director of the Centre for International and Defence Policy at Queen's University.

Stéphane Roussel is professor of Canadian foreign and defence policy at l'École nationale d'administration publique (ÉNAP) in Montreal.

Mark B. Salter is professor of Political Science at the School of Political Studies at the University of Ottawa.

Anita Singh is a SSHRC post-doctoral fellow at the Munk School of Global Affairs at the University of Toronto.

Claire Turenne Sjolander is professor of Political Science at the School of Political Studies and vice-dean of Graduate Studies in the Faculty of Social Sciences at the University of Ottawa. She is the recipient of the University of Ottawa's Excellence in Education Award for 2008–9 and the International Studies Association's Distinguished Scholar Award for 2012.

Heather A. Smith is professor of International Studies in the Department of International Studies at the University of Northern British Columbia. She is a 3M National Teaching Fellow (2006) and a two-time UNBC Teaching Excellence Award winner.

Rebecca Tiessen is associate professor of Military Psychology and Leadership at the Royal Military College of Canada, and currently holds the Canada Research Chair in Global Studies and Leadership.

INTRODUCTION

Conversations without Consensus — Internationalism under the Harper Government

Heather A. Smith and Claire Turenne Sjolander

Prime Minister Stephen Harper has rejected the long tradition of internationalism, diplomacy, multilateralism and peacekeeping that has defined Canada's role in the international community since the end of the Second World War. . . .

. . . [T]he Harper government . . . continues to erase from its memory Canada's storied history as a force of moral good and peacemaker within the international community. (Fulton, 2006: 17)

Former Conservative prime minister Joe Clark recently accused Mr. Harper of turning his back on a six-decade tradition of "effective internationalism." Liberal foreign affairs critic Bob Rae says we have lost the sense of humanitarian leadership we once had. (Ivison, 2007: 1)

[W]hat we—and the rest of the world—get is empty posturing and crassly self-serving rhetoric from political leaders who seem to have no shame about using Canadian soldiers as pawns and photo ops while paying lip service to the ideals of internationalism. ("Afghan Mission," 2007: 10)

Canada has a proud history of internationalism. That tradition would be well-served by this country assuming a bigger role in the global war against poverty and AIDS. ("Buttress . . . " 2006: 20)

Within months of the Conservative Party led by Stephen Harper coming to office, cries that "Canada's new government" was betraying Canada's internationalist past were being heard and repeated. While hardly the only public commentary suggesting a similar turn in Canadian foreign policy, Linda McQuaig's populist condemnation of the Harper government, *Holding the Bully's Coat: Canada and the U.S. Empire* (2007), heralded the death of Canadian internationalism. Full of praise for Lester B. Pearson's contributions to developing United Nations peacekeeping and for Lloyd Axworthy's land mines treaty,

McQuaig condemned the Harper government for "enabling a regime [the Bush administration in Washington, DC] that is considered by many around the world to be the major obstacle to peace and security" (2007: 1). Far from being a nation that had championed internationalism, the United Nations, and UN peace-keeping, Canada under Stephen Harper's government was painted by McQuaig as being an obstacle to the very peaceable outcomes it once advocated as the most committed internationalist on the world stage.

This volume finds its origins in the discussions about whether or not—or the extent to which—the election of Stephen Harper's Conservative government in 2006 marked a fundamental shift in Canadian foreign policy. Would this now truly be the end of liberal internationalism?[1] Did the election of the Conservatives mark a new era in Canadian foreign policy? Were the contentions of—and concerns about—this emerging new era legitimate or overstated? If there was to be a new era in foreign policy, would it be defined by a new overarching idea to replace the idea of internationalism? If so, what would this new idea be, how would it be different from internationalism, and, if different, how could that difference be explained?

Despite suggestions that the election of the Harper government had trans-lated into a rejection of Canadian internationalism, the idea of internationalism remained—and arguably remains—a prevalent one, at least in our classrooms. As such, the volume was also motivated by the contrast between the outcry of the punditry as to internationalism's demise and the tenacity with which our students embraced such a mythical (?) internationalist representation of Canada's role and place on the world stage. We were struck by how our students were astounded and often shocked by the classroom discussion of foreign policy realities—such as the significantly diminished participation of Canada in UN peacekeeping missions over the past two decades—that clashed with their firmly entrenched internationalist worldviews. Our students seemed to embrace a nostalgic image of Canada—the helpful fixer, the peacekeeper, the altruistic good international citizen. In addition to their inevitable surprise over the decline in Canada's peacekeeping commit-ments, they also seemed astonished that Canada's role in Afghanistan was, until very recently, primarily a combat one, that Canada was and is an international environmental laggard, and that its foreign aid budgets had diminished steadily over the years—all well in advance of the election of Stephen Harper.

The declaration of the death of internationalism as well as its tenacity in the minds of our students leads us to ask about the resilience of the idea (and ideal?) of internationalism in the Canadian imaginary. After all, the rhetorical use of in-ternationalist tropes by the previous Liberal governments had served to obfus-cate practices and policies that were less than internationalist, despite the fact that they were still deployed (Black, 2009; Smith, 2009; Turenne Sjolander, 2009). Internationalism was consistently used for strategic purposes by these Canadian governments as a means of fostering domestic support for their foreign policies while simultaneously deflecting criticism. Would internationalism play the same role under the Harper government; would it be used rhetorically to build sup-port for policy even if the content of the policies themselves revealed little of the internationalist orientations of old? If internationalism can be used to justify policies that seem to deviate from internationalist ideals, at least as they are interpreted in the Canadian imaginary, what is Canadian internationalism? What does internationalism mean?

These questions motivate us as editors and motivate the authors of this volume. The authors here assembled are drawn from a variety of theoretical perspectives, career experiences, regions, and areas of policy interest. As editors, we did not prescribe any working definition of internationalism. We did not ask authors to address or debate the merits or limitations of a particular definition of internationalism. We did not require the authors to return to historical interpretations of internationalism. Rather, we asked the authors to come to the question in their own way, to address the ideas and practices of internationalism from their varied perspectives. As such, we hoped to build the foundation for a conversation between and among authors whose theoretical orientations reflect the diversity of the field. To facilitate this conversation, we did ask the authors to think about whether or not their understanding of internationalism had somehow changed—in rhetoric or practice—since the Harper government came to power, at least in the policy area their chapter was addressing. If they concluded that a change had taken place, we asked that they reflect upon how and why that change might have occurred. Finally, we asked the authors to reflect on what their analyses of internationalism told us about Canada in the contemporary world.

The intended absence of a common theoretical framework or definition of internationalism allowed our authors the full range of interpretation and resulted in chapters that are both engaging and, at times, surprising. These chapters provide us with unique, compelling, and theoretically original interpretations of Canada in the world through the prism of multi-faceted understandings of internationalism. As readers will note, these chapters provide competing understandings of what constitutes internationalism, competing interpretations of the relevance of internationalism to current policy practices, and quite dramatically different interpretations of the analytical value of the construct of internationalism itself.

Despite—and more likely, precisely because of—this lack of a predetermined central theoretical framework or a prescribed definition of internationalism, the contributions to this volume quite naturally engage in a dialogue with one another on a variety of themes, and it is the varied perspectives on these themes that frame the conversations in this volume. These conversations touch on the current relevance of internationalism for the practice and analysis of Canadian foreign policy (whether or not internationalism is in decline or has been abandoned by the Harper government), the prospects for the emergence of a new dominant idea framing Canada's foreign policy, the influence of domestic sources of foreign policy on the discursive use and political practice of internationalism, as well as the way in which a focus on domestic sources of foreign policy can open the door to a deeper problematization of the foreign/domestic divide.

Given that we asked authors to assess the relevance of internationalism and whether or not it had changed in discourse or practice under the Harper government, it should come as no surprise that one of the key themes in the volume addresses the current state and characteristics of internationalism. The evaluations put forward by the authors reveal little in the way of consensus, however; internationalist rhetoric and practice seem to vary depending on specific policy areas and the interplay between domestic and political factors.

Several of the authors in this volume (Nossal, Massie and Roussel, Boucher, Copeland, and Lui) argue that *liberal* internationalism is in decline or has been abandoned altogether and that this is particularly clear in the Harper era. For these authors, internationalism has historically been associated with explicitly liberal values (such as peace, freedom, justice, and democracy) often promoted and promulgated by Liberal governments. In order to make their persuasive "declinist" arguments, each of the authors begins with a starting point or benchmark, for each needs to identify the point from which internationalism has declined. Despite the lack of an imposed common definition of internationalism, several authors in the volume adopt a variation of the definition drawn from Kim Richard Nossal, Stéphane Roussel, and Stéphane Paquin's 2011 *International Policy and Politics in Canada* or from one of Nossal's other works. The use of these definitions allows the authors to point to the areas where the Harper government's foreign policy appears to deviate from internationalist practice or internationalist ideals. And while authors such as Daryl Copeland deploy other benchmark definitions in providing their own list of the characteristics of internationalism, all the authors who are engaged in the declinist/abandonment conversation provide us with clear guidelines of what they believe constituted liberal internationalism under previous administrations.

Consistent with these assessments of the state or health of internationalism as a guiding framework or dominant idea in Canadian foreign policy, some of the contributors to this volume identify the origins of the decline of internationalism with the Liberal government of Jean Chrétien. Described elsewhere as an era of "internationalism lite" (Nossal, Roussel, and Paquin, 2011: 143), it is with the Chrétien government rather than with the current Conservative government that authors such as Kim Richard Nossal, Justin Massie, and Stéphane Roussel associate the preliminary dismantling of the liberal internationalist tradition. For his part, Daryl Copeland describes liberal internationalism as making its last gasp during the Chrétien era, thus situating the origins of the internationalist decline in an earlier period. In contrast, Andrew Lui and Jean-Christophe Boucher both associate the decline of the liberal internationalist tradition primarily with the strategic choices made by the Harper government.

While evidence of the decline or abandonment of liberal internationalism makes up a central theme in this volume, it is not the only interpretation offered to readers. David Black assesses the decline of *humane*, rather than liberal, internationalism in his contribution. The chapter by Claire Turenne Sjolander, while pointing to some of the assumptions concealed in the use of such internationalist discourse, provides evidence that internationalist rhetoric is alive and well in the speeches and statements of Prime Minister Harper addressing Canada's mission in Afghanistan. Veronica Kitchen examines the practices of actors not often considered in discussions of internationalism, such as sub-national governments and transnational actors. In her chapter on the Arctic and climate change, Heather Smith critiques the hidden assumptions of internationalism as an analytical tool without even engaging in the debate about the currency of internationalism under the Harper Conservative government. Mark Salter, as well as Krystel Carrier and Rebecca Tiessen, rejects internationalism as an analytical concept; instead these authors draw upon international political sociology and gender analysis to frame their respective analyses. Consequently, while the decline or abandonment of internationalism may be a dominant theme in this volume, it is a contested theme and reveals contested approaches to the understanding and interpretation of Canadian foreign policy.

Given that several of the authors argue that internationalism has been abandoned, is in decline, or has somehow changed, an obvious question arises: what next? Is a new dominant idea framing Canada's foreign policy on the rise? If not internationalism, what is the future direction of Canadian foreign policy likely to be? Just as was the case with the chapters assessing the current state of internationalism, there is no consensus among the chapters on what the future will look like. Kim Richard Nossal argues that no new dominant foreign policy idea is emerging from the Harper government to replace internationalism; rather, the foreign policy of the current government is primarily driven by the desire to promote a domestic partisan agenda. In contrast, Justin Massie and Stéphane Roussel argue that the seeds of a new dominant idea can be seen in the emergence of neocontinentalism, while Jean-Christophe Boucher argues that there has been a shift from liberal to realist internationalism. Daryl Copeland calls for the emergence of some form of post-Pearsonian internationalism, and Paul Gecelovsky identifies the emergence of an evangelical Christian internationalism of personal responsibility. For his part, David Black seems to see (and lament) a future without humane internationalism, yet Anita Singh applauds the shift away from neo-hegemonic internationalism and sees opportunities for continued improvement in Indo-Canadian relations. Andrew Lui's assessment of the future of Sino-Canadian relations is not so positive.

The diversity of assessments of the role, function, presence, decline, abandonment, and future of liberal internationalism under the Conservative government reminds us, as several of the volume's contributors do, that internationalism is a slippery analytical concept that is and has been subject to multiple interpretations. The analytical elasticity of the concept could be grounds for some to dispense with or abandon the concept altogether, arguing that it provides little analytical guidance. For us, however, the multiple interpretations of internationalism are reminders to not take central ideas for granted, as has too often been the case with the concept of internationalism in the study of Canadian foreign policy. We must, as Cynthia Enloe (2004) reminds us, remain curious about ideas that are protected by labels such as "traditional" or "classic" or "natural." Concepts espoused to be at the core of the discipline or at the heart of what Canada is in the world need to be questioned. We may use different starting points and we may come to different conclusions, but if we don't remain curious about concepts such as internationalism, what then do we become as scholars of Canadian foreign policy?

A third theme that is found in many of the chapters concerns the influence of domestic sources of foreign policy and the way in which we problematize the foreign/domestic divide. Regardless of whether an author in this volume argues that internationalism is in decline, has been abandoned, has been mutated, or still has some sort of currency as a discursive frame, almost all authors point to the domestic sphere as an important source explanation. These domestic sources are governmental, societal, or a combination of both. For example, in his assessment of the emergence of an evangelical Christian-inspired variant of internationalism, Paul Gecelovsky identifies both influential Christian organizations and the personal views of Prime Minister Harper as sources of this shift. Justin Massie and Stéphane Roussel argue that the sources of the emerging rival dominant idea of neocontinentialism can be found in part in the values adopted by our current political leaders and the growth of neoconservatism as an ideology in Canada. The values adopted by current political leaders are also used to explain the chilled relations between Canada and China (Lui) and the regressive Conservative policies on maternal and child health (Carrier and Tiessen). Anita Singh highlights the importance of the Indo-Canadian community in shaping the improved relations between Canada and India. Political partisanship and a desire to break fundamentally with the (partisan) Liberal past are the reasons for the abandonment of liberal internationalism, according to Kim Richard Nossal. Daryl Copeland points to a combination of governmental and societal sources for the abandonment of internationalism. Focusing on the decline of humane internationalism, David Black points to domestic sources as explanatory variables. Both Copeland and Black, for example, link the changes they observe to the Canadian public—described as disinterested by Copeland and as disillusioned by Black.

What is so interesting about the prevalence of arguments pointing to domestic sources of foreign policy change is that they fly in the face of the agency-denying claims that "internationalism is in our DNA" (see Nossal, chapter 2). Paul Gecelovsky captures this well in the opening paragraphs of his chapter; drawing from the work of James Eayrs (1971), he observes that policymakers have more freedom than they are willing to admit to and are less constrained than they wish us to believe. Traditional understandings of Canadian foreign policy often focus on external circumstances and constraints. Understandings that paint Canada as a state with little room for manoeuvre must be re-examined in light of the predominance of societal explanations for change identified in this volume. As Claire Turenne Sjolander points out, one of the frequent consequences of the use of internationalist rhetoric has been the depoliticization of Canadian foreign policy—the presentation of political practice as a "given" which cannot be challenged because it stems from an unalterable reality "out there." In the case of the Afghanistan mission, this depoliticization has been most successful in silencing—or in making invisible—the opposition of the political left in Canada.

Further, both Heather Smith's chapter on the Arctic and climate change and Mark Salter's chapter on citizenship, borders, and mobility point to the limitations of using internationalism as a central organizing frame in Canadian foreign policy precisely because this blinds us to alternative ways of conceptualizing the "foreign" (too often arbitrarily distinguished from the "domestic"). Salter cautions us that internationalism is inherently state- and territory- (boundary) centric and therefore conceals the extent to which the ideas, agents, and practices of foreign policy are being transformed. For her part, Smith reminds us that internationalism constructs our conceptual lenses as well as our political practices and conceals the many ways in which climate change is having an impact on lives lived in the Arctic, thus artificially limiting what is included in our study of "foreign" policy. Implicitly, many of the chapters in this volume point to the potential of democratic debate and citizen engagement as sources of change in foreign policy practice and as sources of debate on what is "foreign" in the first instance. Assumptions about what a middle power can and cannot do are being challenged by the Conservative government—and often quite purposefully—as it draws on societal understandings and critiques of Canada's role in the world more responsive to Conservative political priorities. Foreign policy does not emerge fully formed from nowhere; the definition of Canada in the world is not static and may well be under (re)construction as we speak.

Beyond the debates about the decline (or not) of internationalism or the importance of domestic sources of foreign policy, this volume also speaks to us about the discipline of Canadian foreign policy and the nature of its boundaries. Drawing from Heather Smith's chapter on internationalism, the Arctic, and climate change, we adopt an organizing framework that organizes chapters according to "internationalism from the inside" and "internationalism from the outside." For Smith, this distinction is broadly consistent with Robert Cox's (1986) often-cited dichotomy of problem-solving versus critical theory. For Cox, both these forms of theorizing were useful and necessary. For this volume, his insights apply broadly.

The chapters in the first section of the volume view internationalism from the inside and tend to adopt state-centric approaches, focus on state actors, and use conceptual frameworks or theoretical approaches that have been long-standing or have become well-known within the boundaries of the study of Canadian foreign policy. Several of the chapters in this section focus on domestic sources of explanation for change (the area where they witness change). The authors in this section typically would not be considered "critical theorists" by those who structure the debates in the broader field of international relations, but they are certainly critical of the orientation of the Canadian government, sometimes implicitly, sometimes explicitly. In this first section of the volume, we find chapters that reinterpret, critique, or redefine internationalism using analytical practices that are familiar within the established confines of Canadian foreign policy as an academic field.

The second section of the volume includes authors we categorize as working on internationalism from the outside. Consistent with Robert Cox (1986: 207), they typically seek to stand outside the world order, and as such, they problematize theory and perspectives by asking "for whom" the concept of internationalism speaks—in a general sense. The authors in this section tend to draw on theoretical approaches from outside the core of Canadian foreign policy (CFP) texts, and as such, their work is often labelled "alternative" or "non-traditional." Some might even argue that by definition some of these scholars are "not doing CFP" and have little to contribute to the understanding of the discipline.[2] It is our contention, however, that one can find Canadian foreign policy operating in unusual places and sites that are too often disregarded. The authors in this section of the volume problematize internationalism, interrogate it for its concealed perspectives, and, in some instances, reject internationalism outright as a lens by which to understand and interpret Canadian foreign policy.

The adoption of this inside/outside schema could be interpreted by some as reflecting the editors' desire to make some grand statement about divisions in the discipline. Nothing could be further from the truth. The use of inside/outside is designed to show difference, not division. Moreover, as readers will see, while we've used inside/outside as an organizing concept, some chapters do not sit easily in either space; rather, the authors, intentionally or not, engage in analyses that cross the inside and the outside (see Kitchen, chapter 10) or reflect the fluid rather than the dichotomous nature of the schema (see Smith, chapter 1).

Taken as a whole, the volume reveals that while there are important differences in the way we understand and use internationalism, these differences allow us to share in a conversation that celebrates a diversity of approaches and perspectives. We are aware that there is a risk in bringing together such a variety of approaches to the concept of internationalism. Critical scholars might argue that there are too many mainstream chapters in the volume and that we are thereby reinforcing the prevalence of certain approaches in the field of Canadian foreign policy. Mainstream scholars might question the inclusion of chapters with more critical and perhaps uncommon orientations to the study of CFP. This volume began, however, with conversations among scholars who posed a common question about the shape of contemporary internationalism, rather than posit a common answer. For us, this project has never been about coherence or consensus. It's about an exchange of ideas. It's about respect for the scholarly project, broadly speaking, in the interpretations that are provided. The volume stands as a tribute to a community that respects diversity regardless of different opinions and views and methods and theories. This perspective is central to the orientation of this volume—it is why we are so gratified that so many colleagues embracing different views have come together within its pages.

⌈Chapter 1 focuses on teaching internationalism.⌋ In this chapter, Heather Smith provides readers with a detailed analysis of some of the literature on internationalism she used in one of her Canadian foreign policy classes (thus providing components of a literature review that might otherwise typically be in an introductory chapter). However, this chapter is more than a list of readings taught, it is also an interrogation of the idea of inside/outside, with the author reflecting not only on the physical location of the chapter itself (at the beginning of a volume when it would typically be assigned to an appendix) but also on the way her course reading lists may reinforce an inside canon that she as a critical feminist scholar may not wholly embrace. Her analysis shows how the inside and outside are fluid and not absolute categories and how we as scholars and teachers may occupy both spaces—sometimes simultaneously. Ultimately, Smith argues that her task as a teacher is not to create students in her own likeness; rather, her task is to provide the students with a survey of the field that covers both the core and the alternative—the inside and the outside. Students ultimately should be encouraged to choose their own paths.

In the second chapter of the volume, Kim Richard Nossal assesses "the degree to which the Harper government has abandoned traditional internationalism." To make this assessment, he begins by defining internationalism as having five characteristics: responsibility to play a constructive role in the management of conflicts, multilateralism, involvement in international institutions, support for international institutions using national resources for the system as a whole, and an emphasis on international law (Nossal, Roussel, and Paquin, 2011: 135–41). He then draws examples from Canadian foreign policy on Afghanistan, the Arctic, climate change, and the failed Canadian quest for a UN Security Council seat in 2010, and argues that while internationalism under the Harper government is no longer a dominant idea in CFP, it has not been replaced by a new "ism," such as continentalism or isolationism. Rather, according to Nossal, contemporary Canadian foreign policy is driven by one central idea: "the idea that the primary purpose of international policy is to advance a domestic partisan agenda."

In chapter 3, Justin Massie and Stéphane Roussel associate themselves with the "declinist school," arguing that internationalism is on the decline. Unlike Nossal, however, they do observe the emergence of a rival dominant idea: neocontinentalism. They argue that "the neocontinenalist approach in CFP is increasingly becoming the external expression of a growing domestic neoconservatism," and thus like other authors in this volume, they trace foreign policy change primarily to domestic sources. Their chapter points to seven key elements of neocontinentalism that are evident in the foreign policy of the Harper government: the borrowing of values associated with conservatism, the belief that Canada is a foremost power or principal power, a pessimistic conception of human nature, a realist-inspired sense of the national interest, a willingness to use force, admission that the United States is Canada's most important ally, and a downgrading of the importance of international institutions as vehicles for the advancement of Canadian interests. And while they argue that neocontinentalism is not *the* dominant idea guiding Canadian foreign policy, they do contend that we are witnessing the "twilight of internationalism."

In contrast to those who favour a declinist interpretation of internationalism, Jean-Christophe Boucher argues that "Stephen Harper's foreign policy remains true to Canada's internationalist tradition, even if identified more strongly with realism." At the heart of chapter 4 is the assumption that both realist and liberal variants of internationalism have existed in Canadian foreign policy. With the arrival of the Harper Conservatives, however, we see a shift in emphasis from liberal internationalism to realist internationalism, but not an abandonment of internationalism altogether. For Boucher, the realist shift is characterized by the primacy of domestic imperatives and interests, as well as a suspicion of grand moral principles. Realist internationalism is more modest and pragmatic than its liberal counterpart. In support of his argument, Boucher examines the purposeful Canadian evacuation of the principle of Responsibility to Protect (R2P) from Canadian foreign policy. The rejection of R2P, according to Boucher, is an example of realist internationalism and a reflection of the Conservative views that R2P is ill-conceived, lacking in international support, and generally not in Canadian interests.

Canada-India relations under the Conservative government are the focus of chapter 5. Anita Singh argues that the "slow success of the Canada-India relationship under Harper is due to his government's shift away from paternalistic internationalism towards mutually beneficial economic relations." She regards internationalism, as embraced by previous Canadian governments, as having been part of a hegemonic and neo-imperialist vision of the world—a vision that undermined Canada-India relations. Canada treated India as a junior partner, sought to impose Canadian values on India, and judged Indian actions and policies through a Canadian lens. In turn, India saw Canadian behaviours and policies as incompatible with its core national interests. With the arrival of the Harper government and a shift away from this paternalistic behaviour, Canada-India relations are slowly improving. In Singh's view, this case shows us that "there is an inverse relationship between the success of Canada's bilateral relations with developing countries and a foreign policy driven by internationalism."

Chapter 6 also focuses on a bilateral relationship, that of Canada and China. Like Singh and other authors in this volume, Andrew Lui observes a movement away from internationalism by the Harper Conservatives. Unlike Singh, however, he does not consider this break with the past as a strategy that has enhanced the Canada-China relationship. Lui observes that Canada seems disengaged and at times intransigent where China is concerned. Part of his explanation for this foreign policy posture is that Canada is now focused on more traditional partners, such as the United States and the European Union. This shift in focus is coupled with a human rights policy that promotes a tougher stance on human rights and supports the kind of disengagement he observes. Part of the problem, Lui argues, is that internationalism provided a framework for engagement in the past. With the rejection of internationalism, however, the Harper government is lacking any kind of conceptual framework for its international policy, including its policy towards

China. In this, Lui echoes some of the observations made by Nossal in his chapter. Ultimately he shows us that "the Harper government has ignored the new realities of China's rise, and thus its abandonment of internationalism as a role-based approach to Canadian foreign policy has eroded Ottawa's ability to engage with and influence Beijing."

Paul Gecelovsky begins chapter 7 with an observation already discussed in this introduction: policy-makers have more freedom than they are willing to admit to and are less constrained than they wish us to believe. He links this observation about policy-maker agency to an assessment of the influence of the prime minister's evangelical Christian faith on Canadian foreign policy, and argues that we are witnessing the emergence of a faith-based personal responsibility internationalism. This new variant of internationalism, added to "Harper's unwavering confidence in himself to lead, his control over all aspects of policy, and the support of a growing and vocal group of Christian organizations for a foreign policy predicated on a specific reading of biblical principles[, has] worked to bring concerns of faith, more directly and prominently, into Canadian foreign policy decision-making." Drawing on examples from Conservative policy towards Israel as well as from policy changes on the issue of women's reproductive rights in development funding, Gecelovsky shows how a confluence of forces have resulted in a foreign policy orientation supportive of traditional views on values and the family.

"What has happened to Canada? We don't recognize you any more." This statement is part of a conversation repeated by Daryl Copeland in the introduction to chapter 8. In this chapter, Copeland shares with us an insider's view of internationalism. A member of the Canadian Foreign Service for almost 30 years, he observes and describes the steady decline in internationalism as a vision guiding Canadian foreign policy. During the Axworthy era, internationalism was in its last gasp, and with the advent of Stephen Harper, it is now is nothing more than "spectral." Copeland argues that "[w]herever Canada is now going internationally, it bears little resemblance to where it has been." Canada's declining internationalist engagement in the world, combined with both the decline in the capacity and status of Foreign Affairs and International Trade Canada and the Canadian public's declining interest in Canada in the world, is a marker of this unfortunate change. Copeland concludes his chapter, however, by opening the door to a post-Pearsonian narrative, and he finds hope (or seems to find hope) in the non-state sector and popular forces, as well as in the greater possibilities for networking that together might create diplomatic alternatives.

Focusing on citizenship, borders, and mobility, Mark Salter in chapter 9 of this volume turns traditional foreign policy assumptions on their head, claiming that "traditional foreign policy analysis relies on an antiquated and obsolete model of the state that assumes that borders are isometric with territorial boundaries." Salter draws theoretical inspiration from International Political Sociology (IPS) to show readers that practices of statecraft and security occur in spaces and places that are lost from our view when we focus on multilateralism or middlepowermanship.

In the case of citizenship and passports, for example, he shows us that the "issuance of passports . . . is a site for the construction of citizens." In terms of borders, we are prompted to consider spaces such as US preclearance in Canadian airports—spaces that require us to rethink the location of borders. In his assessment of mobility, Salter focuses on visas and how visa processes result in the categorization of the deserving and the undeserving. Ultimately, his chapter offers us a glimpse of foreign policy in unexpected locations—or, at least, locations that are unexpected if we adopt mainstream frameworks of analysis.

[In chapter 10, Veronica Kitchen expands our understanding of foreign policy in unexpected locations while simultaneously problematizing internationalism.] Like Massie and Roussel, Kitchen focuses on the Canada-US relationship, but in contrast to Massie and Roussel, she investigates internationalism in the context of that relationship and asks: "Is it possible to reconcile the seeming incompatibility of internationalism with the bilateral North American security relationship?" In response to this question, Kitchen deconstructs internationalism and assesses internationalism not only in the context of state-to-state relations, but also as it manifests itself in the practices of sub-national governments and transnational actors. She concludes that "internationalism is not consistently present in the North American relationship under Stephen Harper's government." However, the "securitization of everyday spaces has meant that new actors have authority in security policy, which now transcends the distinction between foreign and domestic policy." In some instances, these new actors have engaged in practices consistent with internationalism. Through this innovative analysis, Kitchen challenges dichotomous thinking about internationalism and continentalism and reminds us that state-centric black-boxed analyses leave out everyday actors who are regularly engaged in foreign policy, broadly understood.

Similar to Salter's adoption of a theoretical lens outside the mainstream of Canadian foreign policy literature, Krystel Carrier and Rebecca Tiessen, in chapter 11, draw inspiration from an alternative lens: gender analysis. In their chapter, they critically examine the Conservative government's Muskoka Initiative on maternal, newborn, and child health. Their analysis paints a dire picture of the state of gender equality and shows us that the Conservative government has quite purposefully edited "gender equality" out of Canadian foreign policy, in part as an effort to appeal to a conservative domestic constituency. Carrier and Tiessen also debunk Canadian government claims of leadership in maternal health and show that these claims are both misleading and hypocritical. Finally, they reveal the implications of this evacuation of gender when they examine the case of maternal health in South Sudan. When gender considerations are divorced from maternal health, the social, political, and cultural impediments to maternal health are left unexamined, thus ensuring that the maternal health projects for women in South Sudan are ineffective and unsustainable.

[In chapter 12, positioning herself as a critical scholar, Heather Smith reflects on the implications of coming to the core of the field of Canadian foreign policy.]

She argues that the use of internationalism as a framework may shape and predetermine the results of her analysis and thus undermine the critical project that informs her work. Has her use of internationalism made her insufficiently curious about the embedded assumptions that inform internationalism? In an effort to think critically about internationalism, she draws inspiration from the work of Robert Cox and seeks to stand "outside" internationalism in order to assess the workings of the "concealed perspective" that informs it. She argues that there are at least three components to the concealed perspective of internationalism: it is state-centric, it lacks a human dimension, and it assumes race neutrality. She goes on to demonstrate how these same components of the concealed perspective inform the government and mainstream discourse on the Arctic and climate change, thus showing the practical implications of how the concealed perspective can limit our imaginable possibilities (Beier and Wylie, 2010: xii).

[In chapter 13, David Black turns his attention to Canadian foreign policy towards Africa as articulated by the Harper government.] In so doing, he points to the relative decline of humane internationalism. His chapter shows how the continent of Africa is increasingly outside of and marginal to the interests of the Harper government. By way of explanation, he notes that Africa has never been an area of interest of the prime minister—a prime minister (and party) more interested in aid efficiency than global justice. Equally, the Commonwealth is not an area of interest for the current government. However, Black argues that to fully understand the shift away from Africa and global social justice, we need to look to the decline over time of humane internationalism and the permissive and enabling domestic environment in which these changes have taken place. The trends he observes, he reminds us, are neither new nor confined to the Conservatives. To explain the ongoing decline of humane internationalism, we need to consider the weakness of public support for foreign aid, the changing face and place of organized religion, the decline of radical solidarity politics, and the shift from state-centric humane internationalism to individualistic global citizenship.

[Drawing on post-colonial insights, chapter 14 by Claire Turenne Sjolander provides an analysis of "representations of Canada's mission in Afghanistan since 2006 as found in the speeches of Canadian political leaders, particularly in those of the prime minister, in order to unpack the ideas (and ideals) embedded in the use of internationalist rhetoric in contemporary Canadian foreign policy."] Turenne Sjolander shows us how the tropes of internationalism invoked in speeches by the prime minister serve to construct Canadian identity while simultaneously constructing "others." She challenges us to consider constructions of Canada as a moral exemplar bringing Western values to Afghanistan and as the good international citizen rescuing Afghan women and children who are ahistorically cast as having no agency. Not only does Turenne Sjolander's analysis stand in contrast to volume contributors such as Anita Singh, who argues that the current variant of internationalism is less imperialist than in the past, but her analysis reminds us that the speeches of Stephen Harper are value-laden and replete with constructions of Canada informed by assumptions that are gendered, racialized, and colonial.

In the conclusion of the volume, we, as co-editors, return to the inside/outside theme and reflect on the multiple constructions of internationalism found in the volume and the implications of those constructions for our understanding of Canadian foreign policy. We are mindful of the signals being sent by the Conservative government that suggest a dismantling of internationalism, but we remind readers that internationalism is an elastic concept and that there is little consensus on its meaning. We argue that "how internationalism is understood, interpreted, and deployed in thought and practice mirrors the divide between 'inside' and 'outside'—inside the boundaries of Canada and outside; inside the state, as bureaucratic and policy actors, and outside, as scholars and academics; inside the core of the discipline and outside." The complexity of internationalism becomes clear when we understand it to refer both to a set of political practices and to different political and societal discourses that contribute to the construction of Canadian identity. As practice and as discourse, the meanings that emerge in the unpacking of the concept of internationalism are myriad. Whether internationalism is dead, dying, abandoned, dormant, dismantled, or irrelevant remains as contested as the multiple meanings associated with its practice and discourse.

Taken together, these chapters paint a complex and multi-faceted picture of internationalism in Canadian foreign policy under the Harper government. As a set of ideas and policy practices, internationalism shapes both the way in which Canada acts in the world and the ways in which we as scholars interpret and assess such action. In the end, the question is less one of what internationalism "is" under the Harper (or any other) government than it is one of what internationalism permits and what it conceals in Canadian foreign policy. By engaging us in a variety of different theoretical journeys and by presenting us with a variety of compelling case studies, the authors in this volume invite us to look at internationalism from different perspectives—all critical—in order that we might begin to unpack a concept that has for so long, and so profoundly, shaped the study and practice of Canadian foreign policy and the imaginary of Canada itself.

Notes

1   It is of course important to note that many Canadian foreign policy commentators had long decried the death of Canadian internationalism; as Nossal's chapter in this volume points out, these concerns were raised since the 1970s under Prime Minister Trudeau and escalated throughout the mandate of the Chrétien government—Lloyd Axworthy's land mines treaty notwithstanding.

2   While at a conference in Denmark in the summer of 2011, the editors of this volume, having presented their respective chapters, were privately criticized by a member of the Canadian Foreign Service for understanding "nothing" about Canadian foreign policy. As with other work that does not adopt "traditional" approaches to the study of CFP, such an easy dismissal is not uncommon.

References

"Afghan Mission More Important Than Photo-ops." 2007. *Star-Phoenix* [Saskatoon], 10 October, 10.

Beier, J. Marshall, and Lana Wylie. 2010. "Introduction: What's So Critical about Canadian Foreign Policy?," in J. Marshall Beier and Lana Wylie, eds, *Canadian Foreign Policy in Critical Perspective*. Don Mills, ON: Oxford University Press, xi–xix.

Black, David. 2009. "Out of Africa? The Harper Government's New 'Tilt' in the Developing World." *Canadian Foreign Policy/La politique étrangère du Canada* 15, 2: 41–56.

"Buttress Ottawa's AIDS strategy." 2006. *Toronto Star*, 10 August, 20.

Cox, Robert W. 1986. "Social Forces, States and World Orders: Beyond International Relations Theory." In Robert O. Keohane, ed., *Neorealism and Its Critics*. New York: Columbia University Press, 204–54.

Eayrs, James. 1971. *Diplomacy and Its Discontents*. Toronto: University of Toronto Press.

Enloe, Cynthia. 2004. *The Curious Feminist: Searching for Women in a New Age of Empire*. Berkeley: University of California Press.

Fulton, Bill. 2006. "Harper's Staunch Defence of Israeli Bombing Ignores Canada's Tradition as Peacekeeper." *Edmonton Journal*, 4 August, 17.

Ivison, John. 2007. "Harper's Anti-doctrine: A Nuanced Foreign Policy, but a Foreign Policy Still." *National Post*, 28 November, 1.

McQuaig, Linda. 2007. *Holding the Bully's Coat: Canada and the U.S. Empire*. Toronto: Doubleday Canada.

Nossal, Kim Richard, Stéphane Roussel, and Stéphane Paquin. 2011. *International Policy and Politics in Canada*. Toronto: Pearson Education Canada.

Smith, Heather A. 2009. "Unwilling Internationalism or Strategic Internationalism? Canadian Climate Policy under the Conservative Government." *Canadian Foreign Policy/La politique étrangère du Canada* 15, 2: 57–77.

Turenne Sjolander, Claire. 2009. "A Funny Thing Happened on the Road to Kandahar: The Competing Faces of Canadian Internationalism?" *Canadian Foreign Policy/La politique étrangère du Canada* 15, 2: 78–98.

PART I

Internationalism from the Inside

1

Teaching Internationalism: Bringing Canada and the World into the Classroom

Heather A. Smith

For many of us, a survey course on Canadian foreign policy (CFP) is not complete without a week or two dedicated to the concept of **internationalism**. As this volume shows, there is certainly any number of readings we could select to fill those weeks. So what readings do you use? And after those readings have been selected, do you ponder the implications of the readings you left out? Are there readings you dismiss outright? How do you situate the topic of internationalism in the course? Do you give lectures on internationalism? Or do you hold classroom discussions about internationalism? How do you facilitate those discussions? What do you want your students to know about internationalism? Do you want them to be able to simply define internationalism? Do you want them to be thinking critically about internationalism? When you teach internationalism, what do you teach? How do you teach?

This volume is dedicated to interrogating the meanings of internationalism. So too is this chapter. But the content here is different: the questions are posed from a different starting point. The point of this chapter isn't to focus on a case study of internationalism in practice in the policy sphere. It isn't mostly about whether or not the Harper government is internationalist. This chapter is nonetheless still about internationalism in practice—in the classroom.

For some, a chapter on teaching internationalism, especially one identified as "Chapter 1," will seem strange because teaching, and in turn writing about teaching, is seen to be outside the academic project. Too frequently, the scholarship of teaching and learning is not regarded as research and is thus artificially disassociated from "what counts" as a contribution to our field. Indeed, reviewers for this volume suggested that the editors move this chapter to the end and identify it as an appendix—outside of and separate from the "scholarly" chapters. Teaching as appendix—here we have disciplinary norms exerting their power to place teaching in a space on the outside and at the end of the volume while simultaneously labelling the chapter in such a way as to render it extraneous.

As editors, we decided to "flip the script," so to speak. Rather than place teaching at the end of the volume—in an appendix, away from the "real" content of the book —we have placed this chapter at the beginning. We did this for two reasons. First, as readers will note, the Introduction quite explicitly rejects the adoption of one overarching definition of internationalism, in large part because this project was guided by the desire to expose the lack of consensus on the idea. However, we are mindful of the fact that our unwillingness to choose one definition over another will be troubling to some. Consequently, this chapter, through a discussion of teaching, provides a survey of the competing definitions of internationalism. In this way, this chapter supplements the Introduction.

The second reason for placing a chapter on teaching at the beginning of the volume relates to our adoption of the "inside/outside" metaphor, introduced in the Introduction. As noted above, teaching is too frequently treated as something outside our research. However, teaching is not outside the discipline. Our classroom is as much a space of politics and power as the House of Commons or the United Nations. Just as the statements and speeches of our prime minister shape a discourse, affect policy practices, and construct an image of Canada in the world, so too do our syllabi and our teaching practices. As I've argued elsewhere (Smith, 2010), in our teaching we define the boundaries of our field in 13 weeks. Teaching is very much on the inside—it is a practice and a place where we create and recreate the discipline. Consequently, it matters what we teach and how we teach internationalism.

This chapter focuses on internationalism in practice as performed, legitimized, or problematized in the teaching sphere, and aims to prompt reflection about teaching practices. I hope to encourage faculty to consider the politics of our teaching, to ponder how we contribute to the shaping of a discipline both through the construction of course outlines and in the act/s of teaching. We need to reflect on the images of Canada and the world that we present to our students. And while this chapter may seem to be solely directed at faculty, it isn't. Students, too, should reflect on what they are being taught. They should also ask about what they are not being taught and wonder why, and if they don't know why they are being taught about internationalism, they should ask. Students are not merely receptors of teaching: they are their own agents of learning.

In the next section, I turn to a description of a fourth-year course on "Canadian foreign relations."[1] For the iteration of the course discussed below, which I taught in 2009, I focused on the theme of internationalism. Drawing on the small body of literature related to "the state of the discipline" and "teaching Canadian foreign policy," I then assess the content of my course to see how the content fits into the broader disciplinary trends. However, an assessment of the content tells only half the story. An identification of content only tells us what is being taught, it doesn't tell us how the content is being taught or why the content is being organized in particular ways. Given this, I then spend some time reflecting on my teaching practices with the end of identifying the values that inform my performance of the discipline. Rather uncomfortably, I observe that my outline seems to have an orientation towards content that is unabashedly and traditionally on the "inside." The discomfort comes from the fact that my pedagogical orientation and my research are both informed by critical and feminist approaches, and I wonder if I am somehow doing a disservice to critical and feminist questions by focusing on the dominant discourses on internationalism. And so, at first glance, a contradiction exists between the scholarly me and my teaching content.

However, consistent with critical and feminist pedagogy, my teaching is rooted in my desire that the students respect diversity, in theory and in practice. I teach students the canon and the alternative literature; I encourage them to think critically about all the voices before them and to choose their own theoretical path. Consequently, to argue that my scholarship and teaching are contradictory misses the connection. In much of my scholarship I have been very critical of the way the dominant discourse excludes voices of those on the margins or the way the discipline is shaped in such a way as to delegitimize or undermine the contributions of feminist and critical theorists. If I exclude the "inside," or canon, and if I tell students the only way forward is to be a critical theorist, then I become a gatekeeper. Rather, I want to encourage students to find their own paths. While I'm not entirely comfortable with the dominance of the canon in my course, I will not deny my students access to the breadth of the field—my teaching politics does not include imposing closure on perspectives that do not mimic my own scholarly predilections. My "inside" content is informed by my "outside" theoretical orientation and critical pedagogical practices.

What Do I Teach?

If teaching is a political act, the expression of our politics is found in our course outlines. As I have argued elsewhere, "how we shape our course outlines is a disciplining practice and those outlines send signals to students about what is authoritative and valued" (Smith, 2010: 12). Consequently, the textbooks we assign, the readings we include, and the topics we address matter.

There is no required content for my fourth-year Canadian foreign relations seminar. The instructor only has to focus on a particular issue or theme in Canadian foreign policy. I focused on internationalism in the last iteration of this course, and I began with the theme of dominant ideas. The concept of dominant ideas allows us to focus on the ideational component of Canadian foreign policy, and it is sufficiently elastic so as to allow us to assess dominant ideas "that shaped the ways Canadians have conceived of their relations with the rest of the world" (Nossal, Roussel, and Paquin, 2011: 119) from a variety of perspectives. In addition, dominant ideas are "intangible and latent," "persist over time [but] they are not static or immutable"; they "evolve, change and are sometimes replaced by very different ideas" (119). Using dominant ideas as a concept that grounds the course allows us to look at internationalism as both an evolving and contested concept.

After "dominant ideas," we turn to "middle-power internationalism at the beginning," which includes the Gray Lecture (St Laurent, 1947) and analyses of the

Gray Lecture by historians Hector Mackenzie (2007) and Adam Chapnick (2007). These two articles, in addition to the original Gray Lecture, provide readers with detailed analyses of the context in which the Gray Lecture was delivered. Chapnick and Mackenzie raise fundamental questions about the original intent of the speech and the way the speech has been subject to interpretations over time that attach a meaning to it that may not have otherwise been intended. Chapnick argues that the speech was originally about citizenship and may not be as revolutionary as some seek to suggest. Mackenzie (2007: 159) raises the questions of whether the speech marked "a departure in CFP and the rhetoric associated with it and to what extent did it simply represent a reaffirmation of Canada's values and interests in international affairs"; he ultimately argues that the speech was more about continuity than change.

Taken together, the Mackenzie and Chapnick pieces remind us of the need to be mindful of the historical context in which ideas emerge. They point to the original intent of the speech, as well as to the way that speech has been elevated (or perhaps manipulated) to become central to the post-war definition of ourselves. Their depth of analysis provides a good counterpoint to the one or two lines often dedicated to the speech in textbooks. As well, looking at the full speech can also help students see how scholarly interpretation can often result in the misrepresentation or exclusion of key elements of the speech, such as the excision of the reference to Christian values from contemporary analyses (Michaud, 2007). Finally, their analyses also function to provide a baseline for some assessment of change over time of key concepts associated with internationalism.

After "middle-power internationalism at the beginning," I turn to the articulation of middle-power internationalism as witnessed during the Trudeau and Mulroney years. For this week, I have students read Denis Stairs (1992) on reviewing foreign policy during the Trudeau era, the classic John Holmes (1984) article "Most Safely in the Middle," and Michael Tucker's (1980) assessment of the evolution of internationalism. Taken as a group, the Stairs, Holmes, and Tucker readings provide us with competing interpretations of Canada in the world in the late 1960s and early 1970s. For most of our students this is ancient history, but the respective interpretations pose valuable questions. Presaging his 1994–5 article titled "Will and Circumstance and the Postwar Study of Canada's Foreign Policy," the Stairs chapter assesses the role of systemic change, domestic pressure, and the prime minister in shaping both the content and long-term impact of the review. In his assessment of the "power of conditions over the power of choice" (Stairs, 1994–5: 12), Stairs concludes that the most important variable is international systemic change and argues that "the policy outputs would have been the same had Mr. Pearson remained in office, and had the review never been held" (1992: 201). For a class focusing on change over time, the embedded **agent-structure debate** one finds in the Stairs piece is a crucial question for students to consider.

In "Most Safely in the Middle," former Canadian diplomat John Holmes engages the debates in the early 1980s about the currency of the concept of middle power. Articulating a position from the "inside," he challenges both left nationalist and principal power constructions of Canada. This piece is a lucid contribution to the role and status debate, and for me its value lies in its relationship to the other selections included in this week's readings. As with Stairs (and not surprisingly), there is an embedded agent-structure assumption found in his discussion of "room for manoeuvre" (Holmes, 1984: 372). Holmes states: "The range of Canadian foreign policies is considerably more restricted by basic geo-political-economic and cultural factors than critics and opposition spokesmen [sic] assume, and the room for radical change is circumscribed" (372). In addition, the Holmes piece clearly establishes that "middle power" – and, by extension, internationalism – is not some fluffy moralizing do-gooder orientation but rather a set of behaviours based on a "hardheaded calculation of national interest" (369). Holmes reminds us to see our foreign policy behaviours as purposeful and strategic rather than as some accumulation of behaviours rooted in an overly altruistic view of the world.

The third and final reading for this week on internationalism in the 1970s and early 1980s is the introduction to Michael Tucker's *Canadian Foreign Policy: Contemporary Issues and Themes* (1980). In the introduction to the volume, Tucker defines internationalism as "an exercise of collaboration on the part of Canadian governments, groups or individuals with like-minded governments or peoples elsewhere" (1980: 1–2). He identifies an evolution from functional internationalism to middle-power internationalism to Trudeauvian internationalism while simultaneously arguing that all forms of internationalism "shared a common aim. This has been the enhancement of interests or values commonly shared with others outside Canada, with a view to helping create or sustain a better world order" (2). Tucker regards internationalism as "enlightened behaviour."

The value of including the Tucker reading is that its characterization of internationalism stands in contrast to the perspectives that inform both the Stairs and Holmes readings. The Tucker contribution appears to embrace the more altruistic characterization of Canada in the world that Holmes, in particular, rejects. The Tucker piece also provides us with a definition of internationalism that is vastly more inclusive in terms of who practises internationalism. In the latter part of the chapter, Tucker (1980: 16) discusses **public internationalism**, which he associates with the Canadian public. Thus, broadly consistent with Veronica Kitchen's contribution to this volume, Tucker sees individuals and groups outside the formal foreign policy institutions as participants in the practice of internationalism.

Moving from the Trudeau era, I provide some coverage of the Mulroney era by including Denis Stairs's (2001) opening chapter in the Nelson Michaud and Kim Richard Nossal (2001) volume on Canadian foreign policy between 1984 and 1993. Similar to the readings identified above, this chapter by Stairs asks: "[T]o what extent was the conduct of Canada's foreign policy in the period of the Conservative government from 1984–1993 a reflection of the political orientation of the Progressive Conservative party and the predilections of its leaders, and to what extent was it a product of insistent imperatives arising from circumstances … at home and abroad" (2001: 26). He follows this question by asking whether Canada was an

architect or an engineer—that is, were Canadians "architects of their foreign policies, creating them (as it were) afresh" or "engineers, installing bridges of standard
design over rivers that almost anyone in power would have to cross?" (2001: 27).
Stairs concludes, consistent with the Holmes and Stairs pieces identified above,
that the external environment remains critical to an understanding of CFP in the
Progressive Conservative era and that the political orientation of the government
was less so. As noted by the editors (Michaud and Nossal, 2001: 294), in the conclusion of the volume, "the Mulroney Conservatives were more 'engineers' than
'architects.'"

The value of the Stairs piece for discussions of internationalism is the assumed
continuity of Canada's foreign policy regardless of the party in power. Like other
pieces included in this analysis, it raises questions about manoeuvrability and the
way different variables affect (or don't) the Canadian federal government's ability
to shape or reshape who and what Canada is in the world. The chapter also functions as a foil to the pieces included in the section focusing on the Chrétien era.

While moving through what are essentially prime ministerial eras, I bend the
rules a bit when I include Cranford Pratt's (1990) discussion of humane internationalism in the same section as Kim Richard Nossal's (1998–9) "Pinchpenny
Diplomacy" and Don Munton's (2002–3) "Whither Internationalism." Pratt's
assessment of the degree to which humane internationalism motivates the devel-
opment-related policies of the middle power was published in 1990, thus written in
advance of the Chrétien era. The latter two articles, of course, have as their primary
focus the Chrétien era. Taken together, these three articles identify competing definitions of internationalism and provide competing assessments of the relevance
of internationalism in the 1990s. These articles also show students that Canadian
foreign policy can be assessed from multiple theoretical perspectives.

For students of Canadian foreign policy, Cranford Pratt represents one of the
most important voices from the "outside." Working from an explicitly normative
position, Pratt expresses a grave concern for the state of world – in particular, the
global south – and regularly reminds us of our obligations to others. Pratt's analysis of internationalism focuses on the concept of humane internationalism, which
he defines as "an acceptance that the citizens and governments in the industrialized world had ethical responsibilities towards those beyond their borders who are
suffering severely and who live in abject poverty" (Pratt, 1990: 5). As will be seen
below, like Munton, Pratt identifies variants of internationalism, all captured along
a spectrum of humane internationalism. The three variants identified by Pratt are
radical internationalism, reform internationalism, and liberal internationalism.
Ultimately, Pratt is pessimistic about the extent to which humane internationalism
has had an impact on the foreign policy orientations of countries such as Canada
and Sweden (Pratt 1990: 149; see also Black, chapter 13).

In "Pinchpenny Diplomacy," Kim Richard Nossal defines internationalism as
having four characteristics. First, he makes reference to multilateralism as a component of internationalism, although it is not given as much attention as his latter

three components: community, good international citizenship, and voluntarism. For Nossal, "internationalism is, at bottom, directed towards creating, maintaining, and managing community at a global level" (Nossal, 1998–9: 98). Good international citizenship, he writes, "suggests that a country's diplomacy can be directed toward ameliorating the 'common weal' by taking actions explicitly designed to achieve that end" (99). Finally, internationalism is understood to be a "voluntaristic form of diplomacy. . . . [I]t is an entirely optional form of statecraft—in the sense that one could get by without engaging in it" (100). With this definition as his starting point, Nossal (1998–9) argues that the Chrétien era witnessed a dismantling of internationalism, or at least a reduced emphasis on volunteerism and good international citizenship. Ultimately, he is critical of what he sees as a meanness of spirit in Canada's orientation to the world.

In contrast, Don Munton's (2002–3) study investigates the question of the continued relevance of internationalism, especially in light of critiques offered by scholars such as Nossal (1998–9), Pratt (1989), and Jean-François Rioux and Robin Hay (1998–9). Munton, seeking to examine Canadian public attitudes, focuses on public internationalism. Unlike Tucker, discussed above, Munton does not equate public internationalism with citizen activism or with individuals as active agents of internationalism. Rather, he defines public internationalism as "citizen support for active involvement in international affairs, both bilateral and multilateral, embodying a significant commitment of resources and a concern for the common interest and for world order" (Munton, 2002–3: 161). Munton goes on to argue that there are "four main dimensions of internationalist attitudes ... active internationalism, economic internationalism, liberal-conservative internationalism, and independent internationalism" (161), and that each of these "dimensions are distinguished in terms of where and how resources should be committed and which common interests should be pursued and in what order." With this rather all-inclusive definition of internationalism in hand, Munton, in contrast to those fretting about the decline of internationalism, concludes that the Canadian public is still "strongly internationalist" (177). He states: "[C]ontrary to speculations of some analysts, there does not seem to have been a general decline in public internationalism over the 1990s" (177).

After taking students across 50 or so years of history, I turn to some of the critical interrogations by a cohort of scholars who started to be published in the 1990s. I begin with Mark Neufeld. Building off the work of Cranford Pratt, Neufeld articulates a vision of Canada and the world based on a Gramscian interpretation that challenges us to think about the way in which mainstream theories of Canadian foreign policy "facilitate the smooth working of existing social and political arrangements" (Neufeld, 1995: 10). Neufeld traces the evolution of the concept of Canada as a middle power and describes the middle power as a regulative idea that "oriented the Canadian state to a role supportive of the hegemonic world order" (17). The concept of middle power also had important domestic functions, including the creation of a "domestic consensus in support of extensive involvement in the maintenance of the international order" and the reinforcement of "the notion that the social order within Canada's border was an essentially just one" (17). Neufeld ultimately focuses on the creation of a limitationist notion of middle power that begins during the Mulroney era, but which, he argues, became a "regular feature of official discourse" under the Chrétien government (23).

I also include the work of David Black and Claire Turenne Sjolander (1996: 8) on multilateralism. Like Neufeld, they problematize a concept associated with or treated as embedded in internationalism. Drawing from a neo-Gramscian framework, they deconstruct the discourse of multilateralism and problematize the idea of "new multilateralism." Through their analysis, Black and Turenne Sjolander encourage readers to reflect on how the "Canadian preoccupation with multilateralism ... has always masked inconsistencies and contradictions in Canada's international economic relations and in the construction of the multilateral (hegemonic) world order" (8). Black and Turenne Sjolander also call attention to the gap between the meanings associated with multilateralism and the practice of multilateralism. They observe a widening of the gap between meaning and practice and argue that "its evolving practice may well exacerbate the inequalities in the emerging world order, and undermine multilateralism itself. Thus there is a need to transcend simplistic valuations of multilateralism as inherently 'good'" (9).

To add an explicitly feminist perspective, I include my chapter "Disrupting Internationalism and Finding the Others" (2003) from *Feminist Perspectives on Canadian Foreign Policy* (Turenne Sjolander, Smith, and Stienstra, 2003). In that chapter, I start by adopting a definition of internationalism offered by Kim Nossal (1998–9) in his "Pinchpenny Diplomacy" article and then problematize the concept. I argue that "multiple types of othering ... are embedded in the concept of internationalism" and that internationalism functions in ways to strategically deny domestic practices that disrupt assumptions about Canadian benevolence, openness, and good international citizenship. Our colonial past is rarely recognized, migrants are constructed as threats, and nature is commodified (Smith, 2003). I conclude by stating: "We must not assign a naturalness to internationalism and its component parts. We must question concepts such as good international citizenship. We need to think critically about the ways in which the construction of internationalism translates itself into the management of who is part of a community. We must challenge the implied benevolence of Canadian behaviour at home and abroad" (39).

These three pieces are important contributions to the literature on internationalism. As a group, they represent the growth of critical scholarship in the field and, like Pratt before them, remind students that there are multiple valid vantage points from which to assess Canadian foreign policy. Black and Turenne Sjolander and Smith challenge various components of internationalism and thereby expose the complexity often embedded in overly simplified definitions. They show us that we should not take internationalism as a given, easily understood and easily measured. The pieces expose the ways and means in which internationalism can be colonial, gendered, and regulative. All the pieces offer examples of Canadian foreign policy from the outside. It is interesting to note, as well, that none of the pieces were published in either *International Journal* or *Canadian Foreign Policy*. This, I would argue, may be a reflection of the lack of space, at the time, in the mainstream journals for alternative perspectives and the choices of sites of publishing the authors felt were open to them.

Finally, I conclude the fourth-year course with a discussion of Harper and internationalism. Interestingly, when the course was delivered in the fall of 2009, there wasn't a lot of literature on Harper and internationalism (which was one of the prompts for this volume). Perhaps because his government seemed intent on beating up the Liberals and rejecting the Liberal legacy, scholars didn't see internationalism as a worthwhile topic of study. Or perhaps it was assumed that the Conservatives would be short-lived, and thus there would be no "era" to speak of— only a Harper "blip" that wouldn't have long-term repercussions on CFP. However, Claire Turenne Sjolander, David Black, and I were curious about the idea of internationalism during the Harper era. As a starting point to what is now this volume, we presented papers on Harper and internationalism at the International Studies Association meeting in 2009. These three papers, on Harper and Afghanistan (Turenne Sjolander, 2009), the Harper government and overseas development assistance (Black, 2009), and climate change policy under the Harper government (Smith, 2009), were subsequently published in *Canadian Foreign Policy* and became the readings for the Harper era in my fourth-year course. All three articles have a critical orientation and complement earlier critical work on Canadian foreign policy. As well, the Black and Turenne Sjolander pieces functioned as starting points for the chapters these authors have contributed to this volume.

After several weeks of readings related to internationalism that I assign, the students become the course designers—in a manner of speaking. They have to assign readings to their classmates and give presentations on some theme or issue area related to internationalism. Together, they have 13 weeks of internationalism and Canadian foreign policy. That, then, is my fourth-year course, as taught in 2009. However, one might ask: what is the value of looking at one course outline? As will be seen in the next section, it may be one course outline, but it raises interesting questions about the discipline more broadly.

And So ... at First Glance ...

When I consider the content of my course, as identified above, I'm actually quite struck by the degree to which it is weighted in favour of the "inside" of the discipline. I see a tendency to reinforce the dominant trends in the field, more than to disrupt them. For example, the content is written mostly by men. This is consistent with the discipline more broadly. For example, all the most-used texts in the field are written by men, according to Kirton (2009: 556). Every author listed in association with the top 10 books in the field identified by Kirton is a man. And it's not just the authors of the textbooks. Consider, for example, whom they cite.

A quick scan of the citations in these textbooks will confirm the dominance of scholarship by men in the field.

A course outline dominated by male scholars reflects the dominance of men in publishing in the field of Canadian foreign policy (Cornut, Smith, and Roussel, 2010). And so while I think these are first-rate textbooks that introduce students to the field, I have to wonder if I signal to students that CFP is written by and about men. By focusing on traditional debates, as opposed to feminist debates or critical CFP, it's almost as if I preordain the male-dominated image of the world, creating feminist and critical approaches as the "other," placing my own preferred theoretical orientation on the margins or bottom rungs (Enloe, 1996) of the discipline. If I adopted and used *Feminist Perspectives on Canadian Foreign Policy* (Turenne Sjolander, Smith, and Stienstra, 2003) – which I have done in previous iterations of the courses – students would read a book with all women scholars and feminists. If I included the Marshall Beier and Lana Wylie (2010) volume on *Canadian Foreign Policy in Critical Perspective*, students would be exposed to innovative and creative theorizing that challenges common understandings of CFP written by both male and female scholars. My intent is neither to essentialize nor to dichotomize the world of CFP into male and female. My point is simply to suggest that the dominance of the "core" of the field in my course outline produces an image of the field that even I, as a feminist scholar, find problematic. By focusing on traditional debates, I potentially, even if unintentionally, reinforce assumptions about who writes Canadian foreign policy.

Also as a result of my focus on traditional debates, my course is dominated by **positivist** theoretical analyses. While there are readings that include some reference to race, such "Disrupting Internationalism" (Smith, 2003), the absence of a distinctly post-colonial perspective is almost shocking. A couple of feminist articles provide an entry point into the broader literature. Critical literature is also included. But it seems the core still dominates.

What is interesting, in a rather unfortunate way, is that my dismay about the positivist/"inside" theoretical dominance in my course would seem misplaced to some. The norm is to focus on the core. In spite of my concerns, my course includes readings and approaches that are rarely covered in other courses and thus is unconventional by many standards. However, the course is not sufficiently unconventional for my own standards because I feel that I privilege the core over alternative approaches. For example, according to Claire Turenne Sjolander's (2007) evaluation of the field, the core areas tend to include Canadian-American relations, trade, and defence. I don't feel that a CFP course is incomplete without a week dedicated to each of these topics. I may include them, depending on the way the course is designed. Inclusion of the United States is done through the readings, as it is ever present in much of what we write. I have included case studies on areas such as human security, climate change, Arctic sovereignty, and overseas development assistance, and my inclusion of the environment as a topic on course outlines (Turenne Sjolander, 2007), as well as any gender and critical theory, is unusual (Smith, 2010). In that regard, I'm including content that does not generally get adopted in many classes across the country. Another thing that strikes me about my course outline is that it is very "Canadian." All my readings are written by Canadian scholars located at Canadian universities. There are indeed volumes (Bothwell and Daudelin, 2009; Gattinger and Hale, 2010) that include chapters and articles either by Canadian scholars located outside Canada or scholars of different nationalities who may offer a slightly different perspective on Canada and the world. Given my concerns about how "Canadian" my course is, I may need to turn to texts such as these; however, these are not texts I've used because they are often quite time-bound and/or are too focused on one particular theme, to the detriment of others. This said, questions can be raised about the implications of my very Canadian-centric course outline. Am I guilty of the parochialism and navel-gazing that David Black and I were critical of in 1993 (Black and Smith, 1993)?

In part there is some parochialism—my course outline is a lot of Canadians talking to each other (sort of). It certainly would be possible to include some readings by scholars and practitioners looking at Canada from the outside. However, the worries that David Black and I expressed in 1993, about a lack of debate between scholars, limited cumulation, a lack of innovative theorizing (which at the time we articulated in very liberal terms), are not quite as pressing as they were over 15 years ago. For example, we (Black and Smith, 1003: 770) suggested more serious consideration of approaches that helped us move beyond the idiosyncratic and parochial ones that dominated CFP. My course outline challenges some of the idiosyncrasy and parochialism through the inclusion of critical and feminist approaches. The critical and feminist articles introduce students to Coxian and Gramscian theorizing through Neufeld and Black and Turenne Sjolander, and to the work of feminist theorists such as Marysia Zalewski (1996, 2006), Cynthia Enloe (1996), and Christine Sylvester (2007) through the inclusion of pieces written by Canadian scholars who cite their work. Indeed, these are cases where the insights of scholars of international relations (IR) have been applied to Canadian cases by Canadian scholars, but they are important contributions that mark some minimal progress in the field, at least in terms of diversity. They show that there is room for new directions.

The absence of any attempt in my course to view CFP or Canadian international policy in an interdisciplinary fashion is also lamentable. For someone in an interdisciplinary department, the dominance of my home discipline in this course troubles me. It troubles me because it flies in the face of recommendations I've been party to or made elsewhere. In the chapter on pedagogy in *Feminist Perspectives on Canadian Foreign Policy*, Claire Turenne Sjolander, Deborah Stienstra, and I argue for an expanded understanding of CFP:

> By expanding how we understand Canadian foreign policy, we need to rely on a variety of sources, including those from other disciplines or from interdisciplinary studies. We may need to read critiques of immigration policy from disability studies or women's studies. We may need to draw on the work

of aboriginal scholars and their understandings of the world that evolved over centuries of nationhood...In short, we need to go beyond "Canadian foreign policy" texts—whether they are part of the canon or the growing list of alternatives. (Turenne Sjolander, Smith, and Stienstra, 2003: 16)

My scholarship is increasingly interdisciplinary, but it would appear the way I construct my CFP course is not.

Course content matters. It sends signals about what is valued in the discipline. My course is dominated by core questions and positivist epistemologies, even if I do include readings that problematize the mainstream. How do I explain this pattern? After all, if I am asking others to reflect on the implications of their class content, surely I can reflect on my choices for content.

In part, I think my course reflects the resilience of the core. The questions of power, status, and role have dominated the field in theory and practice ever since the end of the Second World War. These are the concerns of a state, and ours is a field with a state at the heart of its analysis. The starting point of our analyses is typically the state, and we have too often had our analyses shaped by that starting point. Early critical work focused on critiques of the state and engaged the mainstream, too often using the basic terms of reference of the mainstream. The value of starting with questions central to the core was that critical and feminist scholars offered different visions of internationalism, or overseas development assistance, or human security. At the same time, perhaps we let the agenda of what constituted the appropriate topics of CFP be determined by others, as opposed to creating our own agendas. This is changing. Critical and feminist scholars are now defining their own research agendas, but the core remains intact.

The core is resilient, and maybe I do need to rethink what I teach in my course. However, I also know that looking at the content of a course outline only provides half the picture. There is so much more to a course than the readings. An assessment of content doesn't tell us how a subject is taught. It doesn't tell us about the values and intentions that shape the teaching. The reason I organize readings as I do has meaning. The way I encourage students to question readings has meaning. My politics aren't just about what is in print, they are also about practice.

How and Why I Teach

When we design our courses, content is shaped in part by our assumptions of what constitutes the discipline. Time, resources, course requirements, availability, and access to resources also influence our course outlines, but our course outlines are markers of "what matters." How we teach Canadian foreign policy, however, also matters. If we lecture from a podium, detached from our students, and deliver material in an authoritative manner and prescribe particular definitions as the best or the preferred, we send signals to our students about what counts as knowledge and whose knowledge counts. The knowledge that counts is the "truth" that is identified by the professor—who is the authority. What is required of our students in that context is that they receive the knowledge that we deliver. If my course is delivered in this manner, then I would argue that the dominance of core content is reinforced by a traditional "stand and deliver" method of teaching.

But that isn't the case. In my classes, I meld a variety of teaching strategies in ways that seek to push students to think critically, to question each other and me, to simultaneously respect the past and see how assumptions of continuity can and should be challenged. These are my politics. And my politics are not necessarily obvious at first glance—they are not obvious in the listing of content in my course outline.

As a starting point for many of my courses, whether they focus on Canadian foreign policy or on gender and international studies, I introduce students to some of the broad analytical questions that are central to the course. So while week one in my course outline inevitably reads "Introduction to the Course," it should really read: "Questions at the Heart of the Course." The questions posed on that first day in a CFP course typically include: What do you think Canadian foreign policy is? Why study Canadian foreign policy? I also include the question: How should one study Canadian foreign policy? From the beginning, I introduce students to the idea that Canadian foreign policy is a contested field and numerous approaches help us to understand Canada in the world. Often, I present them with Robert Cox's problem-solving/critical theory framework (1986). This framework provides students with a means by which to organize and interpret some of the readings that they will do later in the class. The early introduction of Cox's framework also signals to the students that they will be required to think theoretically and to look at the assumptions that inform the articles they are reading. Reading to learn facts, dates, and definitions is not enough in my classroom.

It is not always easy for students to get their heads around this framework, especially if their studies prior to the course have treated Canada or things Canadian in an unproblematic manner. Interestingly, students often find it easier to understand problem-solving theory because it relates to realism as taught in their lower-division courses, but somehow critical theory is a bit of a mystery. This said, when I taught the course in the past year, several of the students were already well versed in theory and saw themselves as budding critical theorists. So for them, the Coxian framework was welcome.

To say that I introduce my students to the problem-solving/critical theory framework is not to suggest that I expect my students to become critical theorists. If that were the case, my course outline would look vastly different. My course outline includes a number of classic works in the field and articles representing diverse perspectives on internationalism because I believe our students should have a sense of the evolution of our field and should have a respect for our history. Sometimes my students resist reading some of the "classics" because they don't see the relevance of an article from the 1980s to their current busy cellphone-dominated lives. Yet, I tell them that questions asked in the past often remain very relevant today. I also tell my students that there are insights to be found in all types of articles adopting approaches different from their own predilections and my scholarly preference.

If I wanted to create a cohort of critical scholars, I would not spend so much time teaching internationalism. I spend time teaching the concept of internationalism because the concept is treated by many scholars as a core idea in the field and yet it is fundamentally contested. And I believe that my task as a teacher is to teach both the constructed core and the alternative approaches to Canadian foreign policy. Therefore, I introduce them to competing definitions of internationalism and students are required to compare and contrast definitions of internationalism. Students need to see that internationalism is a contested idea. Students will not be able to get the sense of contestation if we only give them one definition and then move on to the next topic in the course.

We can teach our students that there is "one way" to look at internationalism, or we can teach them about diversity. I choose to teach about diversity. And in presenting that diversity of voices in our discipline, I hope that students then learn to respect a diversity of voices—to not impose intellectual closure on an approach because they assume it won't work for them. And I hope this respect for diversity is translated into their lives outside my classroom space.

My task is to expose my students to the field, to give them choices, to support their intellectual agency, rather than to impose a view of the field that excludes approaches that I don't adopt in my own work. I am not willing to impose closure on the work of others in ways that mimic the marginalization of critical and feminist approaches.

I also encourage students to claim their own agency as learners. I don't lecture. They do this work in groups. I do support them as they work together. They are not set out alone to work through these articles, but I work more as a facilitator of learning rather than as an authoritative voice telling them which is the best perspective. This approach isn't always the most comfortable for students who are often trained that the lecture-style format is the only way to learn, but it does give them a push to claim their agency as learners, to trust their own instincts, to engage in debate with their peers, and to take intellectual risks. There are few intellectual risks for our students when they are only taking notes.

There is one final teaching activity I use that I think encourages learners' agency, encourages some risk-taking, and reinforces a respect for multiple voices. In both of my CFP classes, I invite some members of my scholarly community to participate. For those who study and teach CFP in close proximity to other universities or in large departments, inviting colleagues into your classrooms may not pose any logistical difficulties. That's not true in my case, given the rather remote location of my university. However, over the last several years, I have had Kim Nossal, Claire Turenne Sjolander, David Black, and Adam Chapnick speak with my students—not to my students. Via teleconferencing, they have become part of our classroom discussions. For this exercise, the scholars above are invited to speak to a piece of their scholarship that is an assigned reading for the class. The students are required to prepare questions in advance, and then we call the scholar on the day we are studying his or her work. My colleagues have been most gracious about sharing their time and their views, and the students are always better prepared for these classes than any other. I think that the degree of student preparation is correlated to their sense that talking to an academic is a risky venture and so they need to ask "good" questions. Somehow, the inclusion of these scholars as "people" with real voices and not just as words written in an academic article changes the dynamic for the students. This exercise brings the field into the classroom and provides students access to scholars in a way that is unconventional—quite literally, the outside is brought inside.

The values that inform my teaching shape the way the content is delivered. My students don't end up with one definition of internationalism. They don't sit and write down notes that they then regurgitate on a final exam. They are exposed to competing views of key concepts. They are encouraged to think about and around the meaning of those competing views. They are introduced to a diverse set of scholars, and consequently, they are provided with a number of ways to consider Canada in the world. They are encouraged to be critical of generalizations, to be sceptical of myth claims, and, perhaps most significantly, to be agents of their own learning.

So What and Who Cares . . .

A chapter on teaching and learning in a Canadian foreign policy volume is rare—too rare. Too often we treat our scholarship as separate from our teaching, but this distinction isn't unique to Canadian foreign policy or Canadian political science. Our institutions function on the basis of those distinctions, and we are assessed as though they were separate and unique categories. The reality, however, is that our assumptions about what constitutes the field, what is acceptable knowledge, what are acceptable ways of knowing, and whose voices matter are found in both our scholarship and our course outlines. A few pieces (Turenne Sjolander, 2008; Turenne Sjolander, Smith, and Stienstra, 2003; Smith, 2010) provoke us to think about teaching, but more needs to be done. As argued here, it is clear that an assessment of course outlines only gives us part of the story. I wonder how others teach Canadian foreign policy. What teaching strategies do they use and why? Do scholars who embrace critical theory teach differently than scholars who adopt a liberal approach to their scholarship? Are there common features in our teaching? And if you don't include feminist and critical approaches, why not? What does that tell your students? What does that say about your view of the field? It would be intriguing to see qualitative work done on this question.

I also have to wonder what our students think. I know from experience that my learning objectives for my students—such as respect for diversity—may all be well and good but my students may take away something completely different from the class. What I teach isn't always what they learn. So we need to ask them. We need to ask our students what they are learning. We need to ask them, after taking one of our courses, what is their lasting impression of the field. Only our students can really tell us what it is that they have come to understand to be CFP.

There are still outstanding issues for me, as a result of writing this chapter. I continue to ponder the resilience of the core. Kim Richard Nossal (2000: 110) has suggested that with the Canadianization of IR we will witness a growth of post-nationalist theoretical perspectives. Post-positivists, feminists, and critical theorists will alter the teaching and scholarship about Canada and the world. Maybe the addition of the Beier and Wylie (2010) volume marks that shift. It is unquestionably an important contribution to the field, but I wonder if, when some-one makes another list of the top 10 used textbooks, it will make an appearance, or whether the current list will remain largely unchanged. I am sceptical of Nossal's prediction of the future, but time will tell. I think the core questions of power, status, and role will continue to hold sway because they are the questions and con-cerns of the state and we are preoccupied, for better or worse, with the Canadian state.

I began this chapter by asking about internationalism. In my reflections about teaching internationalism, I've interrogated on my own teaching practices and my teaching politics. These reflections have resulted in broader questions about the discipline and my part in it. I am a scholar who regards herself as "outside" the canon, engaging in research that is "alternative," but who has a significant portion of content in her course outlines that would be seen as "inside." For me, the inclu-sion of the inside is just as important as the inclusion of the outside. Together they make a whole—they provide our students with a sense of the diversity in the field. And so, let me ask: What does your course outline say about CFP? How do you perform the field?

Key Terms

agent-structure debate   positivist
internationalism   public internationalism

Study Questions

1. Why should a chapter on teaching be included in a volume on Canadian foreign policy? What are the arguments against the inclusion of a chapter on teaching? Why does it matter?
2. What are the implications for students' understanding of Canada in the world if they are only provided one definition of internationalism? What is the value of providing multiple definitions of internationalism?

3. Look at your course outline and consider whether your course reinforces the core or shares with you the spectrum of approaches. Why does it matter how a course outline is constructed?
4. If you were to design a course on Canadian foreign policy, what themes and debates would you focus on? Why?

Note

1   I also teach a third-year Canadian foreign policy survey course that does include some of the same readings noted here, but because it is a survey course, there are also other debates covered. For example, I include the role and status debate (Molot, 2007; Bratt and Kukucha, 2007; Nossal, Roussel, and Paquin, 2011; Holmes, 2007; Dewitt and Kirton, 2007), the domestic sources debate (Pratt, 2007; Nossal, 2007), as well as a discussion of the state of the discipline (Sjolander, 2007; Kirton, 2009; Turenne Sjolander and Smith, 2010; Smith, 2010).

References

Beier, Marshall, and Lana Wylie, eds. 2010. *Canadian Foreign Policy in Critical Perspective.* Don Mills, ON: Oxford University Press.

Black, David R. 2009. "Out of Africa? The Harper Government's New 'Tilt' in the Developing World." *Canadian Foreign Policy/La politique étrangère du Canada* 15, 2: 41–56.

Black, David R., and Heather A. Smith. 1993. "Notable Exceptions? New and Arrested Directions in Canadian Foreign Policy Literature." *Canadian Journal of Political Science* 24, 4: 745–74.

Black, David R., and Claire Turenne Sjolander. 1996. "Multilateralism Reconstituted and the Discourse of Canadian Foreign Policy." *Studies in Political Economy* 49 (Spring): 7–35.

Bothwell, Robert, and Jean Daudelin. 2009. *Canada Among Nations, 2008: 100 Years of Canadian Foreign Policy.* Montreal and Kingston: McGill-Queen's University Press.

Bratt, Duane, and Christopher Kukucha, eds. 2007. *Readings in Canadian Foreign Policy*, 1st ed. Don Mills, ON: Oxford University Press.

———, eds. 2011. *Readings in Canadian Foreign Policy*, 2nd ed. Don Mills, ON: Oxford University Press.

Chapnick, Adam. 2007. "The Gray Lecture and Canadian Citizenship in History." *American Review of Canadian Studies* 37, 4: 443–56.

Cornut, Jérémie, Heather A. Smith, and Stéphane Roussel. 2010. "On the Margins? Women and Gender in the Study of Canadian Foreign Policy." Paper presented at the annual meeting of the Canadian Political Science Association, Montreal, June 2010, 11–12.

Cox, Robert W. 1986. "Social Forces, States and World Orders: Beyond International Relations Theory." In Robert O. Keohane, ed., *Neorealism and Its Critics*, 204–54. New York: Columbia University Press.

Dewitt, David, and John Kirton. 2007. "Three Theoretical Perspectives." In Bratt and Kukucha, 2007: 27–45.

Enloe, Cynthia. 1996. "Margins, Silences and Bottom Rungs: How to Overcome the Underestimation of Power in the Study of International Relations." In Steve Smith, Ken Booth, and Marysia Zalewski, eds, *International Theory: Positivism and Beyond*. Cambridge: Cambridge University Press, 186–202.

Gattinger, Monica, and Geoffrey Hale. 2010. *Borders and Bridges: Canada's Policy Relations in North America.* Don Mills, ON: Oxford University Press.

Holmes, John W. 1984. "Most Safely in the Middle." *International Journal* 39 (Spring): 366–88.

———. 2007. "Most Safely in the Middle." In Bratt and Kukucha, 2007: 9–21.

Kirton, John. 2009. "The 10 Most Important Books on Canadian Foreign Policy." *International Journal* 64, 2: 553–64.

Mackenzie, Hector. 2007. "Shades of Gray? The Foundations of Canadian Foreign Policy in World Affairs in Context." *American Review of Canadian Studies* 37, 4: 459–73.

Michaud, Nelson. 2007. "Values and Canadian Foreign Policy-Making: Inspiration or Hindrance?" In Bratt and Kukucha, 2007: 341–56.

Michaud, Nelson, and Kim Richard Nossal. 2001. "Diplomatic Departures? Assessing the Conservative Era in Foreign Policy." In Nelson Michaud and Kim Richard Nossal, eds, *Diplomatic Departures: The Conservative Era in Canadian Foreign Policy, 1984–1993*. Vancouver: University of British Columbia Press, 290–5.

Molot, Maureen. 2007. "Where Do We, Should We, or Can We Sit? A Review of Canadian Foreign Policy Literature." In Bratt and Kukucha, 2007: 62–75.

Munton, Don. 2002–3. "Whither Internationalism?" *International Journal* 58, 1: 155–80.

Neufeld, Mark. 1995. "Hegemony and Foreign Policy Analysis: The Case of Canada as a Middle Power." *Studies in Political Economy* 48: 7–29.

Nossal, Kim Richard. 1998–9. "Pinchpenny Diplomacy: The Decline of 'Good International Citizenship' in Canadian Foreign Policy." *International Journal* 54, 1: 88–105.

———. 2000. "Home-Grown IR: The Canadianization of International Relations." *Journal of Canadian Studies* 35, 1: 95–114.

———. 2007. "Analyzing Domestic Sources of Canadian Foreign Policy." In Bratt and Kukucha, 2007: 163–75.

Nossal, Kim Richard, Stéphane Roussel, and Stéphane Paquin. 2011. *International Policy and Politics in Canada*. Toronto: Pearson Education Canada.

Pratt, Cranford, ed. 1989. *Internationalism under Strain*. Toronto: University of Toronto Press.

———. 1990. "Has Middle Power Internationalism a Future?" In Cranford Pratt, ed., *Middle Power Internationalism: The North-South Dimension*. Montreal and Kingston: McGill-Queen's University Press, 143–67.

———. 2007. "Dominant Class Theory and Canadian Foreign Policy: The Case of the Counter-Consensus." In Bratt and Kukucha, 2007: 176–95.

Rioux, Jean-François, and Robin Hay. 1998–9. "Canadian Foreign Policy: From Internationalism to Isolationism." *International Journal* 54, 1: 57–75.

St Laurent, Louis. 1947. "The Foundations of Canadian Policy in World Affairs." In R.A. MacKay, ed., *Canadian Foreign Policy 1945–1954: Selected Speeches and Documents*. Toronto: McClelland & Stewart, 388–99.

Smith, Heather A. 2003. "Disrupting Internationalism and Finding the Others." In Claire Turenne Sjolander, Heather A. Smith, and Deborah Stienstra, eds, *Feminist Perspectives on Canadian Foreign Policy*. Don Mills, ON: Oxford University Press, 24–39.

———. 2009. "Unwilling Internationalism or Strategic Internationalism? Canadian Climate Policy under the Conservative Government." *Canadian Foreign Policy/La politique étrangère du Canada* 15, 2: 57–77.

———. 2010. "Disciplining Nature of the Discipline." In Marshall Beier and Lana Wylie, eds, *Canadian Foreign Policy in Critical Perspective*. Don Mills, ON: Oxford University Press, 4–14.

Stairs, Denis. 1992. "Reviewing Foreign Policy, 1968–1970." In Don Munton and John Kirton, eds, *Canadian Foreign Policy: Selected Cases*. Scarborough, ON: Prentice Hall, 189–204.

———. 1994–5. "Will and Circumstance and the Postwar Study of Canada's Foreign Policy." *International Journal* 50, 1: 9–39.

———. 2001. "Architects or Engineers? The Conservatives and Foreign Policy." In Nelson Michaud and Kim Richard Nossal, eds, *Diplomatic Departures: The Conservative Era in Canadian Foreign Policy, 1984–1993*. Vancouver: University of British Columbia Press, 25–42.

Sylvester, Christine. 2007. "Anatomy of a Footnote." *Security Dialogue* 38, 4: 547–58.

Tucker, Michael. 1980. *Canadian Foreign Policy: Contemporary Issues and Themes*. Toronto: McGraw-Hill Ryerson.

Turenne Sjolander, Claire. 2007. "Two Solitudes: Canadian Foreign Policy/Politique étrangère du Canada." *Canadian Foreign Policy/La politique étrangère du Canada* 14, 1: 101–8.

———. 2009. "A Funny Thing Happened on the Road to Kandahar: The Competing Faces of Canadian Internationalism?" In *Canadian Foreign Policy/La politique étrangère du Canada* 15, 2: 78–98.

Turenne Sjolander, Claire, and Heather A. Smith. 2010. "The Practice, Purpose and Perils of List Making." *International Journal* 65, 3: 751–62.

Turenne Sjolander, Claire, Heather A. Smith, and Deborah Stienstra. 2003. "Engaging in the Possibilities of Magic: Feminist Pedagogy and Canadian Foreign Policy." In *Feminist Perspectives on Canadian Foreign Policy*. Don Mills, ON: Oxford University Press, 12–21.

Zalewski, Marysia. 1996. "All These Theories Yet the Bodies Keep Piling Up: Theories, Theorists and Theorising." In Steve Smith, Ken Booth, and Marysia Zalewski, eds, *International Theory: Positivism and Beyond*. Cambridge: Cambridge University Press, 340–53.

———. 2006. "Distracted Reflections on the Production, Narration, and Refusal of Feminist Knowledge in International Relations." In Brooke Ackerly, Maria Stern, and Jacqui True, eds, *Feminist Methodologies for International Relations*. Cambridge: Cambridge University Press, 42–61.

2 The Liberal Past in the Conservative Present: Internationalism in the Harper Era

Kim Richard Nossal

Internationalism has been a central element of Canadian foreign policy since the end of the Second World War. It features prominently in explanations of the policies pursued in the decades immediately following the war (Keating, 2002; Chapnick, 2005). Indeed, so deeply entrenched did the internationalist approach to foreign policy become in Canada that it could readily be described as a **dominant idea** (Nossal, Roussel, and Paquin, 2011: 135–41), a dominance widely acknowledged, even among those who are critical of the idea. (See, for example, Smith, chapter 12; Turenne Sjolander, chapter 14; Smith, 2003.)

But perhaps because of that entrenched dominance, internationalism has come to be featured equally prominently in normative debates over the direction of Canadian foreign policy (Munton, 2002–3). In the late 1970s, Sandra Gwyn bemoaned the decline and fall of "Canada's Golden Age of Internationalism," asking, "Where are you, Mike Pearson, now that we need you?" (quoted in Chapnick, 2008–9: 210). In the late 1980s, scholars like Cranford Pratt wondered aloud whether it was possible for Canada to embrace a "refurbished humane middle power internationalism" (1990: 155). In the 1990s and early 2000s, a persistent line of criticism of the Liberal government of Jean Chrétien was that it was abandoning Canada's traditional commitment to internationalist policies (Rioux and Hay, 1998–9; Nossal, 1998–9; Cohen, 2003).

Likewise, a common theme in commentary on the foreign policy of the Conservative government of Stephen Harper has been the expression of regret over what is often termed the "abandonment" of internationalism by that government after 2006. The view that the Harper Conservatives have abandoned Canada's traditional **Pearsonian internationalism** is shared by commentators across an extraordinarily wide spectrum of opinion. For example, in her 2007 screed on Canada's putative contribution to the American empire, *Holding the Bully's Coat*, Linda McQuaig (2007: 1) asserted that "we've moved from being a nation that has championed internationalism, the United Nations and UN peacekeeping to being a key prop to an aggressive U.S. administration operating outside the constraints of international law." McQuaig's extreme and vituperative antipathy towards the

Harper Conservatives is clearly not widely shared in Canada—at least judging by the millions of votes cast for Conservative candidates in the 2006, 2008, and 2011 elections—but her observation that Canada no longer champions internationalism as it once did is echoed by a range of more serious and substantial foreign policy commentators (Fowler, 2010; Fréchette, 2010; Welsh, 2010; Siddiqui, 2010; Heinbecker, 2010; Paris, 2011: 26–8).

The purpose of this chapter is to assess the degree to which the Conservative government under Stephen Harper has abandoned traditional internationalism in its foreign policy. Assessing Conservative foreign policy initiatives using some commonly accepted characteristics of an internationalist approach to global politics, I conclude that we have indeed seen little evidence of the internationalism that was the dominant idea in both the discourse and the practice of Canadian foreign policy in the decades after the end of the Second World War. We have not even seen what has been called **internationalism lite**, the favoured approach of the Chrétien Liberal government (Nossal, Roussel, and Paquin, 2011: 143; also see Keating, 2006). Rather, we have seen the articulation of a set of ideas rarely expressed openly in Canadian foreign policy: a Manichaean view of the world (Paris, 2011).

Following the May 2011 election that gave the Conservatives a majority, the prime minister outlined his views of foreign policy. In an interview with *Maclean's*, Harper asserted that Canadian foreign policy had to be made for a "dangerous world" that was marked by "a struggle between good and bad"; in such a dangerous environment, "the real defining moments for the country and for the world are those big conflicts where everything's at stake and where you take a side and show you can contribute to the right side" (Whyte, 2011). Thus, he told a Conservative Party convention, his government would take "strong, principled positions in our dealings with other nations"; the purpose was not "just to go along and get along with everyone else's agenda. It is no longer to please every dictator with a vote at the United Nations" (Harper, 2011).

But it can be argued that there is another "idea" that is driving contemporary Canadian foreign policy: the idea that the primary purpose of international policy is to advance a domestic partisan agenda. In other words, since 2006, foreign policy has had an important strategic purpose, and that has been to advance Harper's broader overall goal of remaking Canadian politics by making the Conservatives the dominant political party in Canada. That Harper is seeking to effect a long-term transformation of Canadian politics is clear. As he himself admitted unambiguously in September 2008,

> My long-term goal is to make Conservatives the natural governing party of the country. And I'm a realist. You do that two ways. . . . One thing you do is you pull conservatives, to pull the party, to the centre of the political spectrum. But what you also have to do, if you're really serious about making transformations, is you have to pull the centre of the political spectrum toward conservatism. (Quoted in Behiels, 2010: 118)

In the 2004, 2006, 2008, and 2011 elections, we can see slow but steady progress towards this long-term goal. Although the explanation for the ascendancy of the Conservatives and the decline of the Liberals between 2004 and 2011 is to be found in factors other than international policy, in this chapter I argue that foreign policy has played a not unimportant part in this transformation. As I will show, the Conservatives used international policy unambiguously to advance the broader political goal of displacing the Liberals as Canada's natural governing party, in particular through a concerted effort to break with a past in Canadian foreign policy that is seen as deeply Liberal.

How Internationalist Have the Harper Conservatives Been?

One way to assess whether the Conservative government under Stephen Harper has abandoned internationalism is to examine the main characteristics of an internationalist approach to foreign policy and then to look at the main elements of the foreign policy of the Harper Conservatives and see whether we see internationalist ideas reflected in policy behaviour.

But what is internationalism? As the editors note in the introduction, this volume does not strive for a common definition of internationalism. In this chapter, I suggest that there are five characteristics of this approach—often qualified as "liberal internationalism" to underscore the overtly liberal values and assumptions that underlie it. First, internationalism puts a premium on the idea of each state taking *responsibility for playing* a constructive role in the management of conflicts that will inevitably arise in global politics. Second, an internationalist policy suggests that *multilateralism* is essential for defusing conflicts in international affairs and that therefore states should not act unilaterally in international politics. Third, internationalism places emphasis on involvement with, and support for, *international institutions*, for it is believed that institutionalization promotes multilateralism and dampens the unilateral impulse. Fourth, support for international institutions must be given concrete expression by a willingness to use national resources for the system as a whole. Finally, internationalism suggests an emphasis on international law, which is assumed to enhance the stability of the international system (Nossal, Roussel, and Paquin, 2011: 135–41; also see Keating, 2002; Munton, 2002–3).

If we look at the Canadian government's foreign policy in the years immediately following the Second World War (Holmes, 1979, 1982; Chapnick, 2005), we can clearly see that these ideas animated Canadian foreign policy. Moreover, as Erika Simpson (1999) reminds us, these ideas are evident in the approaches of Lester B. Pearson, Canada's foreign minister from 1948 to 1957. To what extent do we see these ideas reflected in the foreign policy of the Harper Conservatives?

We must preface this discussion with the observation that when the Conservatives came to power in 2006, they demonstrated no serious acquaintance with international affairs. The international policy mindset of the party is perhaps most clearly revealed in the party's 46-page 2006 election platform. This document contained just three short sections on international affairs: defence, trade, and foreign policy writ large, the latter section consisting of a mere 171 words (Conservative Party of Canada, 2006: 44–5), so short that it is possible to quote it in full:

> Canadians are rightly proud of our values of freedom, fairness, and compassion. But too often, Liberal foreign policy has compromised democratic principles to appease dictators, sometimes for the sake of narrow business interests. Foreign aid has been used for political purposes, not to ensure genuine development. We need to ensure that Canada's foreign policy reflects true Canadian values and advances Canada's national interests.
>
> A Conservative government will:
> - Articulate Canada's core values of freedom, democracy, the rule of law, human rights, free markets, and free trade – and compassion for the less fortunate – on the international stage.
> - Advance Canada's interests through foreign aid, while at the same time holding those agencies involved in this area accountable for its distribution and results.
> - Increase spending on Overseas Development Assistance beyond the currently projected level and move towards the OECD average level.
> - Make Parliament responsible for exercising oversight over the conduct of Canadian foreign policy and the commitment of Canadian Forces to foreign operations.
> - Place international treaties before Parliament for ratification.

Indeed, it would appear that those who crafted—or approved—this section of the 2006 platform had little knowledge or understanding of the nature of international politics or foreign policy. Tellingly, none of the many eyes in the Conservative Party who looked at the platform before it went to press appeared to know (or care) that "foreign aid" is a term that is decades out of fashion or that ODA is the acronym for "official development assistance," not "overseas development assistance." In addition, the partisan frame of the platform that focused on the supposed single sin of Liberal foreign policy—having "compromised democratic principles to appease dictators, sometimes for the sake of narrow business interests"—reveals a highly limited understanding of what foreign policy is (or should be) all about.

Certainly there was little evidence in 2006 that the leaders of the Conservative Party of Canada had inherited any of the strong internationalist principles of the Progressive Conservative government of Brian Mulroney from 1984 to 1993 (Michaud and Nossal, 2001; Gecelovsky and Keating, 2001). On the contrary: the 2006 platform—and the superficial level of Conservative discourse during the 2005–6 election campaign—underscored Jeffrey Simpson's observation that Harper came to power "with no experience or apparent interest in the world" and that his party was "without a single frontbencher qualified by experience or interest to become foreign affairs minister" (2006).

To be sure, that was then. Once in power, the Harper cabinet was confronted with the necessity of dealing with a wide-ranging international agenda, and the prime minister himself had to accommodate his schedule to the crowded annual calendar of summit meetings. Moreover, "Canada's New Government" was supported by the massive bureaucratic resources of the Canadian state. In the event, Harper and his government obviously left the jejune simplicities of the 2006 platform behind them. But the platform is a useful reminder of the degree to which the Conservatives arrived in power with a *tabula rasa* when it came to international politics and foreign policy.

Once the Conservatives were in power, the mission in Afghanistan became the central foreign policy preoccupation of the Harper government, so much so that Louise Fréchette, former Canadian ambassador to the UN, former deputy minister of national defence, and former deputy UN secretary-general, openly worried that "we come across as a 'one-note' foreign policy country—Afghanistan, Afghanistan, Afghanistan" (2010: 273). But in fact the Canadian contribution to the Afghanistan mission could be considered an excellent example of contemporary internationalism. The mission was authorized by the United Nations, and the Afghanistan Compact of 2006, which was intended to provide an overarching plan for Afghanistan, was an international agreement involving over 50 countries, including all permanent members of the Security Council. The Canadian contribution to the Afghanistan mission could be constructed as being in the best traditions of Pearsonian internationalism; after all, as Adam Chapnick reminds us, Pearson's internationalism was "far more violent, aggressive and confrontational" than the usual portrait of Pearsonian internationalism widely peddled to Canadians by their elites in the last 40 years (2006: 64). Indeed, when Harper visited Afghanistan at the outset of his mandate in March 2006, his speech committing Canada to the mission even if the going got tough—"Canadians do not cut and run"—sounded what could be interpreted as an internationalist note. Harper claimed that the Afghanistan mission was "in the very best of the Canadian tradition: providing leadership on global issues; stepping up to the plate; doing good when good is required" (Harper, 2006).

But it is clear from the justifications Harper offered for the mission that internationalism cannot be identified as the driver of Canada's engagement in Afghanistan. Rather than try to justify the mission in internationalist terms, the prime minister offered a largely incoherent mishmash of different justifications. He began with the standard "national interest" argument that Canadian security depended on ensuring that Afghanistan did not again become an incubator for terrorist attacks. But he also suggested that Canadian security was affected by the opium trade, which, he said, "wreaks its own destruction on the streets of our country." And he also invoked three other justifications: the importance of a country such as Canada taking a leadership role in global politics, the importance of the humanitarian mission, and the importance of "standing up for Canadian values" (Harper, 2006).

These latter justifications were, in a sense, internationalist (Chapnick, 2006: 65), but when juxtaposed with the others, they did not make much sense. It should be noted, however, that Harper's incoherence in 2006 was not unusual. After studying every speech on Afghanistan given by Canadian ministers from 2001 to 2008, Jean-Christophe Boucher concluded that "the Canadian government's message on Afghanistan has been chaotic for most of the past seven years," with the result that the government "has not succeeded in clearly communicating the logic behind Canada's intervention and actions in Afghanistan" (2009: 718). Boucher's conclusion echoes Robert Fowler's acidic critique that the Afghanistan mission was marked by a "confusion of purpose" (2008: 5).

Moreover, whatever initial enthusiasm Harper had for the mission eventually dissipated. In early 2008, he negotiated a deal with the Liberal opposition to remove Afghanistan from the political agenda by committing Canadian forces to withdraw by 2011—again, a move without any strategic coherence or logic (Nossal, 2009). Likewise, Harper's steadfast commitment to complete military withdrawal by 2011, despite the "surge" embraced by the administration of Barack Obama (Turenne Sjolander, 2010), remained puzzlingly inconsistent with his earlier commitments (Nossal, 2011). Moreover, the last-minute reversal in the face of strong allied pressure in November 2010 underscored the continuing lack of strategic logic of Canada's Afghanistan policy (Nossal, 2010a). In their special report marking the fifth anniversary of the Conservative victory, Paul Wells and John Geddes (2011: 22) note the irony: "Harper's handling of the Afghanistan file reflected a level of incoherence he would not have accepted from a subordinate."

A second priority of the Harper Conservatives has been the Arctic, and here we see an interesting transformation. The Harper government began by following a well-trodden road of Canadian unilateralism that goes back to the articulation of such fanciful notions as the "sector theory" of Canadian claims over Arctic waters in the early twentieth century. The Conservatives played the **Arctic card** from the beginning during the 2005–6 election campaign (Nossal, 2007). Once in power, the Harper government was aggressively unilateral in asserting Arctic ownership, getting into a spat with Denmark over Hans Island and adopting what is usually called a "use it or lose it" approach (Huebert, 2009; Byers, 2009). The government was clearly keen to expand the presence of the Canadian state north of the 60th parallel in order to bolster Canadian claims to sovereignty in the Arctic. To that end, the Conservative government embraced an expansive program of hardware acquisitions, including the creation of a deep-water replenishment facility at an existing port at Nanisivik to extend a Canadian presence in the Arctic during the June–October navigation season; the acquisition of a Polar-class icebreaker; new replenishment ships for the navy; and a replacement for the Aurora CF-140 long-range patrol aircraft. Some of these expensive initiatives have moved ahead, albeit slowly. In August 2008, Harper announced the construction of a heavy Polar-class icebreaker to replace the CCGS *Louis S. St-Laurent*, due to be decommissioned in 2017. Symbolically named the CCGS *John G. Diefenbaker*, after the Progressive

Conservative prime minister who succeeded St Laurent as prime minister in 1957, the Polar-class icebreaker is intended to operate for three seasons of the year. Construction at Nanisivik began in 2010, but was significantly downgraded in 2012 as a budget-cutting measure.

In August 2010, however, the government released a statement on what it called "Canada's Arctic Foreign Policy" (Canada, n.d.). The policy embraced a distinctly multilateral approach to northern policy, focused on a revitalization of Canada's commitment to the Arctic Council and a recognition that the eight states of the circumpolar north "remain best placed to exercise leadership in the management of the region." It should be noted, however, that the nascent internationalism in the new policy came with an edge. In its conclusion, the statement left an iron-fisted reminder in the velvet multilateral glove: "Cooperation, diplomacy and respect for international law have always been Canada's preferred approach in the Arctic. At the same time, we will never waver in our commitment to protect our North."

By contrast, the Harper Conservatives have taken other international policy positions that would not be mistaken for Pearsonian internationalism. Prime among these would be the evolving Canadian position on climate change and greenhouse gas emissions. In opposition, Harper understood that Canada's commitment to reduce greenhouse gas (GHG) emission to 6 per cent below 1990 levels was a commitment that Jean Chrétien had essentially pulled out of thin air at the Kyoto negotiations in 1997. After all, given that Canada's population is *structurally* designed through immigration policy to grow at a massive rate annually, no government of Canada could maintain greenhouse gas emissions at a steady state, much less reduce them, and certainly not to a figure of 6 per cent below 1990 levels (Simpson, Jaccard, and Rivers, 2007). Thus, between 1997 and 2006, when the Conservatives took office, Canada's GHG levels steadily grew, even as the Chrétien government was ratifying the protocol in 2002.

In power, however, the Conservatives somewhat moderated their approach to the Kyoto Protocol. The Harper government announced that while Canada would not meet its Kyoto targets, it would not renounce the Kyoto agreement. At the same time, however, Ottawa started to engage in what Heather A. Smith has called "cowboy diplomacy" in global climate change negotiations, which she characterizes as "regime dismantling" rather than as the regime creating usually associated with internationalism (2008–9: 58, 63). For example, in September 2007, Harper announced that Canada would join the Asia-Pacific Partnership (APP) on Clean Development and Climate, a multilateral group formed in 2005 by Australia, China, India, Japan, Korea, and the United States. Ostensibly designed to be a complement to Kyoto, this grouping included states that had not ratified Kyoto—Australia and the United States—but also parties to the Kyoto Protocol that were very heavy emitters, such as India and China. However, as Smith (2009) notes, the APP as a multilateral institution was not particularly effective at reducing GHG emissions, and it was effectively sidelined with the defeat of John Howard in the November 2007 elections in Australia and the victory of Barack Obama in the 2008 presidential elections in the United States. Moreover, the Conservatives eventually began to play the very same numbers game that they had criticized the Chrétien government for playing. At first, the Harper government adopted what it called a "made-in-Canada, made-for-Canada" approach; the so-called 20/20 target introduced in 2007 sought to reduce Canada's greenhouse gas emissions to 20 per cent below 2006 levels by 2020 (Baird, 2007). In 2010, the Conservatives simply moved Canada's target in line with that established by the Obama administration: 17 per cent below 2005 levels by 2020.

More generally, we cannot see unambiguous evidence that the Harper government feels warmly about the full panoply of international institutions whose meetings he must attend by virtue of his position. By all accounts, he has little enthusiasm for the United Nations as an institution (Fréchette, 2010; Heinbecker, 2010), tending to focus on the corruption, ineffectiveness, and blatant Israel-bashing that are so deeply rooted in that international organization. And even when Harper eventually decided to seek a seat on the Security Council in 2010, his "campaign" was limited to a speech, delivered to the General Assembly in September 2010, that paid appropriate (and unusual) tribute to the long tradition of support for the UN by Canadian governments since the 1940s (Harper, 2010b); he did not make the personal calls that usually are a mark of a Security Council campaign. Indeed, it can be argued that Harper's real views were better reflected in his initial inclination to avoid vying for the seat. But even after he had agreed to seek election, Harper was unlikely to have shared the kind of breathless enthusiasm of Paul Dewar, the foreign affairs critic of the New Democratic Party, who claimed that "[w]e must have a seat on the Security Council, it's in our DNA" (quoted in Slater and Ibbitson, 2010).

Canada's failure to secure election to the Security Council in 2010 can in part be attributable to the lack of the kind of "grand" initiatives that were taken by previous governments, held up (however inappropriately) as exemplars of Pearsonian internationalism and used to bolster the decennial Canadian bid for a non-permanent seat on the Security Council. These would include initiatives taken by the Liberal government of Jean Chrétien in the 1990s (such as the land mines treaty, the International Criminal Court, or the New Partnership for African Development launched at Kananaskis in 2002); by the Mulroney government from 1984 to 1993 (such as its anti-apartheid activism or global environmental initiatives); or by the Liberal government of Pierre Elliott Trudeau from 1968 to 1984 (such as his nuclear suffocation initiative, his co-chairmanship with Mexico of the North–South summit at Cancún in 1981, or the peace initiative of 1983–4).

To date, the most significant global initiative undertaken by the Conservative government has been the global maternal health initiative (see Carrier and Tiessen, chapter 11), launched in January 2010 by Harper in his role as host of the G8 Summit (Harper, 2010a). However, this initiative was immediately mired in controversy when it was revealed that the Canadian initiative explicitly excluded family planning and abortion services. To be sure, within two days Harper had abandoned the family planning exclusion, but because the remaining abortion exclusion lined the Conservative government up with Republicans in the United States, the Democratic Obama administration openly criticized Harper's initiative. At a meeting of G8 foreign ministers, Hillary Rodham Clinton, the US secretary of state, was blunt: "You cannot have maternal health without reproductive health. . . . And reproductive health includes contraception and family planning and access to legal, safe abortion" (quoted in Clark, 2010). David Miliband, the British foreign secretary, also publicly criticized the Canadian government for its stand on abortion. Harper tried to defend his government's position, arguing, "We want to make sure our funds are used to save the lives of women and children and are used on the many, many things that are available to us that frankly do not divide the Canadian population" (Fitzpatrick and Foot, 2010), but the exclusion was to be widely criticized in Canada and elsewhere (Webster, 2010).

In a hunt for evidence of whether internationalist ideas animate the Conservative government, it should be noted that there does exist one speech given by Harper in which he sounds, if not Pearsonian, then at least Holmesian. Speaking to the Council on Foreign Relations in New York in September 2007, Harper explicitly promised that his government would pursue middle-power diplomacy. As he put it, middle powers "step up to the plate to do their part . . . willing to assume responsibilities, seek practical, do-able solutions to problems and who have a voice and influence in global affairs because they lead, not by lecturing, but by example" (Harper, 2007), his words clearly echoing the kind of perspective on "middlepowermanship" in Canadian foreign policy articulated by John W. Holmes (1970, 1976, 1984; also Nossal, 2010b). But, as far as can be determined, this is the only time that Harper used the term "middle power" in his speeches to describe Canada in world affairs; he certainly did not return to this theme in the years after 2007.

Letting Go of the Past: The Abandonment of Liberal Internationalism?

To this point I have sought to find evidence of internationalist ideas in the foreign policy rhetoric and practices of the Harper Conservative government. I have suggested that while there is clear evidence of multilateral engagement, one would be hard-pressed to argue that internationalism has been a guiding idea in the foreign policy realm in Ottawa after February 2006. But why has this dominant idea been so absent in contemporary foreign policy rhetoric or practice?

In assessing this question, it is important to note that no other foreign policy idea has emerged as dominant. The Harper government is clearly not moved by isolationism or continentalism or regionalism as those ideas have manifested themselves in Canadian foreign policy; there is no evident "new" foreign policy idea in formation. It cannot even be concluded that the Conservative government is particularly *conservative* in its foreign policy (Bloomfield and Nossal, forthcoming). And because there is no clear alternative strategic foreign policy perspective articulated or pursued by the Conservative government beyond its embrace of

Manichaeanism, a logical explanation for the absence of internationalism since 2006 is that internationalist discourse and internationalist projects were quietly but purposely laid to rest for partisan political reasons.

In other words, when the Conservatives came to power in February 2006, they brought with them a determination to make a clear and unambiguous break with the past. This was most symbolically reflected in the decision to call themselves "Canada's New Government." Indeed, there is considerable evidence that, in foreign policy, the Conservatives sought policies that would distinguish themselves from their predecessors and encourage Canadians to let go of the past. Most obviously, Harper broke with a long tradition in international policy dating back to 1968, when Pierre Elliott Trudeau, on assuming office, had ordered a review of foreign and defence policy. This practice had been subsequently followed by Joe Clark, Brian Mulroney, Jean Chrétien, and Paul Martin (Nossal, 2006). But to underscore the difference from Martin, who, in his brief time in office, had done little more in the realm of foreign policy than produce an international policy review, the Conservative government pointedly did not initiate a review. Even language that served as reminders of the Liberal era—such as Responsibility to Protect, human security, child soldiers, or international humanitarian law—was excised from the Department of Foreign Affairs and International Trade website; political staffers in both the minister's office and in the Prime Minister's Office made clear that certain words were no longer welcome in official documents (Davis, 2009; Collins, 2009; Berthiaume, 2011). Indeed, Canada's leading role in the NATO (North Atlantic Treaty Organization) intervention in Libya in 2011 provides a useful exemplar of this dynamic at work. Government statements about Libya were carefully crafted so that Canadians would not be reminded of the last time that the Royal Canadian Air Force engaged in a humanitarian intervention—the air campaign against Serbia from March to June 1999 during the Chrétien government.

If this rebranding dynamic was at work in foreign policy, then certainly internationalism—so commonly rendered in Canadian discourse as "Pearsonian internationalism"—would have been a likely target, for internationalism as a policy idea cannot be understood unless it is placed within its historical context. This idea did not spring out of nowhere; rather, it was a response to the dominance of the particular Canadian brand of isolationism of the interwar period from 1919 to 1939. Isolationism as a policy idea had stressed the acceptability—if not the necessity—of avoiding any involvement in the conflicts of global politics; it had legitimized the pursuit of unilateralism; it had attached little importance to international institutions like the League of Nations, except for the prestige that simple membership could bring, and it had been quite acceptable to avoid making any concrete national contributions to international organizations; and finally isolationism had held out little hope for the ability of international law to contribute anything positive to world politics. A view common in Ottawa was that isolationism during the interwar period had contributed to the international system's collapse into systemic war in the late 1930s. In this view, in order to avoid a repetition of this catastrophe, it was necessary that all countries, but particularly the great powers, avoid the policy idea that had contributed to the Second World War. In that sense, internationalism must be seen as the antithesis of interwar isolationism.

Internationalism may have started life as a way of thinking about the world of world politics and, applied in the Canadian context, as a way of thinking about the most appropriate policies for Canada, as a small power aligned with, and allied to, the United States, Britain, and other western European countries, to engage that world. However, as these tenets of internationalism were practised by Canadian foreign policy makers in the decade immediately after the Second World War, and as they became increasingly entrenched in Canadian foreign policy behaviour in the 1960s and 1970s, internationalism as a policy idea underwent an important change. As Don Munton (2002–3) has noted, political leaders in Ottawa increasingly began to recognize that their pursuit of an internationalist foreign policy resonated well among Canadian voters, who appeared to like the self-image of an engaged and responsible middle power contributing to international peace and stability through such activities as peacekeeping and "helpful fixing" (Ichikawa, 1979).

Slowly, what had started out as a foreign policy pursued for essentially foreign policy goals was transformed into a foreign policy pursued for essentially domestic political/electoral goals. By the late 1990s, internationalism had been turned into what Hector Mackenzie has called the "central myth" of Canadian foreign policy (2007: 90–1). Girded by facile tropes about the tenets of internationalism being "in our DNA" (quoted in Nossal, Roussel, and Paquin, 2011: 38), internationalism increasingly became a means to forge a distinct Canadian identity, even if, as Sté-phane Roussel and Chantal Robichaud (2004) remind us, this argument must be carefully nuanced.

Chapnick argues that there is a strong link between the mythologized view that Canadians have of Pearsonian internationalism and the political party that was in power for so much of the period after 1945: "Over the last forty years opportunistic Liberal governments have taken ownership of this popular view of liberal interna-tionalism, leading Canadians to believe that Liberal foreign policy stands for con-tributing positively to world affairs" (2006: 64). Thus, if indeed the Conservatives came to power in 2006 believing that *liberal* internationalism had become *Liberal* internationalism in the popular imaginary, then it is likely that internationalism was subjected to the same rebranding dynamic. In other words, as part of the effort to purge popular perceptions, there was a purposeful abandonment of approaches to policy that smacked of the Liberal era, such as Pearsonian internationalism.

Conclusion

If foreign policy under the Harper Conservatives is interpreted as an out-growth of a *domestic* political/electoral agenda, it makes the apparent disap-pearance of Canada's internationalism more understandable. If indeed liberal internationalism is seen by the prime minister and his senior ministers as a tradition in Canadian foreign policy that is deeply associated with Liberal governments—or even with the Progressive Conservative government of Brian Mulroney (Gecelovsky and Keating, 2001)—then abandoning overt reminders of those traditions becomes an integral part of encouraging Canadians to embrace the Conservative Party.

But if indeed foreign policy has been used primarily for electoral purposes by the Conservative government after 2006, the possibility of recovering that internationalist tradition—a hope expressed in a number of the chapters that follow—is increasingly unlikely. To be sure, such hopes reflect a wider dynamic. On the one hand, the Conservatives' embrace of an explicitly Manichaean worldview, their articulation of a more muscular foreign policy, and their abandonment of the traditional tenets of internationalism have not attracted wide endorsement among the foreign policy elite. On the other hand, however, the new directions in Canadian foreign policy have not inspired the kind of negative reactions among the broader public that might otherwise prompt the Conservative government to change its mind about those directions. And this is likely to be a self-reproducing dynamic: the more the public accepts (or, as importantly, does not reject) the new ideas about Canada's proper role in world affairs articulated by the Conservatives, the less relevant the reminders of a Liberal (if not liberal) internationalist past in Canadian foreign policy will become.

Key Terms

Arctic card
dominant idea
internationalism lite

Manichaeanism
Pearsonian internationalism

Study Questions

1. Looking at the Canadian case, can one establish a relationship between ideas about the nature of world politics and policy outcomes?
2. In what ways did the internationalist approach after the Second World War get transformed in the 1990s, and why?
3. Can the worldview of the Conservative government of Stephen Harper be described as ideological?
4. Why did Pearsonian internationalism become so entrenched as what Hector Mackenzie terms a "central myth" in Canadian foreign policy?
5. How was the Arctic card played by Prime Minister Harper's predecessors, John Diefenbaker, Pierre Elliott Trudeau, and Brian Mulroney?

References

Baird, John. 2007. "Remarks: Regulatory Framework." 25 April [delivered in Toronto, 26 April]. At http://www.ec.gc.ca/default.asp?lang=En&n=6F2DE1CA-1&news=389E60E0-1E29-462A-B9AF-02A00CAC7AA9.

Behiels, Michael D. 2010. "Stephen Harper's Rise to Power: Will His 'New' Conservative Party Become Canada's 'Natural Governing Party' of the Twenty-First Century?" *American Review of Canadian Studies* 40, 1: 118–45.

Berthiaume, Lee. 2011. "Language Changes Were 'Suggestions,' Diplomats Say." *Embassy Magazine*, 9 March. At http://www.embassymag.ca/page/view/language-03-09-2011.

Bloomfield, Alan, and Kim Richard Nossal. Forthcoming. "A Conservative Foreign Policy? Canada and Australia Compared." In James Farney and David Rayside, eds, *Comparing Canadian Conservatism*.

Boucher, Jean-Christophe. 2009. "Selling Afghanistan: A Discourse Analysis of Canada's Military Intervention (2001–2008)." *International Journal* 64, 3: 717–33.

Byers, Michael. 2009. *Who Owns the Arctic? Understanding Sovereignty Disputes in the North.* Vancouver: Douglas & McIntyre.

Canada. n.d. [2010]. *Statement on Canada's Arctic Foreign Policy: Exercising Sovereignty and Promoting Canada's Northern Strategy Abroad.* At http://www.international.gc.ca/polar-polaire/assets/pdfs/CAFP_booklet-PECA_livret-eng.pdf.

Chapnick, Adam. 2005. *The Middle Power Project: Canada and the Founding of the United Nations.* Vancouver: University of British Columbia Press.

———. 2006. "Caught in-between Traditions: A Minority Conservative Government and Canadian Foreign Policy." In Andrew F. Cooper and Dane Rowlands, eds, *Canada among Nations 2006: Minorities and Priorities.* Montreal and Kingston: McGill-Queen's University Press, 58–75.

———. 2008–9. "The Golden Age: A Canadian Foreign Policy Paradox." *International Journal* 64, 1: 205–21.

Clark, Campbell. 2010. "Clinton's Tough Diplomacy Stings Ottawa." *Globe and Mail*, 30 March. At http://www.theglobeandmail.com/news/politics/clintons-tough-diplomacy-stings-ottawa/article1517805/.

Cohen, Andrew. 2003. *While Canada Slept: How We Lost Our Place in the World.* Toronto: McClelland & Stewart.

Collins, Michelle. 2009. "'Gender Equality,' 'Child Soldiers' and 'Humanitarian Law' Are Axed from Foreign Policy Language." *Embassy Magazine*, 29 July. At http://www.embassymag.ca/page/view/foreignpolicy-7-29-2009.

Conservative Party of Canada. 2006. *Stand Up for Canada: Federal Election Platform.* Ottawa. At http://www.cbc.ca/canadavotes2006/leadersparties/pdf/conservative_platform20060113.pdf.

Davis, Jeff. 2009. "Liberal Era Diplomatic Language Killed Off." *Embassy Magazine*, 1 July. At http://www.embassymag.ca/page/view/diplomatic_language-7-1-2009.

Fitzpatrick, Meagan, and Richard Foot. 2010. "Harper Defends Maternal Health Project Funding Minus Abortions for Third World Countries." *Vancouver Sun*, 27 April.

Fowler, Robert R. 2008. "Alice in Afghanistan." *Literary Review of Canada* 16, 1: 3–5.

———. 2010. "Speaking Text: Reflections on Africa and Other Canadian Foreign Policy Issues." Liberal Party Policy Conference, Montreal, 28 March. At http://davidakin.blogware.com/100328.Fowler.Can150.pdf.

Fréchette, Louise. 2010. "Canada at the United Nations: A Shadow of Its Former Self." In Fen Osler Hampson and Paul Heinbecker, eds, *Canada among Nations: 2009–2010: As Others See Us.* Montreal and Kingston: McGill-Queen's University Press, 265–74.

Gecelovsky, Paul, and Tom Keating. 2001. "Liberal Internationalism for Conservatives: The Good Governance Initiative." In Michaud and Nossal, 2001: 194–206.

Harper, Stephen. 2006. "Address by the Prime Minister to the Canadian Armed forces in Afghanistan." 13 March. At http://www.pm.gc.ca/eng/media.asp?category=2&id=1056.

———. 2007. "PM Addresses the Council on Foreign Relations." New York, 25 September. At http://www.pm.gc.ca/eng/media.asp?category=2&id=1830.

———. 2010a. "Canada's G8 Priorities." Ottawa, 26 January. At http://www.pm.gc.ca/eng/media.asp?id=3093.

———. 2010b. "PM Highlights Canada's Role on the World Stage." New York, 23 September. At http://www.pm.gc.ca/eng/media.asp?category=2&id=3672.

———.2011. "Prime Minister Stephen Harper's 2011 Convention Speech." Ottawa, 13 June. At http://www.conservative.ca/press/news_releases/prime_minister_stephen_harper_s_2011_convention_speech.

Heinbecker, Paul. 2010. *Getting Back in the Game: A Foreign Policy Playbook for Canada*. Toronto: Key Porter Books.

Holmes, John W. 1970. *The Better Part of Valour: Essays on Canadian Diplomacy*. Toronto: McClelland & Stewart.

———. 1976. *Canada: A Middle-Aged Power*. Toronto: McClelland & Stewart.

———. 1979. *The Shaping of Peace: Canada and the Search for World Order, 1943–1957*, vol. 1. Toronto: University of Toronto Press.

———. 1982. *The Shaping of Peace: Canada and the Search for World Order, 1943–1957*, vol. 2. Toronto: University of Toronto Press.

———. 1984. "Most Safely in the Middle." *International Journal* 39, 2: 366–88.

Huebert, Rob. 2009. "Canadian Arctic Sovereignty and Security in a Transforming Circumpolar World." *Foreign Policy for Canada's Tomorrow* 4 (July). At http://dspace.cigilibrary.org/jspui/bitstream/123456789/23862/1/Canadian%20Arctic%20sovereignty.pdf.

Ichikawa, Akira. 1979. "The 'Helpful Fixer': Canada's Persistent International Image." *Behind the Headlines* 37 (March): 1–24.

Keating, Tom. 2002. *Canada and World Order: The Multilateralist Tradition in Canadian Foreign Policy*, 2nd ed. Don Mills, ON: Oxford University Press.

———. 2006. "A Passive Internationalist: Jean Chrétien and Canadian Foreign Policy." In Lois Harder and Steve Patten, eds, *The Chrétien Legacy: Politics and Public Policy in Canada*. Montreal and Kingston: McGill-Queen's University Press, 124–41.

Mackenzie, Hector. 2007. "Canada's Nationalist Internationalism: From the League of Nations to the United Nations." In Norman Hillmer and Adam Chapnick, eds, *Canadas of the Mind: The Making and Unmaking of Canadian Nationalisms in the Twentieth Century*. Montreal and Kingston: McGill-Queen's University Press, 89–109.

McQuaig, Linda. 2007. *Holding the Bully's Coat: Canada and the U.S. Empire*. Toronto: Doubleday Canada.

Michaud, Nelson, and Kim Richard Nossal, eds. 2001. *Diplomatic Departures: The Conservative Era in Canadian Foreign Policy, 1984–1993*. Vancouver: University of British Columbia Press.

Munton, Don. 2002–3. "Whither Internationalism?" *International Journal* 58, 1: 155–80.

Nossal, Kim Richard. 1998–9. "Pinchpenny Diplomacy: The Decline of 'Good International Citizenship' in Canadian Foreign Policy." *International Journal* 54, 1: 88–105.

———. 2006. "Les objectifs politiques des examens de politique étrangère: Étude comparée de l'Australie et du Canada." *Études internationales* 37, 2: 57–69.

———. 2007. "Defense Policy and the Atmospherics of Canada-U.S. Relations: The Case of the Harper Conservatives." *American Review of Canadian Studies* 37, 1: 23–34.

———. 2009. "No Exit: Canada and the 'War without End' in Afghanistan." In Hans-Georg Ehrhart and Charles C. Pentland, eds, *The Afghanistan Challenge: Hard Realities and Strategic Choices*. Montreal and Kingston: McGill-Queen's University Press, 157–73.

———. 2010a. "Making Sense of Afghanistan: The Domestic Politics of International Stabilization Missions in Australia and Canada." Paper to Association for Canadian Studies in Australia and New Zealand, University of New England, Armidale, NSW, 5 July. At http://post.queensu.ca/~nossalk/papers/Nossal_2010_Making_Sense.pdf.

————. 2010b. "'Middlepowerhood' and 'Middlepowermanship' in Canadian Foreign Policy." In Nikola Hynek and David Bosold, eds, *Canada's Foreign and Security Policy: Soft and Hard Strategies of a Middle Power*. Don Mills, ON: Oxford University Press, 20–34.

————. 2011. "America's 'Most Reliable Ally'? Canada and the Evanescence of the Culture of Partnership." In Greg Anderson and Christopher Sands, eds, *Forgotten Partnership Redux: Canada-U.S. Relations in the 21st Century*. Amherst, NY: Cambria Press, 375–404.

Nossal, Kim Richard, Stéphane Roussel, and Stéphane Paquin. 2011. *International Policy and Politics in Canada*. Toronto: Pearson Education Canada.

Paris, Erna. 2011. "The New Solitudes." *The Walrus* 8, 2: 22–30.

Paris, Roland. 2011. "What Is Stephen Harper Afraid Of?" *Embassy Magazine*, 20 July. At http://embassymag.ca/page/printpage/paris-07-20-2011.

Pratt, Cranford. 1990. "Has Middle Power Internationalism a Future?" In Cranford Pratt, ed. *Middle Power Internationalism: The North-South Dimension*. Montreal and Kingston: McGill-Queen's University Press, 143–67.

Rioux, Jean-François, and Robin Hay. 1998–9. "Canadian Foreign Policy: From Internationalism to Isolationism." *International Journal* 54, 1: 120–42.

Roussel, Stéphane, and Chantal Robichaud. 2004. "L'État postmoderne par excellence? International-isme et promotion de l'identité internationale du Canada." *Études internationales* 35, 1: 149–70. At http://www.erudit.org/revue/ei/2004/v35/n1/008451ar.html.

Siddiqui, Haroon. 2010. "World Passes Judgment on Harper's Foreign Policy." *Toronto Star*, 14 October.

Simpson, Erika. 1999. "The Principles of Liberal Internationalism According to Lester Pearson." *Journal of Canadian Studies* 34, 1: 75–92.

Simpson, Jeffrey. 2006. "Canada's Biggest Challenge Never Made It into the Election." *Globe and Mail*, 24 January, A27.

Simpson, Jeffrey, Mark Jaccard, and Nic Rivers. 2007. *Hot Air: Meeting Canada's Climate Change Challenge*. Toronto: McClelland & Stewart.

Slater, Joanna, and John Ibbitson. 2010. "PM Hails Canada as Model Global Citizen in UN Pitch." *Globe and Mail*, 24 September.

Smith, Heather A. 2003. "Disrupting Internationalism and Finding the Others." In Claire Turenne Sjo-lander, Heather A. Smith, and Deborah Stienstra, eds, *Feminist Perspectives on Canadian Foreign Policy*. Don Mills, ON: Oxford University Press, 24–39.

————. 2008–9. "Political Parties and Canadian Climate Change Policy." *International Journal* 64, 1: 47–66.

———— . 2009. "Unwilling Internationalism or Strategic Internationalism? Canadian Climate Change Policy under the Conservative Government." *Canadian Foreign Policy/La politique étrangère du Canada* 15, 2: 57–77.

Turenne Sjolander, Claire. 2010. "The Obama Charm? Canada and Afghanistan under a New US Administration." *American Review of Canadian Studies* 40, 2: 292–304.

Webster, Paul C. 2010. "Canada's G8 Health Plan Receives Praise and Criticism." *The Lancet* 375, 9726 (8 May): 1595–6.

Wells, Paul, and John Geddes. 2011. "What You Don't Know about Stephen Harper." *Maclean's*, 7 February: 14–27.

Welsh, Jennifer. 2010. "Immature Design." *The Walrus* 7, 5: 26–31.

Whyte, Kenneth. 2011. "In Conversation: Stephen Harper." *Maclean's*, 5 July. At http://www2.macleans.ca/2011/07/05/how-he-sees-canada%E2%80%99s-role-in-the-world-and-where-he-wants-to-take-the-country-2/.

3 The Twilight of Internationalism? Neocontinentalism as an Emerging Dominant Idea in Canadian Foreign Policy

Justin Massie and Stéphane Roussel*

As conventional wisdom would have it, internationalism has dominated the intellectual landscape of Canadian foreign policy (CFP) since the Second World War (Nossal, Roussel, and Paquin, 2011: 135–41). On many occasions, however, its decline has been predicted, such as in 1969, when the newly elected Pierre Elliott Trudeau called for a more realistic approach to foreign policy, or after the Cold War, when the traditional roles played by middle powers were questioned. This chapter can be associated with this "declinist school" (see Nossal's, Copeland's, and Boucher's chapters in this volume), not because it predicts a new agony of internationalism, but because it contemplates the emergence of a rival—**neocontinentalism**—based on an alternative set of ideas. This is not to say that the currently displayed features of the latter have replaced internationalism to the point of forming a new strategic culture, but merely that neocontinentalism must be considered as a serious rival dominant idea.

Indeed, we argue that a new set of ideas is emerging in the field and practice of Canadian foreign policy, one loosely based on the tenets of traditional **continentalism**, yet one sufficiently different to deserve the prefix "neo." At the outset, continentalism was an approach based on the idea that the destiny of both the Canadian state and Canadian society is inextricably linked to that of the United States. It is therefore in Canada's national interest to align itself openly with its southern neighbour. The continentalist doctrine, understood as such, had for a long time remained essentially a foreign trade policy associated with North American free trade, although from time to time until the mid-twentieth century, some nationalist Canadians saw in continentalism, or in a close relationship with the United States, an alternative to the shackle of the British Empire (Clarkson, 2011: 90). Nevertheless, outside the commercial realm, the formal idea of continentalism remained conceptually underdeveloped (Clarkson, n.d.). Indeed, in the field of Canadian foreign policy, there are few references to continentalism as a doctrine

* The authors would like to thank Frédérick Gagnon (Department of Political Science, Université du Québec à Montréal) and Frédéric Boily (Campus St-Jean, University of Alberta) for their useful insights.

of foreign policy. Further, despite the fact that the practice and basic operational principles of continentalism in matters of defence were laid in 1938, they were only rarely conceptualized as being continentalist and, as practices and principles, were not associated with other aspects of foreign policy (such as diplomacy and trade).

The evolution from continentalism to neocontinentalism rests partly on another shift, this one taking place in the broader field of Canadian politics, from **conservatism** to neoconservatism, or, to put it otherwise, from Toryism to the "Calgary School." The neocontinentalist approach in CFP is increasingly becoming the external expression of a growing domestic neoconservatism. In this sense, domestic politics is playing a direct role in the emergence of new ideas about the place and the role of the country at the international level.

Ideology, Dominant Ideas, and Strategic Culture in Canadian Foreign Policy

Is foreign policy mainly driven by interests, pragmatism, and material factors? One relatively shared understanding of CFP is that partisanship and political parties do not make a significant difference in the conduct of foreign policy. This may be a legacy of the Cold War period, during which the major political parties in Canada (the Liberals and Conservatives) shared similar conceptions of the place and role of Canada in the international arena (Nossal, Roussel, and Paquin, 2011: 275–6). Even after the Cold War, the consensus seems to hold with respect to the substance of Stephen Harper's policies vis-à-vis those of his Liberal predecessors (Bow and Black, 2008–9). In the same vein, Bloomfield and Nossal argue that the Harper government has "abandoned a foreign policy based on dogmatic principles in favour of a more pragmatic approach." Indeed, "it can be argued that Canadian foreign policy since 2006 has been guided by a single over-riding principle, to the exclusion of other, more dogmatic, ideas: to do what is necessary to make the Conservative Party of Canada the country's 'natural governing party'" (2010: 1–2; see also Black, 2009; Murrett and O'Reilly, 2010; Nossal, chapter 2).

In short, **ideology**, defined as a "system of political thought arising out of, and reflecting, the economic, political, and cultural experience of particular social groups," is often thought of as a weak explanatory variable for CFP, and this is despite the fact that ideologies "function to integrate these groups and to mobilize them for political action—against competing groups and their ideologies" (Jahn, 2009: 415). Countering the effects of ideology and partisanship, pragmatism and Canada's geostrategic position can explain the significant stability of its foreign policy since the 1940s (Stairs, 2001: 26; Buteux, 1994).

Other political scientists, however, appear to conclude the exact opposite: that ideology remains an important factor in the (international) behaviour of the Conservative government. They see not only a shift in rhetoric (or style), but also a true societal change underlying an institutionalizing trend of (neo)conservative thoughts and policies. In analyzing the 2011 federal election, some observe "hints . . . that the Conservative success was a product of coverage focused mainly on issues of the right—the economy, foreign affairs and crime," as well as of a deliberate Conservative effort to keep "the base happy and appealing to a greater proportion of sympathetic voters on the centre right" (Soroka, Cutler, Stolle, and Fournier, 2011: 71, 77). This ideological shift, according to sceptics and proponents of the Harper government, has led to a distinctive approach to foreign policy based on the Calgary School movement (Boerger, 2007; Nadeau, 2010). As Adam Chapnick notes, "contemporary articulations of Canadian foreign policy are encouraging a move away from the country's traditional conservative roots to a more radical conservatism" (2005: 648). From this perspective, ideology seems to matter and may help explain the alleged distinctiveness of Conservative CFP under a Harper government.

While it is possible to argue the general importance of ideology as a determining variable of foreign policy, it remains difficult to demonstrate the direct causal links between ideology and specific decisions. This is largely because the values, beliefs, and principles comprising an ideology may not necessarily be applicable to the international level; they may suggest multiple foreign policy postures, and specific decisions may have multiple explanatory causes. Despite these caveats, we contend that the ideological shift in Canada's societal and political landscape has contributed, at least in part, to another shift, this one in Canadian foreign policy. We argue that major changes in Canada's international behaviour and strategic thinking are attributable to a changing domestic ideological landscape.

To make that argument, we must first distinguish ideology from dominant ideas and strategic culture. **Strategic culture** refers to those "distinctive, dominant, and persistent systems of ideas and practices regarding international security [writ large] held by a socio-political community" (Massie, 2009: 628–9; Haglund, 2004: 485; Longhurst, 2004: 17). The notion of strategic culture thus encompasses ideology (and other ideational factors) as well as concrete policy actions and decisions in a semi-permanent and consistent ensemble. Stated otherwise, new thoughts *and* policies must be discernible and consistent with one another for a new strategic culture to become a dominant "way of thinking and doing" foreign policy within a socio-political community. A strategic culture necessarily includes core constitutive elements, most notably a definition of Canada's place and role in the world, its values and interests, and an operational code (or a strategy linking ends with means). We thus conceive strategic culture not as a cause of foreign policy, but as a heuristic device to help us understand ideationally driven change and continuity with regard to states' international security policy-making. Ideologies necessarily impact a state's strategic cultures, but they do not constitute their sole causal factor. Compared to internationalism, continentalism, and Atlanticism (Massie, 2009), neocontinentalism has not reached the same level of dominance. What seems clear, however, is that (1) neocontinentalism is the expression of a new neoconservative ideology with regard to foreign policy, and hence (2) it can be characterized as an *emerging* "dominant idea."[1]

From Conservatism to Neoconservatism

Conservatism refers to a political attitude located on the right of the political spectrum. According to Alain Noël and Jean-Philippe Thérien (2008), the fundamental distinction between the left and right in this dichotomy is a different attitude towards the notion of equality. While those on the left believe it is possible to buffer social and economic disparities through reforms or radical changes, those on the right are more sceptical or defiant about the ability to correct these disparities through measures they would see as social engineering. Believing that attempts to correct these inequalities could bring worse consequences than those they aim to correct, those on the right prefer to have faith in "natural" (re)ordering.

As with any ideology, conservatism comes in various flavours, yet certain core values remain distinctively associated with it. Socially, tradition and religion are usually central elements. Their importance is nurtured by the belief that human life is a constant battle between "good" and "evil," no matter its origin (divine or deriving from human nature) (Boily, 2010: 19; see also Gecelovsky, chapter 7). Economically, conservatism is usually associated with free trade and a minimalist role for the state. Governmental interventions in the economic realm must be reduced to a minimum, while private initiatives help provide public goods. Politically, one of the central values of conservatism is the maintenance of law, order, and stability. Given their pessimistic conception of human nature, conservatives consider that conflicts and violence (including war) are inevitable and that the state must be ready to cope with them. Strong justice, police apparatus, and military institutions are considered necessary to deal with internal and external sources of insecurity. For this reason, conservatism accepts the reinforcement of state power, even if it contradicts the economic principle of a minimalist state (Boily, 2010: 19–20). Finally, consistent with its faith in tradition and preference for a stable natural order, conservatism usually calls for the preservation of the status quo or, alternatively, for a review of past behaviour to find solutions to contemporary problems. In this sense, conservatism values stability, cautiousness, and prudence over new ideas.

While some of these basic values may be applied to foreign policy, conservatism remains a general political doctrine, not necessarily designed to guide a state's foreign policy in a clear, consistent, and unidirectional path (Bloomfield and Nossal, 2010). Nevertheless, it is possible to trace some clear links between the general doctrine and its application to the realm of foreign policy. For instance, the commitment to a free market may lead to positive attitudes towards free trade, while the values of law and order may justify support for a greater defence effort.

A clearer application of conservative values to foreign policy can be found in British Canadian imperialism. As journalist Charles Taylor (1982) shows, there is a rich conservative tradition in Canadian politics. Inherited from its British counterpart, conservatism was a dominant ideology in the Canadian political landscape of the early twentieth century. At its origin, Canadian conservatism displayed a strong external relations dimension, associated first and foremost with imperialism (and the idea that Canada was part of a wider entity, the British Empire, and thus that guiding values and behaviour should reflect and promote imperial interests). In this sense, early Canadian conservatism represented the rejection of the American version of liberalism and republicanism, a central principle of early Toryism (Roussel, 2004: 125–7; Bickerton, Gagnon, and Smith, 2002, 38–9), which David Bell confusingly referred to as 'conservative liberalism" (1995: 116).

To what extent is conservatism still present in contemporary Canadian politics? For the political right, recent developments on the Canadian federal scene might signal renewed faith: the creation of the Reform Party in 1987 and, subsequently, of the Canadian Alliance in 2000, followed by the merger with the Progressive Conservative Party in 2003 to create the new Conservative Party. The Reform and the Alliance were the products of protest movements in the West against a political party system traditionally favouring the "centre of Canada" (Ontario and Quebec) and deemed unrepresentative of the demands and concerns of the West. In the late 1980s this feeling of alienation found new ideological expression in the neoconservative movement that was gaining visibility and legitimacy in other countries, especially in the United States (Miousse, 2007). Indeed, the Reform/Alliance Party was frequently labelled "neoconservative" (Bickerton, Gagnon, and Smith, 2002: 185–7; Leuprecht, 2003; Boily, 2007: 40–9). Because the movement offered a new synthesis of conservative ideas (as was the case for its American counterpart), the adjective was usually ascribed to the Reform and the Alliance, but many of the latter's leaders took key positions in the Conservative Party that emerged after the 2003 fusion. It is thus most likely that some ideas of the Reform/Alliance percolated into the Conservative Party that has been in government since January 2006.

Canada's neoconservative movement was ideologically and intellectually fuelled by a more or less consistent group of academics and intellectuals dubbed the "Calgary School." The Calgary School includes personalities such as Tom Flanagan, Barry Cooper, Rainer Knopff, David Bercuson, Roy Rempel, and Ted Morton. As represented by them, the most important distinctive feature of Canadian neoconservatism is its commitment to tax reductions and the limitation of the role of the state as an economic and social agent. While not prominent, religious beliefs are also present in some debates, such as those on abortion and same-sex marriage. Most noteworthy, neoconservatism puts forth the idea that "evil" exists and that it is the duty of the citizens and their leaders to act according to "what is right" (Boily, 2007: 45–7; Bickerton, Gagnon, and Smith, 2002: 199–200). For example, Foreign Minister John Baird declared at the United Nations General Assembly that "9/11 was a stark reminder that evil exists, that life is fragile, that freedom has enemies, and that the poison of radical terrorism is real" (2011).

Another distinctive theme in the writings of the Calgary School is the fatigue regarding Quebec's demands and/or specificities. While its criticisms of Quebec are mostly raised regarding constitutional and economic issues (Bercuson and Cooper, 1991; Crowley, 2009), they also concern the realm of foreign policy, since many "debatable" decisions (such as the refusal to take part in the Iraq War and to participate in the American missile defence system, as well as Harper's Afghanistan policy) were allegedly made because of Quebec opposition (Granatstein, 2004: 193–4; 2007; 2008: 87–8; cf. Boucher and Roussel, 2008; Massie, Boucher, and Roussel, 2010).

Lastly, neoconservatives have expressed a clear desire to reinforce the application of law and order in Canada. At the domestic level, this means tougher attitudes towards criminality, especially through punitive measures and policies. At the international level, Canadian neoconservatives express distrust towards international organizations (especially the UN), moral fanaticism against threats to Western liberal democracy and Christian values, unqualified belief in the benefits and benevolence of US hegemony, as well as faith in the use of force as a legitimate tool of statecraft. As will be made clear below, neoconservatives advocate a specific foreign policy objective for Canada: that of achieving the status of being the United States' closest partner and most reliable ally.

Continentalism in Canadian Foreign Policy

The above-mentioned values are part of what we call 'neocontinentalism," an emerging dominant idea that is gaining prominence as internationalism's strongest ideological rival because of the ascent of neoconservatism in Canada. Neocontinentalism, however, must first be distinguished from traditional continentalism. The latter was once a dominant idea in Canadian international politics (Kohn, 2004; Smith, 1994), which has been mostly preoccupied with culture and trade rather than security, diplomacy, and defence. Traditional continentalism essentially refers to the vast and multifaceted network of exchanges (goods, people, ideas, etc.) between Canadian and American societies and its positive consequences for both societies and governments. It can be seen as an unintentional societal and economic phenomenon rather than as a deliberate political project or governmental strategy designed to meet explicit political objectives.[2] It was, in short, the product of perceived necessities arising because of Canada's unique geographic location.

If continentalism was clearly not a *political* project, it could be considered as a *trade* strategy, designed to maximize the benefits of Canada's geographic location, with the promotion of a Canada-US free trade agreement being the core element of that strategy. It was also one of the rare issues of foreign relations on which Grits and Tories clearly disagreed. Liberals were traditionally more inclined to promote free trade and closer relations with the United States, which was conceived as a counterweight to the British Empire. Conservatives, on the other hand, remained the voice of British imperialism in Canada until the Second World War, if not until the mid-1950s (Nossal, Roussel, and Paquin, 2011: 129–30). Even after the last trace of imperialism in Canadian foreign policy had vanished (the watershed event here was probably the Suez Crisis in 1956), Conservatives remained defiant in the face of Canada's relationship with the United States. The prevalence of continentalism can be seen in the thinking of major conservative intellectuals such as Donald

Creighton and George Grant (Taylor, 1982; Grant, 1965). Conservatives defended a conception of the Canadian identity that was based on Canada's British roots and stood in opposition to the United States, while the Liberals held a conception of Canada that that was far more critical of the British Empire and was ready to accept a closer relationship with the United States. In a word, from the time of Confederation to the mid-1960s, Liberals were more continentalist than the Conservatives regarding trade and alliances within the North Atlantic Triangle (Brebner, 1945; McKercher and Aronsen, 1996).

With respect to security and defence, continentalism gained prominence as a rival to Canada's contending strategic cultures, Atlanticism and internationalism (which are often considered the same) (Nossal, Roussel, Paquin, 2011: 275–6; Massie, 2009). In contrast to continentalism, internationalism is usually described as a *liberal* strategic culture:

> Internationalism is sometimes described as "liberal"—for two reasons. Some use it because this approach was initially formulated and implemented by Liberal governments, particularly the government of Louis St Laurent. But the adjective is also used because internationalism takes as its starting point the application of political liberalism to global politics. Not only is internationalism founded on liberal values (such as peace, freedom, justice, and democracy), but the means to promote it are inspired by some of the key tenets of liberal philosophy: individual rights, equality, rule of law, transparent systems of governance and the management of economic exchange. Moreover, because the majority of Canadians value these principles, internationalism generates considerable consensus. (Nossal, Roussel, and Paquin, 2011: 136)

Liberal internationalism, in the Canadian context, acknowledges a responsibility to take an active part in world affairs, the virtue of Western-led multilateralism, a will to commit significant domestic resources to international affairs, and faith in liberal international institutions, including international law and the free market.[3] Yet one could astutely point out that many CFP initiatives in the area of defence do not fall within such a strategic culture. This is because of a contending strategic culture—continentalism—also at work in CFP.

Prime among continentalist initiatives are the 1940 Ogdensburg Agreement and the creation of NORAD (North American Aerospace Defense Command) in 1957–8, which both significantly tied Canadian security to American security. One response to such apparent deviances from internationalism has been to emphasize the fact that they were embedded in an internationalist logic, according to which international institutions were thought to provide a counterweight and a safeguard against the excessive American influence to which a close Canada-US relationship would inevitably lead (Roussel, 2004: 197–200). A second response has been to stress that these initiatives were not perceived as elements of a wider strategy designed to achieve general foreign policy objectives—in contradistinction to some other initiatives, such as the creation of the United Nations or NATO (North Atlantic Treaty Organization), which were explicitly designed to implement internationalist and Atlanticist agendas. The continentalism that was displayed during the Second World War and the Cold War was not part of a well-thought-out strategy but a "force of nature" against which Canada could do little, according to John Holmes, a key internationalist thinker (1985: 25). Continentalism, in other words, lacked a clearly defined worldview; a specific definition of Canada's values, interests, and place in the world; and the proper means by which to achieve them. The security and defence initiatives associated with continentalism were merely pragmatic responses to Canada's geostrategic position and threat environment, rather than products of a (conservative) ideology. Indeed, an increasingly benign international environment helps to explain the ability of Canadian governments to exert "strategic dissent" vis-à-vis US security initiatives such as the ballistic missile defence (BMD) system (Nossal, 2011).

The shift towards continentalism as a dominant idea in Canadian strategic thinking was made possible by the accession to power of the Conservative Party led by Brian Mulroney in 1984. During his campaign to gain the leadership of the Conservative Party, at a moment when Prime Minister Trudeau's nationalistic trade policies were souring relations with the Reagan administration, Mulroney promised to improve Canada's relations with the United States dramatically. Canada, he said, would be a "better ally, a super ally" of the United States. The new leader also promised to be tougher against the Soviets than the Liberals had been, and to make Canada "first class in conventional defence" (quoted Michaud and Nossal, 2001: 9). In 1985, a year after his election, Mulroney put forth the idea that it was time to negotiate a free trade agreement with the United States.

Pro-America, anti-Soviet, an emphasis on defence—all of these attitudes can be associated with conservatism and continentalism. Nevertheless, once in power, Mulroney and his ministers adopted a much more balanced tone and adapted their policy accordingly. If they launched the negotiations for a free trade agreement, they were not the super ally they promised to be. If they were very critical of the Soviet Union, even after Mikhail Gorbachev launched glasnost and perestroika, they did not confront Moscow as hard as one could have expected. And if they published a White Paper on defence containing a long list of new military acquisitions, they were also the ones who sacrificed that list on the altar of deficit reduction. In other words, the Mulroney Conservatives did not put forth an ideologically based continentalist foreign policy.

While Mulroney's foreign policy revealed sympathies with continentalism in the area of trade, it remained explicitly committed to a revamped version of liberal internationalism (Canada, 1986). As Denis Stairs puts it, "certainly [the Conservatives] have not been successful in identifying a *distinctive* vision—one, that is, that would distinguish the Conservative view from those of their adversaries or even from the ones inherent in the eclectic expectations of the attentive population at large" (2001, 28; emphasis in original). All in all, it is very difficult to contend that the Mulroney government was distinctively "conservative" in the ideological sense of the word, at least in the realm of foreign and defence policy. Ideology is thus rarely (if ever) considered a significant explanation of Mulroney's foreign policy (cf. Chapnick, 2005).

The Rise of Neocontinentalism

The attacks on the United States of 11 September 2001 and their impact on Canada's prosperity and security have given a second life to continentalism in Canadian foreign policy. The trade dimension remains central, but new security elements have been added to the original discourse. A notable illustration of this expansion is contained in one of the key neocontinentalist blueprints of CFP, Michael Hart's *From Pride to Influence* (2008). Hart, a leading scholar of trade policy (see Hart, 2002), applies his continentalist trade perspective to the realms of security and defence. He argues that, given a growing North American economic interdependence, new threats to international security (terrorism, rogue states, weapons of mass destruction), and US unipolarity, Canada must align its foreign policy with that of the United States. This is the only way, he contends, that Canada can maintain its security and prosperity while gaining influence and pride on the world stage.

The neocontinentalist relationship between trade and security is also articulated in the concept of a "security perimeter." Briefly stated, the security perimeter involves a standardization of procedures in Canada and the United States with respect to traffic coming from the rest of the world, the purpose being to facilitate the reduction of controls *between* the two countries (see Kitchen, chapter 10). Although the concept was originally put forth by Canadian officials, it became part of the American vocabulary in 2000. After 9/11, despite repeated calls by the American ambassador to Canada, Paul Cellucci, the expression "security perimeter" was officially banned by the Chrétien government because of its political implications—namely, that any standardization process would be, in fact, the Americanization of Canadian procedures. The idea nonetheless survived among Canadian commentators, especially economists, and within the business community. Proposals in favour of a new comprehensive arrangement with the United States flourished (e.g., meeting American security requirements in order to reduce the need for extensive controls at the border and to secure access to the US market for Canadian exports). These "big ideas," linking trade and security, marked a renewed interest for a continentalist approach to Canadian foreign policy (Roussel, 2002). Most importantly, they added to it a distinct worldview, a definition of Canada's place and role in the world, Canadian values and interests, and an operational code. Indeed, a favourable context provided continentalism with the ideological content necessary to generate neocontinentalism.

During the Chrétien era, however, Ottawa was regularly under criticism for its pusillanimity in international affairs and its habit of not backing its word with concrete actions. The human security agenda was, for instance, denounced as purely declaratory (Nossal, 1998–9), supported with few resources. Despite several military commitments around the world (ex-Yugoslavia, Somalia, Haiti), the Canadian Armed Forces were neglected and their budget dramatically reduced during the struggle against the deficit; they never fully recovered under the Chrétien government, even after September 2001.

Many of the criticisms of Chrétien's attitude towards the United States came from authors sympathetic to continentalist ideas (e.g., Granatstein, 2002; Gotlieb, 2004). Despite some distinctions, their views seem consistent with those of a group of intellectuals more closely associated with neoconservatism, the Calgary School. It is the synthesis of these views that can be labelled "neocontinentalism." Because the Harper government has been described as having implemented some of the Calgary School's precepts, it is worth examining neocontinentalism in light of the Harper government's foreign policy to date.

Neocontinentalism can be understood as being composed of seven core constitutive elements. Only after the effective implementation of a critical mass of these elements in Canadian foreign policy can one argue that internationalism has been replaced by a new neocontinentalist strategic culture. The following constitutive elements thus represent a preliminary attempt to delineate an "ideal type" for the purpose of illustrating what a neocontinentalist foreign policy would represent. The Harper government's foreign policy, while sympathetic to some of those elements, cannot yet be argued to contain them all.

First, neocontinentalism borrows some of the values associated with conservatism from the economic (free trade, laissez-faire, individual rights, minimal fiscal burden), political (law, order, stability, and state integrity and sovereignty), and social dimensions (tradition, religion, family). Neocontinentalism's worldview and prescriptions must, at a minimum, be consistent with these values. At first glance, Harper's "tough on crime" agenda, tax cuts, and child-care benefit plan, to name but a few, seem to illustrate the actual implementation of ideologically driven Conservative policies (Snow and Moffitt, 2011).

A second constitutive element relates to Canada's position in the world. Neocontinentalism rests upon a deep dissatisfaction with Trudeau's and Chrétien's foreign policies, which have been criticized as having sabotaged Canada's status and position on the international stage. Hence, Canada's most important duty is to restore Canadian status and position in the international hierarchy by substantially investing in its military and diplomatic capabilities (Boerger, 2007: 123–30). More to the point, neocontinentalists believe that Canada is a "foremost power," depicting it as a state with a huge potential of influence on the international stage if it plays its cards well and accepts the responsibilities that come with such rank. This, of course, is consistent with Stephen Harper's characterization of Canada as an "energy superpower" (Hester, 2007) as well as a "strong, reliable partner" to the United States (Canada, 2008: 4).

A third element, consistent with the pessimistic conception of human nature inherent to conservatism, is that the world is a dangerous place, with many potential enemies that must be neutralized or checked. Canada cannot be considered a safe haven for terrorists and other potential threats—a concern largely fuelled by the attacks in New York and Washington. Neocontinentalists are more likely than internationalists to adopt a Manichaean conception of the world, with the "good" found on one side and the "bad" on the other. Those who fall on the wrong side of this divide are those who do not respect the law, democracy, and tradition defined in Western/liberal terms. In fact, Prime Minister Harper praised Colombia for its democratic political system, whereas he demonized Iran and chastised Russia for their aggressive behaviour (O'Grady, 2009).

A fourth constitutive element is that while neocontinentalists speak in terms of power relations and national interest, they are more likely to be guided by principles and values than by a pragmatic and dispassionate (i.e., realist) assessment of the national interest. In this sense, neocontinentalists share with liberal internationalists a deep commitment to the promotion of democracy, human rights, and the rule of law. As Mr Harper made clear in an April 2003 speech:

> We [Conservatives] understand that the great geopolitical battles against modern tyrants and threats are battles over values. . . . Conservatives must take the moral stand, with our allies, in favour of the fundamental values of our society, including democracy, free enterprise and individual freedom. This moral stand should not just give us the right to stand with our allies, but the duty to do so and the responsibility to put "hard power" behind our international commitments. (Harper, 2003a)

Harper maintained this policy even after acceding to power. Indeed, in his 2008 Speech from the Throne, he urged Canada to stand ready to defend aggressively against threats to its fundamental values, for "[o]ur national security depends on global security. Our Government believes that Canada's aspirations for a better and more secure world must be matched by vigorous and concrete actions on the world stage" (Harper, 2008).

A fifth element flows from the two previous ones. Since the world is dangerous and power relations are a key feature of the international system, force is a legitimate tool to secure the international order and to neutralize and/or punish those who threaten the US-dominated order. This is a central element of any strategic culture, and assessing that element is crucial to distinguishing between the two cultures (Johnston, 1995). Liberal internationalists are willing to use force, but under stricter conditions than neocontinentalists require. The former believe it is necessary to secure a consensus among key Western allies (e.g., the United States, the United Kingdom, France, Germany), as well as to comply with international law. This means that any use of force must be backed by a United Nations Security Council resolution. Neither of these criteria applies to the neocontinentalist approach. The United States (and to a lesser extent the UK) is the only ally on which Canada should really count. In addition, international institutions like the

UN are almost insignificant for neocontinentalists. A relaxed understanding of the conditions under which it is necessary to use military force logically means a conception of international politics that gives a significant role to the armed forces. The corollary is that the armed forces must be given the proper resources to perform their duty, which means a relatively higher defence budget. As will be discussed below, Harper made this clear in his stand in favour of Canada's participation in the Anglo-American–led war against Iraq in 2003.

A sixth and crucial constitutive element is the explicit admission that Canada's closest partner and most important ally is the United States. Canada's prosperity largely depends on its immediate access to the American market. The same is true with respect to security. Since at least the 1938 "Kingston Dispensation," Canadian security has been inextricably tied to that of its southern neighbour (Haglund and Fortmann, 2002; Massie, 2007; Barry and Bratt, 2008; see also Kitchen, chapter 10). But neocontinentalists push the idea of close relations with the United States a step further than traditional continentalists do. Not only is free trade and minimal (yet necessary) defence cooperation needed, but the "relationship with the United States is the indispensable foundation of Canadian foreign policy in all its dimensions" (Hart, 2002–3). Stephen Harper's remarks during a press conference with President Obama are illustrative of this: "[T]he view of this government is unequivocal: threats to the United States are threats to Canada. There is no such thing as a threat to the national security of the United States which does not represent a direct threat to this country" (Harper, quoted in Davis, 2009). Given such interdependence, it follows that it is in Canada's self-interest to remain, as Harper's defence strategy puts it, a "strong, reliable partner" to the United States, both in North America and abroad (Canada, 2008).

Neocontinentalism thus suggests that Canada should nurture its "special" relationship with the United States outside its traditional continental setting, notably by supporting US military operations overseas. This was made clear by Harper during the crisis over the Iraq War. In March 2003, he stood in the House of Commons to argue that "[w]e should be there with our allies when it counts against Saddam Hussein" (Wells, 2007: 10). He explicated his position—and incidentally its underlying neoconservative bent—later in the *National Post*. His op-ed illustrates quite clearly the importation of neoconservative ideas, originally associated with the Reform/Alliance, into the Conservative Party. It also serves to illustrate many of the other five constitutive elements discussed above.

For this failure [to take part in the war against Iraq], Canadians have suffered not necessarily an immediate economic loss, but a reminder of our growing irrelevance on the world stage. We are losing, as a consequence, our ability to exert influence on the events and the allies that will shape our future. . . . We need more flexible and aggressive methods to promote our underlying interests and values in the world. . . . The time has come to recognize that *the United States will continue to exercise unprecedented power* in a world where international rules are unreliable and where the security and advancing of the free, democratic order still depend significantly on the possession and use of military might. The basis for entering into an ad hoc coalition is not our relationship with the United States per se. The reason to consider the United States is that, fundamentally, we share the same fundamental values in a dangerous world. But more deeply, we share common interests on multiple levels to an extent experienced by no two other countries. . . . In fact, *Canada's greatest asset on the international stage is our unique relationship with the United States*—the fact that we just happen to share values and interests with the world's sole superpower. Not only can we advance our own interests in concert with the United States, the opportunity exists to strengthen Canadian influence on the Americans, and thus enhance our sovereignty in ways that no encirclement strategy could plausibly do. (Harper, 2003b; our emphasis)

For Canada to achieve its primary foreign policy objective—that is, "to re-establish Canada as a serious partner for United States"—neocontinentalists focus almost exclusively on hard power. As Harper further explained:

Bluntly, some of these [policies] involve the ability to deploy hard power. First, we must take seriously our own and continental security, rather than just push the entire burden on to the United States. We need to engage actively in the continental missile defence program to ensure Canada has a voice in its own air security. Second, we need to rebuild our military capacity to diverse and effective levels. Third, we need to ensure that Canada is never again perceived as a potential source of threats through a long-overdue reform of our border controls and refugee programs. (Harper, 2003b)

In other words, Canada's neocontinentalism holds that Canada should become the best ally of the United States through military means. Indeed, rather than seeing the US as a threat to Canadian sovereignty, neocontinentalists conceive the southern neighbour as a benevolent hegemon. It follows that Canada should not seek to constrain its actions through multilateral institutions, but rather conceive of US hegemony as an opportunity for greater influence on world affairs. As Colin Robertson put it, "Real influence also depends on being a reliable partner in collective security and helping the U.S. bear the global burden of primacy, as we did by putting boots on the ground in Afghanistan, planes in the air over Libya and taking a lead role in the reconstruction of Haiti" (2011). This faith in bilateralism is partly because neocontinentalists are usually sceptical of the ability of multilateral institutions to implement foreign policy objectives. Such institutions are thought not to possess the necessary teeth to impose order, or worse, it is feared that they may impose constraints on those who are willing to maintain and restore international order, as was allegedly the case during the invasion of Iraq (Boerger, 2007, 133–5).

Conclusion

In our assessment of an ideologically driven conservative foreign policy in Canada, we have argued that a new set of ideas pertaining to Canada's place and role in the world has emerged in the last decade or so, one we label "neocontinentalism." The emergence of neocontinentalism is mostly driven by a shifting political and ideological landscape in Canada, from conservatism and liberalism to neoconservatism. While neocontinentalism has not yet materialized sufficiently or reached the intellectual consensus needed to deserve being conceptualized as a strategic culture, it does represent an emerging dominant idea in Canadian foreign policy. It rests on a distinctive ideology and departs in significant ways from both traditional continentalism and liberal internationalism. In this sense, the practice and study of Canadian foreign policy may witness, in the medium term, the twilight of internationalism.

Key Terms

continentalism

neocontinentalism

conservatism

strategic culture

ideology

Study Questions

1. What are the main differences between a pragmatic and an ideologically driven foreign policy?
2. To what extent can the Mulroney government's foreign policy be labelled conservative?
3. What are the most defining constitutive elements of neocontinentalism?
4. To what extent can the Harper government's foreign policy be labelled neocontinentalist?
5. What are the main differences between a liberal internationalist, a continentalist, and a neocontinentalist foreign policy?

Notes

1   The concept of dominant ideas has for the most part been used to describe internationalism. It usually refers to a relatively consistent set of values, preferences, attitudes, and beliefs held by a socio-political community with regard to foreign relations (Noël, Thérien, and Dallaire, 2003; Nossal, Roussel, and Paquin, 2011; Munton and Keating, 2001; Perreault, 2011).

2   This has held true, with the possible exception of the position of the Clear Grits, who advocated Canada's admission to the Union (see Roussel, 2004: 127–30), or Canada nationalists of

the 1930s, who were hoping to find in the relations with the United States a counterweight to
the British influence.

3   In this chapter, we are using the definition of Canadian internationalism offered in Nossal,
Roussel, and Paquin (2011: 136) not only because it is largely accepted by many CFP specialists,
but also because it was explicitly presented as a "dominant idea," if not as a strategic culture
(see Massie, 2009; Roussel and Robichaud, 2004).

References

Baird, John. 2011. "Address by the Honourable John Baird, Minister of Foreign Affairs, to the United
Nations General Assembly." New York City, 26 September. At http://www.international.gc.ca/
media/aff/speeches-discours/2011/2011-030.aspx?lang=eng&view=d.

Barry, Donald, and Duane Bratt. 2008. "Defense against Help: Explaining Canada-U.S. Security Relations." *American Review of Canadian Studies* 38, 1: 63–89.

Bell, David V.J. 1995. "Political Culture in Canada." In Michael S. Whittington and Glen Williams,
eds, *Canadian Politics in the 1990s*. Toronto: Nelson, 105–28.

Bercuson, David J., and Barry Cooper. 1991. *Deconfederation: Canada without Quebec*. Toronto: Key
Porter Books.

Bickerton, James, Alain-G. Gagnon, and Patrick J. Smith. 2002. *Partis politiques et comportement
électoral au Canada: Filiations et affiliations*. Montreal: Boréal.

Black, David. 2009. "Out of Africa? The Harper Government's New 'Tilt' in the Developing World."
Canadian Foreign Policy/La politique étrangère du Canada 15 (Summer): 41–56.

Bloomfield, Alan and Kim Richard Nossal, 2010. "A Conservative Foreign Policy? Canada and Australia
Compared." *Canadian Political Science Association*, Montreal, 3 June.

Boerger, Anne. 2007. "Rendre au Canada sa puissance: La politique étrangère et de défense canadienne
vue de l'Ouest." In Frédéric Boily, ed., *Stephen Harper de l'École de Calgary au Parti conservateur*.
Québec: Presses de l'Université Laval, 121–46.

Boily, Frédéric. 2007. "Le néoconservatisme au Canada: Faut-il craindre l'École de Calgary?" In
Frédéric Boily, ed., *Stephen Harper de l'École de Calgary au Parti conservateur*. Québec: Presses de
l'Université Laval, 27–53.

———. 2010. *Le conservatisme au Québec*. Québec: Presses de l'Université Laval.

Boucher, Jean-Christophe, and Stéphane Roussel. 2008. "From Afghanistan to 'Quebecistan': Que-
bec as the Pharmakon of Canadian Foreign and Defence Policy." In Jean Daudelin and Daniel
Schwanen, eds, *Canada among Nations 2007: What Room for Manoeuvre?* Montreal and Kingston:
McGill-Queen's University Press, 128–56.

Bow, Brian, and David Black, eds. 2008–9. "Political Parties & Foreign Policy." *International Journal*
64, 1: 7–88.

Brebner, J. Bartlet. 1945. *North Atlantic Triangle: The Interplay of Canada, the United States, and Great
Britain*. New York: Columbia University Press.

Buteux, Paul. 1994. "Sutherland Revisited: Canada's Long-Term Strategic Situation." *Canadian
Defence Quarterly* 24, 1: 5–9.

Canada. 2008. *Canada First Defence Strategy*. Ottawa: Department of National Defence.

Canada, Parliament of. 1986. *Independence and Internationalism: Report of the Special Joint Committee
on Canada's International Relations*. Ottawa: Supply and Services Canada, June.

Chapnick, Adam. 2005. "Peace, Order, and Good Government: The 'Conservative' Tradition in Canadian Foreign Policy." *International Journal* 60, 3: 635–50.

Clarkson, Stephen. 2011. "Update: The Choices That Were Made and Those That Remain." In Duane
Bratt and Christopher J. Kukucha, eds, *Reading in Canadian Foreign Policy: Classic Debates and
New Ideas*. Don Mills, ON: Oxford University Press, 87–92.

————. n.d. "Continentalism." *The Canadian Encyclopedia*. At http://www.thecanadianencyclopedia. com/index.cfm?PgNm=TCE&Params=A1ARTA0001890.

Crowley, Brian Lee. 2009. *Fearful Symmetry: The Fall and Rise of Canada's Founding Values*. Toronto: Key Porter Books.

Davis, Jeff. 2009. "Harper Hits Mark with Border Security Message." *Embassy Magazine*, 25 February. At http://embassymag.ca/page/view/obama_visit_canada-2-25-2009.

Gotlieb, Allan. 2004. *Romanticism and Realism in Canada's Foreign Policy*. Benefactors Lecture. Toronto: C.D. Howe Institute.

Granatstein, Jack L. 2002. "A Friendly Agreement in Advance: Canada-U.S. Defence Relations, Past, Present, and Future. " *C.D. Howe Institute Commentary* 166 (June): 22.

————. 2004. *Who Killed the Canadian Military?* Toronto: HarperCollins.

————. 2007. *Whose War Is It? How Canada Can Survive in the Post-9/11 World*. Toronto: HarperCollins.

————. 2008. "Multiculturalism and Canadian Foreign Policy." In David Carment and David Bercuson, eds, *The World in Canada: Diasporas, Demography, and Domestic Policy*. Montreal and Kingston: McGill-Queen's University Press, 78–91.

Grant, George. 1965 [2004]. *Lament for a Nation: The Defeat of Canadian Nationalism*. Montreal and Kingston, McGill-Queen's University Press.

Haglund, David G. 2004. "What Good Is Strategic Culture?" *International Journal* 59, 3: 479–502.

Haglund, David G., and Michel Fortmann. 2002. "Canada and the Issue of Homeland Security: Does the Kingston Dispensation Still Hold?" *Canadian Military Journal* 3, 1: 17–22.

Harper, Stephen. 2003a. "Rediscovering the Right Agenda." *Citizens Centre Report Magazine* 30, 10 (June).

————. 2003b. "A Departure from Neutrality." *National Post*, 23 May: A18.

————. 2008. "Protecting Canada's Future." *Speech from the Throne*. Government of Canada, 19 November 2008. At http://www.speech.gc.ca.

Hart, Michael. 2002. *A Trading Nation: Canadian Trade Policy from Colonialism to Globalization*. Vancouver: University of British Columbia Press.

————. 2002–3. "Lessons from Canada's History as a Trading Nation." *International Journal* 58, 1: 25–42.

————. 2008. *From Pride to Influence. Towards a New Canadian Foreign Policy*. Vancouver: University of British Columbia Press.

Hester, Annette. 2007. "Canada as the 'Emerging Energy Superpower': Testing the Case." Canadian Defence and Foreign Affairs Institute. At http://www.cdfai.org.

Holmes, John. 1985. "Remarks before the Standing Committee on External Affairs and National Defence." Ottawa, 10 October.

Jahn, Beate. 2009. "Liberal Internationalism: From Ideology to Empirical Theory—And Back Again." *International Theory* 1, 3: 409–38.

Johnston, Alastair Iain. 1995. "Thinking about Strategic Culture." *International Security* 19, 4: 32–64.

Kohn, Edward P. 2004. *This Kindred People: Canadian-American Relations and the Anglo-Saxon Idea, 1895–1903*. Montreal and Kingston: McGill-Queen's University Press.

Leuprecht, Christian. 2003. "The Tory Fragment in Canada: Endangered Species?" *Canadian Journal of Political Science* 36, 2: 401–16.

Longhurst, Kerry A. 2004. *Germany and the Use of Force*. Manchester: Manchester University Press.

McKercher, B.J.C., and Lawrence Aronsen, eds. 1996. *The North Atlantic Triangle in a Changing World: Anglo-American-Canadian Relations, 1902–1956*. Toronto: University of Toronto Press.

Massie, Justin. 2007. "Canada's (In)dependence in the North American Security Community: The Asymmetrical Norm of Common Fate." *American Review of Canadian Studies* 37, 4: 493–516.

————. 2009. "Making Sense of Canada's 'Irrational' International Security Policy. A Tale of Three Strategic Cultures." *International Journal* 64, 3: 625–45.

Massie, Justin, Jean-Christophe Boucher, and Stéphane Roussel. 2010. "Hijacking a Policy? Assessing Quebec's 'Undue' Influence on Canada's Afghan Policy." *American Review of Canadian Studies* 40, 2: 259–75.

Michaud, Nelson, and Kim Richard Nossal, eds. 2001. *Diplomatic Departures: The Conservative Era in Canadian Foreign Policy, 1984–93*. Vancouver: University of British Columbia Press.

Miousse, Benoît. 2007. "*The West Wants In*: Les revendications de l'Ouest comme vecteur de renouvellement de la droite canadienne." In Frédéric Boily, ed., *Stephen Harper de l'École de Calgary au Parti conservateur*. Québec: Presses de l'Université Laval, 9–26.

Morton, Ted. 2003. "A New Quebec Alberta Alliance?" *National Post*, 20 May. At http://www.tedmorton.ca.

Munton, Don, and Tom Keating. 2001. "Internationalism and the Canadian Public." *Canadian Journal of Political Science* 34, 3: 517–49.

Murrett, Colleen, and Marc J. O'Reilly. 2010. "Canada's Defiant Arctic Policy: Emblematic of a New Era in Canadian Foreign Policy or an Example of Stephen Harper Realpolitik?" Paper presented at the annual conference of the International Studies Association, New Orleans, 17 February.

Nadeau, Christian. 2010. *Contre Harper*. Montreal: Boréal.

Noël, Alain, and Jean-Philippe Thérien. 2008. *Left and Right in Global Politics*. Cambridge: Cambridge University Press.

Noël, Alain, Jean-Philippe Thérien, and Sébastien Dallaire. 2003. "Divided over Internationalism: The Canadian Public and Development Assistance." *Cahiers du CPDS*, February.

Nossal, Kim Richard. 1998–9. "Pinchpenny Diplomacy: The Decline of 'Good International Citizenship" in Canadian Foreign Policy.' *International Journal* 54, 1: 88–105.

———. 2011. "America's 'Most Reliable Ally'? Canada and the Evanescence of the Culture of Partnership." In Greg Anderson and Christopher Sands, eds, *Forgotten Partnership Redux: Canada-U.S. Relations in the 21st Century*. Amherst, NY: Cambria Press, 375–404.

Nossal, Kim Richard, Stéphane Roussel, and Stéphane Paquin. 2011. *International Policy and Politics in Canada*. Toronto: Pearson Education Canada.

O'Grady, Maria Anastasia. 2009. "A Resolute Ally in the War on Terror." *Wall Street Journal*, 28 February, A9.

Perreault, François. 2011. "The Arctic Linked to the Emerging Dominant Ideas in Canada's Foreign and Defence Policy." *Northern Review* 33 (Spring): 47–67.

Robertson, Colin. 2011. "Advancing Canadian Interests with the US." *Embassy Magazine*, 4 May. At http://www.embassymag.ca/page/view/robertson-05-04-2011.

Roussel, Stéphane. 2002. "Pearl Harbor et le World Trade Center: Le Canada face aux États-Unis en période de crise." *Études internationales* 33, 4: 667–95.

———. 2004. *The North American Democratic Peace: Absence of War and Security Institution-Building in Canada-US Relations, 1867–1958*. Montreal and Kingston: McGill-Queen's University Press.

Roussel, Stéphane, and Chantal Robichaud. 2004. "L'État post-moderne par excellence? Internationalisme et promotion de l'identité internationale du Canada." *Études internationales* 35, 1: 149–70.

Smith, Allan. 1994. *Canada: An American Nation?* Montreal and Kingston: McGill-Queen's University Press.

Snow, Dave, and Benjamin Moffitt. 2011. "Straddling the Divide: Conservatism and Populism in Harper's Canada and Howard's Australia." Paper prepared for the Canadian Political Studies Annual Conference, Wilfrid Laurier University, Waterloo, 16–18 May.

Soroka, Stuart, Fred Cutler, Dietlind Stolle, and Patrick Fournier. 2011. "Capturing Change (and Stability) in the 2011 Campaign." *Policy Options*, June-July: 70–77.

Stairs, Denis. 2001. "Architects or Engineers? The Conservatives and Foreign Policy." In Nelson Michaud and Kim Richard Nossal, eds, *Diplomatic Departures: The Conservative Era in Canadian Foreign Policy, 1984–93*. Vancouver: University of British Columbia Press, 25–42.

Taylor, Charles. 1982 [2006]. *Radical Tories: The Conservative Tradition in Canada*. Toronto: Anansi.

Wells, Paul. 2007. "Stephen Harper's Twisted Walk Back on Iraq." *Maclean's*, 29 January, 10.

4

The Responsibility to Think Clearly about Interests: Stephen Harper's Realist Internationalism, 2006–2011

Jean-Christophe Boucher

Since Louis St Laurent's Gray Lecture in 1947, Canadians have assessed and judged their government's foreign policy by the standards of internationalism. The Conservative government of Stephen Harper, first elected in 2006 after 12 years of Liberal domination in Ottawa, has not escaped the inevitable comparison with the internationalist tradition. Many scholars, commentators, and practitioners have argued that, since 2006, the government of Canada under the Conservative Party has abandoned or, even worse, betrayed the sacred laws of internationalism (see Nossal, chapter 2). Two main criticisms have been expressed in the literature to support such a claim. First, some authors have argued that Stephen Harper has forsaken the internationalist tradition by moving Canada towards continentalism. In this context, the Conservative management of foreign affairs appears to be concerned mostly with Canada's relations with the United States. Frédéric Mérand and Antoine Vandemoortele (2009), for example, contend that through his speeches and actions Harper is a radical continentalist, systematically aligning himself with Washington. The second main line of criticism posits that Harper strays from the internationalist tradition when he aligns Canada's international policy with domestic imperatives for electoral, partisan interests. Some, such as Paul Heinbecker (2010), attribute this pragmatic shift to Canada's domestic political environment; for example, Conservative pundits have used foreign policy as a wedge issue with which to divide the electorate and the Liberal Party in the hope of attaining for the Conservatives a House of Commons majority and, ultimately, of making the Conservative Party of Canada the natural governing party of the future.

On the whole, these criticisms of Stephen Harper's foreign policy rest on the assumption that, since 2006, the Conservatives have altered Canada's stance on international issues fundamentally. However, assessing change in foreign policy behaviour, and particularly the shift away from internationalism, remains a daunting task. As a dominant idea in international policy, internationalism is "both intangible and latent: even if one can claim that they [dominant ideas] exist, it is difficult to *demonstrate* that they exist, for the simple reason that they are generally not expressed; and they are not expressed because, being dominant, they are so rarely challenged" (Nossal, Roussel, and Paquin, 2011: 119; emphasis in original). Furthermore, the instrumentalization of internationalism renders an assessment of the latter's proper nature in Canadian international politics hazardous. As Evan Potter (2009) observes, liberal internationalism has become a distinctive Canadian brand that particularizes Canada's image abroad and, for the most part, has been adopted by both domestic and international publics. As Claire Turenne Sjolander rightly recognizes, "Liberal internationalism has become, in a significant sense, a Canadian *brand* which reflects the best of Canadians to themselves at home at least as much as it promotes an image of Canada abroad" (2009: 79). In many ways, brands have a tendency to outgrow their actual product, and a strong brand will remain impervious to changes despite a significant modification of the merchandise. There is a general tendency on the part of politicians and practitioners to use the internationalist brand even when the product does not fit the idea (Hampson and Oliver, 1998; Nossal, 1998–9, 2005; Cohen, 2003; Stairs, 2003a; Gotlieb, 2004; Granatstein, 2004). For these reasons, claims that the Harper government's handling of Canadian international affairs has abandoned or, even worst, betrayed the sacred laws of internationalism merit particular attention.

In this chapter, I argue that since the election of Stephen Harper's Conservative government in 2006, Canada has taken a "realist" stance towards foreign policy issues. Far from turning its back on a well-entrenched foreign policy tradition, however, the Harper government still embraces internationalism, albeit in a more modest, pragmatic fashion. This realist shift acknowledges the primacy of domestic imperatives and interests in the determination of Canada's foreign policy positioning and priorities. In addition, the Conservatives are suspicious of any association with grand moral principles that would, in effect, steer the conduct of foreign policy away from national interests. In attempting to shed light on the specifics of Canadian internationalism under a Conservative government, I will first discuss the multiple interpretations of the concept of internationalism as reflected in the literature. Without such conceptual groundwork, discussions on the adequacy, or lack thereof, of the Conservatives' foreign policy with respect to interpretations of internationalism are bound to remain unfocused. Second, I will show how, in some respects, Stephen Harper's foreign policy remains true to Canada's internationalist tradition, even if identified more strongly with realism.

The Conceptual Mirage of Internationalism(s) in Canadian Foreign Policy

Internationalism, as a concept, remains illusive and under-specified. No sustained intellectual discussion pertaining to Canadian foreign policy can fully emancipate itself from the conceptual ball and chain bequeathed by the pioneers in Canada's international activity (such as Lester B. Pearson, O.D. Skelton, Escott Reid, Hume Wrong, and John Holmes). As many authors have noted, internationalism remains a conceptual mirage (Molot, 1990; Black and Smith, 1993; Nossal, 1998–9; Munton and Keating, 2001; Turenne Sjolander, 2009; Munton, 2002–3; Gotlieb, 2004). As a notion, it is often vague and ill-defined, allowing scholars, commentators, and politicians to see only what they are yearning for. While there is no shortage of definitions or usages of "internationalism" in the literature, there is no widely accepted conceptual understanding of the term. In fact, the wealth of notions associated with "internationalism"—such as Pearsonian, human, passive, new, liberal, economic, realist, conservative, or constructive—implicitly signals an overall confusion over what scholars actually mean by the word. As Don Munton (2002–3) ably notes, for lack of an operative definition, scholars often settle to ask "Whither internationalism?" when evaluating a specific Canadian government's international behaviour.

Much of the conceptual uncertainty shrouding "internationalism" stems from the tendency to confuse ends and means with respect to Canada's foreign policy behaviour. As Max Weber writes in *Objectivity in Social Science and Social Policy*, "All serious reflection about the ultimate elements of meaningful human conduct is oriented primarily in terms of the categories 'end' and 'means'" (2011: 49). In brief, Weber holds that humans desire something either for itself or as a means of achieving something else more highly desired. In the study of international relations, authors have generally identified two broad conceptions of states' finality: realist or idealist. On the one hand, in following a *realist* interpretation, states can pursue "egoistical" ends based on their comprehension of their national interests, defined in terms of security, prosperity, or cultural imperatives. On the other hand, according to a more *idealist* reading, states can pursue altruistic ends based on their membership in an international community and **cosmopolitan values** such as "the satisfaction of global or human needs; … the respect of universal human rights; and the importance of moderation, communication, generosity, and cooperation in international affairs" (Melakopides, 1998: 4–5).

There are two common misconceptions associated with this realist-idealist dichotomy. The first is that a realist understanding of international relations is empty of any moral considerations. Many realist authors, at least from the classical realist school of thought, have argued that the interests of states are not restricted to material issues and confined to security or economic dimensions. To this effect, Hans Morgenthau warns, "A discussion of international morality must guard against … underestimating it by denying that statesmen and diplomats are moved by anything but considerations of material power" (1948: 225). Classical realists have stressed the legitimacy and importance of values in the conduct of foreign policy. E.H. Carr (1954) asserts the significance of "ordinary morality," while Morgenthau (1948) analyzes the role of "emotions" and Raymond Aron (1984) the tandem *gloire—idée*, in the practice of international relations. Nevertheless, these sets of values are put in perspective by the arguably ethnocentric ethical caveats of particular states. In the words of Morgenthau, "[T]here is an enormous gap between the judgment we apply to ourselves and our own actions, and the universal application of our own standards of action to others" (1948: 246). Hence, a realist understanding of international relations does offer some space for values to influence actors; it contests, however, the universal propensity of such values.

The second misconception, as Welsh (2005) and Heinbecker (2011) have noted, is that cosmopolitan values and the interests of states are not always in opposition; they often coincide and sponsor the same policies. There is, however, an underlying hierarchy to the logic of the egoistical-altruistic interest. Realist scholars have argued that when push comes to shove, states will promote their own interests to the detriment of other ideals (Carr, 1954; Aron, 1984; Morgenthau, 1948). As E.H. Carr writes, "The accepted standard of international morality in regard to the al-truistic virtues appears to be that a state should indulge in them in so far as this is not seriously incompatible with its more important interests" (1954: 159). Idealists, for their part, have instead argued that normative considerations should prevail in cases where interests and moral imperatives diverge. In essence, the realist-idealist interpretation follows two distinct understandings of the preferable end pursued by states.

Both of the traditions identifying distinct end-means logics for Canada's in-ternational behaviour have been present in Canada's internationalist narrative. Internationalism, as a specifically Canadian way of conducting foreign policy on the international stage, is not inconsistent with either liberal or realist interpreta-tions of international relations. Allan Gotlieb expresses the dual finality pursued by Canada's foreign policy: "One pole ties us to hard reality, *Realpolitik* if you will, and makes us want our governments to protect the national interests when it deals with other states. . . . In contrast to the pole of realism, there is another pole that attracts Canadians to an idealistic vocation. Its advocates tend to have a visionary, at times almost romantic, approach to our position in the world" (2004: 1). In this light, internationalism in Canadian foreign policy appears to be a two-headed monster: one head represents the liberal ideals of global citizenship and values-based for-eign policy, while the other maintains realist notions of national interests (either economic, security, or cultural) and a case-by-case approach to foreign policy. The generalized dissatisfaction with the conventional interpretation of international-ism, an interpretation that in effect emphasizes the liberal outgrowth, stems from the recognition that internationalism has not always had *only* a values-based for-eign policy temperament. Lester B. Pearson himself (Chapnick, 2005b; Gotlieb, 2004; Stairs, 2001, 2003b) noted that "Canadian value-laden pronouncements in external affairs have never been meant to be taken entirely seriously" (Chapnick, 2005b: 649) and that Canadian foreign policy should remain flexible and prag-matic, incorporating two "realist" dispositions (Simpson, 1999).

In its most general sense, internationalism is a foreign policy attitude supporting the idea that Canada should actively engage in international affairs through multilat-eral relationships while pledging significant resources to shared interests and world order. Therefore, in this minimal sense, the concept of internationalism encompasses three necessary and jointly sufficient conditions: (1) multilateralism, (2) a sense of responsibility towards international affairs, and (3) respect for the international rule of law. One will note that I have mostly been loyal to Holmes's (1970) interpretation of internationalism, identified as a "cooperation of nations in the common interest" and the collaborative effort "to achieve the international agreements which fortify the world structure" (cited in Munton and Keating, 2001: 526). Additionally, I have purposefully avoided certain terms that are sometimes associated with internationalism, such as "middlepowermanship" or "functionalism." To include such concepts in a definition of internationalism is problematic; middlepowermanship with respect to Canada, for example, suggests more a recognition of Canada's status or power than an actual attitude towards foreign policy (Molot, 1990; Black and Smith, 1993; Neufeld, 1995; Keeble and Smith, 1999; Munton and Keating, 2001). At best, some could argue that Canada's internationalist point of view is a consequence of its status in the world order, but not an actual consequence of internationalism. Likewise, the functionalist argument (according to which Canada should be awarded status and consequently decision-making relevancy on specific international issues [such as atomic energy or Arctic concerns] as a function of the importance of its interests and competency in the matter) is an offshoot of an internationalist attitude. It is only in an internationalist mindset that functionalism actually takes on any meaning as a specific Canadian foreign policy; internationalism, however, does not need a functional argument to be conceptually consistent (Chapnick, 2005a).

That being said, the first necessary condition associated with the notion of internationalism, and probably the least contentious, is Canada's *support and preference for multilateral dealings* where more than two states engage in a collaborative relationship to define or diffuse political issues (Nossal, Roussel, and Paquin, 2011; Nossal, 1998; Keating, 2002). For Tom Keating (2010), we must distinguish between the idea of **multilateralism**—"a belief about how to conduct one's affairs in a world of states and of how these states should conduct their affairs" (9)—and the practice of multilateralism. As a necessary condition of internationalism, multilateralism is limited to its "instrumental" understanding, or in Keating's words, to the practice of multilateralism.[1] As such, advocating for multilateral cooperation in Canadian foreign policy suggests neither a leap of faith nor an ideology. The necessity for Canada to contribute to and promote multilateral cooperation derives from two rational arguments. First, most internationally relevant issues are better addressed in multilateral forums. Paul Heinbecker expresses this reality impeccably by pointing out that "for international security, for trade and finance, for health and environmental protection, for human rights and human development—in sum, for the totality of modern life—multilateral cooperation is indispensable" (2004: 794). Considering Canada's limited capacity to commit resources to foreign affairs issues, it is only through multilateral institutions that it can confront international concerns by pooling its resources with those of other states. Second, through multilateralism, states can counterbalance the undue influence of other states by widening their room for manoeuvre on the international stage and by pre-emptively limiting or shaping future engagements (see Massie and Roussel, chapter 3). As many have recognized, multilateral cooperation is the principal strategy that Canada can adopt to balance the disproportionate, but unavoidable, influence of the United States on its foreign policies.

The second necessary condition characterizing internationalism is a *sense of responsibility towards international affairs*. In his 1998 article, Nossal defines this condition as actions "directed towards creating, maintaining, and managing community at a global level" (98). This element of internationalism represents the idea that Canada has an obligation to participate actively in world affairs given its enviable economic, political, and social position. The origin of this sense of responsibility can stem either from a moral obligation towards a loosely termed "international community" or, instead, from the realization that such responsibility is, in fact, in Canada's self-interest. Indeed, Canada remains highly dependent on a relatively stable international environment and has no choice but to participate in enterprises whose purposes are to maintain an international system that is largely to Canada's advantage. Furthermore, this duty to engage in international affairs also logically involves the need for the government of Canada to invest significant resources in foreign policy portfolios such as defence, diplomacy, and development aid. If Canada were to lack the necessary tools to act on the international stage, the "responsibility" requirement of internationalism would be devoid of sense.

The third and final necessary condition for a general concept of internationalism as applied to Canadian foreign policy is a commitment to *bolster and respect international law*. When supporting and promoting international law, states attempt to limit the capacity of nations to act arbitrarily in the international system. Lacking the power, either military, economic, or cultural, to compete in an *ad hoc* international community unconstrained by international legislation, Canada has every interest in relying on the rule of law. In this sense, internationalism means that Canada should engage internationally and enter into legally binding agreements in every form possible, ranging from trade treaties (either through the World Trade Organization or bilateral free trade agreements) to the use of force in conformity with international institutions. Internationalism also means that Canada will and should use the relevant international organs to settle international disputes and to promote its national interests, instead of acting alone and imposing its views.

Table 4.1 captures the nature of internationalism as means and as an instrument of state foreign policy, as well as the dual nature of the ends of internationalism, linked to the cosmopolitan "values versus interests" debate. Both liberal and realist internationalisms remain alive in Canadian foreign policy and in essence are subsumed in the debate about values and interests. They are the two poles between which scholars, practitioners, commentators, and the public debate Canada's place in the world and how the Canadian government should conduct its international relations.

TABLE 4.1 Necessary conditions of internationalisms

Internationalism

- Multilateralism
- Sense of responsibility towards international affairs
- Respect for and promotion of international rule of law

Liberal internationalism	Realist internationalism
• Cosmopolitan values	• National interests

According to Dewitt and Kirton (1983), liberal internationalism is a "constant co-operative endeavour to enhance universal values through the steady development of a more institutionalized and just international order." We can associate liberal internationalism with what scholars have called "humane internationalism" (Pratt, 1989), active internationalism (Munton and Keating, 2001), or Pearsonian internationalism (Tucker, 1980). As such, there is the belief that internationalism is a strategy that seeks to achieve such goals as being a "good international citizen" and promotes cosmopolitan ideals. The notion of "good citizenship," Nossal tells us, involves the suggestion that "a country's diplomacy can be directed towards ameliorating the 'common weal' by taking actions explicitly designed to achieve that end' (1998: 99). Good citizenship entails more than just concrete actions such as making a commitment to international aid, participating in peacekeeping, or promoting fairness in trade relationships; it involves a fundamental conviction that Canada is part of an international community, a community that is essentially perfectible. Thus, there is a teleological underpinning to liberal internationalism. The good citizenship condition encompasses the view that Canada's foreign policy should work towards the betterment of international society, placing, in essence, the community's interests at the vanguard of international policy-making. A cosmopolitan ideal-based foreign policy refers to the idea that Canada's foreign policy should adhere to specific intrinsic values, such as human rights, democracy, and good governance, and should promote these values through specific policies. These values are to serve as a guide, a moral compass dictating Canada's stance on such international matters as war and peace, international aid, and economic equality (Pratt, 1989). In this light, proponents of liberal internationalism see Canada as a "norm-entrepreneur," a model country whose example other nations can follow (Riddell-Dixon, 2004; Welsh, 2004; Axworthy, 2003). A cosmopolitan-based foreign policy is ethical in nature. It does more than just promote the rule of law; it aligns a country's foreign behaviour with ethical rules irrespective of the consequences.

Realist internationalism, for lack of a better term, is a dominant idea according to which Canadian foreign policy should be aligned with the country's national interests. Given the evolving nature of these interests, such a foreign policy should be conducted on a case-by-case basis. Nonetheless, the internationalist foundation of this foreign policy asserts forcefully that national interests, however egoistical in nature, can best be met through a commitment to multilateralist cooperation (in an instrumental sense), a sense of responsibility, and support for international law. A realist understanding of internationalism puts the emphasis on the importance of Canadian national interests in defining foreign policy priorities. Although national interests are a source of much debate among scholars—either on what exactly constitutes Canadian national interests (Granatstein, 2003) or which strategy (continentalism or internationalism) can best achieve these interests—a realist perception of internationalism focuses on such notions as "sovereignty and independence, national security and economic growth" (Gotlieb, 2004: 2). A realist conception of foreign policy is character-ized by case-by-case policy-making that emphasizes the contextual and ephemeral nature of international politics, with domestic and foreign imperatives changing dramatically across time. Hence, realists consider that encasing Canada within an *a priori* set of principles would essentially limit the country's ability to adapt to an evolving international environment.

Branding Stephen Harper's Internationalism

Under Stephen Harper, Canada's foreign policy has remained internationalist in nature. Since 2006, the Conservative management of international relations has been conducted mostly through multilateralism, with a special preference for like-minded forums such as the North Atlantic Treaty Organization (NATO) or the G8 and G20. There is also a clear sense that only through its active engagement in the world can Canada address important issues such as prosperity and security. As Harper acknowledges, "the thing that's probably struck me the most ... is not just how important foreign affairs/foreign relations is, but in fact that it's become almost everything" (Whyte, 2011: 3). The promotion of the international rule of law is probably the weakest link in the Conservatives' internationalism. Nonetheless, Canada has been quite active in signing free trade agreements, concluding accords with such countries as Colombia, Peru, Jordan, and Panama and conducting major negotiations with the European Union and India. In many ways, this trend is consistent with policies of previous Canadian governments. What is particular to the Conservative government of Stephen Harper, however, is its strong realist shift towards an emphasis on the need to act in accordance with Canada's national interests and to limit Canada's commit-ment to cosmopolitan values.

In his Conservative convention speech of 2011, Stephen Harper outlined his understanding of foreign policy:

> Re-equipping the military is just the tip of the iceberg when it comes to making Canada a meaningful contributor in the world. We also have a pur-pose. . . . And that purpose is no longer just to go along and get along with everyone else's agenda. It is no longer to please every dictator with a vote at the United Nations, and I confess that I don't know why in the past attempts

to do so were ever thought to be in Canada's national interests. . . . Now we
know where our interests lie, and who our friends are, and we take strong,
principled positions in our dealings with other nations—whether popular
or not.

We can clearly discern the strong realist inclination in this passage, particularly
in the notion that the purpose of Canada's foreign policy should be aligned with
its national interests. Despite the speech being such a strong statement, however,
discerning a distinct "Conservative" foreign policy brand is a difficult enterprise,
primarily because the Conservative government has been quite circumspect on
foreign policy. Although there are rumours of a "new" foreign policy position
document to be presented, as of 2012, the Harper government has declined to
publish a White Paper that would summarize and identify foreign policy challenges
and priorities. As Nossal (chapter 2) notes, the absence of a clear foreign policy
document, one that would outline a distinct philosophy towards international
affairs, signals how little the Conservatives understood foreign policy before 2006.
This betrays a preference for dealing with international issues on an "à-la-pièce"—or
case-by-case—basis, thus leaving the government room to manoeuvre in
implementing political initiatives that would reflect changing international and
domestic imperatives. In this context, we have to rely on available sources such
as the *Canada First Defence Strategy* and the Conservatives' electoral platforms of
2006, 2008, and 2011.

The *Canada First Defence Strategy* is an important document reflecting on
foreign policy. Although officially unveiled by Prime Minister Harper in May
2008, the document had been a position paper developed by Gordon O'Connor
before the Conservative Party took power in Ottawa in 2006. Furthermore, both
the 2006 and 2008 electoral platforms mention that an elected Harper government
would implement the *Canada First* strategic plan. *Canada First* is still considered to
be the main foreign policy document of a distinctively Conservative international
agenda.[7] Needless to say, a defence policy is not equivalent to a foreign policy, but
such a focus on defence and security betrays the genuinely realist inclination of
the Harper government. Themes of anarchy, uncertainty, sovereignty, security, and
responsibility, all notions associated with a classical realist interpretation of international relations, are well entrenched in the *Canada First* document. For example,
the introduction legitimizing a new defence strategy for Canada clearly signals a
realist understanding of the world: "Today we live in an uncertain world, and the
security challenges facing Canada are real. Globalization means that developments
abroad can have a profound impact on the safety and interests of Canadians at
home. . . . Canadians expect and deserve no less than a highly capable military
that can keep them safe and secure while effectively supporting foreign policy
and national security objectives" (Government of Canada, 2008: 7). In hindsight,
Canada First articulates a realist conception according to which security imperatives are paramount in the conduct of international politics, overshadowing other

issues such as foreign aid and even trade. Thus, *Canada First* stresses a willingness to improve Canada's defence capabilities in the hope that the Canadian Forces can "deliver excellence at home, be a strong and reliable partner in the defence of North America, and project leadership abroad by contributing to international operations in support of Canadian interests and values" (2008: 7).

Were one to examine the Conservative federal election platforms of 2006, 2008, and 2011, one would be surprised at the sparseness of foreign policy proposals. As Nossal (2007 and chapter 2) notes, in the 2006 election platform entitled *Stand up for Canada*, only 3 out of the 60 priorities identified by the Conservative Party of Canada pertain explicitly to foreign policy: advancing Canadian values and interests on the world stage, defending Canada, and creating jobs through international trade. In fact, these 3 priorities (representing only 2 pages out of the 46-page platform) are mentioned at the end of the document, as if to symbolize how little importance was to be accorded to international politics. Essentially, the 2006 platform expresses the party's desire to align foreign policy with Canadian values, broadly defined in terms of freedom, fairness, and compassion, while advancing Canadian national interests. The document also advocates strengthening Canada's defence capabilities through large-scale investments, and encourages free trade–oriented policies.

Although a tad more explicit, the 2008 Conservative electoral platform, patriotically named *The True North Strong and Free: Stephen Harper's Plan for Canadians,* underlines 6 foreign policy concerns among 74 priorities. In terms of values and foreign aid, the 2008 document expresses the Conservative government's willingness to promote Canada's democratic ideals abroad, as well as to continue its support for international development by increasing foreign aid allocations. With respect to defence policy, the 2008 electoral platform emphasizes the need to defend Canada's Arctic sovereignty, build on the *Canada First* defence strategy, and support the Afghanistan mission until 2011. Finally, the Harper platform specifies that Canada would try to focus its international trade initiatives on emerging markets such as China, Mongolia, Mexico, India, and Brazil.

In its 2011 election platform titled *Here for Canada*, the Conservative Party puts forward two main priorities with respect to foreign policy: first, to promote economic prosperity by encouraging international trade, and second, to defend Canadian sovereignty by strengthening the Canadian Armed Forces and by defending Canada's interests in the Arctic. In this, the 2011 platform is consistent with previous documents. In terms of promoting Canadian values, however, the 2011 document abandons earlier themes such as the promotion of democracy and focuses instead on defending religious freedoms, supporting developing countries, and promoting maternal, newborn, and child health. Nevertheless, these priorities are in fact subsumed under the "stand on guard for Canada" umbrella, which suggests either confusion (how is international aid and promoting maternal health a subcategory of Canada's security interests?) or the securitization of issues about which the 2011 platform offers no arguments (see Carrier and Tiessen, chapter 11).

In retrospect, the 2006, 2008, and 2011 Conservative platforms remain unimaginative and vague. Despite this, the idea that Canada needs to promote its interests abroad, mainly in terms of economic prosperity and security, is consistently asserted and identified as a foreign policy priority of the Conservative government. From the *Canada First* document and the 2006, 2008, and 2011 electoral platforms, we see an implicit realist interpretation of Canada's international affairs. As Nossal (chapter 2) remarks, there is little sign of liberal internationalism in these texts. Clearly, Conservatives have explicitly argued and conducted a more egoistical foreign policy than have previous governments. Nevertheless, the internationalist inclination—where international affairs are managed mostly through multilateralism, a sense of responsibility towards the welfare of nations, and the promotion of the international rule of law—remains, on the whole, alive with Stephen Harper.

The Responsibility to Think Clearly: Coming to Terms with R2P

The Conservative government's unwillingness to come to terms with the "Responsibility to Protect" doctrine (R2P) is a second indication of the realist shift in Canada's commitment to internationalism. The decision of the Conservative government to limit Canada's affiliation with the R2P initiative is probably the best example of how this realist transition is perceived in Conservative circles. More than just a rebranding exercise on the part of the Conservative government in an effort to eradicate the Liberal legacy in foreign policy, as some have tried to suggest (Davis, 2009), the decision to disengage Canada from R2P is emblematic of an attempt to re-centre Canada's foreign policy on egoistical interests and values. Conservatives argue that Liberals, particularly during Lloyd Axworthy's tenure at the Department of Foreign Affairs and International Trade (DFAIT) between 1996 and 2000, have embarked on a creative spiral of tentative norms creation emphasizing the need to remodel the traditional conception of security and promote a foreign policy focused on human security and the responsibility of nations to protect endangered populations, irrespective of state sovereignty. This led critics to a cynical evaluation of Canadian foreign policy: Ottawa appeared to be willing to "wimp out" on concrete international engagements while holding a moralizing discourse that aggravated friends and foes alike (Nossal, 1998; Hampson and Oliver, 1998).

The R2P principle has evolved since it was first developed by the International Commission on Intervention and State Sovereignty (ICISS) and sponsored by the government of Canada in September 2000. Within the context of the human security agenda, the **Responsibility to Protect** was broadly defined as "the idea that sovereign states have a responsibility to protect their own citizens from avoidable catastrophe, but that when they are unwilling or unable to do so, that responsibility must be borne by the broader community of states" (ICISS, 2001: 8). According to Ban Ki-moon's *Implementing the Responsibility to Protect: Report of the Secretary-General*, published in 2009, R2P rests on three pillars:

1. the primary responsibility of states to protect their own populations from the four crimes of genocide, war crimes, ethnic cleansing, and crimes against humanity, as well as from their incitement;
2. the international community's responsibility to assist a state to fulfill its R2P; and
3. the international community's responsibility to take timely and decisive action, in accordance with the UN Charter, in cases where the state has manifestly failed to protect its population from one or more of the four crimes. (Bellamy, 2010: 143)

From R2P's inception in 2000 to the 2005 World Summit, where it received official endorsement from the international community, Canada had always been at the forefront of discussions on the conceptualization and implementation of the doctrine. Then prime minister Paul Martin, speaking at the high-level meeting of the sixtieth session of the United Nations General Assembly in 2005, acknowledged and congratulated the Canadian lineage of R2P (Martin, 2005). At least in words, successive Liberal governments of Jean Chrétien and Paul Martin endorsed R2P. In the late spring of 2005, months after Martin's address at the United Nations, the Liberal government released its foreign policy White Paper, *Canada's International Policy Statement* (IPS), subtitled "A Role of Pride and Influence in the World," which outlined Canada's "Responsibilities Agenda." According to this document, Canada's international policy would be attentive to five responsibilities: "to protect" by holding governments accountable and to intervene to prevent humanitarian tragedies; "to deny" by preventing terrorists and irresponsible governments from acquiring weapons of mass destruction; "to respect" by helping build lives of freedom for all people; "to build" by providing development assistance packages that encourage the independence of recipients in their own development; "to the future" through sustainable development and management of public goods (IPS, Diplomacy: 20). In many ways, Liberal internationalism expressed itself through the R2P agenda by proposing Canadian support for cosmopolitan ideals, promoting good citizenship, and favouring the betterment of the global public good.

However, when the Conservative Party of Stephen Harper took office in February 2006, Canada's overt support for the R2P agenda was reconsidered. As soon as the spring of 2007, senior Conservative policy staffers asked top brass from DFAIT to eliminate every mention of R2P from official and unofficial policy statements. This request was also forwarded to the Canadian representation at the United Nations in New York, where diplomats were asked to stop referring to or engaging in the Responsibility to Protect agenda. These directives stemmed more from the Prime Minister's Office (PMO), which controlled much of official speech writing on foreign policy issues, than from the office of Foreign Affairs Minister Maxime Bernier, who directed the day-to-day operations at DFAIT. Concomitant with notifying public servants of Canada's decision to forgo its support for R2P, Conservatives embarked upon a "cleansing" operation, systematically eliminating references to R2P in memos, notes, PowerPoint presentations, and official documents (Davis, 2009). Despite strong opposition from the DFAIT bureaucracy at home and abroad, the Conservative government remained convinced that R2P was an ill-thought principle that opened the door to misuse and abuse from states; that the international community had neither the will nor the capacity to implement such a grand objective; and that Canada's involvement in R2P was not in the country's best interests.[3]

From the Conservative government's perspective, the principle of R2P is conceptually suspect. At the very least, there are a number of conceptual problems associated with R2P that have not yet been addressed in international forums. First, there is a propensity in the R2P initiative to impose a social order that many could perceive as imperialistic or Western-centric. R2P rests on the notion of a global community with shared and universal values, including respect for human rights (in the sense of a respect for the moral and physical integrity of the human being), an individualist conception of freedom, the sanctimony of the rule of law, the peaceful nature of democracy, and so on. These represent a Western interpretation of moral order, an order not necessarily shared by most nations. In this respect, the Conservatives' attempt to disengage Canada from the R2P initiative is, in many ways, an un-conservative endeavour.[4]

Second, while R2P is quite clear on when the international community should intervene in another country's internal affairs (to prevent genocide, war crimes, ethnic cleansing, and crimes against humanity), what worries Conservatives is the actual applicability of such wide-ranging principles. Ethical discussions surrounding R2P should never have been based on the extreme case, but rather on situations more limited in scope—events where genocide, war crimes, ethnic cleansing, or crimes against humanity criteria are not easily identifiable. Accusations of genocide or other such crimes have been the norm in UN General Assembly speeches and have proved useful in invoking the responsibility of the international community to intervene, but this is where the R2P principle remains lacking. We generally have a good idea of what constitutes a clear case of genocide, yet we are still uncertain as to how R2P could or should apply to more limited cases. In practice, we have already seen events where R2P was invoked without there being a clear association with the four crimes listed above. Since 2005, many countries have appealed to R2P in dubious instances that, in effect, sap the overall legitimacy of the principle. For example, R2P was invoked during the Russian intervention in Georgia in 2008; by the French to support intervention in Myanmar after the passing of the cyclone Nargis in 2008; by the Palestinian Authority, Qatar, Iran, and the World Council of Churches during the Gaza crisis in 2009; by India, Norway, and the Global Centre for R2P for the Sri Lankan dealings with the Tamil insurrection in 2008–9; for the North Korean crisis; and finally by the Myanmar government in exile for Myanmar's handling of its ethnic minorities (Bellamy, 2010). In all these cases, the R2P principle was abused either because the R2P criteria did not apply (Myanmar, Sri Lanka, North Korea) or because the principle was used to provide a "moral" glitter to egoistical interests (Georgia, Gaza). As an epistemic society, we still have no clear understanding of where and when R2P should be applied, and this ambiguity fosters and encourages exploitation of the principle. The Conservative government has made it quite clear that its international actions, even in cases such as NATO's Libyan intervention, should not be justified in terms of R2P. As Deepak Obhrai, the Conservative member of Parliament for the riding of Calgary East, warned during the House of Commons debate on Libya on 14 June 2011, "[W]e [the government of Canada] want to see this as a Libyan-led solution and not one that is affected by military action under the responsibility to protect" (Government of Canada, 2011).

With respect to the relevance of R2P to national interests, the Harper government estimates that Canada has neither the capacity (in terms of resources to commit to international aid), the conflict prevention diplomacy, or the deployable military personnel to participate effectively and contribute to a fully grown R2P agenda. As Nossal states, "[T]he Responsibilities Agenda, if one were to take it seriously, commits Canada, and thus Canadians, to a vast project of global reform, change, and commitment. Any one of the Responsibilities—let alone all five together—would overwhelm any government in Ottawa that tried to embrace them" (Nossal, 2005: 42). Furthermore, Conservatives consider that Canada should not constrain its foreign policy with international norms that are not obligatory, where free riders can benefit without paying the cost to maintain such norms, and where there is so little international consensus, especially among the "great powers." Canada should be able to carry out a case-by-case foreign policy, advocating its values when it sees fit and remaining free to act in accordance with its interests—which are not always the same as those of the international community.

Conclusion

On many issues, Stephen Harper's conduct of foreign policy since 2006 has been characterized by an inclination towards a stronger "realist" interpretation of internationalism. Although the Conservative government has tried to promote an international policy that is centred on Canadian national interests and involves a case-by-case conception of foreign affairs, it has not completely abandoned Canada's affection for internationalism. In this context, Harper's foreign policy remains true to a broad conceptualization of internationalism defined by multilateralism, a sense of responsibility to act in international affairs, and a respect for and commitment to promote the international rule of law. Nonetheless, what differentiates Conservative foreign policy from that of the previous Chrétien and Martin governments is its strong scepticism about a cosmopolitan interpretation of foreign policy. From 2006 to 2011, the Harper government committed itself to a general improvement of funding for foreign policy departments such as DFAIT, DND, and the Canadian International Development Agency (CIDA). Also, Conservatives have sought to re-centre Canadian foreign policy on a stronger realist understanding of the world by limiting the normative discourse that had characterized the last 20 years of Liberal administration. Ironically, Michael

Ignatieff had already summarized this perspective in a 2004 publication in which he noted that, during the first decade after the end of the Cold War, "[o]ur ventures were more deeply undergirded by illusions of imperial omnipotence than we knew, more underwritten by unquestioned assumptions about our goodness than was prudent; and our failure to sustain decent ends *with* adequate means leaves open to question just how deep our commitment to these ends actually was" (2004: 553–4).

The decision by the Harper government to revisit Canadian official support of the principle of R2P illustrates this desire to realign Canadian foreign policy with realist internationalism. As I have argued, Conservative pundits perceive the "Responsibility to Protect" package as a perfect example of a Canadian foreign policy that is focused on a moralistic, values-based discourse, when Canada's capacity actually to endorse such principles remains disputable. In this context, Conservatives express the need to think clearly about Canadian interests and not to make an official commitment (such as by making an engagement to R2P a centrepiece of Canada's foreign policy) to principles that are still being developed. Also, Conservatives believe that Canada has a responsibility to be honest and not to be constrained by moral principles that it cannot, considering its capacities and political will, fully implement.

Finally, in this chapter, I have tried to nuance, either explicitly or implicitly, two general assumptions related to Stephen Harper's conduct of Canadian foreign policy, the first being that the determination of Conservative foreign policy is mainly directed by partisan considerations, and the second, that the Conservatives have pushed Canada's international policy towards a radical continentalism that, in effect, adopts policies in total alignment with Washington's. In this context, the attempt of the Harper government to disengage Canada from R2P can be seen as a perfect example. To begin with, linking R2P with partisanship is difficult, since for the partisanship argument to be consistent, it is necessary either that the issue has an important electoral weight or that it can be used as a wedge to disrupt a rival's party cohesion. In both cases, Harper's rejection of R2P appears to fail to support the partisanship argument. Canada's defence of R2P on the international stage and as a foreign policy statement is not an electoral issue among the Canadian population (with the possible exception of educated voters interested in foreign policy), and R2P is not a serious wedge issue inside the Liberal Party. Further, with respect to the continentalist argument, it is difficult to see how Canada's rejection of R2P serves American interests or, at least, helps to improve Canadian-US bilateral relations. Americans have not been particularly supportive of the R2P agenda at the United Nations, but the issue has never been an irritant between Ottawa and Washington. In hindsight, Canada's rejection of R2P is better explained by the return to realist internationalism, which puts Canada's national interests at the centre of foreign policy decision-making and favours the case-by-case conduct of international affairs. The realist internationalism expressed in the Conservative government's foreign policy since 2006 is the result of its philosophical stance on Canada's place and responsibility in the world.

Key Terms

realist internationalism

responsibility to protect

cosmopolitan values

multilateralism

Study Questions

1. Define and discuss the distinction between liberal internationalism and realist internationalism.
2. How are the policies of the Conservative government of Stephen Harper a reflection of realist internationalism?
3. What are the main themes developed in the Conservative electoral platforms of 2006, 2008, and 2011?
4. What are the main objections of the Harper government towards the Responsibility to Protect agenda?
5. Do you think Canada should centre its foreign policy on its national interests or its values? In the event of a conflict between these imperatives, which should be given precedence and why?

Notes

1   Following Keating (2002, 2010), the traditional definition of multilateralism in Canadian foreign policy is cosmopolitan in nature. Multilateralism is conceived as an end in itself, not as a means to advance particular policy agendas.
2   When conducting interviews with senior political advisors and public servants for this chapter, I asked on many occasions if we could expect a specific Conservative White Paper outlining the Harper government's foreign policy priorities. In response, I was consistently referred, almost apologetically, to the *Canada First* document.
3   Confidential interviews conducted with senior Conservative advisors at DFAIT, the Department of National Defence, and the PMO; multiple interviews ranging from July 2008 to September 2011.
4   As Adam Chapnick (2005) notes, the volition to export and impose social order internationally is fundamentally a small-c conservative idea (see also Massie and Roussel, chapter 3).

References

Aron, Raymond. 1984. *Paix et guerre entre les nations*. Paris: Calmann-Levy.

Axworthy, Lloyd. 2003. *Navigating a New World: Canada's Global Future*. Toronto: Knopf Canada.

Bellamy, Alex J. 2010. "The Responsibility to Protect—Five Years On." *Ethics and International Affairs* 24, 2: 143–69.

Black, David R., and Heather Smith. 1993. "Notable Exceptions? New and Arrested Directions in Canadian Foreign Policy Literature." *Canadian Journal of Political Science* 26, 4: 745–74.

Carr, Edward H. 1954. *The Twenty Years' Crisis 1919–1939*. London: Macmillan.

Chapnick, Adam. 2005a. *The Middle Power Project: Canada and the Founding of the United Nations*. Vancouver: University of British Columbia Press.

————. 2005b. "Peace, Order, and Good Government: The 'Conservative' Tradition in Canadian Foreign Policy." *International Journal* 60, 3: 635–50.

Cohen, Andrew. 2003. *While Canada Slept: How We Lost Our Place in the World*. Toronto: McClelland & Stewart.

Conservative Party of Canada. 2006. *Stand Up for Canada*. At http://www.cbc.ca/canadavotes2006/leadersparties/pdf/conservative_platform20060113.pdf.

————. 2008. *The True North Strong and Free: Stephen Harper's Plan for Canadians*. At http://www.scribd.com/doc/6433536/Stephen-Harpers-Plan-for-Canadian.

————. 2011. *Here for Canada: Stephen Harper's Low-Tax Plan for Jobs and Economic Growth*. At http://www.conservative.ca/media/ConservativePlatform2011_ENs.pdf.

Davis, Jeff. 2009. "Liberal-Era Diplomatic Language Killed Off." *Embassy Magazine* 1 July. At http://embassymag.ca/page/view/diplomatic_language-7-1-2009.

Dewitt, David, and John Kirton. 1983. *Canada as a Principal Power*. Toronto: Wiley.

Gotlieb, Allan. 2004. *Romanticism and Realism in Canada's Foreign Policy*. Benefactors Lecture. Toronto: C.D. Howe Institute.

Government of Canada. 2011. *House of Commons Debates*. Vol. 146, no. 008, 1st Session, 41st Parliament, 14 June.

————. 2005. *Canada's International Policy Statement: A Role of Pride and Influence in the World*. Ottawa: Supply and Services Canada.

————. 2008. *Canada First: Defence Strategy*. Ottawa: Supply and Services Canada.

Granatstein, Jack L. 2003. *The Importance of Being Less Earnest: Promoting Canada's National Interests through Tighter Ties with the U.S.* Benefactors Lecture. Toronto: C.D. Howe Institute.

————. 2004. *Who Killed the Canadian Military?* Toronto: HarperCollins.

Hampson, Fen, and Dean Oliver. 1998. "Pulpit Diplomacy: A Critical Assessment of the Axworthy Doctrine." *International Journal* 53, 3: 379–406.

Harper, Stephen. 2011. *Prime Minister Stephen Harper's 2011 Convention Speech*. June. At http://www.conservative.ca/press/news_releases/prime_minister_stephen_harper_s_2011_convention_speech.

Heinbecker, Paul. 2004. "Multilateral Cooperation and Peace and Security." *International Journal* 59, 4: 783–800.

————. 2010. *Getting Back in the Game: A Foreign Policy Playbook for Canada*. Toronto: Key Porter Books.

Holmes, John. 1970. *The Better Part of Valour*. Toronto: McClelland & Stewart.

ICISS (International Commission on Intervention and State Sovereignty). 2001. *The Responsibility to Protect*. Ottawa: International Development Research Centre.

Ignatieff, Michael. 2004. "The Seductiveness of Moral Disgust." *Social Research* 71, 3: 549–68.

Keating, Tom. 2002. *Canada and World Order: The Multilateralist Tradition in Canadian Foreign Policy*, 2nd ed. Don Mills, ON: Oxford University Press.

————. 2010. "Multilateralism: Pass Imperfect, Future Conditional." *Canadian Foreign Policy/La politique étrangère du Canada* 16, 2: 9–25.

Keeble, Edna, and Heather A. Smith. 1999. *(Re)defining Traditions: Gender and Canadian Foreign Policy*. Halifax: Fernwood Press.

Martin, Paul. 2005. *Statement by the Right Honourable Paul Martin Prime Minister of Canada to the High-Level Meeting of the Sixtieth Session of the United Nations General Assembly*. New York, 16 September.

Melakopides, Costas. 1998. *Pragmatic Idealism: Canadian Foreign Policy 1945–1995*. Montreal and Kingston: McGill-Queen's University Press.

Mérand, Frédéric, and Antoine Vandemoortele. 2009. "L'Europe dans la culture stratégique canadienne, 1949–2009." *Études internationales* 40, 2: 241–59.

Molot, Maureen Appel. 1990. "Where Do We, or Should We, or Can We Sit? A Review of Canadian Foreign Policy Literature." *International Journal of Canadian Studies* 1, 2: 77–96.

Morgenthau, Hans. 1948. *Politics among Nations: The Struggle for Power and Peace*. New York: McGraw-Hill.

Munton, Don. 2002–3. "Whither Internationalism?" *International Journal* 58, 1: 155–80.

Munton, Don, and Tom Keating. 2001. "Internationalism and the Canadian Public." *Canadian Journal of Political Science* 34, 3: 517–49.

Neufeld, Mark. 1995. "Hegemony and Foreign Policy Analysis: The Case of Canada as a Middle Power." *Studies in Political Economy* 48 (Autumn): 7–29.

Nossal, Kim Richard. 1998. "Foreign Policy for Wimps." *Ottawa Citizen*, 23 April, A19.

———. 1998–9. "Pinchpenny Diplomacy: The Decline of 'Good International Citizenship' in Canadian Foreign Policy." *International Journal* 54, 1: 88–105.

———. 2005. "Ear Candy: Canadian Policy toward Humanitarian Intervention and Atrocity Crimes in Darfur." *International Journal* 60, 4: 1017–32.

———. 2007. "Defense Policy and the Atmospherics of Canada-U.S. Relations: The Case of the Harper Conservatives." *American Review of Canadian Studies* 37, 1: 23–34.

Nossal, Kim Richard, Stéphane Roussel, and Stéphane Paquin. 2011. *International Policy and Politics in Canada*. Toronto: Pearson Education Canada.

Potter, Evan. 2009. *Branding Canada: Projecting Canada's Soft Power through Public Diplomacy*. Montreal and Kingston: McGill-Queen's University Press.

Pratt, Cranford, ed. 1989. *Internationalism under Strain: The North-South Policies of Canada, the Netherlands, Norway, and Sweden*. Toronto: University of Toronto Press.

Riddell-Dixon, Elisabeth. 2004. "Walking the Talk: A Prerequisite for Effective Multilateralism in the Twenty-First Century." In Graham F. Walker, ed., *Independence in an Age of Empire: Assessing Unilateralism and Multilateralism*. Halifax: Centre for Foreign Policy Studies, Dalhousie University, 113–23.

Simpson, Erika. 1999. "The Principles of Liberal Internationalism According to Lester Pearson." *Journal of Canadian Studies* 34, 1: 75–92.

Stairs, Denis. 2001. "Canada in the 1990s: Speak Loudly and Carry a Bent Twig." *Policy Options*, January–February.

———. 2003a. "Myths, Morals, and Reality in Canadian Foreign Policy." *International Journal* 58, 1: 239–56.

———. 2003b. "Challenges and Opportunities for Canadian Foreign Policy in the Paul Martin Era." *International Journal* 58, 4: 481–506.

Tucker, Michael. 1980. *Canadian Foreign Policy: Contemporary Issues and Themes*. Toronto: McGraw-Hill Ryerson.

Turenne Sjolander, Claire. 2009. "A Funny Thing Happened on the Road to Kandahar: The Competing Faces of Canadian Internationalism?" *Canadian Foreign Policy/La politique étrangère du Canada* 15, 2: 78–98.

Weber, Max. 2011. *Methodology of Social Sciences*. New Brunswick, NJ: Transaction Publishers.

Welsh, Jennifer. 2004. *At Home in the World: Canada's Global Vision in the 21st Century*. Toronto: HarperCollins.

———. 2005. "Reality and Canadian Foreign Policy." In Andrew F. Cooper and Dane Rowlands, *Canada among Nations 2005: Split Images*. Montreal and Kingston: McGill-Queen's University Press, 23–46.

Whyte, Kenneth. 2011. "How He Sees Canada's Role in the World and Where He Wants to Take the Country." *Maclean's*, June. At http://www2.macleans.ca/2011/07/07/how-he-sees-canada%E2%80%99s-role-in-the-world-and-where-he-wants-to-take-the-country/.

5 Internationalism in Canada-India Bilateral Relations under Stephen Harper

Anita Singh

Canada-India relations have suffered massive fluctuations since India gained its independence in 1947. Though in the 1950s and 1960s India was a darling of Canada's development aid program, its 1974 "peaceful" nuclear tests marked an apex in negative relations between the two countries. While the Mulroney, Chrétien, and Martin governments only half-heartedly pursued bilateral relations, the Harper government has prioritized India in its emerging-markets strategy, taking proactive steps to improve the economic, cultural, and political climate between the two countries.[1] Concerted efforts through various ministries—Citizenship and Immigration, Finance, Natural Resources, and Foreign Affairs—have resulted in long-overdue progress in the bilateral relationship, evidenced by steady (albeit slow) growth in bilateral trade; numerous memoranda of understanding in science and technology, earth sciences, and higher education; the Canada-India Nuclear Cooperation Agreement (NCA); and, most importantly, diplomatic reciprocation from the Indian government.

Why has the Harper government been successful in improving Canada-India relations where previous governments have failed? While India's economic growth, the normalization of its nuclear program, and its growing involvement in world affairs are partially responsible for improvements in bilateral relations, these factors do not adequately account for the shifts attributed to the Conservative government's foreign policy. Thus, this chapter argues that the slow success of the Canada-India relationship under Harper is due to his government's shift away from paternalistic internationalism and towards mutually beneficial economic relations—a shift that has also involved delinking India from both "Af-Pak" and China.

To make this case, this chapter shows how highly internationalist periods of Canadian foreign policy during (and immediately after) the Cold War damaged the Canada-India relationship. During this time, India perceived Canada as having a neo-imperialist agenda. Given its history under the British, India was wary of any forms of Western imperialism in its foreign policy; thus the Harper government's success with India comes from a departure from Canadian internationalism as manifested during the Cold War. The chapter concludes with the suggestion that there is an inverse relationship between the success of Canada's bilateral relations with developing countries and a foreign policy driven by internationalism.

Internationalism in Early Canada-India Relations[2]

This chapter's central argument focuses on internationalism as a moralistic endeavour that uses foreign policy to impose Western values on developing states. It argues that an internationalist foreign policy reinforces (rather than improves, as some versions of internationalism claim to do) North-South divisions and traditional hierarchies between Western and non-Western states. Relatedly, attempts to divorce internationalism from its ethical connotations—as Munton and Keating argue (2001: 531), "broadly defined, [internationalism] has not only a behavioural element, but also an ethical one" (as if the concept could actually be unpacked into its behavioural and ethical components)—dilute the negative impact of internationalism's moral superiority on Canada's foreign relations.

Canada emerged from the post–Second World War period with a new foreign policy identity that ushered in the "golden period" of internationalism. Given the horrors of the Second World War, both the prime minister and the minister of external affairs showed an unwavering commitment to "the betterment of mankind" through their support for "internationalist norms and institutions" (Nossal, 1998–9: 89; Rioux and Hay, 1998: 60). Evidence of this proactive role was highlighted by institutional changes within Canada that led to the creation of the specific position of "Secretary of State for External Affairs" (which divorced External Affairs from the jurisdiction of the prime minister) and increased Canada's diplomatic corps in several regions of the world (Mansur, 1992: 50).

Despite the consensus that identifies the post-war period as "highly internationalist," only a few scholars have made a strong commitment to an exact definition of internationalism. John Holmes (1970), an early proponent of internationalism, left the door open for a broad conception of internationalism, rejecting attempts to define the concept. For Holmes, internationalism took different forms, each defined by a modifier—such as pure internationalism, active internationalism, new and tougher internationalism, soft-minded internationalism, American New Deal internationalism, and Canadian internationalism. Holmes famously argued against "tidy" definitions, which he saw as counterproductive to the conduct of world affairs (1970: 63). Similarly, "tidy" definitions were unable to capture the acute intertwining between internationalism and Canada's domestic political culture. As Rioux and Hay argue, "internationalism would be difficult to uproot without undermining the very identity of the country" (1998: 61). Munton and Keating (2001: 517) stop short of calling internationalism a foreign policy "religion" but argue that it is an attractive baseline for international decision-making.

Centrally, internationalism was an approach to foreign policy that favoured the current international order. Kim Nossal (1985: 53) observes that early internationalism (particularly under St Laurent and Pearson) had four major components: "taking an active involvement in, and assuming some responsibility for, the management of international conflict; working multilaterally toward international order; making commitments to international institutions; and committing resources for the betterment of the international system as a whole." Because the concept centred on multilateral action, there was an assumption that its goals were based in collective interests. In other words, it was assumed that collective participation of states also brought tacit acceptance of Canadian foreign policy goals as a "force for good" in the international system.

Most critical assessments of Canadian internationalism do not address the neo-imperialism inherent in the values Canada projects. Instead, most criticisms focus on Canada's departure from internationalist goals, such as Kim Nossal's (2005) review of Prime Minister Martin's decision to remain uninvolved in the Darfur humanitarian crisis—focusing on the inconsistency between the Canadian government's internationalist rhetoric and its practice. Similarly, Evan Potter (1996) argues that limited resources mean that Canada should embrace a selective internationalism, one focused on its strengths in diplomacy and negotiation. However, Potter also stops short of questioning whether Canada's internationalism-driven "niche diplomacy" is welcome within the international community. As discussed later in this chapter, the imposition of internationalism on Canada's relations with India resulted in negative relations between the two states for three interrelated reasons.

Internationalism as a Hegemonic Exercise

First, internationalism is seen as a system-preserving approach to international relations, promoting a world order heavily dependent on the maintenance of American hegemony and the Western sphere of influence. Don Munton and Tom Keating offer that "at the bare minimum, internationalism comprises participation and involvement internationally ... It encompasses participation with a commitment of resources toward a purpose: the pursuit of international order" (2001: 526). Particularly within the Cold War, internationalism's system-maintaining properties are noted by various scholars. Alain Noël, Jean-Philippe Thérien, and Sébastien Dallaire suggest that "[b]efore anything else, Canada's development assistance policy ... served to strengthen the geostrategic and economic bases of the liberal order established in the postwar period" (2003: 5). Similarly, David Black and Claire Turenne Sjolander note that Canada's economic activity during the Cold War "was supportive of the bases of *Pax Americana*, despite the fact that the unequal basis of the order was becoming clearer" (1996: 10). In other words, maintaining the current international order required consistency in the hierarchy between states. In particular, Canada's relationships with developing states, such as India, were pursued in a way that inherently retained the hierarchy between the states. In its relationship with Canada, India felt that it should be an equal partner and thus took offence at being treated as a junior partner (Nayar and Paul, 2003).

After India gained independence in 1947, observers saw great potential in relations between New Delhi and Ottawa—indeed, many saw Canada and India as natural allies—and Escott Reid, Canada's then envoy to India, boldly suggested that the two enjoyed a "special relationship" (1981: 24). India was an important test case for Canada's newly formulated internationalist foreign policy. Ottawa's early policies were based on an image of India as a poverty-stricken, uneducated country (this perception has informed Canada's self-positioning towards India until very recently). In contrast, India, having just emerged from a long history of colonialism, was loath to come under—even indirectly—patronage by any other state, a position that it emphasized repeatedly.[3] Due to these differences in outlook, the similarities in India and Canada's shared international interests were exaggerated to fit the image of a special relationship. Instead of improving the relationship between the two countries, Canada's policy created differences in political outlook, national interests, and alliance structures between the two countries (Rubinoff, 2002).

The challenges introduced by Canada's affinity for institutional and multilateral conflict-resolution mechanisms became clear within the first few years of the bilateral relationship. In 1950, Canada sponsored the United Nations (UN) Resolution 80, which called for a plebiscite in Kashmir to determine which state—India or Pakistan—controlled the region (Touhey, 2007). Canada's fears rested on the assumption that conflict over Kashmir would damage newly formed relationships within the Commonwealth. However, India solidly rejected the resolution as international interference in a domestic matter, particularly because a plebiscite in Pakistan's favour would lend support to the **two-nation thesis** that justified the latter's formation and would undermine India's identity as a secular state. Canada assumed that its decision to involve the UN in Kashmir would have wide support within India. However, Canada did not understand that India would perceive these actions as a neo-colonial attempt to control the geopolitical outcomes of South Asia.

Imposition of Western Values

Canadian internationalism was also determined by "international values," or "international interests," that reflected the hegemonic international structure of the time. Michael Tucker argues that internationalism is the "enhancement of interests and values commonly shared with like-minded peoples and governments everywhere" (1980: 2). In her assessment of Tucker's definition, Leigh Sarty recognizes the "distinctly moral overtone" in Canadian internationalism, in which Canadians take "pride in a purportedly selfless commitment to internationalist principles" (1992: 755), where Canada's role in world affairs was pursued as a "good international citizen." As Cooper, Higgott and Nossal suggest, middle-power internationalism is based on the tendency of middle powers "to pursue multilateral solutions to international problems, their tendency to embrace compromise positions in international disputes, and their tendency to embrace notions of 'good international citizenship' to guide their diplomacy" (1993: 19). In the same vein, Cranford Pratt (1990: 3) differentiates internationalism from the evils of realism, viewing the latter as dictated by "geopolitical, economic or other traditional foreign policy interests." Instead, Pratt's internationalism—upholding "the common good" in order to improve the well-being of developing states—treats the needs of developing states based on Western-defined matrices of "development." However, Pratt's work stops short of questioning the values projection that, this chapter argues, underlies Canadian internationalism.

This values projection became evident when Canadian and Indian interests clashed in 1954 when both countries became members of the International Control Commission (ICC), a body established to oversee the partition of Vietnam, elected to represent the West, the East, and the **non-aligned bloc** (Poland was elected to represent Eastern interests in the ICC). Differences in Canada's and India's perspectives became increasingly apparent during negotiations. India saw Canada as an apologist for the American sphere of influence, while Canada saw India as excusing the actions of Eastern Communist regimes. Similarly, in 1956, while Canada and India were working together to resolve the Suez Crisis, the Soviet military moved to crack down on a popular uprising against its occupation of Hungary. Despite India's declared neutrality, it was conspicuously quiet on the Soviet action, which raised the ire of Canadian officials. In both cases, Canada assumed that its bilateral assistance to India would procure congruence in their foreign policies. In comparison, India maintained its policy of compartmentalization and did not see why its foreign policy should be determined by its development assistance donors.[4]

Following disagreements during the negotiation of the Nuclear Non-Proliferation Treaty (NPT) throughout the 1960s, discontent between the two countries grew after India's nuclear test on 18 May 1974. In a particularly drastic response, Canada suspended all diplomatic relations and all bilateral assistance except for food aid. This hard-line reaction was fuelled by Canada's anger over India's betrayal of the terms of the bilateral Atoms for Peace Agreement, since it was obvious that some enriched nuclear material had come from Canadian reactors. Further, India's nuclear test was considered an embarrassment to Canada's commitment to peaceful nuclear energy—in essence, due to Canada's failure to monitor compliance, to assure verification, and to insist on safeguards for the CANDU reactors. India's test was a direct challenge to the recently negotiated and Canada-championed NPT, which had come into effect in 1968 (Kauskik, 1979; Bratt, 1996). Canadian sanctions were then made permanent after concerns arose when Prime Minister Indira Gandhi declared a "state of emergency" in 1975. Ashok Kapur calls this the period of "benign neglect," when—paradoxically—Canada's interest in South Asia waned just as the region's importance in world affairs began to grow (Kapur, 1991: 62). Ryan Touhey (2007: 742–3) blames the impasse on a lack of personal interest on the part of successive prime ministers, as vividly illustrated by the fact that no high-level Canadian representatives visited India between 1955 and 1983.

For India, Canada's severe response was emblematic of the values projection inherent in internationalism. Indian policy-makers have questioned the inherent bias of the nuclear non-proliferation regime because of its discriminatory nature, as it determines legitimacy based on timing; had India held its nuclear tests before the cutoff date, it would have had full rights as a nuclear weapons state (Talbott, 1999). Moreover, India did not agree that current nuclear states are more deserving of nuclear status and responsibility or that they necessarily have more stable domestic regimes. During the negotiations of the NPT, India furthered its case against discrimination, claiming that the NPT limits "non-nuclear weapons states" (NNWS) from horizontal proliferation while allowing "nuclear weapons states" (NWS) to proliferate vertically. As an example of this values hierarchy, Indian commentators have argued that the NPT regime is a "nuclear white man's burden," since its intended outcome has codified and legitimized a power imbalance between states (Subrahmanyam, 1974: 11). Not only are NWS the only powers that can legitimately possess nuclear weapons, they have also self-appointed themselves as the nuclear protectors of the international system against rogue states, terrorist cells, and other nuclear threats.

Convenient Internationalism

The end of the Cold War challenged Canadian policy-makers with the task of creating a new foreign policy. On the one hand, policy-makers were expected to simultaneously identify a new place for Canada's national interests and address demands for the development of a "new internationalism" (Black and Turenne Sjolander, 1996: 7). On the other, this new foreign policy was expected to fall within the fiscal constraints imposed by previous decades of deficit spending. The combination of these factors resulted in a confused foreign policy, with rhetorical commitments but without resulting action. In this vein, Kim Nossal has accused the Chrétien government of "pinchpenny" diplomacy, marked by a "meanness of spirit that delegitimizes the voluntaristic acts of 'good international citizenship'" (1998: 89). Evan Potter and Janice Stein famously called for a "niche diplomacy" approach to foreign politics, where the focus should lie in the "areas where there is a clear and identifiable Canadian interest and where Canada's international policy decisions and programmes can have a maximum impact" (Stein, 1994: 11; Potter, 1996: 25).

However, even before the fiscal austerity measures of the 1990s, Canada had long practised a "convenient" internationalism that resulted in its selective engagement in global conflicts. While Canada imposed resolutions on India over Kashmir and India's nuclear development, it had a muted response to Indian prime minister Indira Gandhi's request for a humanitarian intervention when West Pakistan launched a military operation against East Pakistan during the 1971 Bangladesh War of Independence. Canadian policy-makers argued that Canada had abstained from becoming involved in the resolution of this conflict because it wished to avoid escalating the conflict and challenging the unity of the Commonwealth alliance.

Further, Canada assumed it would be offered a mediation role after the conflict ended.[5] Yet, India's perception was that Canada did not enter the conflict because it did not want to antagonize the United States, which supported a unified Pakistan, despite the genocidal activities of the Pakistani army in Bangladesh. Only a single apology emerged from Canada for its decision. Heath MacQuarrie, member of Parliament for Hillsborough, Prince Edward Island, stated, "[Canada] did not do as much as we could or perhaps should have done" (Haider, 2005: 325). Canada's inaction was ironic considering its internationalist interest in conflict resolution and peacekeeping in the region.

By the early 1990s, very little had changed. Canadian policy-makers were interested in India's economic transformation, the product of privatization and deregulation measures as well as investment schemes (Ahluwalia, 2002: 67).[6] Recognizing the potential in India's new economy, Canada conducted three high-level missions to India: International Trade Minister Roy MacLaren in 1994, Secretary of State for Asia Raymond Chan, also in 1994, and "Team Canada" in 1996. Team Canada, led by Prime Minister Jean Chrétien and including 300 business people, numerous provincial premiers, and trade officials, sought to match India's market requirements with existing Canadian capabilities (Canada, Team Canada Mission, 1996; Tremblay, 2003). The delegation signed 75 trade contracts worth approximately C$3.4 billion (Stackhouse, 1996: B1; Speirs, 1996: A11).

In addition to the economic agenda, Foreign Affairs Minister Lloyd Axworthy introduced a human security–focused foreign policy based on the principles of good international citizenship, multilateralism, and humanitarianism. In line with this policy orientation, Canada responded harshly to India's challenge to international non-proliferation norms through its nuclear test in May 1998. Canada's response was especially severe in comparison to that of other Western states—it recalled its high commissioner, cancelled Canadian International Development Agency (CIDA) programs, suspended trade talks, opposed India's request for World Bank loans, challenged its bid for a seat on the United Nations Security Council (UNSC), and took an anti-India stance at G8 meetings (Rubinoff, 2002: 850). Axworthy's foreign policy manifested itself in a personal crusade against violators of international norms, including India. While advocating isolation and punishment for India, the foreign minister enforced his perspective through economic sanctions, which Canada maintained for longer than any other state.

As anticipated, India's new nuclear capabilities were also severely condemned by the major and middle powers, including the United States, the European Union, and Japan (Nayar and Paul, 2003).[7] However, Canada's response was unique for two reasons. While the rest of the world lifted the sanctions after several months, Canada maintained its punitive measures for nearly three years. It became evident that Canada's sanctions had very little effect on India, since years of neglect meant that bilateral trade amounted to only a few hundred million dollars a year—a particularly small amount in comparison to India's growing trade with Europe, Asia, and the United States—leaving little room for punitive measures. The bilateral economic relationship had weakened to such an extent that the Indian government no longer saw Canada as essential for its economic growth and humanitarian development.

While Canada expressed an economic interest in India, its decision to punish India for its nuclear transgressions was driven by international norms of non-proliferation and residual feelings of betrayal dating back to 1974. India's high commissioner in Canada argued that this response was due to a residual negative opinion of India in Canada, where Canada continued to treat India as the junior partner in the relationship, negotiating in a high-handed manner informed by moral condemnation (Verma, 2000). This is particularly significant because it is a position that has been costly for Canada's economic engagement with this emerging power.

A look at Canada's relationship with India during the Cold War reveals the impact on India of Canada's internationalist foreign policy goals. India's stubbornness with respect to negotiating Kashmir unilaterally, its challenge to the nuclear non-proliferation regime in 1974, and its decision to intervene unilaterally in East Pakistan (Bangladesh) sheds light on the contradiction between Canada's internationalist interests and India's perception of these foreign policy goals. For example, Canada expected India to welcome UN involvement in South Asian conflicts (particularly Kashmir and Bangladesh) and to respect the norms of non-proliferation, but from India's perspective, Canada's foreign policy goals were an attempt to impose Western-determined preferences on India's core national interests. As shown in the following section, the Harper government's shift away from internationalism has effectively brought Canadian and Indian economic interests into alignment and divorced Canada's India policy from that of other states in the region, particularly China's and Pakistan's.

Internationalism and the Canada-India Bilateral Relationship under Stephen Harper

For the first few months after the 2006 election, there was a notable absence of a Conservative foreign policy "direction," particularly with respect to such emerging powers as India and China. The government's lack of attention to India and China was emblematic of a larger foreign policy challenge, described by John Kirton (2007, 12B) as "ignorant isolationism," given the prime minister's "lack of knowledge or interest in international affairs. With India's economic ascendance attracting new economic partners, Canada's attempts to engage India were not as successful as those of the United States and the EU countries" (Kapur and Raghubeer, 2010). Overall, the Harper government's foreign policy–related decisions have been largely reactive to international events, one example being its response to the Israel-Lebanon conflict in June 2006 as described by David Black in chapter 13.[8] This section describes the gradual development of the Harper government's foreign policy towards India and how its economic focus on bilateral relations signifies a break with previous practices of internationalism.

Role of the Indo-Canadian Community

The Harper government's early policy towards India was driven by domestic rather than foreign policy considerations. Owing to their slim electoral victory in 2006, the Conservatives made an "obvious effort to move beyond the old Reform image of being less than positive toward Canada's ethnic minorities" (Munton, 2010) and focused on improving relations with immigrant communities, including (if not especially) Indo-Canadians, given their concentration in traditional Liberal-voting constituencies. Thus, early into its first term, the government set up the Air India Inquiry for two important strategic reasons. First, recognizing the Indo-Canadian community's dissatisfaction with the 2005 Air India trial, the Conservatives could use the Air India Inquiry to synchronize the security concerns of the Indo-Canadian community with the government's terrorism policy, particularly after the 2006 Mumbai train blasts (Clark, 2007; Whitaker, 2007). The Harper government also received support from Indo-Canadians for adding the Tamil Tigers to Canada's list of terrorist groups. Second, the Harper government was able to show the Indian government that it was taking action on Canadian-grown **Khalistan** separatism,[9] which continues to be a major bilateral issue for the Indian government.

Then, in May 2006, the government included its first set of changes to immigration policy in the federal budget, halving the landing fee for new immigrants from $975 to $490. This new fee was favourably received by Indo-Canadians because of the large number of family-class applications submitted by members of the community (Siddiqui, 2008; Goar, 2008: AA06). Further changes to immigration policy occurred in 2008, when Immigration Minister Diane Finley announced a new policy to ease the backlog at overseas consulates, giving priority to business-class and professional immigrants. The prime minister himself commented at an Indo-Canadian gathering that the changes to the Immigration and Refugee Protection Act would improve access and increase efficiency for skilled Indian immigrants. He argued that immigration reforms were necessary to "get skilled workers into the country earlier, help families get reunited sooner, [and] provide the Canadian economy with the human capital it needs" (Coutts, 2008: A4; MacCharles, 2008: A1). During a 2010 trip to India, Minister Jason Kenney tied these domestic issues to foreign policy, expressing "the need to take action against fraudulent immigration consultants, improve visa processing time, encourage immigration from Indian students to Canada, and build stronger connections between Indian and Canadian businesses" (Taylor, 2009).

Prime Minister Harper's visit to India in November 2009 highlighted the connection between Indo-Canadians and his government's foreign policy. During the ceremonial trip, he visited the Golden Temple in Amritsar and the Chabad House and made an appearance on a popular dance reality show. The trip was seen by some to have been blatantly **ethnopolitical**, designed to curry the favour of ethnic groups in Canada. For example, the Golden Temple was the site of the Indian Army's Operation Blue Star in 1984, where an attempt to corner Khalistani separatists hiding within the compound resulted in the deaths of hundreds of worshippers. The event was an important catalyst for some Canadian Sikhs who continue to support the separatist movement. Similarly, the Chabad House was one of the sites attacked during the Mumbai terrorist attacks in November 2008. Both the Indo-Canadian and Canadian Jewish communities responded favourably to the prime minister's decision to visit the Chabad House.

Indo-Canadians were also key stakeholders in the development of the government's economic strategy towards India. Community leaders in the Canada India Foundation, the Indo-Canada Chamber of Commerce, and the Canada-India Business Council were in close contact with the government through business meetings, overseas travel, Indian ministerial visits, consultation sessions, and personal relationships. Through their government connections, these diaspora groups were able to outline the potential areas for improving the Canada-India relationship, which included energy exploration and production, technology, infrastructure, and education. More importantly, the Indo-Canadian community *excluded discussion about bilateral opportunities* that would be sources of conflict between Canada and India. Canada's Indo-Canadian community was resolutely focused on areas suitable for economic cooperation between the two countries. More specifically, Canada avoided policies that would typically be considered internationalist, particularly policies involving "mediation" or "avoidance" of conflict in the region, such as in Kashmir, Pakistan, or Afghanistan (Nossal, 1985: 53). This decision favoured efforts to promote improved economic relations between the two states. In this way, even without a clear plan to engage India, the Harper government had already indicated a new direction for the bilateral relationship.

Internationalism has had a long connection with Canadian society and domestic groups. Cranford Pratt argues that internationalism is "an acceptance by the citizens of industrialized states that they have ethical obligations towards those beyond their borders and that these in turn impose obligations upon their governments" (Pratt, 1990: 59). The Harper government's dependence on the Indo-Canadian community (as well as other immigrant groups) was the first indication of departure from internationalism and also a shift from its inherent neo-imperialism. Engaging Indo-Canadian groups—albeit for narrowly defined economic and electoral interests—offered a way for Canadian policy-makers to understand what India's interests would be within the bilateral relationship. Critically, this allowed the Harper government to avoid imposing *predetermined internationalist* interests onto India (such as development aid, multilateral solutions to Kashmir, and Cold War politics), as was previously the case in Canada-India relations. Further, the Conservative government used domestic policies—support for tighter immigration and terrorism laws—to create foreign policy space for the management of its relationship with India. While this did not mean that Canadian foreign policy decisions were divorced from larger domestic interests, it did mean that decision-making was not singularly dependent on an internationalist vision of what India's interests should be within the bilateral relationship.

Economic Improvements

It took a year after the 2006 election for the first ministerial delegation to visit India, but since then, the Prime Minister's Office and a small group of federal ministers have centrally coordinated the relationship between the two states.[10] In March 2007, Ted Menzies, parliamentary secretary to then trade minister David Emerson, led an economic mission to India. This trip marked both a symbolic and a productive beginning towards improved India-Canada relations, with the objective of establishing the framework for a future free trade agreement (FTA) between the two countries. As agreed within the Department of International Trade, pursuing an FTA would take place "on an incremental basis" (Obhrai, 2010), and thus Menzies was to suggest a Foreign Investment Promotion and Protection Agreement (FIPA), aimed at providing greater certainty for "Canadian firms with existing investments in India, as a first step toward an eventual free trade agreement" (*Deccan Herald*, 2010). Given the difficulties in establishing a business in India, the FIPA makes important guarantees for businesses interested in establishing a presence in India.

The next significant official visit to India—in January 2008—took over a year to materialize. However, it was an important visit, as Maxime Bernier was the first minister of foreign affairs to visit India in five years. Bernier's meetings with India's ministers of commerce and industry and external affairs focused largely on trade issues and economic engagement. At a meeting with Finance Minister Pranab Mukherjee, Bernier was questioned about Canada's support for an India-specific exemption at the Nuclear Suppliers Group (NSG) and the International Atomic Energy Agency (IAEA) in order to resume nuclear trade.[11]

By the summer of 2008, the government signalled its first nuclear-related policy shift towards India. As indicated above, India's history of nuclear proliferation required an exemption at the IAEA and the NSG. Canada's position was difficult. Its allies had indicated their support for the India exemption, but the exemption undermined Canada's own policy of non-proliferation and disarmament. Further, a vote in favour of India would mute Canada's long-standing criticism and symbolize an explicit acceptance of India's nuclear program.

Despite these challenges, Canada voted in favour of the India exception in 2008 and in the following year began its own negotiations for a nuclear transfer deal. Given the history of negative relations between Canada and India—particularly in the field of nuclear politics—signing the Nuclear Cooperation Agreement (NCA) was possible because of a perceptual shift within the government. For Canada, India had been a nuclear pariah state, outside the behavioural norms of the non-proliferation regime (Mistry, 2006). In order to justify its divergence from this long-standing position, government efforts were directed towards creating a link between economic benefits and nuclear power, with the effect of *normalizing* nuclear power by comparing it to wind, electric, and fossil energy sources. In this vein, these efforts had the additional effect of *legitimizing* India's nuclear program within the context of energy production.

Beginning 2009 with a renewed electoral mandate, the Harper government continued its plan to improve relations with India. International Trade Minister Stockwell Day travelled to India on three separate occasions to open Canadian trade offices in Hyderabad (January), Kolkata (September), and Ahmedabad (September) (DFAIT, 2009; McCarthy, 2009: B11; *Indian Express*, 2009). In addition to the trade offices, Day was involved in negotiations with both his Indian counterpart, Kamal Nath, and the Indian prime minister concerning improvements to the meagre bilateral trade relationship between India and Canada.

In the first six months of 2010, two other ministers—Finance Minister Jim Flaherty and Minister of Citizenship and Immigration Jason Kenney—also travelled to India. While Kenney's trip dealt with the desirability of streamlining immigration policies (estimates suggest a current backlog at Canadian visa offices of over one million applications), Flaherty met with Indian Finance Minister Pranab Mukherjee and Montek Singh Ahluwalia, deputy chair of India's Planning Committee, to coordinate the G20 positions on issues related to post-recession economic stability. The trip was meant to highlight similarities between Canada and India in their efforts to weather the global economic recession, placing particular emphasis on the stability of Canada's banking sector, the country's economic stimulus plans, and its fiscally conservative growth philosophy.

During a three-year period (between 2007 and 2009), over 19 ministerial-level trips were conducted to India. Minister Day rearticulated the message central to these foreign visits in 2007: "[S]ix of us [ministers] have been up and down [to] India in the last six months. How much more do you want to know that we want to engage?" (Clark, 2009: A6). During these visits, several major policies were announced, including the NCA, the FIPA, and the **Comprehensive Economic Partnership Agreement** (CEPA). The culmination of these efforts was Prime Minister Manmohan Singh's visit to Canada in June 2010 for the G20 Summit—the first visit of a sitting Indian prime minister in 37 years. These efforts have brought Canada and India to a historic zenith, since at this meeting both countries finally signed the NCA, reversing 35 years of nuclear policy and giving Canada access to India's $100-billion energy program (*Globe and Mail*, 2010; *Hindustan Times*, 2010).

India has also reciprocated Canada's gestures towards an improved bilateral relationship. Since 2007, Indian Minister of Road Transport and Highways Kamal Nath has visited Canada on three separate occasions. Other visiting dignitaries have included former president Dr Abdul Kalam, Minister for Communications and Information Technology Sachin Pilot, and Minister of Commerce and Industry Anand Sharma (Canada, 2010). Economically, the most obvious improvement in Canada-India relations is the growth in trade, which has doubled since the 2006 election from $2 billion to $4.14 billion in 2009 (Canada, Department of Finance, 2011). While the scale of trade remains small, its steady and impressive growth during the Conservative government is significant. It reflects increased business confidence in both the Indian economy and the Canadian government's commitment to bilateral relations.

Stephen Harper: An Internationalist in Wolf's Clothing?

How do contemporary economic relations with India fit within Canadian internationalism? Theoretically, broadened versions of the concept have attempted to include Harper's economic bilateralism. Don Munton offers a modified version—"economic" internationalism—in which "high priority [is given] to international trade and investment and to closer economic ties with other countries bilaterally and multilaterally" (2002–3: 141). While the definition certainly fits Canada's economic relationship with India under Stephen Harper, there are challenges to the economic internationalism that Munton presents. First, this definition does not explain how economic internationalism differs in its objectives from other theories of international political economy. Economic realist literature, for example (see Gilpin, 1984), agrees that bilateral economic relations inherently maintain the international economic system in a state's national interest. While it is not necessary that internationalism be indefinitely tied to related concepts such as humanitarianism, middlepowerism, and multilateralism, it is difficult to see how economic internationalism maintains any connection to these other forms of internationalism.

Herein lies the challenge of "fuzzy" internationalism, as the addition of a modifier could be adopted to explain any foreign policy. Broad conceptualizations of internationalism that can incorporate all foreign policies limit internationalism's usefulness as a theoretical tool (Legro and Moravcsik [1999] make this argument about expanded versions of realism). Further, broad approaches are poorly equipped to define a policy-relevant theory for Canadian foreign policy. The conceptual limitlessness of internationalism is a challenge for even the most dedicated policy-makers, as the breadth of the concept introduces important limitations on Canada's middle-power resources (Cooper, Higgott, and Nossal, 1993). Thus, these limited resources have resulted in a middle-power foreign policy focused on "gain[ing] special influence in functional areas where their interests have appeared strongest" (Wood, cited in Chapnick, 1999: 73–4). However, other authors, such as Denis Stairs, question the adequacy of a functionalist explanation, challenging the assumption that "middle powers will not only exhibit similar tactical repertoires, but also common objectives and purposes" (1998: 271).

Given these theoretical inadequacies, this chapter questions the utility of expanding the concept of internationalism so that it might include the Harper government's foreign policy towards India. This chapter suggests, as an alternative, that Canada's current bilateral relations with India indicate a departure from internationalism; otherwise, the inclusion of Harper's foreign policy within the framework of internationalism would require an expansion of the concept—the limits of which are highlighted above.

Developments in the Canada-India economic relationship have focused solely on bilateral improvements. Unlike Canada's relationship with China, where trade policy has often been tied to the improvement of human rights, the Canada-India economic relationship has focused on mutual benefits. Further, the diaspora connection allows for a grassroots focus on improved economic relations, including supporting small- and medium-sized businesses (SMEs), easing red tape for investment opportunities, and improving knowledge and skills transfer between the two countries. Mutually beneficial economic objectives have equalized the hierarchical relationship that once existed.

Additionally, this chapter argues that the Harper government has been successful in re-engaging India because it does not treat India with the neo-imperialism inherent in previous iterations of internationalist Canadian foreign policy. Kim Nossal offers important objections to the values projection that, instead of guiding foreign policy, was *turned into* Canada's foreign policy objectives by the government in Ottawa (2004: 12–14). He argues that values projection included an agenda that was overly ambitious (requiring too many resources), concealed a tendency to be hypocritical, and resulted in an "imperialism of values" approach to foreign policy (14). This last objection played a particularly important role in the negative relations between Canada and India over the 60 years up to 2006. In contrast, the Harper government has successfully removed values projection from its relationship with the Indian government. This is not to say that the Harper government does not engage in values projection elsewhere in its foreign policy, but the Canada-India relationship has become economically important enough to avoid additional liabilities from internationalism.

Importantly, the moral imperative and values imposition traditionally found in the Canada-India relationship has been muted by the government's decision to focus on the economic side of the nuclear trade deal. The Nuclear Cooperation Agreement, for example, was treated as a trade deal and not a security-related agreement. At its most basic level, the agreement allows businesses to place contracts for the trade of nuclear technology and material (particularly but not exclusively uranium). The deal is aimed at increasing India's nuclear energy supply to help meet the country's growing energy demands (India, 2008). India's ambitious nuclear goals are constrained by its limited domestic uranium resources, as well as by trade restrictions imposed by the Nuclear Non-Proliferation Treaty. Indeed, without the help of imports, India's nuclear scientists estimate that the country could max out its nuclear energy production by 2020.[12] The Indian government now estimates that it will be spending $100 billion on its nuclear industry over the next 10 years. For energy-starved and uranium-poor India, the nuclear industry provides the resources to fuel the economic growth of its massive population. For Canada, the nuclear deal links a crucial domestic industry to one of the largest nuclear markets in the world.

In addition to the obvious economic links, there is also an important connection between the nuclear deal and other important improvements in Canada-India bilateral relations. Generally, the removal of trade barriers and the facilitation of trade between the two countries— through such mechanisms as the Foreign Investment Promotion and Protection Agreement and the Comprehensive Economic Partnership Agreement—also directly affect the success of the nuclear trade.

The damage done by "imperialist" internationalism is particularly important given the new power dynamic between the two countries. Historically, with its weak economy and developmental challenges, India has had to work to gain Canada's attention and goodwill. However, the improvement of the Indian economy and its growing global reach have placed the onus on Canada to gain India's attention. Canada, in fact, continues to have a limited profile in India. Ted Menzies, parliamentary secretary to the minister of international trade, has argued that "[India] has lots of choices [for trade] and it is up to Canada, and Canadians, to step up and become preferred partners" (Chase, 2007).

The Harper government has almost exclusively focused on economic relations with India. However, as the relationship between Canada and India continues to grow, the government's exclusive reliance on economic relations undermines the potential to craft a more comprehensive strategy for improving the bilateral relationship. There are several possible areas for future engagement, given their shared history in combatting terrorism, including the Khalistan and Tamil Tigers separatist movements. In addition, while India has not been willing to support NATO's military efforts in Afghanistan, it has committed $1.2 billion towards reconstruction efforts and is Afghanistan's largest Asian donor (BBC News, 2009; Bajoria, 2009). Canada's military withdrawal from Afghanistan in 2011 has increased the scope for cooperation between the two countries, although there is also a stark absence of sustained cooperation across other aspects of international politics. For example, India has long lobbied for a permanent seat on the UN Security Council, and hence Canada's support for the concept of expanding UNSC permanent membership would be an important public declaration of the Canada-India relationship. Simply put, the bilateral relationship will continue to stagnate until Canada's economic efforts are buttressed by more substantive political and security overtures.

The possible growth of the Canada-India bilateral relationship leads to a more significant issue. In many ways, the economic focus of that relationship inherently skews the analysis of this chapter away from internationalism as a potential explanation for the Harper government's foreign policy. However, with the inevitable growth of the Canada-India relationship and additional areas for cooperation, it will be interesting to see if internationalism will eventually be reintroduced into the bilateral relationship—and if so, at what price?

Key Terms

two-nation thesis	ethnopolitical
non-aligned movement/bloc	Comprehensive Economic Partnership
Khalistan	Agreement (CEPA)

Study Questions

1. This chapter suggests that improved relations between Canada and India come at the cost of internationalist principles. Is this a necessary trade-off? Why or why not?
2. Other than the economic justification examined in this chapter, what are the other reasons that Canada should pursue a relationship with India?
3. In a democratic country, should diaspora groups have an influence on Canada's foreign policy towards their home states? What are the challenges and benefits associated with their involvement?
4. Can Canada's bilateral relations be successfully built on "single-issues" policies, such as economics? Or do you think that successful bilateral relationships should be more nuanced? What does this say about the potential for Canada-India relations?
5. This chapter concludes that economic internationalism has very little connection to the fundamentals of internationalism. Why do you agree or disagree with this conclusion?

Notes

1   Andrew Lui's discussion of Canada-China relations in chapter 6 provides an interesting comparison for the Harper government's emerging-economies strategy.

2   While internationalism has competing conceptualizations, this chapter assesses the effect of internationalism as evidenced by Canadian foreign policy in the early Cold War period. As explained in this section, internationalism at the time was distinctly tied to Canada's interest in establishing an ethical foreign policy, being a good international citizen, and improving the well-being of developing states. Temporally, this internationalist turn in Canadian foreign policy coincides with the start and decline of Canada-India relations. Eventual changes in Canada's internationalist foreign policy were not important to Canada-India relations because the relationship had already deteriorated to a dysfunctional level. This trajectory is explained throughout this chapter.

3   Heather Smith's chapter in this volume asks the very question that challenged Canada-India relations at this time, as the impact of colonialization was a defining experience for India's international interactions. As Smith observes in chapter 12, "Starting with a vision of the world where race is rendered irrelevant, where colonial pasts and presents are not interrogated is problematic."

4   Claire Turenne Sjolander's discussion (chapter 14) of the Suez Crisis importantly juxtaposes Canada's "virtuous" internationalist goals with perceptions held by states outside the Western sphere of influence, such as India.

5   Canada never did assume a mediation role in the post-conflict negotiations, largely because India preferred the negotiations to take place bilaterally, without external interference. The outcome of this summit resulted in the Simla Agreement, which has been the basis for the current line of control in Kashmir.

6   India's gross domestic product (GDP) growth rate rose from 3 to 6 per cent. By the year 2000, India saw growth rates as high as 10 per cent.

7   In addition to Canada, these self-identified middle-power states included Australia, Norway, and Sweden. China advocated full sanctions against India and limited sanctions against Pakistan.

8 The Harper government's foreign policy ignorance is also discussed by David Black (chapter 13) in relation to Latin America and development assistance.

9 Khalistan separatists wish to see the creation of an independent state for Sikhs.

10 The first scheduled trip to India, in early January 2007, by Immigration Minister Monte Solberg was interrupted due to a cabinet shuffle. This early lack of attention paid to India compares unfavourably with foreign trips to Brazil, Mexico, Pakistan, and Afghanistan by Foreign Affairs Minister Peter MacKay and trips to the United States, Mexico, China, and Switzerland by Minister of International Trade David Emerson (Urquhart, 2007).

11 Under the terms of the NPT, India's previous violations of the treaty would make it ineligible for nuclear trade even for peaceful purposes. Thus, the 40 members of the Nuclear Suppliers Group were required to agree to an India-specific exemption to this clause.

12 As India's foreign ministry noted, "[T]he truth is that we were desperate ... if this agreement had not come through we might as well have closed down our nuclear reactors and by extension our nuclear program" (Srivastava, 2005).

References

Ahluwalia, Montek S. 2002. "Economic Reforms in India since 1991: Has Gradualism Worked?" *Journal of Economic Perspectives* 16, 3: 67–88.

Bajoria, Jayshree. 2009. "Backgrounder: India-Afghanistan Relations." 22 July. At http://www.cfr.org/publication/17474/indiaafghanistan_relations.html.

BBC News. 2009. "India: Afghanistan's Influential Ally." 9 October. At http://news.bbc.co.uk/2/hi/7492982.stm.

Black, David, and Claire Turenne Sjolander. 1996. "Multilateralism Re-constituted and the Discourse of Canadian Foreign Policy." *Studies in Political Economy* 49 (Spring): 7–36.

Bratt, Duane. 1996. "Is Business Booming? Canada's Nuclear Reactor Export Policy." *International Journal* 51, 3: 487–505.

Canada. 2010. *Joint Statement by Canada and India on the Occasion of the Visit to Canada of Minister Anand Sharma, Minister Commerce and Industry of India.* Ottawa, 24 September. At http://www.canadainternational.gc.ca/india-inde/.

Canada, Department of Finance. 2010. *Speech by the Honourable Jim Flaherty, Minister of Finance, at a Luncheon Hosted by the Confederation of Indian Industry.* Mumbai, India. At http://www.fin.gc.ca/n10/10-048_1-eng.asp.

Canada, Team Canada Mission. 1996. "Confederation of Indian Industry." 10 January. At http://www.tcm-mec.gc.ca/india96-en.asp.

Chapnick, Adam. 1999. "The Middle Power." *Canadian Foreign Policy/La politique étrangère du Canada* 7, 2: 73–82.

Chase, Stephen. 2007. "Ottawa Pitching Trade Deal to India." *Globe and Mail*, 12 March, A1.

Clark, Campbell. 2007. "PM Raises Stakes in Bid to Extend Security Powers." *Globe and Mail*, 23 February, A4.

———. 2009. "Canada, India Near New Era of Trade." *Globe and Mail*, 6 October, A6.

Cooper, Andrew, Richard A. Higgott, and Kim Richard Nossal. 1993. *Relocating Middle Powers: Australia and Canada in a Changing World Order.* Vancouver: University of British Columbia Press/University of Melbourne Press.

Coutts, Matthew. 2008. "Immigration Backlog 'Holds Us Back,' PM Says." *National Post*, 19 April, A4.

Deccan Herald. 2010. "FIPPA will Conclude Soon: Canadian Minister." 15 September. At http://www.deccanherald.com/content/96630/fippa-conclude-soon-canadian-minister.html.

DFAIT (Department of Foreign Policy and International Trade). 2008. "Minister Bernier Concludes Successful Meetings in India." 12 January. http://www.international.gc.ca/media/aff/news-communiques/2008/385765.aspx.

————. 2009. "New Trade Office in India and WTO Meeting." 4 September. At http://www.international.gc.ca/commerce/visit-visite/india-2009-inde.aspx.

————. 2011. "Canada-India Relations." 12 December. At http://www.canadainternational.gc.ca/india-inde/bilateral_relations_bilaterales/canada_india-inde.aspx.

Gilpin, Robert. 1984. "The Richness of the Tradition of Political Realism." *International Organization* 38, 2: 287–304.

Globe and Mail. 2010. "Canada-India: These Nukes Are Good Nukes." 29 June, A6.

Goar, Carol. 2008. "Finley's Bill Side-Swipes Kenney." *Toronto Star*, 7 April, AA06.

Haider, Zaglul. 2005. "Unfolding Canada-Bangladesh Relations." *Asian Survey* 45, 2: 325.

Hindustan Times. 2010. "Canada Becomes India's Ninth Civil Nuclear Energy Partner." 28 June. At http://www.hindustantimes.com/Canada-becomes-India-s-ninth-civil-nuclear-energy-partner/Article1-564200.aspx.

Holmes, John. 1970. *The Better Part of Valour.* Toronto: McClelland & Stewart.

India, Office of the Prime Minister. 2008. "Key Questions on the Nuclear Initiative." At http://www.pmindia.nic.in/.

Indian Express. 2009. "Canada Opens Trade Office, Expects to Double Business." 26 September. At http://www.indianexpress.com/news/canada-opens-trade-office-expects-to-double/521842/.

Kapur, Ashok. 1991. "Canada and India." In Arthur Rubinoff, ed., *Canada and South Asia: Political and Strategic Relations.* Toronto: University of Toronto, Centre for South Asian Studies, 53–63.

Kapur, Ashok, and Naresh Raghubeer. 2010. "Harper—India's Best Friend." 25 June. At http://www.calgaryherald.com/business/Harper+India+best+friend/3199280/story.html.

Kauskik, Brij Mohan. 1979. "Indo-U.S. Nuclear Dialogue: The Present Status." *Strategic Analysis* 2, 10: 356–60.

Kirton, John. 2007. Lecture 12B: "The Harper Years." At http://www.kirton.nelson.com/student/documents/312-12b-2006.pdf.

Legro, Jeffrey W., and Andrew Moravcsik. 1999. "Is Anybody Still a Realist?" *International Security* 24, 2: 5–55.

McCarthy, Shawn. 2009. "Canada and India Vow to Deepen Ties." *Globe and Mail*, 21 January, B11.

MacCharles, Tonda. 2008. "PM Defends Immigration Changes; Harper Said He Is Ready to Go to the Polls on the Issue." *Toronto Star*, 19 April, A01.

Mansur, Salim. 1992. "Canada and Pakistan: At the Beginning." In Arthur G. Rubinoff, ed., *Canada and South Asia Political and Strategic Relations.* Toronto: Centre for South Asian Studies, 38–52.

Mistry, Dinshaw. 2006. "Diplomacy, Domestic Politics and the U.S.-India Nuclear Agreement." *Asian Survey* 46, 5: 675–98.

Munton, Don. 2002–3. "Whither Internationalism?" *International Journal* 58, 1: 155–80.

————. 2010. Professor of International Studies, University of Northern British Columbia, personal correspondence, 3 September.

Munton, Don, and Tom Keating, 2001. "Internationalism and the Canadian Public." *Canadian Journal of Political Science* 34, 3: 517–49.

Nayar, Baldev Raj, and T.V. Paul. 2003. *India in the World Order: Searching for Major-Power Status.* Cambridge: Cambridge University Press.

Noël, Alain, Jean-Philippe Thérien, and Sébastien Dallaire. 2003. "Divided over Internationalism: The Canadian Public and Development Assistance." *Cahiers du CPDS*, no. 03-02 (February).

Nossal, Kim Richard. 1985. *The Politics of Canadian Foreign Policy.* Scarborough, ON: Prentice-Hall.

————. 1998–9. "Pinchpenny Diplomacy: The Decline of 'Good International Citizenship' in Canadian Foreign Policy." *International Journal* 54, 1: 88–105.

————. 2004. "The World We Want? The Purposeful Confusion of Values, Goals and Interests in Canadian Foreign Policy." Canadian Defence and Foreign Affairs Institute. Occasional Paper. At http://www.cdfai.org/PDF/The%20World%20We%20Want.pdf.

————. 2005. "Ear Candy: Canadian Policy toward Humanitarian Intervention and Atrocity Crimes in Darfur." *International Journal* 60, 4: 1017–32.

Obhrai, Deepak. 2010. Parliamentary Secretary for Foreign Affairs and International Trade. Telephone interview, Calgary, 16 September.

Potter, Evan. 1996. "Niche Diplomacy as Canadian Foreign Policy." *International Journal* 52, 1: 25–38.

Pratt, Cranford, ed. 1990. *Middle Power Internationalism: The North-South Dimension.* Montreal and Kingston: McGill-Queen's University Press.

Reid, Escott. 1981. *Envoy to Nehru.* Don Mills, ON: Oxford University Press.

Rioux, Jean-François, and Robin Hay. 1998. "Canadian Foreign Policy: From Internationalism to Isolationism?" *International Journal* 54, 1: 57–75.

Rubinoff, Arthur G. 2002. "Canada's Re-engagement with India." *Asian Survey* 42, 6: 838–55.

Sarty, Leigh. 1992. "*Sunset Boulevard* Revisited? Canadian Internationalism after the Cold War." *International Journal* 48, 4: 742–77.

Siddiqui, Haroon. 2008. "Demographic Changes Fuel Our Foreign Policy." *Toronto Star*, 24 February. At http://www.thestart.com/comment/article/306144.

Speirs, Rosemary. 1996. "PM's Asian Trip Called an $8.6 Billion Success." *Toronto Star*, 19 January, A11.

Srivastava, Sanjeev. 2005. "Indian PM Feels Political Heat." BBC News, 25 July. At http://news.bbc.co.uk/2/hi/south_asia/4715797.stm.

Stackhouse, John. 1996. "Indian Deals Herald 'New Era': Steel, Textile, Diesel Contracts Produce Big Day for Canadian Business with Subcontinent." *Globe and Mail*, 15 January, B1.

Stairs, Denis. 1998. "Of Medium Powers and Middling Roles." In Ken Booth, ed., *Statecraft and Security: The Cold War and Beyond.* Cambridge: Cambridge University Press, 270–88.

Stein, Janice Gross. 1994. "Canada 21: A Moment and a Model." *Canadian Foreign Policy/La politique étrangère du Canada* 2, 1: 9–13.

Subrahmanyam, K. 1974. *The Indian Nuclear Test in a Global Perspective.* New Delhi: India International Centre.

Talbott, Strobe. 1999. "Dealing with the Bomb in South Asia." *Foreign Affairs* 78, 2: 110–22.

Taylor, Lesley Ciarula. 2009. "Canada Plans to Admit More Foreign Students." *Toronto Star*, 20 February. At http://www.thestar.com/news/canada/article/590819.

Touhey, Ryan. 2007. "Canada and India at 60: Moving beyond History." *International Journal* 62, 4: 733–52.

Tremblay, Reeta Chowdhari. 2003. "Canada-India Relations: The Need to Re-engage." Asia Pacific Foundation of Canada's Roundtable on the Foreign Policy Dialogue, 27 March.

Tucker, Michael. 1980. *Canadian Foreign Policy: Contemporary Issues and Themes.* Toronto: McGraw-Hill Ryerson.

Urquhart, Ian. 2007. "Everyone Has Caught India Fever." *Toronto Star*, 8 March. At http://www.thestar.com/columnists/article/188875.

Verma, Rajnikanta, High Commissioner for India in Ottawa. 2000. "Canada-India Relations: Building on Experience." *Conference Proceedings: Canada-India Relations after the Nuclear Tests in 1998: A New Beginning or a New End?* University of Waterloo, May.

Whitaker, Reg. 2007. "Security and Politics." *Globe and Mail*, 26 February.

6

Sleeping with the Dragon: The Harper Government, China, and How Not to Do Human Rights

Andrew Lui →overseas human & rights
exceeding domestic hum
rights

China is no stranger to international scrutiny when it comes to **human rights**. The country's meteoric economy, its growing international prominence, and its share of media attention over events such as the Beijing Olympic Games are but a few of the factors that maintain an intense global spotlight on the Chinese regime. Interest in China has thus fuelled debate—and international condemnation—over how Chinese authorities deal with human rights at home and abroad. Among a leading group of states, Canada has issued persistent challenges to the Chinese regime on its human rights commitments. Correspondingly, Beijing has been receptive to Ottawa's human rights concerns insofar as Ottawa's criticism was being couched within a broader mandate to strengthen Sino-Canadian ties across the board. Canada's approach to the rising power has therefore been grounded in a policy of engagement. And, until recently, engagement has served Canada's interests effectively as the bedrock of Sino-Canadian relations from its official recognition of the People's Republic of China (PRC) in 1970 onwards.

Prime Minister Stephen Harper's Conservative government, however, has made a striking break with past doctrine and ignited a storm of controversy over its China policy. From the onset of the Conservatives' taking power in February 2006, the Harper government's "tough-on-China policy" caused a sharp deterioration in diplomatic relations, raising serious concerns about the prudence of instigating what has become one of the frostiest periods in the history of Canada-China affairs (Jiang, 2007; Simpson, 2008). Put bluntly, Harper's strategy of "cool politics, warm economics" has resulted in considerable shortfalls (Evans, 2008a). By all measures, if not pursuing a strategy of outright *dis*engagement, the Harper government appears to be engaged in little more than intransigence.

So where did things go wrong? More importantly, are the existing disparities between Beijing and Ottawa irreconcilable, thereby signalling a structural turning point in bilateral relations, or can Canada's position be renewed through diplomatic compromise and more adept engagement? Instead of relying exclusively on historical, descriptive, or anecdotal narratives, this chapter offers a conceptual analysis of the qualitative distinctions between the Conservative approach to human rights in Canadian foreign policy (CFP) and Sino-Canadian relations, on the one hand, and the general blueprints that were drafted under earlier administrations, on the other. It begins with the assumption that rigorous attention to China policy is vital to the contemporary study of CFP. Getting China policy right may be exceedingly difficult, according to Paul Evans (2008b: 131), but it is also fundamentally important. Already, China's global expansion in reach and power has made it the second-largest trading partner of Canada and the United States. Amid other trends and developments, though, an analytical appraisal of the Sino-Canadian relationship is key because of its relative immaturity. Outspoken entrepreneur Jim Balsillie (2008) admonishes that "[i]f ever there was a time to change our way of thinking about the world, this is that time. And if ever there was a world power we needed to understand better, it is China." Whether or not one appreciates his flair for the provocative, there is an underlying consensus that much between Beijing and Ottawa is getting lost in translation despite the rising significance and density of bilateral ties. This chapter therefore seeks to explore these sources of contention in part because scholarly attention to China policy clearly lags behind the complex realities of the Sino-Canadian relationship.

Furthermore, understanding the human rights factor in this relationship has become central to CFP, as evidenced by the Harper government's ardent attempts to isolate China through the Conservatives' particular brand of values-driven foreign policy.[1] These core values, according to the 2006 Speech from the Throne, centre on freedom, democracy, the rule of law, and human rights (Government of Canada, 2006). To advocacy groups such as Amnesty International (AI), however, the Conservatives' track record on human rights is not only arbitrary and inconsistent but also serious cause for concern. The group remonstrates that "Canadian leadership in the struggle to shore up human rights protection around the world, a proud record built up over many decades, has recently begun to slip" (AI, cited in Barthos, 2007). Indeed, Harper's obstinacy over the high-profile detention of Omar Khadr in Guantanamo Bay, his support for forging new partnerships with rights-abusing countries like Colombia, and his reticence about the genocide in Darfur are only a few of the complaints that rights groups have lobbied against him. This record calls into question the credibility of these values while making a disproportionate focus on China all the more conspicuous. China certainly has its share of growing pains. Nonetheless, it is not the *only* country with systemic human rights problems. The fact that multifarious bilateral relations were made superficially contingent on human rights—unlike any other in which Canada is engaged—is a puzzling development in CFP that merits analytic scrutiny.

This chapter has two primary aims. First, it assesses Canada's international human rights policy with respect to China in order to establish the specific policy discrepancies between the Harper government and its predecessors. Emblemized by clashes over Tibet and Huseyin Celil—two cases which will be explored later in this chapter—the *ad hoc* peculiarities of Harper's China policy in fact signify a deliberate and more extensive shift in geopolitical emphasis. In particular, Harper has broken from past initiatives in steering away from China and the Asia Pacific. The current directive falls instead on making deeper investments in the US relationship, strengthening old bonds with Britain and the European Union (EU), and possibly forging new ones with emerging markets in Latin America and India. Second, this chapter shows, in turn, how this geopolitical shift is indicative of a significant change in CFP in terms of the Conservatives' (somewhat experimental) strategic direction. Although novelty and innovation in foreign policy are not to be discouraged, Harper has opted to eschew the internationalist foundations of Canadian foreign policy in the absence of a competing framework. This void is unprecedented, according to Kim Nossal (chapter 2), as the Conservatives have subsumed international policy under a domestic partisan agenda fixated on one strategic purpose: to supplant the Liberals as the "natural governing party" of Canada.

This chapter argues, then, that the Harper government's public animosity towards China can be traced to this abandonment of internationalist principles. More than just a general ideology, internationalism provided the rubric for a role-based approach to foreign affairs that allowed Canada to assert its identity, expand its foreign markets, and mitigate against excessive US influence. The choice facing Canadians in the twenty-first century, however, concerns whether or not Canada will be successful in asserting a similar role as China rises as a global power. The Harper government, in its deliberate geopolitical shift away from China and the Asia Pacific, has unfortunately eroded Canada's ability to meet this challenge, instead reverting back to an emphasis on traditional partners or attempting to forge stronger ties within the Americas. In essence, this clear deviation from internationalist underpinnings is both harmful and untenable. It appears to be rooted, moreover, in a narrow ideological brand of policy formulation that systematically ignores the realities of contemporary international relations as well as a judicious vision of Canada's role in the world. Redressing these shortfalls in Canadian foreign policy will mean, in the final instance, that Canada must adapt to sleeping with elephants and dragons alike.

The Harper Doctrine on Human Rights and China

Previous governments have been anything but shy in rebuking China on human rights. Yet previous governments, including those under John Diefenbaker and Brian Mulroney, also insisted that denunciation be accompanied by engagement. Strengthening bilateral relations at a variety of diplomatic levels and across an array of concurrent objectives remained the persistent mantra of Ottawa's China policy, with little or no partisan distinction. Even while human rights issues entered the bilateral equation in the 1980s, most passionately over the Tiananmen Square crackdown in June 1989, the core strategy of deeper engagement with China was scarcely affected (Gecelovsky and Keenleyside, 1995). Continuity was the ensuing hallmark in the transition from Brian Mulroney to Jean Chrétien. In what Allan Thompson (1994) describes as the **Chrétien doctrine on human rights**, closer commercial ties would be pursued parallel to rather than contingent on genuine differences and concerns over human rights. Accordingly, the post-Tiananmen period witnessed both exponential growth in bilateral trade and direct, multi-level talks on human rights issues (Khondaker, 2007).

Sceptics may doubt the sincerity of these talks, pointing to the imbalance in the Chrétien government's policy in favouring rhetorical or symbolic gestures over substantive sanctions against the Chinese regime. Bruce Gilley, for instance, reproaches this course of statecraft in arguing that "Canada has become complacent and spiritless in its foreign policy, a position we [Canadians] often rationalize to ourselves through appeals to commercial gain and empirically unsound relativism about human rights" (2008: 128). Gilley goes on to say that Ottawa has unwittingly caused its own irrelevance in bilateral affairs because the soft approach on engagement and human rights, rehearsed by successive governments since 1970, has eroded the power and influence of Canada to effect positive change in China (128–9). Others, such as Charles Burton (2007), object to Chrétien's style of **quiet diplomacy**—confidential, closed-door dialogues between ministerial officials—charging that it did not lead to any discernible improvement in the realization of human rights in China. Burton also (2006) charges that the prominent Canada-China Bilateral Human Rights Dialogues, which began in 1997 and concluded in 2006, were too formal, too scripted, and too far removed from human rights problems on the ground.

Unfortunately, these arguments discount the comprehensive purpose of engagement with respect to Canada's international relations with the People's Republic. In a direct reply to Gilley, Paul Evans contends that Canada's

> China policy was largely about opening China to the broader world including international institutions, was based upon clear principles (albeit ones that did not give precedence to the projection of Canadian values), and was a major success. It was popular among the public, a large majority of politicians, and Canada's coterie of foreign policy analysts and Asia scholars. Generally, the Canadian approach was echoed by virtually every other Western government. (2008b: 134)

Over the past decades, Canada's role in engaging China went beyond serving domestic self-interests, at one extreme, or attempting to compel the Chinese regime to immediately adopt sweeping democratic reforms, at another extreme. The Canadian position from 1970 to 2006, however imperfect, sought instead to cultivate balanced relations with an important world player in its transition away from international isolation and exclusion.

Playing this role was not problem-free. Even Canadian officials admit to diminishing returns on the bilateral human rights dialogues, which had stagnated since their inception. Nonetheless, Canada's role of engagement also enjoyed remarkable success. Its bilateral relations with China were the envy of most other states when then Chinese premier Zhu Rongji affirmed in 1998 that "Canada is our best friend in the whole world" during one of Chrétien's Team Canada ventures. Beneath the rhetoric, nonetheless, a successful engagement policy would eventually lead to additional dividends in the form of a new **strategic partnership**. Announced in the twilight days of the last Liberal government under Paul Martin, this partnership was intended to pave the way for high-level talks on crucial bilateral and global issues, including trade, investment, energy, human rights, and the environment (York and Freeman, 2007). The initiative was supported enthusiastically on both sides of the Pacific, signalling ever closer bilateral ties.

Given this backdrop, it is undeniable that, since 2006, relations have soured considerably. As Bill Schiller (2009) observes, "Prime Minister Stephen Harper appeared to have stumbled with the Canada-China relationship almost from the day he was elected in 2006." Harper had attained a minority government with little or no foreign policy experience among his ranks of Conservative MPs. The now infamous example of former foreign minister Maxime Bernier is a case in point. It could be said that the Conservatives, like any unseasoned government, were simply experiencing their share of growing pains as they learned the ropes of statecraft from a precarious minority position. Upon closer inspection, however, the actions of the Harper government are clearly more systematic. In fact, the **Harper doctrine on human rights** and China signals a deliberate and more extended shift in geopolitical emphasis away from China and the Asia Pacific in favour of forging closer ties with the United States, strengthening old bonds with Britain and the EU, and possibly establishing new ones with emerging markets in Latin America and India.

To begin with, the Conservative government under Stephen Harper sought to deliver on a promise to take a tougher stance against the Chinese regime. This promise, made while the Conservatives were in opposition, was meant to correct what the party perceived as Liberal failures to advance Canadian values in a myopic pursuit of commercial interests. As a direct snub to both the Liberals and the Chinese, Harper told reporters en route to the November 2006 APEC (Asia-Pacific Economic Cooperation) summit in Vietnam that "I don't think Canadians want us to sell out our values, our beliefs in democracy, freedom and human rights. They don't want us to sell that out to the almighty dollar" (cited in Laghi, 2006). This retort was made largely as a tit-for-tat response to President Hu Jintao's initial cancellation of Canada-China talks at the APEC summit over Harper's hard-line stance on Tibet and Huseyin Celil. These controversies illustrate that by making bilateral relations thus contingent on intractable differences, the Harper government is not following a principled approach to foreign policy per se, but is making a conscious attempt to steer Canada's international relations in a different direction.

Harper's policy on Tibet appears at first glance to invoke the debates of the 1950s and early 1960s. Following China's Communist revolution, Canada's foreign policy elite, in tandem with international counterparts, deliberated on the question of Tibetan independence. Although Lester B. Pearson, then secretary of state for external affairs, is noted for his incipient sympathy for the idea of a sovereign

Tibet, Canada's position eventually coalesced with the international consensus that Tibet remain an official part of the People's Republic of China (Davis, 2009). Prime Minister Diefenbaker (cited in Davis, 2009) echoed this position in 1960 in a letter to the Dalai Lama while maintaining that "the Canadian delegation [at the UN General Assembly] will be receptive to all initiatives seeking to ensure respect of the human rights of the people of Tibet." Harper, for one, has publicly acknowledged his admiration for Diefenbaker and his achievements. Renewing support for Tibet could be regarded as likening his policies to Diefenbaker's.

Nevertheless, it is important to remember that even Diefenbaker sought deeper engagement with China by establishing bilateral trade with the PRC through the approved sale of wheat on credit. Canada's relations with China during this period were duly affected by Cold War considerations. At the time, Canada's conception of human rights was not nearly as "universal" as it is today (Schabas, 1998). Along with other Western states, Canada favoured civil and political rights over economic, social, and cultural rights, which often made the outward condemnation of Communist countries' performance on human rights issues a matter of Cold War rivalry. Canada ultimately adopted a status quo position that fell far short of the diplomatic recognition of Tibet. The Harper government has therefore gone further than any previous government on this issue by awarding the Dalai Lama honorary citizenship—a move likely pushed by the prime minister and the evangelical Christian wing of his caucus (York and Laghi, 2006). Former Conservative trade minister David Emerson (cited in Martin, 2006) was clearly puzzled by these developments, complaining that "[i]t's like our China policy is made in Tibet." The complex bilateral relationship, worth over $50.8 billion in two-way trade in 2009, was thereby held to be contingent on specific issues or grievances like the Tibetan situation (Government of Canada, 2010).

Similar diplomatic squabbling over Huseyin Celil has, at times, brought bilateral relations to a virtual standstill. The Canadian immigrant of Uighur descent, born in the Xinjiang Autonomous Region, was incarcerated in China on terrorist-related charges in 2006. Ever since, Celil has been refused the diplomatic recourse ostensibly guaranteed by bilateral agreements, as Chinese officials continue to disavow his Canadian citizenship. Abandoning the usual tactic of quiet diplomacy, Harper made Celil's plight "the improbable centerpiece" of Canada-China relations leading up to the 2006 APEC summit (Gillis, 2006). What began as a consular issue thus became a critical touchstone for normalizing bilateral relations. Only after years of failure has Harper accepted a change in strategy on the Celil case, turning in May 2009 to the services of John Kamm, an American businessman turned activist (Clark, 2009b). Most remarkably, Kamm's reputation as a human rights advocate was built on his success with low-key, bottom-up approaches that could not be more different from the highly public, top-down strategies favoured by the Conservative government. Rather than admitting to a foreign policy blunder altogether, Harper has attempted to salvage his China policy by outsourcing quiet diplomacy to a private third-party firm.

Moreover, the examples of Tibet and Huseyin Celil highlight the conspicuous discrepancy between the Conservatives' China policy and the glaring absence of the Harper government's support for human rights in other areas of international relations. These trends suggest that Harper's values-driven or principled approach to foreign policy is simply a pretext for expediency. As already mentioned, Harper's resolve to repatriate Celil is entirely inconsistent with his refusal to repatriate Omar Khadr—the Canadian citizen, captured as a 15-year-old enemy combatant by US forces in Afghanistan, who pleaded guilty to war crimes in exchange for a definitive sentence and the eligibility to return to Canada in 2011. This now infamous case breaks with Canada's commitment to the UN Convention on the Rights of the Child, which is supposed to protect child soldiers from prosecution. As Robert Wolfe (cited in Taylor, 2007) remarks, the Conservatives openly "scold China on Tibet, yet you would never catch Harper making nasty comments about Guantánamo." Also, in line with their refusal to sponsor a UN resolution calling for a moratorium on the death penalty, the Conservatives have moved away from the common practice of seeking clemency for Canadian expatriates sentenced to execution abroad (Barthos, 2007). The Harper government has also remained reticent on the issue of Darfur, lacking any coherent strategy for dealing with what has been defined as genocide, described as the worst humanitarian disaster thus far in the twenty-first century, and identified in *Canada's International Policy Statement* (2005) as a priority area (Government of Canada, 2005).

In further contrast to the China example, Harper has sought improved relations with Colombia and other emerging markets in Latin America despite widespread allegations of state atrocities (see David Black's chapter in this volume regarding the Harper government's new emphasis on Colombia and other Latin American countries notwithstanding widespread criticism from civil society groups). Indeed, Harper's official visit to Colombia in 2007 was the first ever by a sitting Canadian prime minister since diplomatic relations were established in 1953. En route to his four-country tour of Latin America and the Caribbean, which included stops in Chile, Barbados, and Haiti, Harper defended the government's new geopolitical emphasis on Latin America, arguing that it would be untenable to prohibit trade talks until human rights conditions were ideal. He stated explicitly with regard to Colombia, "We are not going to say, 'Fix all your social, political and human-rights problems and only then will we engage in trade relations with you.' . . . That's a ridiculous position" (Harper, cited in Freeman, 2007). The discrepancies between the Conservatives' Latin American policy and their China policy are startling, not because previous governments were ever immune to charges of inconsistency, but because the Conservatives claimed that their Liberal predecessors were not consistently values-driven or principled *enough*. On the whole, these geopolitical shifts under the Harper doctrine are indicative of a significant change in CFP in terms of the Conservatives' strategic direction, which essentially calls for the abandonment of the internationalist foundations of Canadian foreign policy.

Whither Internationalism? Harper Meets the Asian Dragon

In the absence of a competing framework, the withering of internationalism under the Harper doctrine has left Canada's China policy in disarray. Gone is the strategic partnership—a term that Harper refuses to use in connection with China—and here to stay are puzzling questions about why Harper embarked on a rather drastic change in Ottawa's strategic direction and why this change led ultimately to such disastrous outcomes (York and Freeman, 2007). Observers such as journalist Jeffrey Simpson (2009) blame the Conservatives' "puerile partisanship" and "stunning ignorance of the world," which made them want to be different just for the sake of being different (also see Jiang, 2007). While Simpson's claim obviously appeals to the converted, it offers few analytically useful clues regarding the linkage between the withering of internationalism and the withering of Canada-China relations. Exploring this linkage is key to understanding the pitfalls of the current government as well as the medium- to longer-term contours of Canada's geopolitical future with China and other relevant countries.

Unfortunately, internationalism is a rather slippery concept. John W. Holmes is often credited with the scholarly prominence of internationalism in post-war Canadian foreign policy. Yet Holmes often uses the term with numerous qualifications, such as pure internationalism, active internationalism, liberal internationalism, wider internationalism, new and tougher internationalism, soft-minded internationalism, comfortable internationalism, and internationalist nationalism (Munton and Keating, 2001: 526). He thereby seems to relish some degree of conceptual ambiguity in the term. In Holmes's footsteps, Kim Nossal offers a more precise definition of internationalism in describing its chief objective as the avoidance of war, seeing it as equivalent to its antithesis, isolationism, in aim but differing in method. Nossal (1985: 53) argues further that internationalism is comprised of four interconnected factors: (1) an active involvement in and responsibility for the management of interstate conflict; (2) a willingness to forgo the advantages of unilateral action for the broader interests of the community of states; (3) support for multilateralism; and (4) a willingness to act on prior commitments by mobilizing national resources for the betterment of the international system as a whole.[2] As such, internationalism is best depicted as a particular role-based *style* of foreign policy—how a state operates within the system of states rather than what, precisely, it does (also see Gecelovsky, 2009).

For several important reasons, then, post-war circumstances were responsible for cementing internationalism as the foundation of Canada's foreign policy outlook. Most crucially, internationalism would provide a structure for Canada, so dependent on international trade, to expand its foreign markets while concurrently avoiding excessive US dominance. On this first point, John Holmes (1976: 30) once argued—with piercing relevance today—that "Canada is vulnerable because it is a country with a small population, enormous territory, and vast resources. It is dependent upon a world safe for commerce." It had become clear in the aftermath of the Second World War that the customary pattern of trade between Canada and Britain would not survive into the post-war era, thereby signalling the definitive end of the special relationship of the colonial era (Holmes, 1979: 80–90). As such, internationalism provided Canada with a conceptual basis with which to pragmatically address its post-war economic needs in a period of rapidly growing Canada-US ties.

Second, in the face of patent economic benefits, the significance of this new trade pattern ran the risk of eclipsing Canada behind the emerging colossus to the south. Pierre Trudeau famously likened this predisposition to the tribulations of a mouse with an elephant. Indeed, while post-war Liberal governments accepted this reality and sought pragmatic solutions in dealing with the United States, Diefenbaker emphasized stronger ties to Britain and the Commonwealth as the solution to offset US predominance. With the clarity of hindsight, Diefenbaker's gambit was a failure. His attempts were shunned by Britain and did little to curb growth in Canada-US commerce (Bothwell, 2007: 146–50). By contrast, internationalism was meant to help Canada establish and pursue a specific role within the international order according to functionalist principles—a role that would be more important than that of the smaller powers but less so than that of the great powers. According to John Holmes, Canadians "must, however, have some conception of our role in the world if we [Canadians] are to be an independent state at all" (1966: 28). Role-based thinking thus provided a natural way for Canada to assert an independent, internationalist identity. Canada's fundamental task in the post-war period was to proclaim that Canada mattered in international relations through the now familiar archetype of a middle power. These lessons, though rooted in the past, retain their resonance in the present.

Today, Canada has reached a critical juncture that bears striking similarities to the geopolitical quandary with which the country was faced in the post-war period between the emerging US superpower, on the one hand, and Britain and the Commonwealth, on the other. As Robert Cox (2005) notes, Canadians and their governments are in a constant dilemma over whether Canada's orientation should be geared more towards "the United States or the world." But this dilemma has been made ever more complex with the rise of a new power on the international stage. Specifically, the choice to be made today concerns Canada's orientation towards China. Canada is faced now with the challenge of learning to live peacefully and prosperously with an Asian dragon in addition to the American elephant to which Canadians are more accustomed.

The Harper government, in its deliberate geopolitical shift away from China and the Asia Pacific, has made a deliberate decision to revert back to the practice of strengthening ties with "traditional" partners. Harper is thus attempting to mirror Diefenbaker's policies but in a much more extreme fashion, with the Asian dragon in lieu of the American elephant. And, in the absence of new ideas, he seems to be willing to entertain expedient if inconsistent and short-term partnerships with less-than-savoury regimes (see chapters by Nossal and Black in this volume for further discussion of the Harper government's unambiguous break from international policies that tend to be identified with the Liberal "brand"). Yet one of the biggest disappointments with the Harper doctrine is not that the Conservatives deny the salience of internationalist principles altogether, but rather that Harper has appropriated the rhetoric of internationalism when speaking to select audiences only to abandon in application the consistent, role-based approach to foreign affairs that internationalism would afford. Speaking in New York to the US Council on Foreign Relations in September 2007, Harper (cited in Hurst, 2007) declared that "middle powers who can step up to the plate to do their part" are in high demand given the complexities of contemporary international relations. He went on to say that middle powers are those states "who are willing to assume responsibilities, seek practical, do-able solutions to problems and who have a voice and influence in global affairs because they lead, not by lecturing, but by example" (Hurst, 2007).

Beneath the rhetoric, however, the Harper government has neither led by example nor sought doable solutions to the complex problems of human rights and good governance—especially in the case of China. In fact, Harper's China policy eschews internationalism, since middlepowermanship, so "deeply connected to the internationalist approach to foreign policy," was meant to actively engage, reinforce, and strengthen the multilateral bonds that are vital to the stability of the international system (Nossal, Roussel, and Paquin, 2011: 55). Harper's China policy appears instead to be accomplishing just the opposite at a time when China's human rights record is improving and when other states have pursued deeper engagement with the rising power. The US Council on Foreign Relations (cited in Simpson, 2007), for instance, recently issued a report stating that, despite flashpoints of disagreement, "China's overall trajectory over the past 35 years of engagement with the United States is positive. Growing adherence to international rules, institutions, and norms—particularly in the areas of trade and security—marks China's integration [into international society]." China watchers universally agree that the Chinese people are considerably freer today than at any other point in their history. Across almost all human rights measures, China has made notable progress in terms both of citizens' (subjective) perceptions of improvement and absolute (objective) indicators.

Using recent survey data, Tianjian Shi and Diqing Lou (2010: 175–6) find that the majority of Chinese citizens believe that civil and political rights have improved significantly since 1979. Even Canadian diplomats in Beijing, in a confidential report obtained by the *Globe and Mail*, agree that China is achieving "incremental progress" on human rights issues and is projected to make a "steady forward movement" in the foreseeable future (York, 2007). Randall Peerenboom derives similar conclusions, contending after a rigorous qualitative assessment of rights performance in China that, by and large, "citizens are happy with their lives, optimistic about the future, and relatively satisfied with the government on the whole, largely because the government has been successful at maintaining stability and improving the living standards of most people" (2005: 148).[3] These reports contradict the Harper government's harsh—if not extreme—approach to Sino-Canadian relations.

Harper's China policy has thus come under fire for being misguided or unworkable. Derek Burney, for instance, claims that the Conservatives' outlook on China "has tended to concentrate somewhat erratically on the two bookends of trade and human-rights issues with not much productive dialogue on either, and with a large gap between the two" (2009). Similarly, Wenran Jiang (2009: 907), Mactaggart research chair at the University of Alberta's China Institute, notes that the Conservatives have exaggerated the human-rights-versus-trade argument in treating the two issues as mutually exclusive—something that future governments must avoid. Yet Daniel Bell (2007) charges that while Canada-China trade may have suffered under Harper's tenure, the Harper doctrine has also harmed the prospects for human rights in the People's Republic. Bell contends that if advancing human rights were the government's genuine aim, Canada would be engaging China on issues such as poverty reduction and environmental protection, as hundreds of millions of Chinese are most affected by the concomitant threats to human dignity associated with these issues. On human rights and other global issues, Kenneth Roth (2010), director of Human Rights Watch, shows even greater disdain for the Harper doctrine in arguing that Canada once "punched above its weight. It was a nation to be contended with. . . . Now, unfortunately, when it comes to the international arena, Canada is barely punching at all."

Whether or not one agrees with these challenges, Canada could nonetheless be playing a far more constructive role while better fulfilling domestic interests. When Canada abandoned internationalism and a role-based identity in foreign affairs, progress on human rights in China and Canada's domestic interests have both languished. Errol Mendes (2007), a legal scholar at the University of Ottawa, believes that Canada has played, and can continue to play, a key role in legal reform. He argues that a more constructive, role-based engagement would be

> to persuade China that its crucial interests in expanding its economy, its development agenda and its trade and commercial links are dependent on building the foundation blocks of any human rights system in the world— namely, the rule of law and an independent professional judiciary that does not resort to any form of coercion, let alone confessions obtained by torture.

Concurrently, former prime minister Paul Martin hinted that strong bilateral relations with a prosperous China could, in turn, benefit the domestic interests of Canada as a country that relies on international trade and a healthy global economy. To avoid another recession, Martin (cited in Martin, 2006) foretold in 2006 that Ottawa "better start knocking on Beijing's door."

Given the depth of the subsequent global recession, Martin's warning carried particular resonance. Much of the world recorded negative growth, but China's booming economy, though it slowed, continued to grow—albeit from double-digit expansion down to 8.7 per cent annualized growth in 2009. Several economic indicators have shown that China was the most resilient amongst the major world economies in recovering from the economic crisis (MacKinnon, 2009a). Many analysts and observers will be watching closely to see how Beijing will translate its relative economic might into a broader ploy for global influence. Paul Evans (2008a) downplays rumours that a new "Beijing consensus" will emerge, although he does state emphatically that "China is not just affected by the meltdown; it has a major role in how it plays out. When America sneezes, China, like Canada, catches a cold. The difference is that China is now in a position to prescribe the medicine and help build the hospital where the patients will be treated." The only problem, for Canada, is the disrepair of the bilateral relationship.

Fortunately, there are encouraging signs that the Harper government is learning from past mistakes, if only somewhat belatedly. Wenran Jiang points out that Canada's China policy prior to the Harper government was "rather consistent and nonpartisan" (2009: 892). As a consequence, Harper's initial missteps with China have necessitated nominal remedies on the part of Canadian officials. Foreign Minister Lawrence Cannon and International Trade Minister Stockwell Day were both sent in early 2009 on a China excursion in an attempt to mend broken fences and to pave the way for Harper's first state visit in December of that year. The prime minister was subsequently chastised by Chinese premier Wen Jiabao (cited in Galloway, 2010) for waiting "too long" to visit China, raising serious "problems of mutual trust." Nevertheless, Harper's corrective measures prompted Chinese officials to lift the roadblocks that had prevented Canada from receiving "approved destination status" for Chinese tourists; as a consequence, Chinese tourism to Canadian destinations is projected to increase by 50 per cent by 2015 (Clark, 2009a).[4] This gesture by Chinese officials also served as a prelude for President Hu Jintao's corresponding state visit to Canada in 2010. During his tour, President Hu stressed the need for Canada to renew the bilateral strategic partnership from a longer-term perspective that would look to areas of cooperation and mutual gain (Galloway, 2010).

In an attempt to formulate a less partisan approach to Canada's China policy, Canadian officials have offered subtle acknowledgements that bilateral relations with China had indeed been damaged over human rights issues, Tibet, and Harper's decision not to attend the Beijing Olympic Games. Minister Cannon, at the time of his visit, signalled a "forward-looking" desire to revive the Canada-China Bilateral Human Rights Dialogue, which the Conservatives had cancelled in 2006, citing their ineffectiveness, albeit under a different name. The excuse, according to Cannon, is that he "[doesn't] like using the words human-rights dialogue" but would "want to propose a mechanism whereby everybody will feel comfortable as we move forward" (cited in MacKinnon, 2009b). Hopefully, few would remember that Beijing officials were not in any discomfort before the dialogues were cancelled in the first place.

Overall, the Harper doctrine has failed to serve either Canadian domestic interests or the human rights of Chinese citizens. Even with nominal corrections, a critical reappraisal of the Harper doctrine is essential. Pundits, for example, have often cited partisanship and lack of CFP experience amongst Conservative ranks as mainsprings of Harper's China policy and the ultimate reasons for its failure. Yet a deeper analysis of the Harper government's disengagement from China and the Asia Pacific—and subsequent attempts to bolster ties with countries like the United States, India, and Colombia—reveals that partisanship and inexperience only go so far to explain the origins and intent of the Harper doctrine. Certainly, Harper's "war on the civil service" (Macdonald, 2010) has fuelled speculation that ideology rather than evidence drove much of the Conservatives' policy-making process. As one commentary put it, the Harper government "has shown little propensity to respect its [the civil service's] professionalism and expertise, and often seems uninterested in the advice of public servants; it prefers them to simply carry out political orders, playing the role of mechanics" (Globe Editorial, 2009). By dismissing evidence and expert advice, however, the Harper government has fashioned a China policy that seems rooted in a values-based persuasion that bears little resemblance to the realities of contemporary international relations.[5] All told, inexperience might explain the Harper government's poor grasp of *les affaires d'états*; partisanship might then explain the Conservatives' suspicion of the civil service. But it takes something akin to arrogance to make such extreme policy decisions in the absence of a more judicious vision of Canada's role in the world.

In effect, Harper and his caucus grossly overestimated their agency—that is, their influence or power over the Chinese regime—while underestimating the structural constraints imposed by China's rising power and global reach on a wide range of international issues (see, for example, Dahl, 1957; Wendt, 1987; Strange, 1996; Lukes, 2004; Barnett and Duvall, 2005). China is set, for instance, to become the world's largest trading nation. The country will remain an important driver of global trade for both developed and underdeveloped countries. Most pertinent for Canada are the structural effects of these shifts in global trade patterns. As Wenran Jiang warns, "[I]f the trajectory of US-China trade growth in the last decade holds for the next," *ceteris paribus*, "China will soon overtake Canada in its total volume of trade with the US. . . . Canada's China challenge is not across the Pacific but right in its largest traditional market" (2009: 896). Disengagement will not change the realities of these trade patterns. Nor will deeper engagement with other countries.

Thus, given the acute shortfalls of the Harper doctrine, the Conservative government was forced into adopting somewhat more balanced, pragmatic measures in its dealings with Beijing. But despite recent overtures, the Harper government's China policy can only be characterized as *ad hoc* or reactionary in the absence of systematic attention to the medium- or long-term ramifications of Chinese growth. Canada's China policy lacks, in other words, an underlying blueprint that could replace the internationalist one that Harper eschewed. Certainly, policy-makers must be cautious when borrowing from the scripts and playbooks of the past (Jervis, 1976, 1988).

Internationalism had nonetheless served as a pillar of Canadian foreign policy for decades precisely because of its flexibility and capacity for innovation. At the very least, internationalism afforded a role-based approach to foreign policy by which Canada could assert its identity, expand its foreign markets, and mitigate against excessive great-power influence. These are goals that still appeal to basic Canadian interests. A renewed look at internationalist principles would simply strengthen Canada's position, offering the foundations that would allow it to regain an active, engaged role in Sino-Canadian affairs. How Canada and other countries choose to respond to China's rise will inevitably affect a wide range of issues, from changes in global trade patterns to emerging human rights concerns.

Conclusion

Stephen Harper's China policy may seem perplexing. By most accounts, it is difficult not to look upon this policy as anything but a blunder. Under the Conservative government, Ottawa made deliberate choices in adopting an untenable position that eschewed the internationalist foundations of Canadian foreign policy and thereby yielded little or no gains for Canada or for China. It would be an exaggeration, however, to blame the failures of Harper's China policy merely on partisanship or inexperience, as is often the case. An analysis of Conservative policies has shown that these failures are the product of a conscious—albeit injudicious—attempt to curb Chinese power in Sino-Canadian relations by steering Canada either towards traditional partnerships or towards new ones in the Americas. The Harper government has ignored the new realities of China's rise, and thus its abandonment of internationalism as a role-based approach to Canadian foreign policy has eroded Ottawa's ability to engage with and influence Beijing.

As a consequence, there are lessons to be drawn from the bankruptcy of the Harper doctrine, lessons that bear a curious resemblance to failed policies from the past—particularly those under John Diefenbaker and concerning what he perceived to be the dilemma of Canada's future vis-à-vis the United States and Britain. When asked on one occasion by an American professor, "Does the future of Canada lie with the United States or the United Kingdom?," O.D. Skelton skilfully replied, "It does not seem to have occurred to the gentleman ... that the future of Canada might perhaps lie with Canada" (cited in Hillmer, 2004–5: 110).[6] Historical lessons suggest that choosing between two extremes—whether between human rights and trade or between one superpower and another—entailed a false dichotomy in the pursuit of Canada's multifaceted domestic and global interests. Canadians need not make the same mistake in the twenty-first century with China.

Clearly impressed with the rise of China, Paul Evans claims that "China has become more self-confident, more sophisticated, more assertive and frequently more constructive in international institutions" (2008b: 135). Despite these achievements, it is important to remember that China still faces numerous obstacles and challenges in the years ahead. Canada can play a constructive and important role by engaging China and the Chinese people throughout this transition process. Past achievements will not guarantee peaceful and prosperous relations with the Asian dragon. Rather than risk irrelevance by disengaging with important global players, Canadians and their CFP officials must borrow a page from O.D. Skelton in realizing that the future of Canada, and the opportunity to live peacefully and prosperously with the Asian dragon, does not lie as much with Washington or Beijing as it does with Ottawa.

Key Terms

human rights   Chrétien doctrine on human rights
quiet diplomacy   Harper doctrine on human rights
strategic partnership

Study Questions

1. Is the pursuit of human rights in Canadian foreign policy driven merely by values or are other factors also at play?
2. What are the limitations of trade and engagement with regard to the promotion of human rights abroad?
3. To what extent should trade-offs between human rights and other foreign policy priorities be allowed in the conduct of Canada's international relations?
4. What are the implications of Sino-Canadian relations for Canadian foreign policy more broadly vis-à-vis other emerging powers or regional blocs in contemporary international relations?
5. Are foreign policy 'corrections' imposed by the structure of international relations or do they come about when state leaders and other decision-making agents recognize the failures of previous policies?

Notes

1   For a general sense of the values-driven foreign policy proposed by the Conservative government, see Government of Canada, "Speech from the Throne to Open the First Session of the Thirty-Ninth Parliament of Canada" (2006); and Government of Canada, "Speech from the Throne to Open the Second Session of the Thirty-Ninth Parliament of Canada" (2007).

2   For a comparison, also see the updated text by Kim Richard Nossal, Stéphane Roussel, and Stéphane Paquin, *International Policy and Politics in Canada* (Toronto: Pearson Education Canada, 2011). This latest volume, translated into French from Nossal's 1985 text and then updated and retranslated back into English, adds a fifth element to the definition of internationalism, namely respect for international law. For the purposes of this chapter, however, Nossal's earlier definition will suffice if only because the element of international law is not as

pronounced. This conception of internationalism, I would argue, remains an extremely useful and relevant one because of its emphasis on a role-based conception of foreign policy and its explicit contrast with isolationism.

3 Randall Pereenboom, director of the Rule of Law in China program at UCLA's Foundation for Law, Justice and Society, reached these conclusions after conducting a survey of rights performance in China that included physical integrity rights and derogation of rights in times of emergency; civil and political rights such as freedom of thought, freedom of speech, freedom of the press, pornography, and freedom of assembly; social and economic rights such as poverty alleviation, health and education; good governance and the rule of law; law and order; women's rights; and cultural and minority rights.

4 China is also expected to be the world's largest outbound market for tourists by 2020 with an estimated 100 million travellers annually.

5 For an insightful and provocative discussion on how political leaders foster erroneous beliefs about the virtue and moral superiority of Canadian values, see Denis Stairs, "Myths, Morals, and Reality in Canadian Foreign Policy," *International Journal* 58, no. 2 (2003): 239–56.

6 Cited in Norman Hillmer, "O.D. Skelton and the North American Mind," *International Journal* 60, no. 1 (2004–5): 93–110.

References

Balsillie, Jim. 2008. "Canada-China Relations Are in Need of an Urgent Overhaul." *Globe and Mail*, 27 October, A15.

Barnett, Michael N., and Raymond Duvall. 2005. *Power in Global Governance*. Cambridge: Cambridge University Press.

Barthos, Gord. 2007. "Canada's Erratic Moral Voice." *Toronto Star*, 15 December, AA04.

Bell, Daniel A. 2007. "Lecturing the Chinese Won't Promote Human Rights." *Globe and Mail*, 13 April, A17.

Bothwell, Robert. 2007. *Alliance and Illusion: Canada and the World, 1945–1984*. Vancouver: University of British Columbia Press.

Burney, Derek. 2009. "Canada Must Outgrow Its Juvenile Relationship with China: Pragmatic Calculation of Mutual Self-Interest Should be the Driver, Not the Mood Swings of Any Given Day." *Globe and Mail*, 11 April, A13.

Burton, Charles. 2006. "Assessment of the Canada-China Bilateral Human Rights Dialogue." At http://spartan.ac.brocku.ca/~cburton/Assessment%20of%20the%20Canada-China%20Bilateral%20Human%20Rights%20Dialogue%2019APR06.pdf.

———. 2007. "A 'Principled' Approach, Quiet Diplomacy and the Prime Minister's Message to Beijing." *Embassy Magazine*, 14 November. At http://embassymag.ca/page/view/.2007.november.14.burton.

Clark, Campbell. 2009a. "Canada's Reward." *Globe and Mail*, 4 December, A1.

———. 2009b. "Harper Enlists Activist to Help Secure Celil's Release: U.S. Businessman Known for Obtaining Freedom of Political Prisoners in China." *Globe and Mail*, 12 May, A1.

Cox, Robert W. 2005. "A Canadian Dilemma: The United States or the World." *International Journal* 60, 3: 667–84.

Dahl, Robert. 1957. "The Concept of Power." *Behavioral Science* 2, 3: 201–15.

Davis, Jeff. 2009. "Canada Disputed Chinese Claims to Tibet from Start." *Embassy Magazine*, 18 February. At http://embassymag.ca/page/view/chinese_tibet-2-18-2009.

Evans, Paul. 2008a. "Getting China Just Right: 'Cool Politics, Warm Economics' Is the Wrong Recipe for Sino-Canadian Relations." *Globe and Mail*, 20 October, A17.

———. 2008b. "Responding to Global China: Getting the Balance Right." *Canadian Foreign Policy/La politique étrangère du Canada* 14, 2: 131–9.

Freeman, Alan. 2007. "PM Backs Trade Talks amid Rights Furor: Colombia Can't Achieve Peace without Economic Help, He Says." *Globe and Mail*, 17 July, A1.

Galloway, Gloria. 2010. "China's Visit a Hopeful Sign for Strained Canadian Relationship: Talks Just the Beginning of a Greater Economic and Trade Relationship with China." *Globe and Mail*, 25 June, A16.

Gecelovsky, Paul. 2009. "Constructing a Middle Power: Ideas and Canadian Foreign Policy." *Canadian Foreign Policy/La politique étrangère du Canada* 15, 1: 77–93.

Gecelovsky, Paul, and T.A. Keenleyside. 1995. "Canada's International Human Rights Policy in Practice: Tiananmen Square." *International Journal* 50, 3: 564–93.

Gilley, Bruce. 2008. "Reawakening Canada's China Policy." *Canadian Foreign Policy/La politique étrangère du Canada* 14, 2: 121–30.

Gillis, Charlie. 2006. "Touching Off Our China Crisis." *Maclean's*, 4 December, 28.

Globe Editorial. 2009. "A Great Public Servant." *Globe and Mail*, 9 May, A18.

Government of Canada. 2005. *Canada's International Policy Statement: A Role of Pride and Influence in the World.* Ottawa: Department of Foreign Affairs and International Trade.

———. 2006. *Speech from the Throne to Open the First Session of the Thirty-Ninth Parliament of Canada.*

———. 2010. "Trade Data Online." At http://www.ic.gc.ca/eic/site/tdo-dcd.nsf/eng/Home.

Hillmer, Norman. 2004/5. "O.D. Skelton and the North American Mind." *International Journal* 60, 1: 93–110.

Holmes, John Wendell. 1966. "Is There a Future for Middlepowermanship?" In J. King Gordon, ed., *Canada's Role as a Middle Power*. Toronto: Canadian Institute of International Affairs, 13–28.

———. 1976. *Canada: A Middle-Aged Power*. Toronto: McClelland & Stewart.

———. 1979. *The Shaping of Peace: Canada and the Search for World Order, 1943–1957*, vol. 1. Toronto: University of Toronto Press.

Hurst, Lynda. 2007. "On World Stage, a Best Supporting Actor: The PM Touted Canada's 'Middle Power' Status This Week. What, Exactly, Was He Talking About?" *Toronto Star*, 29 September, ID01.

Jervis, Robert. 1976. *Perception and Misperception in International Politics*. Princeton, NJ: Princeton University Press.

———. 1988. "War and Misperception." *Journal of Interdisciplinary History* 18, 4: 675–700.

Jiang, Wenran. 2007. "It's a Mistake to Blow Hot and Cold on China." *Globe and Mail*, 19 January, A13.

———. 2009. "Seeking a Strategic Vision for Canada-China Relations." *International Journal* 64, 6: 891–909.

Khondaker, Jafar. 2007. "Canada's Trade with China: 1997 to 2006." Statistics Canada International Trade Division. At http://www.statcan.gc.ca/pub/65-508-x/65-508-x2007001-eng.htm.

Laghi, Brian. 2006. "Harper Promises He Won't 'Sell Out' on Rights: Moral Stand Trumps Trade with China, PM Says after Snub." *Globe and Mail*, 16 November, A1.

Lukes, Steven. 2004. *Power: A Radical View,* 2nd ed. Houndmills, UK: Palgrave Macmillan.

Macdonald, Nancy. 2010. "The War on the Civil Service." *Maclean's*, 8 February, 16.

MacKinnon, Mark. 2009a. "Much at Stake in Cannon's First Visit." *Globe and Mail*, 9 May, A14.

———. 2009b. "Cannon Seeks New Start in Canada-China Relations: Foreign Minister Hopes Ties Can Become 'Frank, Friendly, Forward-Looking.'" *Globe and Mail*, 13 May, A13.

Martin, Lawrence. 2006. "All Roads Lead to China—Except the Tories.'" *Globe and Mail*, 26 October, A21.

Mendes, Errol P. 2007. "China Won't Yield to Lectures from Us: Top Canadians and Business Leaders Must Persuade Chinese That Their Trade Interests Are Best Served When Beijing Adheres to the Rule of Law." *Toronto Star*, 5 March, A13.

Munton, Don, and Tom Keating. 2001. "Internationalism and the Canadian Public." *Canadian Journal of Political Science* 34, 3: 517–49.

Nossal, Kim Richard. 1985. *The Politics of Canadian Foreign Policy*. Scarborough, ON: Prentice-Hall.

Nossal, Kim Richard, Stéphane Roussel, and Stéphane Paquin. 2011. *International Policy and Politics in Canada*. Toronto: Pearson Education Canada.

Peerenboom, Randall. 2005. "Assessing Human Rights in China: Why the Double Standard?" *Cornell International Law Journal* 38: 71–172.

Roth, Kenneth. 2010. "Canada No Longer Leads on Human Rights." *Ottawa Citizen*, 15 October, A15.

Schabas, William A. 1998. "Canada and the Adoption of the Universal Declaration of Human Rights." *McGill Law Journal* 43: 403–42.

Schiller, Bill. 2009. "Canada, China Headed for 'Very Good Relations' Despite 'Ups and Downs.'" *Toronto Star*, 13 May, A17.

Shi, Tianjian, and Diqing Lou. 2010. "Subjective Evaluation of Changes in Civil Liberties and Political Rights in China." *Journal of Contemporary China* 19, 63: 175–99.

Simpson, Jeffrey. 2007. "Domestic Politics Mustn't Drive Our China Policy." *Globe and Mail*, 25 April, A21.

———. 2008. "The Harperites Are Spinning a Line on China and India." *Globe and Mail*, 23 April, A21.

———. 2009. "The Harperites Come to Terms with China's Reality." *Globe and Mail*, 18 April, A23.

Stairs, Denis. 2003. "Myths, Morals, and Reality in Canadian Foreign Policy." *International Journal* 58, 2: 239–56.

Strange, Susan. 1996. *The Retreat of the State: The Diffusion of Power in the World Economy*. New York: Cambridge University Press.

Taylor, Peter Shawn. 2007. "The Harper Doctrine." *Maclean's*, 5 February, 23.

Thompson, Allan. 1994. "The Chrétien Doctrine Trades Off Human Rights: Canada Will No Longer Publicly Condemn Countries That Persecute Their People." *Toronto Star*, 26 March, B5.

Wendt, Alexander E. 1987. "The Agent-Structure Problem in International Relations Theory." *International Organization* 41, 3: 335–70.

York, Geoffrey. 2007. "China's Human-Rights Record Improving, Report by Canadian Diplomats Say: Document Reveals Foreign-Service Officials Hold Much Rosier View of Beijing Than Does Harper Cabinet." *Globe and Mail*, 19 November, A4.

York, Geoffrey, and Alan Freeman. 2007. "Sino-Canadian Relations Dealt Severe Blow: Apparent Cancellation of Meeting Seen as Reaction to Dalai Lama's Visit." *Globe and Mail*, 9 November, A21.

York, Geoffrey, and Brian Laghi. 2006. "Chinese Puzzled by Aloofness from Ottawa: Missing Meetings and Cancelled Trips Have Cooled Off the 'Partnership,' to Beijing's Concern." *Globe and Mail*, 27 September, A7.

7

The Prime Minister and the Parable: Stephen Harper and Personal Responsibility Internationalism

Paul Gecelovsky

To suggest that Canada's foreign policy has been influenced by a prime minister's personal religious beliefs is not a new, or novel, insight. The religious predilections of leaders such as Paul Martin, Jean Chrétien, Lester Pearson, and John Diefenbaker, among others, had an effect on the policies pursued by their respective governments. Pearson, for instance, was the son of a Methodist minister and practised that religion consistently throughout his life. As well, Chrétien and Martin were both practising Catholics who attended Mass on a regular basis. The personal views of Prime Minister Stephen Harper, it will be demonstrated, have played a more prominent and direct role than those of his predecessors in setting Canada's foreign policy.

Heather A. Smith has noted that "internationalism must be understood as Canada's face to the world" (2003: 30). The Canadian visage is not set in stone but rather is changeable, with government emphasizing specific features at different times. A government's priorities help to establish the contours of the face. This is not to suggest that the Canadian government alone can set the Canadian face. International and domestic events intervene to influence the image. James Eayrs, over 40 years ago, persuasively argued that Canada's foreign policy may be explained by some combination of "Fate and Will" (1971). Substituting "minds" for "will" and "conditions" for "fate," Denis Stairs cogently notes that "causation is the product of a murky combination of the two—not of minds alone, nor of conditions alone, but of the first applied to the second" (1995: 9). In applying "minds" to "conditions" or in the contest between Fate and Will, Eayrs concludes that decision-makers "possess more freedom than they are ready to admit" and, further, that the "constraints upon their freedom are not so onerous as they would have us believe" (82). In short, decision-makers, especially Canadian prime ministers, possess the ability to shape the Canadian face to the world. ✳

How Canada responds to international and domestic events, then, is largely a product of its leadership and their predilections. Kim Richard Nossal has written of how the internationalism of the post-war period was shaped by multilateralism, a commitment to international institutions, the assuming of international responsibility, and "a willingness to enter into prior commitments" (1997: 155). The rationale behind this internationalism was to help secure Canada and the world from once again being thrust into the chaos of war, especially between two nuclear-armed superpowers. [The Canadian face was shaped by war and the desire to secure peace; however, its particular form was etched by successive governments, Liberal and Conservative.]

Similarly, the position and prosperity of Canada in the international economic realm have influenced its face to the outside. The level of government support for humanitarian causes that address poverty and inequality and for the propagation of human rights internationally—what Cranford Pratt refers to as humane internationalism (1989), or Cecilia Lynch, as humanitarian internationalism (1999)—affects the Canadian image. By supporting the removal of government assistance and allowing the market mechanism to operate relatively unfettered by state regulation as a means to overcome poverty and equality—referred to as economic (Munton, 2002–3) or market (Lynch, 1999) internationalism—Canada presents a different face to the world.

[The argument developed herein is that the Canadian face is undergoing significant change at present and that none of the extant variants of internationalism developed by Munton, Lynch, Nossal, or Pratt adequately captures what is happening in Canada.] Internationalism, then, is an elastic concept that relates to the degree and character of Canada's involvement abroad, and thus it is open to new forms as the Canadian image is altered by its government. The current government led by Stephen Harper is undertaking such an alteration; Harper is attempting to carve a new Canadian face crafted according to a blueprint he created based on the notion of **personal responsibility internationalism**.

The chapter is divided into three sections. In the first, the Harper style of foreign policy-making is discussed. As the focus of this study is on how Stephen Harper's religious views have shaped Canada's face to the world, it is important to examine the degree of control exhibited by Harper over the direction and substance of Canadian foreign policy. The second section examines the content of Harper's value system and the confluence of his faith and politics. It is demonstrated that Harper's unwavering confidence in himself to lead, his control over all aspects of policy, and the support of a growing and vocal group of Christian organizations for a foreign policy predicated on a specific reading of biblical principles have all worked, more directly and prominently, to bring concerns of faith into Canadian foreign policy decision-making. The third section of the chapter looks at two areas where Harper's views have had a significant influence on Canada's foreign policy: Israel and women's rights.

The Harper Style of Foreign Policy-Making

The personal views of the leaders are important in determining the tone and substance of Canada's foreign policy. The Prime Minister's Office (PMO) has a range of powers that, if so desired, enable the prime minister to exercise an overwhelming influence on the direction and content of Canada's foreign policy (Gecelovsky, 2011). More than any other prime minister, Harper has sought to obtain control over all matters of policy, both its substance and its communication; therefore, Harper's personal faith is of particular importance in discussions of policy.

With respect to the prime minister himself, Harper has demonstrated a desire for "iron clad message control" (Martin, 2010: 130). This is demonstrated by infrequent press conferences and the use of media lists whereby reporters are required to sign up prior to a press conference if they want to pose questions to the prime minister. Access to Harper has been further restricted by the practice of not allowing photographers to take pictures of the prime minister during speaking engagements; rather, staged pictures of Harper are supplied to the media for publication and/or broadcast.

Beyond the prime minister alone, the Harper government, in 2006, adopted a system of message control that would ensure a consistency and continuity of message across personnel, government and state, and media. The **Message Event Proposal** (MEP) covers all civil servants and Conservative caucus members who want to speak publicly. Sections of the MEP include, *inter alia*, Desired Headline, Strategic Objective, Desired Sound Bite, as well as information pertaining to the speaking backdrop, the ideal event photograph, and the speaker's wardrobe (Martin, 2010: 58). Those addressing the public in any forum must fill out an MEP and submit it for scrutiny and approval by the PMO. The MEP's reach extends to all communications, including a Parks Canada release on the mating season of black bears (Martin, 2010: 58), and requires that questions and answers be scripted beforehand for all presentations given by civil servants and caucus members regardless of location or size of audience.

The Harper style of full control extends to the workings of cabinet and Parliament. Major policy decisions are made and communicated to the Canadian public by the prime minister, leaving the various cabinet ministers to play a much diminished role in government. For the most part, it is the role of cabinet ministers to reinforce the message of the prime minister and to ensure that his agenda is followed. This control even extends to Question Period, where ministers' responses are carefully scripted and rehearsed before the prime minister's approval is given. Whether driven by fear or by commitment, cabinet ministers in the Harper government have stayed on message and followed the policies outlined by the prime minister.

Similarly, Harper's control over the Conservative caucus has been absolute. No public dissension among the ranks is tolerated, as demonstrated by the expulsion of Garth Turner from the caucus. Turner was expelled for venting his displeasure with the prime minister's actions on both his personal blog and in the media. Lawrence Martin, in his examination of the incident, writes that the "Prime Minister wanted to make an example out of Turner, to make it clear [to Conservative parliamentarians] that if you stepped out of line, you stepped into a grave" (2010: 36). The result of this has been that Conservative parliamentarians have toed the party line and, as Tom Flanagan has noted, "religiously follow[ed] the official talking points" set out by the prime minister and the PMO (2010).

At the bureaucratic level, the Harper Conservatives have sought to rein in any freedom to speak publicly that previous governments might have allowed civil servants. All events have to be scripted and controlled via the MEP. Any deviations from the script, or any comments regarded by the government as critical of its performance or policies, will dealt with immediately and harshly. The removals of, *inter alia*, Paul Kennedy as the head of the Commission for Public Complaints Against the Royal Canadian Mounted Police, Peter Tinsley as the head of the Military Police Complaints Commission, Linda Keen as the head of the Canadian Nuclear Safety Commission, and General Rick Hillier as the head of the Canadian Armed Forces were all done, in large part, in response to comments and/or actions each made that were perceived by the Conservative leader as critical of his policies. These removals provide "evidence of a pattern: toe the government line or you're gone" (Tinsley, quoted in Martin, 2010: 234). The pattern was also evident in the resignation of Munir Sheikh from his position of deputy minister of Statistics Canada and in the public maligning of Remy Beauregard when he was president of the International Centre for Human Rights and Democratic Development. The latter suffered a heart attack and died largely as a result of the pressure asserted on him to toe the line.

For Harper, control over and access to information are the "foremost priority" of his government (Martin, 2010: 273). The intense control over policy substance and communication by the prime minister is the Harper style of foreign policy-making. The level of control exercised by Stephen Harper far surpasses that of any previous prime minister—hence the importance of his "operational code" to the Canadian face to the outside.

The Confluence of Faith and Politics

Stephen Harper has been characterized as a "more cerebral than emotive" evangelical Christian (Mackey, 2005: 9). In her study of Harper and the emergence of evangelical Christian groups in Canada, Marci McDonald notes that Harper had spoken publicly of his faith on only two occasions before the 2006 election in which the Conservatives came to power and he assumed the office of prime minister (2010: 20). Since becoming prime minister, Harper has been equally reticent to speak publicly about his personal faith (Malloy, 2011). He did, however, include religious references, usually in the form of "God Bless Canada," at the close of speeches early in his time in office. For example, he referred to God in just over one-quarter of his speeches in his first year as prime minister (22/78 or 28 per cent). This number fell by one-half (11/79 or 14 per cent) in his second year. Since then, he has rarely made reference to God in any speech.

The near silence regarding his personal faith should not be misconstrued as an absence of faith, however. Harper has stated that he "cares more about 'God's verdict' on his life than the judgement of historians" (McDonald, 2010: 48). For Harper, faith in public life needs to be tempered by the politically achievable, and one must be politically strategic and incremental in expressing faith through government policy. When possible, one should act in faith but always be mindful of the political costs of acting. The balance between faith and politics lies at the core of Harper's decision-making.

 In terms of faith, Harper has remarked that "social values" are the source of the "really big issues" that divide societies and of "the great geopolitical battles" among states (Harper, 2003). Unlike the silence accorded his personal religious faith, Harper has been more forthcoming in discussing his values. He outlined his "value system" to an invitation-only audience at Preston Manning's Canada Networking Conference, an annual gathering of Canadian conservative activists. During the 12 March 2009 talk, the prime minister set out the "three Fs" of "faith, family and freedom" that comprise the core of his ethical calculus (McDonald, 2010: 369). Prominent among the three Fs is faith, as it is the lens through which the other two are given definition and meaning.

Faith: The First F in Harper's Value System

While a full rendering of evangelism in Canada is beyond the scope of this chapter, a brief discussion of two broad strains of this movement is necessary for an understanding of the foundational principle upon which Harper's faith is constructed and of the corresponding shift in Canadian foreign policy that has occurred during his tenure. One reading of Christian scripture centres on the notion that individuals are personally responsible for their own position in society. The biblical reference for this perspective is found in the Gospel of Matthew (Actually chapter 25: 14–30) wherein Jesus tells his disciples a parable about three servants who were given gifts by their master of five, two, and one talent(s), respectively. After a lengthy period away, the master returns and the first servant informs him that the initial gift of five talents was invested and now has grown to ten. Similarly, the second man comes forward and tells his master that the two talents have doubled to four. The last servant comes forward and returns only the master's initial gift of one talent, saying that he took the money given to him and buried it in the ground, fearful that he would disappoint his master if he should lose the talent. The master praises the first and second men for their efforts and promotes both of them to positions of higher authority. Conversely, the third man is chastised for his fear, has his one talent taken away and given to the first man, and is cast into "the outer darkness" (Revised Standard Version: Matthew 25: 30). The primary message gleaned from the **Parable of the Talents** is that people are individually endowed by God with certain talents or abilities and are each responsible for using their talents or abilities to their highest level in an effort to obtain success. Each person is personally responsible for making the most of the talents provided by God.

[In the personal responsibility perspective, each individual faces challenges and opportunities and the key is to make correct decisions. States can help people in making decisions by putting in place proper structures that enable people to make decisions in which their talents will be optimized. A person is rewarded according to the extent to which he or she chooses wisely. Society, as a whole, benefits when individuals make proper choices; society is regarded as an agglomeration of individual decisions. Those who do not choose the proper course will not be rewarded, may lose the freedom to make future choices, and may even be punished. It is believed that the lessons gleaned from the Parable of the Talents are applicable to all levels of human conduct, including the international. In sum, it is only those individuals who use their talents in a responsible manner who are rewarded and who are a benefit to society.]

A second reading of scripture reflects not on personal responsibility but on human compassion as the sacred foundation for society. This strain of evangelism in Canada stresses [the responsibility of each person to ensure the well-being and health of other members of the community.] The focus shifts from those who practise responsible behaviour to those who contribute to society through assisting others in need. This evangelical tradition draws on the Gospel of Luke wherein Luke tells us of a traveller who has been robbed, beaten, and left for dead by the side of the road (chapter 10). Two people of high position in society, a priest and a Levite, come upon the traveller and pass by without offering any help. Then, a Samaritan, a person of the lowest standing in the community, comes along and offers the traveller assistance, bandaging his wounds and taking him to an inn to recover. It is "not the hegemonic authority figure of the priest or the Levite bureaucrat who administers aid, but rather a member of the stigmatized Samaritan minority group, who has secured a modicum of success and fosters diffuse reciprocity (paying the innkeeper to care for the victim with a future promise)" (Brysk, 2009: 4). [The message of the **Parable of the Good Samaritan** is that each person should be concerned with the plight and well-being of others regardless of his or her standing or position in the community.] The "transformative element" of the Good Samaritan parable is "cosmopolitanism" and the "defining principle" is that the Samaritan "identifies with the interest of the Other" (4). [In short, we are all part of "a community of fate" and we are only as strong or healthy as the condition in which its lowest members live (4).] ✳

This message of compassion for others formed the core of the teaching and preaching of J.S. Woodsworth and his social gospel movement in Manitoba before the First World War. Woodsworth's message was echoed by Tommy Douglas (also an evangelical minister) in Saskatchewan, where he became premier and, later, leader of the federal New Democratic Party in the 1960s. More recently, this message of compassion provided the spiritual root of the humane internationalist perspective advanced by Pratt (1989) and the inspirational core for many civil society organizations that advocate for more generous international development assistance programs and for the acceptance of universal human rights standards by all governments (see Black, chapter 13).

The personal responsibility position outlined in the Parable of the Talents was advocated by William Aberhart. Aberhart was a fundamentalist Baptist preacher who, in 1935, parlayed his prominence as a radio evangelist in Alberta to the office of premier. He used his weekly radio program to counter the social gospel teachings promoted by Woodsworth and Douglas. Following his death in 1943, Aberhart's message was continued by Ernest Manning, who replaced Aberhart in both the office of the premier and as radio host. Manning's influence was continued through his son, Preston. The younger Manning, in turn, acted as a "spiritual mentor" (Mackey, 2005: 73) to Stephen Harper when Harper began his life in politics as a policy analyst for the fledgling Reform Party under Preston Manning's leadership. [The notions of personal responsibility and of making optimum use of the talents given by God are core tenets of Harper's religious faith and the blueprint by which his foreign policy is constructed.]

Family: The Second F in Harper's Value System

The prime minister supports a traditional definition of marriage. Support for this view of marriage is drawn from Christian scripture, which outlines marriage as an institution between a man and a woman sanctified by God. In the 2004 election campaign, [Harper expressed his opposition to same-sex marriage] (Rayside, 2011: 283). Later, in 2010, he maintained that while he had "no difficulty with the recognition of civil unions for non-traditional relationships," he believed that "in law [Canada] should protect the traditional definition of marriage" (*Globe and Mail*, 8 October 2010). This is in keeping with the notion of personal responsibility outlined above, as it is each family member's personal responsibility to ensure the well-being and health of the family by fulfilling his or her particular role.]

Freedom: The Final F in Harper's Value System Triumvirate

["Free enterprise and individual freedom" are, according to Harper, "fundamental values" that Canada and its allies have a "duty" to defend (Harper, 2003). This perspective is in harmony with the view of the personal responsibility strain of Christianity outlined above. [Freedom in this sense refers to being free from government control or regulation—of having the ability to pursue one's interests to the extent that in doing so one does not prohibit others from pursuing their interests.] This perspective particularly holds for personal and economic matters. People and companies should be allowed to pursue their interests largely unfettered by government policies or regulations. For Harper, the market mechanism is efficient and should be left to its own workings. Government intervention in both personal and economic matters is akin to a reduction in freedom. Individuals should be provided the opportunity to use their own talents to the best of their ability without interference from outside influences, such as the state [Individuals, then, ought to be left on their own to decide on and pursue the course of action they deem makes optimal use of their respective talents, as determined through reflection and prayer] Adherence to this conceptualization of freedom also leads to a reliance on the market mechanism for solutions to societal problems.

Political Concerns

Stephen Harper began his political career by helping to build the Reform Party under the leadership of Preston Manning [Manning played an important role in Harper's "pilgrimage" (Mackey, 2005), mentoring Harper both spiritually and politically. The two, however, differ in one very important way: Manning is a populist and Harper is not. Manning built the Reform Party, from the ground up, to be an expression of populist discontent with the then prevailing status quo in Ottawa. The Canadian government, according to the Reform Party, had become captured by elites and had lost touch with the people of Canada, particularly those in the West. Manning wanted to bring the power back to the people, to restore democracy and balance in Ottawa. Harper, conversely, does not seek to defer to the people but instead prefers to decide on a course of action for Canada on the basis of his own intellect and his personal vision for the country. He wants to lead the public to his policies by the force of his own argument and intellect. He does not follow public opinion to decide policy; he sets policy. Harper believes that he knows what is best for Canada better than the public does.

The Canadian Public

Organizations of the religious right that support the personal responsibility view of Christianity outlined above are a growing political force in Canada (Malloy, 2009; McDonald, 2010). There are no definitive statistics on the size of the evangelical population in Canada owing to disagreements about definition and differences in the polling questions; however, the size of the community is most often cited to be between 10 and 12 per cent of the Canadian population (Bean, Gonzalez, and Kaufman, 2008; Hutchison and Hiemstra, 2009; Malloy, 2011). Though only a small fraction of the overall Canadian population, this group is a very vocal and active subculture within Canada. While Canadian evangelicals have been politically active since the 1980s, the issue of lesbian/gay rights, especially same-sex marriage, galvanized the evangelical community into becoming an active and vocal political force in Canada in the 1990s (Malloy, 2011; Rayside, 2011). Roger O'Toole, in his discussion of religion in Canada in the 1990s, described the Catholic Church at that time as being characterized by "the secularised indifference of the many and the spiritual zealotry of the few," an apt description of the current Canadian populace (1996: 8).

Individual Christians have joined together in groups to communicate their concerns to the government and society. Most of these groups have been created in the last 20 years, and they differ from older Christian organizations in Canada in that they do not tend to shy away from partisan politics and candidate endorsement, with some stretching the boundaries of their tax-exempt charitable status (Matthews, 1989). Most of these organizations—the Watchmen for the Nations; Focus on the Family Canada and its Institute of Marriage and Family Canada; the Canada Family Action Coalition and its Defend Marriage Coalition; the National House of Prayer; the Institute for Canadian Values; REAL Women of Canada; and 4MYCanada, for example—lobby the government to take a stronger stand on issues such as abortion, poverty, and same-sex marriage. Self-Interest groups

One group, 4MYCanada, under the leadership of Faytene Kryskow, has been particularly active and vocal in pressing that government policy be brought more in line with Kryskow's Christian perspective. The group maintains a website that lists the parliamentary bills being 'watched" and instructs interested Canadians on how to engage in the political process, including how to select a candidate, how to inundate a member of Parliament with letters and emails outlining the proper course of action to be taken by the parliamentarian, and how to land a civil service position (McDonald, 2010: 151). Kryskow compiled a list of candidates endorsed by 4MYCanada during the fall 2008 election campaign—10 Liberals and 101 Conservatives (McDonald, 2010: 172). For the spring 2011 election, the group composed a report card for parliamentarians, grading them on the basis of their voting record on "moral issues" (e.g., their position on abortion and same-sex marriage). Based on the parliamentarians' final grades, the group endorsed 6 Liberals and 88 Conservatives on their website (www.4MYCanada.ca).

Christian groups like 4MYCanada have emerged as active and vocal participants in the political process, and their importance is demonstrated by their ability to deliver the votes of their members, which were key to the victory of the Harper Conservatives in 2006, 2008, and 2011 (Malloy, 2009: 360; McDonald, 2010: 71).

Enhancing their political heft, these groups often work together to press government from numerous directions to adopt policies they view as more favourable. They work synergistically in a network to exert maximum pressure on Ottawa. These groups also see themselves as training grounds for a new cadre of young conservative activists skilled in modern communications and lobbying. One of the main forums for this form of activity is the Manning Centre for Building Democracy, where Canadians, especially young Canadians, are "encourage[d] and equip[ped] ... to apply their faith-based values within the political arena." This is what Preston Manning refers to as the "faith-politics interface" (Malloy, 2010). [The goal is to train a new generation of Christians who will move into positions of power in government, industry, law, and the arts and who will bring with them a conservative Christian perspective.]

Another source of support for Harper comes, interestingly, from new Canadians, many of whom do not share his religious views. The Canadian Election Study found that in the 2008 general election fully one-third of immigrants cast a vote for a Conservative candidate. While the Conservatives still trail Liberals in terms of immigrant support (38 per cent of immigrants voted Liberal in 2008), the Liberals experienced a decline of 17 percentage points between the 2000 and 2008 elections. Over this same period, new immigrants increased their support for Conservatives from 16 to 26 per cent, while their support for the Liberals dropped from 83 to 49 per cent (Ibbitson and Friesen, 2010) [While precise data for the 2011 election was not available at the time of writing, there is some evidence of a continued shift away from the Liberals and towards the Conservatives by immigrant communities] This shift in support is in part attributable to immigrants having more socially conservative views, especially on wedge issues such as abortion and marriage.

There is, then, in Canada growing domestic support for a political agenda predicated on a personal responsibility perspective. [Harper's own personal values are to some extent reflected in many of the Christian organizations in Canada.] These groups make up a subset of the population that he can count on for electoral support but one that is not large enough to ensure him a majority government. This leads to a position wherein the Canadian prime minister needs to walk a fine line between courting the vote of these groups and avoiding being regarded by the general populace as having been captured by them—a line he managed to walk in the 2011 election. Harper's value system, predicated on his personal faith, has had, more than for any other prime minister, a direct influence on Canada's foreign policy, and this can be credited to his obsessive control over policy, his belief that he knows what is best for Canada, and the almost guaranteed support of a growing chorus of personal responsibility Christians and people from other religious traditions who hold similar views.] ✳

The Harper Shift

Having discussed Stephen Harper's own balancing of faith and politics, the chapter now turns to a discussion of how this balancing act has influenced Canada's foreign policy, especially with respect to Canada's policy concerning Israel and women's rights. In each of these policy fields, Canada's policy under Harper has shifted to reflect the prime minister's personal convictions. Given the complexities of these policy fields, space does not allow more than an introduction to some of the key issues in each field.

[One of the most noticeable shifts in Canada's foreign policy under the leadership of Stephen Harper was that Canada adopted a much more pro-Israel stance] Canada was one of the first governments to stop funding for Hamas after its 2006 electoral victory in Gaza. This was followed by a "near categorical" defence of Israel's military response to Hezbollah and Hamas attacks throughout 2006 (Sasley and Jacoby, 2007: 189). [In a 2008 speech celebrating Israel's sixtieth anniversary, the Canadian prime minister stated that Israel was Canada's "friend and ally," that Canada "stands side-by-side" with Israel and would "continue to stand with Israel just as I have always said we would" (Harper, 2008).]Canadian support for Israel would remain firm during the December 2008 clash between Israeli and Hamas forces in Gaza and the June 2010 Israeli raid on the flotilla of ships from Turkey. [This unequivocal support for Israel continued through the 2011 G8 meeting, where Harper stood firm against the other members, including US president Barack Obama, insisting that no mention of Israel's 1967 borders be included in the final communiqué] ✳ *going against U.S.*

[The strong Canadian support for Israel has come at a cost, and according to the prime minister, "we have the bruises to show for taking that stand." The "bruises" that Canada suffered refers to the vote lost, in the fall of 2010, to Portugal at the United Nations for a non-permanent seat for Canada on the United Nations Security Council.]This was the first time that Canada had failed in a bid for a seat on the Security Council. Further, Harper has opined that those who claim that Canada has "lost influence" or "lost its balance" or "is no longer seen as an honest broker" are employing a "code for the view that Canada should go back to being ambivalent about our relationship with Israel.' [This is something that a Harper government "will never do" (Harper, 2011).]

Canadian support for Israel has been clear and unwavering. As Ezra Levant has written, Canada's support for Israel has been "outstanding," and "no world leader has been as clear as Harper has been in his support for Israel's right to defend itself" (Levant, 2009). Brent E. Sasley and Tami Amanda Jacoby, in their analysis of Jewish and Arab lobby groups in Canada, note that Canadian Jewish leaders have been "surprised by the strength of Harper's defence of Israel," and have "feared it might undermine their advocacy efforts vis-à-vis the other political parties" (2007: 189). While there are many determinants influencing Canada's policy towards Israel, commentators usually note that Canada's shift in policy in this instance is because Harper's support for Israel is born "out of conviction" (Levant, 2009; Sasley and Jacoby, 2007; McDonald, 2010), not from an assessment of Canadian interests in the region and globally.

The case of KAIROS, a Canadian civil society organization, provides further insight into the workings and effects of Canada's Israel policy. KAIROS is a coalition group of 11 member churches and religious organizations, including Anglican, Christian Reformed, Evangelical Lutheran, Presbyterian, United, Quaker, Catholic, and Mennonite denominations, as well as the Primate's World Relief and Development Fund (KairosCanada.org). The focus of the organization's work is on human rights and sustainable development, and for 35 years, KAIROS has received funding for its activities from both Liberal and Conservative governments. In 2009, government funding to the organization was ended and the group's application for funding for the 2009–12 period was denied. KAIROS has been a vocal opponent of the Conservative government's policies and actions, such as its decision to sign a free trade pact with Colombia; its compliance with continued exploration for oil and gas deposits in Northern Alberta, especially with reference to the effects of this activity on the indigenous population of the region; and the lax Canadian position on climate change (KairosCanada.org). Bev Oda, minister for international cooperation, stated that the decision to end funding for the group was based on KAIROS no longer meeting the new development priorities of the Conservative government announced in February 2009. The government backtracked from this position when it came to light that the application had been prepared with the assistance of civil servants from Oda's department. Jason Kenney, then minister of citizenship, immigration, and multiculturalism, offered another reason for the decision when he stated that groups such as KAIROS were "defunded" due to their leadership role in the boycott, divestment, and sanctions campaign against Israel, a position he equated with anti-Semitism (GlobalTV News, 2009; McDonald, 2010: 350). In fact, KAIROS never advocated that such measures be adopted. It appears that Kenney was confusing Kairos Palestine, a Palestinian-based Christian organization that had called for such initiatives to be adopted a week before Kenney's speech, with KAIROS, a Canadian Christian organization (Payton, 2011).

The KAIROS case took an interesting turn when a copy of the document denying funding to the group was leaked to the press. The document was altered by the insertion of the word "not" between the words "you" and "approve," thereby changing the CIDA (Canadian International Development Agency) recommendation for funding from positive to negative. The CIDA officials who signed the document reported that the word "not" was not on the document when they signed it in September 2009. After Minister Oda had repeatedly denied having any knowledge of how and why the document was altered, it was revealed that she had had a staff member insert the word and the minister's signature on the paper. The details concerning the document only came to light after the Speaker of the House had ruled that Oda had "misled" the House, and after he had referred the matter to the Procedure and House Affairs Committee, charging the committee with drafting a report determining whether or not the minister was in contempt of Parliament (Payton, 2011). The committee's work, however, was disrupted by the May 2011 general election, and it is highly unlikely, given the resulting Conservative majority, that the new Conservative-dominated committee will delve further into the matter.

This Harper shift in government policy to full support of Israel has been supported by a number of influential Christian organizations in Canada (McDonald, 2010). In particular, Dr Charles H. McVety, president of Canada Christian College, founder of the Institute for Canadian Values and the Canada Family Action Coalition, and director of the Defend Marriage Coalition, has been very active and vocal in providing defence for Harper's strong stance on Israel, supporting, for example, Harper's decision to cut off funding to KAIROS. McVety is backed by his close relationship with John Hagee, the controversial American televangelist who is the head pastor of the 19,000-member Cornerstone Church in San Antonio, Texas, and host of weekly radio and television shows that are streamed throughout the globe. In 2006, Hagee founded Christians United for Israel, an organization dedicated to supporting Israel and to lobbying key decision-makers to adopt a similar position vis-à-vis Israel.

A second area in which there has been a discernible shift in Canadian policy under Harper's leadership is the issue of women's rights, particularly with regard to choice in family planning and the definition of marriage. The prime minister's announcement of the Muskoka Initiative at the 2010 G8 meeting in Huntsville committing Canada to provide $2.85 billion over five years to improve maternal, newborn, and child health belies the notion that the Conservative government is weak in its support of women's issues. As the particularities of the Muskoka Initiative are covered in a more detailed and nuanced manner by Carrier and Tiessen (chapter 11), the discussion here will focus on the shift in Canada's policy under Harper.

In 2001, Canada was a member of a like-minded group of states, including Australia, Ireland, Liechtenstein, New Zealand, Norway, and Switzerland, that pressed the United Nations General Assembly to take a progressive position on reproductive rights. Later, in 2004, Canada opposed a UN General Assembly resolution commemorating the tenth anniversary of the Year of the Family because the resolution did not include specific references to women's reproductive rights, as well as to the diversity of family structures (Butler, 2006: 75). Canada, in these two instances, assumed positions contrary to that of the United States, the Holy See, and a group of religiously conservative states, all of which sought to remove similar references in other UN resolutions or declarations or to replace such references with more pro-family concerns.

This situation would change once Harper's Conservatives came to power, however. Domestically, the Harper government introduced a series of bills in the House of Commons in an attempt to severely narrow the range of legal abortions available (Nadeau, 2011; Rayside, 2011). In the 2011 election campaign, when confronted with the abortion issue Harper declared that the Conservatives under his leadership would not open the abortion debate or "bring forward any such legislation and any such legislation that is brought forward will be defeated" (Ibbitson, 2011). It is interesting to note that Harper did not reveal his personal convictions surrounding the issue, but rather made it clear that he was against opening the debate. This has led some commentators to suggest that Harper's position is more political than personal, and that it could change if it was demonstrated that there was domestic support for a shift in policy.

At the international level, the Canadian position on reproductive rights moved from support for women's reproductive rights to a policy of zero tolerance for funding for abortion outside Canada. As noted by Carrier and Tiessen (chapter 11), Harper was able to secure the other parties' agreement to allow each state to set the terms for its contribution to the Muskoka Initiative, knowing the Canadian position would not include funding for abortion or contraception. The decision not to provide funding for abortions outside Canada was explained by Harper as being necessary so as not to provoke dissension among the Canadian people (Nadeau, 2011; Rayside, 2011; Martin, 2010). The decision not to provide funds for abortions places women's lives in greater jeopardy than before, as the funding that was provided previously went towards, among other things, improving sanitation in clinics that provided abortion procedures in less-developed and conflict-riven states—states where Canada had provided a modicum of assistance in the provision of basic health care to women in distress, where Canada played somewhat the role of the Good Samaritan.

Related to the issue of women and their role in society is the role Canada played at the UN in the period before the Harper government. Canada worked towards the acceptance of a broader, more inclusive definition of marriage and did not support, for example, a move by the United States to have marriage defined solely as a union between a man and a woman (Butler, 2006: 67). Under Harper's leadership, however, the Canadian position shifted from support for the broader, more inclusive definition to support for a more narrow, traditional definition.

That this shift towards a more traditional definition of marriage was supported by Harper is not surprising. In 2003, when Harper had secured the leadership of the Conservative Party, after the merger of the Alliance and Progressive Conservative Parties, he met privately with Scott Brison, an openly gay Progressive Conservative MP. Brison was a rising star in the party, holding a position in the shadow cabinet. At the meeting, Harper made it clear to Brison that the new party would not be moved from the Alliance position of limiting the rights of gay couples (Martin, 2010: 244). As noted earlier, this position was reaffirmed in the 2004 election campaign, when Harper expressed his opposition to same-sex marriage, and again in 2010, when he remarked that the traditional definition of marriage should be protected by Canadian law.

The changes in policy concerning the reproductive rights of women and the traditional definition of marriage are partly attributable to support for these moves by groups such as Focus on the Family Canada and its Institute on Marriage and the Family, the Canada Family Action Coalition and its Defend Marriage Coalition, and 4MYCanada. In 2004, Focus on the Family Canada published an online guide outlining every MP's position on same-sex marriage (Malloy, 2011: 151). The issue of same-sex marriage is "unambiguous" for these groups, and it "affects the heart" of their "thinking about family, reproduction and [the Bible's] prohibitions against homosexual acts" (Malloy, 2011: 151). These "strong traditional views of values and family" (Harper, 2003) have worked to coalesce Christian (including evangelical and Catholic), Sikh, Muslim, and Hindu groups across Canada (McDonald, 2010) and the world (Butler, 2006). They have also been used by Conservatives to draw support away from "ethnic communities that traditionally voted Liberal—especially Chinese, South Asian and Italian" (Rayside, 2011: 283). These are wedge issues that divide social conservatives of all faiths and ethnicities from other Canadians.

Conclusion

An examination of the Harper record on foreign policy reveals that none of the existing forms of internationalism accurately captures what is happening in Canada. A new variant of internationalism is needed to reflect the current international policies and behaviour of the Harper government. As others have noted in this volume, there has been a clear movement away from liberal internationalism, beginning with the Chrétien government (Nossal; Massie and Roussel; Copeland) and continuing in the current Harper government (Boucher and Lui). David Black has also posited that there has been declining support within both government and society for humane internationalism. This chapter has argued that a new form of internationalism has emerged, one animated by the social conservative religious values of the prime minister and supported by an active and vocal domestic constituency. The architect of this transformation is Stephen Harper, who, more than any previous prime minister, has controlled the direction and substance of Canadian foreign policy, as well as the activities of the members of his government, including ministers, and civil servants. Harper has demonstrated the vast range of powers available to a prime minister to shape the Canadian face to the world if he has the political will and determination to use them and the desire to build a personal legacy.

In terms of the study of internationalism, [this paper argues for the continued usefulness of the concept and the need to maintain a certain degree of its elasticity.] Internationalism is an elastic concept that relates to the degree and character of Canada's involvement abroad, and thus it is open to new variants as Canada alters its international policies and behaviour. Internationalism should not be narrowly defined as a particular form of state behaviour characteristic of early post–Second World War Canadian foreign policy. To do so would render it a historic concept defining a standard of past behaviour by which Canada's current and future performance may be measured.

In sum, additional work needs to be done to extend the analysis beyond Israel or women's rights to other dimensions of Canada's foreign policy. A propitious place to start would be Canada's official development policy and environmental policy to determine whether a shift towards personal responsibility internationalism has occurred.

Key Terms

Message Event Proposal
Parable of the Talents
Parable of the Good Samaritan

personal responsibility internationalism
the three Fs of faith, family, and freedom

Study Questions

1. What are the key elements of the Parable of Talents?
2. What are the key elements of the Parable of the Good Samaritan?
3. Compare and contrast the Parable of the Talents with the Parable of the Good Samaritan.
4. Do you agree that a shift in Canadian foreign policy towards personal responsibility internationalism has taken place? Why or why not?
5. What, if anything, does personal responsibility internationalism add to the study of internationalism?

References

4My Canada. At http://www.4MYCanada.ca.
Bean, Lydia, Marco Gonzalez, and Jason Kaufman. 2008. "Why Doesn't Canada Have an American-Styled Christian Right? A Comparative Framework for Analyzing the Political Effects of Evangelical Subculture Identity." Canadian Journal of Sociology 33, 4: 899–943.
Bible. Revised Standard Version.
Brysk, Alison. 2009. Global Good Samaritans: Human Rights as Foreign Policy. New York: Oxford University Press.
Butler, Jennifer S. 2006. Born Again: The Christian Right Globalized. Ann Arbor, MI: Pluto Press.

Eayrs, James. 1971. *Diplomacy and Its Discontents*. Toronto: University of Toronto Press.

Flanagan, Tom. 2010. "'Something Blue …': Conservative Organization in an Era of Permanent Campaign." Paper presented at the annual meeting of the Political Science Association, Concordia University, June.

Gecelovsky, Paul. 2011. "Of Legacies and Lightning Bolts Revisited: Another Look at the Prime Minister and Canadian Foreign Policy." In Duane Bratt and Christopher J. Kukucha, *Readings in Canadian Foreign Policy: Classic Debates and New Ideas*, 2nd ed. Don Mills, ON: Oxford University Press, 217–27.

Global TV News. 2009. "Kairos Funding Cut Because of Climate Criticism?" 9 December. At http://www.youtube.com/watch?v=s1ZfgPW2-oA.

Globe and Mail. 2010. "The Quotable Stephen Harper: Not Exactly Churchill but Not Bad Either," 9 October, R24. At http://www.theglobeandmail.com/news/arts/books/the-quotable-stephen-harper-not-exactly-churchill-but-not-bad-either/article1749274/.

Harper, Stephen. 2003. "Rediscovering the Right Agenda: The Alliance Must Commit to Ideals and Ideas, Not Vague Decision-Making Processes: The Canadian Alliance Leader Outlines How Social and Economic Conservatism Must Unite." *Citizens Centre Report* 10 (30 June): 72–7.

———. 2008. "Prime Minister's Speech for Israel's 60th Anniversary." 8 May. At http://pm.gc.ca/eng/media.asp?id=2097.

———. 2011. "Prime Minister Harper Addresses the 5th Action Party of the Canadian Jewish Political Affairs Committee (CJPAC)." 11 March. At http://www.pm.gc.ca.

Hutchison, Don, and Rick Hiemstra. 2009. "Canadian Evangelical Voting Trends by Region, 1996–2008." *Church & Faith Trends* 2, 3: 1–25.

Ibbitson, John. 2011. "Any and All Anti-Abortion Legislation 'Will be Defeated,' Harper Declares." *Globe and Mail*, 21 April. At http://www.theglobeandmail.com/news/politics/ottawa-notebook/any-and-all-anti-abortion-legislation-will-be-defeated-harper-declares/article1994462/.

Ibbitson, John, and Joe Friesen. 2010. "The Growing Ties of Immigrants and Conservatives." *Globe and Mail*, 4 October, A1, A9.

Kairos Canada. At http://www.kairoscanada.org/.

Levant, Ezra. 2009. "Stephen Harper and Israel: Not Crass Political Calculation." *Toronto Star*, 29 May. At www.thestar.com/printarticle/642192.

Lynch, Cecelia. 1999. "The Promise and Problems of Internationalism." *Global Governance* 5, 1: 88–101.

McDonald, Marci. 2010. *The Armageddon Factor: The Rise of Christian Nationalism in Canada*. Toronto: Random House.

Mackey, Lloyd. 2005. *The Pilgrimage of Stephen Harper*. Toronto: ECW Press.

Malloy, Jonathan. 2009. "Bush/Harper? Canadian and American Evangelical Politics Compared." *American Review of Canadian Studies* 39, 4: 352–63.

———. 2010. "The Private Faith and Public Lives of Evangelical MPs." Paper presented at the annual meeting of the Political Science Association, Concordia University, June.

———. 2011. "Canadian Evangelicals and Same-Sex Marriage." In David Rayside and Clyde Wilcox, eds, *Faith, Politics and Sexual Diversity in Canada and the United States*. Vancouver: University of British Columbia Press, 144–66.

Martin, Lawrence. 2010. *Harperland: The Politics of Control*. Toronto: Viking.

Matthews, Robert O. 1989. "The Christian Churches and Human Rights in Canadian Foreign Policy." *Journal of Canadian Studies* 24, 1: 5–31.

Munton, Don. 2002–3. "Whither Internationalism?" *International Journal* 58, 1: 155–80.

Nadeau, Christian. 2011. *Rogue in Power: Why Stephen Harper Is Remaking Canada by Stealth*. Trans. Bob Chodas, Eric Hamovitch, and Susan Joanis. Toronto: Lorimer.

Nossal, Kim Richard. 1997. *The Politics of Canadian Foreign Policy*. Scarborough, ON: Prentice Hall.

O'Toole, Roger. 1996. "Religion in Canada: Its Development and Contemporary Situation." *Social Compass* 43, 1: 119–34. At http: //are.as.wvu.edu/o'toole.html.

Payton, Laura. 2011. "Contempt Debate before MPs Once Again." CBC News, 18 March. At http://www.cbc.ca/news/politics/story/2011/03/18/pol-oda-privilege.html.

Pratt, Cranford. 1989. *Internationalism under Strain: the North-South Policies of Canada, the Netherlands, Norway and Sweden*. Toronto: University of Toronto Press.

Rayside, David. 2011. "The Conservative Party of Canada and Its Religious Constituencies." In David Rayside and Clyde Wilcox, eds, *Faith, Politics and Sexual Diversity in Canada and the United States*. Vancouver: University of British Columbia Press, 279–99.

Sasley, Brent E., and Tami Amanda Jacoby. 2007. "Canada's Jewish and Arab Communities and Canadian Foreign Policy." In Paul Heinbecker and Bessma Momani, eds, *Canada and the Middle East: In Theory and Practice*. Waterloo, ON: Wilfrid Laurier Press and CIGI, 185–204.

Smith, Heather A. 2003. "Disrupting Internationalism and Finding the Others." In Claire Turenne Sjolander, Heather A. Smith, and Deborah Stienstra, eds, *Feminist Perspectives on Canadian Foreign Policy*. Don Mills, ON: Oxford University Press, 24–39.

Stairs, Denis. 1995. "Will and Circumstance and the Postwar Study of Canada's Foreign Policy." *International Journal* 50, 1: 9–39.

8 Once Were Diplomats: Can Canadian Internationalism Be Rekindled?

Daryl Copeland

A few years ago I had lunch with a friend who was then the head of a Canadian Crown corporation. During that meeting we discussed the growing gap between Canada's long-standing image and reputation as an active, enlightened, and committed member of the international community and the more recent manifestation of Canadian **internationalism**, which seems to have waned to the point of near invisibility.

I suggested that when it comes to the management of the nation's brand, coasting for too long on past laurels can prove costly. Surely, at some point, Canada's bluff would be called, perhaps in a very public way, leaving the country vulnerable and exposed with possibly disastrous consequences in terms of credibility and influence. "But, it's already happening," said my guest, who had just returned from a donors' meeting abroad. "After making my statement, a European delegate pulled me aside and asked, 'What has happened to Canada? We don't recognize you any more.'"

Although at the time I never imagined anything quite as excruciating as Canada's failure to secure election to the United Nations (UN) Security Council in the autumn of 2010, this exchange nevertheless confirmed something that I had been feeling with increasing intensity for over a decade. Wherever Canada is now going internationally, it bears little resemblance to where it has been.

Let me declare myself. As a commentator and analyst, conditioned undoubtedly by 30 years in the foreign service, I have developed an attachment to a certain *idea* of Canada's place in the world. While I see no need to lapse into a maudlin and ultimately sterile debate about the existence—or not—of some mythical golden age in Canadian **diplomacy** and foreign policy (Cohen, 2003: 5–21), I do confess to feeling quite comfortable with the notion, however vague, of Pearsonian internationalism. However devalued its contemporary currency, to my mind that term aptly captures Canada's vocation for much of the second half of the twentieth century.

Helpfully fixing. Honestly brokering.

The way we were.

In those days, Canadian internationalism was palpable and its expression could be measured. Canada was a major donor, a leader in multilateral diplomacy, and a pioneer in the making of international organizations. Moreover, this internationalism not only amounted to a willingness and capacity to act and initiate, but was reflected as well in a set of widely shared attitudes and well-developed aptitudes that supported that kind of a global role.

I recognize, of course, that for many Canadians the Pearsonian internationalist label must seem somewhat distant and dated, perhaps even alien. After all, it has been several decades since Canada stood among the most generous aid providers of the Organisation for Economic Co-operation and Development (OECD), or made a large-scale contribution to multilateral peacekeeping, or took the lead on a cooperative initiative intended to treat a major global crisis or issue. Moreover, the demographics and culture of this land have been utterly transformed over the past generation or so—the one half of Toronto's population that was not born there, for example, is unlikely to have any fuzzy and warm feelings about the good old days of Canadian internationalism.

Still, if internationalism is understood as a predisposition towards meaningful engagement with peoples, organizations and states abroad in the pursuit of collaborative international solutions to identified problems and challenges,"[1] then Canada's present *bona fides* are dubious. The country has lost its confidence, its capability, and a substantial degree of its credibility. In certain parts of the NGO (nongovernmental organization) community, Canada is today regarded as a pariah. In 1957 Mr Pearson was awarded the Nobel Peace Prize for his role in resolving the Suez Crisis; in 2009 at the post-Kyoto COP15 conference in Copenhagen, Canada received the Fossil of the Year Award for this country's regressive position on climate change.

The relative decline in Canada's power and influence has been to some extent inevitable given developments elsewhere in the world, including European postwar recovery and integration, the ascent of the BRICs, and so forth. But that alone cannot account for the near invisibility of Canadian diplomacy today. Canada now finds itself in unfamiliar territory. Something fundamental has changed, while something of value may have been lost.

Where are we now, what has happened, and why?

It's complicated.

Can a new narrative be constructed?

Perhaps.

To get at those questions in reference to an assessment of the international policy records of the Chrétien, Martin, and Harper governments, it is necessary first to establish the context by casting a glance a little further backwards.

From Pearson's Peacekeepers ...

Fifty years ago there was a widely shared conviction, both within this country and abroad, that Canada could play a useful part in addressing major international issues and could make a difference in determining the course of world events.

When External Affairs Minister Lester Pearson stepped up to the plate at the United Nations in 1956, his efforts attracted more admiration and support than surprise or derision.[2] Similarly, when Prime Minister Trudeau engineered the opening of China to the West in 1971, or the North-South Summit in Cancun a decade later, it all seemed quite natural. If Trudeau's one-man peace crusade of 1984, intended to promote a "strategy of suffocation" and to bring the superpowers back from the brink of nuclear war, was not universally appreciated, it nonetheless indicated the scope and intensity of Canadian internationalism. Canadian leaders believed that this country had a role to play and could make a worthwhile contribution to international development, peace, and security.

Contrary to the received wisdom, little of that changed during the Mulroney years. If anything, that period represented Canada's last hurrah as an engaged, global player. Although much of the commentary covering that period has focused on Canada-US relations, mainly on account of the Free Trade Agreement (and later the North American Free Trade Agreement [NAFTA]) and the Acid Rain Treaty, there was in fact much more. The list of Canada's contributions includes responding in a timely, compassionate, and comprehensive way to the Ethiopian famine of 1984–6; co-chairing the UN Conference on the Rights of the Child; orchestrating a campaign within the Commonwealth to bring an end to apartheid in Southern Africa; actively opposing the Indonesian occupation of East Timor; negotiating the Montreal Protocol on ozone layer depletion; and organizing the UN Conference on Environment and Development in Rio de Janeiro. That last event alone, popularly referred to as the "Earth Summit," was a diplomatic mega-project. It produced Agenda 21, the Rio Declaration, the Biodiversity Convention, the Statement of Forest Principles, and the first UN Framework Convention on Climate Change. During this period Canada's ratio of gross domestic product (GDP) to aid expenditure peaked at 0.56 per cent, the closest the country has ever come to Pearson's goal of 0.7 per cent.

Other efforts, such as the North Pacific Cooperative Security Dialogue, never found the great-power support required to bring them to fruition, but they were worth a try. With power shifting towards the Asia Pacific with the dramatic rise of China in recent years, even these ventures may come to be seen as historic opportunities lost.

From the end of the Second World War through the 1990s, this country was a significant player in the international system. A variety of factors helped make that possible—Canada's exaggerated economic power and political influence, widespread devastation in Europe and Asia, the Cold War, colonialism and underdevelopment. But these attributes alone do not provide a full explanation. Canada—and Canadians—then had world order goals and they were large: poverty eradication, conflict resolution, environmental protection, the reform of multilateral institutions. Canadian politicians and diplomats took on ambitious, long-term projects because they thought them worth doing and believed Canada capable of delivering the results required.

Progress, when it came, was slow. Risks were high. Costs were considerable. Yet successive governments were bought in to an international policy consensus that was non-partisan and enjoyed a broad popular following. Crucially, they provided the resources necessary to get on with the job. [Political leadership, institutional capacity, and public support were the essential prerequisites.]

It has been only 20 years from Rio to Copenhagen, yet all of that now seems almost impossibly long ago and far away.

. . . to Program Review

The pattern of global engagement sketched above appeared set to continue when Jean Chrétien assumed office as prime minister in 1993. During that government's first mandate, however, two things happened that resulted in a sharp shift away from the post-war modus operandi. The first was the "Fish War" with Spain, which served to introduce the government to the potential inherent in soft power and **public diplomacy.**[3] The second was the establishment of "Program Review," which resulted in massive spending cuts and a radical downsizing of the Canadian state (Bourgon, 2009). International policy instruments—defence, diplomacy, and development—were amongst the hardest hit.

In the 1994 dispute with Spain over North Atlantic fisheries (Sneyd, 2009), [Canada's position and actions—especially the pursuit, boarding, and seizure of the trawler *Estai* in international waters—were predicated on tenuous legal grounds.] Some considered Canada's actions acts of war. It was recognized almost from the start that standard diplomatic defences, such as *démarches*, statements, and speeches, would not be sufficient and that a much broader approach would be required. The decision was therefore taken to move the contest, insofar as possible, into the court of public opinion—much better that than to face being called to the dock at the International Court of Justice in The Hague.

A major international campaign was orchestrated out of Ottawa and was based largely on the principles of public relations, particularly the notion of "earned media." On the day the Spanish were to present their case in New York to a UN conference on "straddling and migratory fish stocks," Canadian fisheries minister Brian Tobin appeared on a barge in the East River opposite UN headquarters and held aloft an undersized fishing net seized from the Spanish trawler. While staff distributed pictures of restricted species found in the hold to a large group of international press, [Tobin presented Canada's environmental and ethical case.] His brash, brilliant stunt made for great visuals and produced headlines everywhere. This amounted to ambushing the Spanish government, and it effectively pre-empted Spain's attempt to condemn and discredit Canada before the UN. It also completely undermined the position of Spanish fisheries minister Luis Atienza, who reportedly withdrew an op-ed that elaborated the complaint against Canada and had been scheduled to run the next day in the *Wall Street Journal*.

A few days later, Royce Frith, Canada's high commissioner to the United Kingdom, had himself photographed amongst a sea of Canadian flags displayed by supportive Cornish fishers who were similarly riled over Spanish fishing practices off the British coast. This event may have been carefully choreographed, but the sentiments were very real and again, the coverage was massive. Public opinion had now been so sufficiently conditioned that Spain dropped its international legal action, fearing that if approached, the justices would balk.

In short, Canada orchestrated an advocacy campaign that used potent images to generate front-page news and backed this up with briefings and presentations on overfishing and resource conservation, on a worldwide basis, 24/7. The strategy worked, and some in government recognized the ingredients of a successful new formula: convince others to want what you want by using the appeal of Canada's generally positive image and reputation (soft power) to connect directly with foreign populations and opinion leaders through the media (public diplomacy).

Canada used a similar approach in 1996 to take the lead in organizing an (ultimately aborted) effort at humanitarian intervention intended to assist refugees displaced by conflict in Rwanda/Zaire (Massey, 1998). Canadian officials prepared the ground by forging coalitions with like-minded states, soliciting the support of NGOs, and promoting the idea of a multilateral rescue mission in the world press. In the end, Canada was likely fortunate that the undertaking proved unnecessary—it would have been an extremely complex and difficult mission, and it came at a time when Canadian resources were being cut. While we will never know what the outcome might have been, we do know that nothing of that nature or magnitude has been attempted by this country since.

Discovering Niche Diplomacy

The Rwanda/Zaire episode, as well as the fish war that preceded it, helped to set the stage for the 1996–2000 tenure of Lloyd Axworthy, the last foreign minister to have a significant personal impact on the nature and direction of Canadian international policy. Axworthy achieved this status mainly through sheer will and by honing the soft power/public diplomacy combination to a fine edge.

Charged with implementing the Program Review expenditure reductions, the new minister could see that the old ways of Pearsonian internationalism were no longer sustainable. But he was not prepared to accept that this meant inaction. To the contrary, Axworthy sought to identify opportunity in adversity, even if faced with opposition on the part of the United States and other major powers. In the campaigns leading to the signing of the treaty to ban land mines in 1997 and the establishing of the International Criminal Court in 1998, the minister attained his objectives by nurturing partnerships with international civil society and similarly inclined countries.[4] He was also much more active than his predecessors in reaching out to the academic community and to NGOs at home and abroad.[5] In all cases, he used the media to great effect.

The same innovative approach, in varying degrees, was seen in initiatives to try to limit the proliferation of small arms, to highlight the plight of children in war zones and curb the use of child soldiers, and to restrict the sale of "conflict diamonds" through the launching of the Kimberley Process Certification Scheme under the auspices of the UN Security Council. Canada also sponsored the International Commission on Intervention and State Sovereignty, whose final report, *The Responsibility to Protect* (IDRC, 2001), though initially overtaken by the events of 9/11, eventually resurfaced and was adopted in principle at the UN Millennium Summit in September 2005.

Taken together, these achievements were artfully—and, in part, retrospectively—packaged by officials of the Department of Foreign Affairs and International Trade (DFAIT) into a remarkably coherent program that came to be known as the Human Security Agenda (McRae and Hubert, 2001). It did not survive for long following Axworthy's departure from office, but it stands as enduring testament to what can be achieved, even during hard times, by the powerful combination of personal ambition, political will, and bureaucratic skill.[6]

The examples cited above illustrate that during the Chrétien years the diplomatic paradigm for Canadian internationalism shifted.[7] Canada had fundamentally downsized its international ambitions, but that recalibration was not translated into a retreat from the field. To be sure, along the way some strategic opportunities were missed.[8] The large-scale, long-range, world-changing engagement of the post-war decades was gone. In its place were special projects and media-friendly diplomatic niches, each with a defined beginning and end (Potter, 1996). Upon completion, the minister simply called a press conference, declared victory, and moved on.

Minister Axworthy certainly had his critics (e.g., Nossal, 1998–9), but he learned, and very quickly, how to make a virtue of necessity. Conventional diplomacy was still necessary, but at a time when Canada's relative power was declining, traditional means were no longer sufficient when it came to influencing foreign governments. That influence was best brought to bear through their publics and through international public opinion, especially when compulsion was not an option and democratization had expanded the scope for exercising influence indirectly. And while the demands associated with this burst of activism imposed significant costs upon DFAIT's already struggling staff, the record of the second half of the 1990s looms larger the further it recedes in time.[9]

Still Making a Difference?

It must be asked: what has been the general direction of this country's international policy in the intervening decade? For the most part, direction has been non-existent, and such action as has been taken could best be described as responsive rather than proactive. Late in the Chrétien period, Canada avoided joining the US-led coalition that invaded Iraq, but in 2002 it went to war in Afghanistan (Stein and Lang, 2007).[10] That commitment was gradually extended, first to 2009 and later, through a deft series of political manoeuvres, to 2011 by Prime Minister Harper. Harper achieved all-party consensus for that decision following the receipt of recommendations presented in the "Manley Report" (Independent Panel, 2008). Among other effects, the Afghanistan campaign has boosted the prominence and fortunes of the Canadian military and has tended to swing Canada's overall international policy mix towards defence at the expense of diplomacy and development.[11]

On issues of Middle East peace, Prime Minister Martin departed from Canada's notionally "balanced" position and began a pronounced tilt towards Israel; this redirection was sharpened by the Harper government, which openly supported the 2006 Israeli incursion into Lebanon, withdrew assistance to Palestinians in the Gaza Strip following the election of a Hamas government there, and was mute on the Israeli campaign to cripple that government in 2008–9. After a very rough beginning, several years into their second mandate the Conservatives came to recognize that cool political relations with China were not conducive to the development of closer trade and investment ties, and they have acted accordingly to restore that relationship.[12] Similarly, after a period of relative inattention, India is once again on the bilateral relations map, and "the world's toughest sanctions" have been imposed on Burma.[13] The release of documents related to possible war crimes in the treatment of Afghan detainees by Canadian military and civilian officials has been stonewalled, while Canadian citizen and child soldier Omar Khadr, whatever his crimes, has been left to martial justice in Guantanamo Bay. When the news of Osama bin Laden's—quite possibly illegal—assassination was announced, and even as the storyline evolved radically, Canada's response was congratulatory (Copeland, 2011b).

Elsewhere, the parliamentary chartered organization known as Rights and Democracy has been gutted, and funding in support of several long-established NGOs reduced (e.g., Canadian Council for International Co-operation) or eliminated (e.g., KAIROS). Planned defence purchases (fighters, ships) and Arctic sovereignty have taken on a new profile. The aid budget has been untied, and in 2010 major emergency humanitarian-relief operations were launched in response to the earthquake in Haiti and the floods in Pakistan. Free trade negotiations have been launched with the EU and concluded with various others, while discussions are underway with the United States on the establishment of a common security perimeter. Relations with Latin America were declared a priority in 2009, and shortly thereafter a visa requirement was slapped on visitors from Mexico.[14]

Multilateralism, traditionally a hallmark of Canadian diplomacy and international policy, figured centrally in the rhetoric of the Chrétien and Martin governments. Apart from their talking a good game and advancing the standing of the G20, however, it can be argued that the Liberal governments did not achieve much (Kirton, 2009–10). In contrast, in their first four years, the Harper government mainly ignored and occasionally disdained multilateral policy and institutions, especially with regard to climate change and the repudiation of the Kyoto Accords.

By the summer of 2010, however, some aspects of this approach appeared to be changing. Canada began actively—and, in the end, unsuccessfully—to pursue a seat on the UN Security Council,[15] and, while hosting the G8/G20 Summits in June 2010, was able bring attention to issues of maternal and child health and fiscal responsibility. The decision to hold the G20 meeting in downtown Toronto resulted in much of the central business district being fenced off and a police riot against protesters. This was not a case study in public diplomacy or branding. Much of the activity was the result of prime ministerial decisions, and most of it would not qualify as internationalist. Meanwhile, a revolving-door succession of foreign ministers over the past decade has left barely a trace of their tenure in office. When John Manley succeeded Lloyd Axworthy in late 2000, he began something called the Foreign Policy Update, but that project was abandoned as a result of his promotion to deputy prime minister in the wake of 9/11. Bill Graham was responsible in 2003 for launching the innovative online *Foreign Policy Dialogue*, which offered Canadians the opportunity to bring the interactive capacity of the Internet to bear on policy development. Yet Graham's formidable knowledge of the content of these files was not matched by a clear sense of where he wanted to take them. Carried over in the portfolio by the Martin government, he was replaced in mid-2004 by Pierre Pettigrew, whose main achievement was to preside over the release of the five-part *International Policy Statement*. Years in the making, this compendium consisted of an overview of, and individual volumes dedicated to, diplomacy, defence, development, and commerce (Government of Canada, 2005). The sweeping and elegantly structured *Statement* recommitted Canada to a more modest iteration of once-robust internationalism, but it was shelved quickly, and with extreme prejudice, following the election of a Conservative minority government in 2006. Thus ended any pretence of a non-partisan approach to international policy. In the interim, as noted by Kim Nossal in chapter 2 no coherent substitute—short of manoeuvring for domestic political advantage—has emerged.

Since January 2006, Ministers Peter MacKay, Maxime Bernier, David Emerson, and Lawrence Cannon have come and gone. Books are unlikely to be written about their legacy. For 30 months Lawrence Cannon carried the torch in a world in which the foreign ministerial competition included the likes of Hillary Clinton and Sergei Lavrov, David Miliband and Bernard Kouchner. Cannon's successor, John Baird, is not generally known for his diplomatic finesse; he faces a steep learning curve in a very tough operating environment. And the internationalist tradition? At a time when Canada is already among the least generous of OECD donors, the aid budget has been frozen (Clark, 2010). The number of Canadian development assistance programs in Africa, a continent in desperate need, has been significantly reduced, and diplomatic missions there have been closed (York, 2009)—this at a time when Africa appears poised for significant growth and recovery (Wallis, England, and Manson, 2011). Canada's once-extensive diplomatic networks on that continent took decades to construct. Their loss will be costly, and the price of any eventual rebuilding high. The government's top three priorities in early 2011—trade and investment with emerging economies; the USA/Americas; Afghanistan—do not in my view qualify as internationalist. The fourth item on that list—asserting Canadian leadership in emerging global governance—has a vaguely internationalist ring, but the content is not fully articulated (DFAIT, 2011).

The Tools of the Trade ...

If the Axworthy years can be seen as a last, almost desperate gasp of Canadian internationalism, however downsized, with very little by way of policy development or initiative in its wake, then some attention must also be devoted to the matter of that third crucial, yet frequently overlooked prerequisite, institutional capacity. It is impossible to practise effective internationalism in the absence of well-functioning and adequately funded international policy instruments, the foreign ministry perhaps foremost amongst them. In that respect, it is one thing that since 2000 a string of ministers have demanded little beyond routine services from DFAIT, but quite another that the department's capabilities have been significantly reduced, a development that began in earnest under Chrétien. Deep cuts were made during Axworthy's four-year tenure—which makes his record of achievement even more remarkable—and that trend, despite a brief respite during the first half of the present decade, has since continued (Collins, 2009).

DFAIT is not alone in facing hard times (Copeland 2004, 2005); foreign ministries (and foreign services) most everywhere have been going through a difficult period (Riordan, 2003, 2007; Armstrong, 2009; Lowy Institute, 2009). These ministries' one-time near monopoly on the management of international policy and relations has been broken, and this can be explained in part by the diminishing importance of states per se in the age of globalization. There has been a debilitating migration of decision-making authority and other high-end functions (e.g., policy advice and development) away from foreign ministries and towards central agencies—in Canada's case the Privy Council Office and the Prime Minister's Office. Centralization within national governments has been accompanied by a shift of power and influence upwards, to supranational institutions; outwards, to other government departments, civil society, business, and even individuals; and downwards, to other levels of government (provincial, state, municipal). In consequence, the prestige and position of foreign ministers have been eroded, with defence ministers and heads of state or government emerging as the principal beneficiaries.

DFAIT's fortunes have reflected these changes (Lang and Morse, 2010). In response, beginning with the ill-fated Corporate Review exercise of the early 1990s, there has been a series of inconclusive attempts at reform and restructuring, most driven not by vision or strategic imperatives, but by the need to cut spending.[16] Then came the pair of particularly disruptive decisions: first, in 2003, to bifurcate the department in order to create a separate trade ministry, and then, in 2006, to reintegrate it with Foreign Affairs just after the separation had been completed. The anxiety, dislocation, administrative overheads, and inefficiencies generated by these sorts of massive reorganization, or the costs in terms of productivity and morale, cannot be overstated.

Although the arrows point mostly in one direction, there have been attempts to break the downward spiral. In 2004 a strategic decision was made at Foreign Affairs Canada to try to turn the adversity associated with the departmental split into an opportunity to create a foreign ministry (as well as diplomacy and foreign service) for the twenty-first century. Rather than a clever or convenient calculation of bureaucratic interest, this exercise was intended to produce a disciplined assessment of the best way forward for the department, and for Canada, in a changing world.

Despite a very promising start, the timing was unfortunate. New resources were withheld following the 2006 election, and the reform initiative, which did not contain a trade component, was among the first casualties of the reintegration.[17]

... Have Been Muted ...

DFAIT has lost not only a significant measure of its decision-making and advisory functions, but also, as a result of the unprecedented micromanagement and central control over all external communications, its voice. This central control has been exercised both through self-censorship, which in recent years has become rampant, and through the post-2007 requirement to pre-clear all public statements by using an Orwellian device known as a Message Event Proposal (Davis, 2010; Simpson, 2010). The combined effect is that Canadian diplomats have been gagged, with devastating consequences.

Public diplomacy, a practice regarded by most observers as basic to diplomatic tradecraft in the twenty-first century, requires of its practitioners not only a high degree of agility and acuity, but also a substantial measure of autonomy in the form of a licence to engage in spontaneous exchange, either in person or through the new or conventional media. If Canadian representatives are to connect directly with publics and opinion leaders abroad in order to exercise persuasion and influence, then genuine dialogue, albeit within the context of broad strategic objectives, must be encouraged. Because all conversations cannot be scripted or their outcomes preordained, diplomats must be accorded the trust and respect required for one to engage credibly without the need to seek headquarters' authorization in advance.[18]

Responsiveness, creativity, comfort with risk, and a willingness to devolve authority should be the hallmarks of contemporary Canadian diplomacy. Instead, they have become its casualties. From a position of leadership in the practice of innovative public diplomacy (PD) during the first half of this decade, Canada has now fallen far behind, while the United Kingdom and the United States, in comparison, have surged ahead, especially in the widespread use of new media applications, including Twitter, Facebook, YouTube, and blogs.[19]

It is sometimes said that a good diplomat stands up not only *for* his or her country abroad, but, when necessary, *to* his or her country at home. The absence of senior management push-back in the face of a raft of harmful central agency decisions over the past few years—many involving the evisceration of the department's once pack-leading prowess in international policy's key sector, public diplomacy—has regrettably become a contemporary DFAIT hallmark. With more spirited, imaginative, and committed leadership, I am convinced that much of what has been lost could have been saved, gains consolidated, and new directions taken.

. . . Or Become Dull

And what of the representational platform abroad, from which any renewed internationalism might be pursued? Like the operation at headquarters, Canada's network of missions abroad has been hollowed out and become shaky. Notwithstanding renewed efforts to redeploy a modest number of staff to the field, deep reductions to the budgets of posts abroad have made the conduct of even rudimentary diplomatic activities most difficult (Berthiaume, 2010).

Some background and context here is essential. I am convinced that in the age of globalization, security is not a martial art. It has less to do with generals and admirals, bombs and guns than it does with finding effective ways to address the needs and grievances of the poor and the excluded. Diplomats, in other words, have to become much more involved in the process of long-term, equitable, and human-centred development, a condition that underpins security.[20] They will require a detailed knowledge of history, advanced language skills, and extreme cultural competence. Perhaps most importantly, diplomats will have to spend much more of their time not only out of the office, but operating "outside the bubble" and even outside the wire in conflict zones and counterinsurgency settings (Copeland and Potter, 2008).

In such instances, political officers especially will have to be capable of swimming, with comfort and ease, in the sea of the people, and never be seen flopping around like a fish out of water when venturing beyond the chancery (see Copeland, 2008). Absent this quality—more easily learned through ground-level world travel or NGO experience than over years spent in Ivy League colleges—there is no way that foreign ministries will be able to generate vital, granular intelligence about place. This often overlooked aspect should be the basis of the foreign ministry's comparative advantage and its ace in the hole vis-à-vis competition with other international policy actors.

Instead, that vital connection to *place* is wilting on the vine.

How is DFAIT coping today? An exercise christened "Strategic Review II" is underway as this book goes to press. That is almost certainly code for further cuts. Under the rubric of *Transformation* (see DFAIT, 2010a), Canadian diplomatic missions are being remade into whole-of-government points of service overseas, with career diplomats often outnumbered by the employees of other government departments. That might be fine—except that too often those dispatched are being exiled from their home departments for reasons having nothing to do with their personal suitability for representational work abroad.

More people are finally being moved into the field—that is clearly needed. Yet this is being accompanied by a new corporate design intended to shift headquarters functions out to missions, a development that will almost certainly have the unintended but pernicious effect of forcing diplomats to behave even more like international policy bureaucrats. If limited numbers of DFAIT staff are called upon to write background and scenario notes, organize meetings, and provide services not only to travelling Canadians, but also internally, there will be precious little time for diplomacy. Instead, those posted abroad will have to spend even more time in their offices and at their desks—exactly where they shouldn't be—talking to others of their ilk about what might be going on outside.

That is a formula for turning allegations about the irrelevance of the foreign service into a self-fulfilling prophecy.

We have seen that foreign ministries are being marginalized and sidelined within government, reduced to the role of landlords and common service providers to other government departments. They are also being degraded from within.[21] In DFAIT's case, the gutting of the power, prestige, and central responsibilities of the department has left in its wake a rather banal crew of remainders, none of which contribute much to the design or delivery of diplomacy. Bureaucratic process and administrative busy-work have overtaken international policy leadership, analysis, and formulation; the administrative tail is wagging the policy dog.

If the senior managers had a vision of their departments' place in the firmament of government, foreign ministries might see themselves as central agencies for the management of globalization, with a crosscutting, catalytic writ vis-à-vis other government departments and authority supported at the highest political levels. They could—and I think should—be at the centre of international policy. But they are not, and they lack the domestic influence, budgetary strength, analytical depth, specialized skills, and subtle, supple capacities required. A foreign ministry whose mandate is under siege and whose workforce is populated by the wrong kind of employee will not be able to develop or implement innovative international policy in difficult environments, especially if under-resourced and disconnected from the levers of domestic power.

Turning the Page ...

Based largely on the assumption that Canada could maximize its influence if it acted in concert with others, internationalism was until about a decade ago believed to serve core Canadian interests. Moreover, that variety of internationalism—as reflected, among other things, in this country's reputation as an honest broker, helpful fixer, and boy scout to the world—was once a significant component of the **national brand**. Like all quality brands, its strength and durability were based not on what we said, but on what we were doing in the world. These days, although that brand retains a measure of its former lustre, it is fading fast.[22] While people from elsewhere continue to covet the prospect of residency here, the basis of this country's appeal has little to do with international policy or performance.[23]

What has become of Canada's once-vaunted global role? Until early in this century, though the nature and scope of Canadian internationalism had certainly changed, this country was nevertheless active. That activism, however, has since succumbed to a perfect storm of conditions. The interrelated combination of an inevitably smaller place in the world, the serial lack of political leadership, a running-down of the capacity and resources of the foreign ministry, and transformed internal conditions have combined to subvert *traditional* Canadian internationalism. Under the guise of a principled stand on the promotion of freedom, democracy, human rights, and the rule of law, Canada's pragmatism has in recent years given way to a highly politicized, even ideological, approach.

In response to the opportunities presented by the emergence of the BRICs and of an increasingly **heteropolar**[24] world order, the government has responded, without any public consultation, by joining in the NATO (North Atlantic Treaty Organization) bombing of Libya in support of the anti-Gaddafi opposition (Copeland, 2011c). Yet the real threats to the planet—climate change, resource scarcity, diminishing biodiversity, collapsing ecosystems—are rooted in science and driven by technology. Reinforcing the garrison, calling in an air strike, or dispatching an expeditionary force won't help with the likes of pandemic disease or species extinction; these challenges are not amenable to military solutions. Dialogue, negotiation, and compromise, on the other hand, will be indispensible. And it is precisely these skills, sadly, that have been ignored or allowed to atrophy.

If it was needed, the humiliating loss to Portugal in the race for election to the UN Security Council in October 2010 provided further and convincing testament to Canada's devalued internationalist currency.[25] The message from the floor of the General Assembly is that the world is no longer buying. The old narrative is exhausted, and attempts at its revival (Harper, 2010) serve mainly to underscore a yawning credibility gap.

The days of coasting on the fumes of Pearsonian internationalism are well and truly over (Copeland, 2010a).[26] The arrival in Ottawa of a Conservative majority government in May 2011, especially in face of the attributes and trends set out in the pages above, offers scant hope for any fundamental change in the nature or direction of Canadian international policy. For the time being at least, and particularly as regards diplomacy, we have dealt ourselves out of the game (Heinbecker, 2010). At the level of government policy and within the apparatus of the state, Canadian internationalism has become spectral.

. . . And Finding a New Way Forward

None of this, however, is to suggest that Canada is without internationalist potential. Immigration, buttressed by trade, travel, tourism, and technology, has transformed Canada from a distant remnant of rival empires into an open-ended possibility, a work in progress in which evolution and accommodation are constant. After almost 150 years, Canada has become a state—of becoming. For better and for worse, we are now the globalization nation.

With the role of the state receding, important aspects of Canada's internationalist future may now reside beyond national, political, or institutional structures. Many countries have the coercive power associated with armed force, but that will never be Canada's strong suit. Nor should it be. Canada's strength, and the source of any future influence, emanates not from the loudness of its voice, the comeliness of its landscapes, or the power of any weapons; rather, this country's appeal resides in the diverse makeup of its communities, in the *souplesse* of its social fabric, and in the openness, generosity of spirit, and outward orientation of its people. Because the *idea* of Canada still evokes a smile rather than a scowl, people will talk to us. The same positive predisposition is not always displayed towards those with a colonial past or imperial present.

With its generally benign image, its unthreatening manner, little historical baggage, and its open, approachable temperament, Canada has something quite unusual to offer. That attraction is cultural and rooted in the population rather than in politics or public administration.[27] This seems to me a unique, but for the most part unrecognized, advantage over the competition. If it is to be harnessed, however, new approaches will be required.

To that end, civil society organizations and various levels of government can, and almost certainly will, play a larger role in defining this country's role and reputation. In so doing, they will be able to draw on Canada's rich variety of resident talent, which includes individuals with the educational, linguistic, and cross-cultural acumen required to function at a high level just about anywhere. When it comes to the complex balancing skills and knowledge-based problem-solving abilities required for mediation, collaboration, and political communication, Canadians are admirably equipped (Hampson and Paris, 2010).

How, then, to tap into this potential and to create a post-Pearsonian narrative? Since, in the globalization age, the most profound challenges facing governments are transnational, according priority to science diplomacy and to providing high-level scientific and technological advice to decision-makers would seem obvious candidates. But these options are conspicuous mainly by their absence from the current discourse (Copeland, 2010a, 2010b, 2010c).

Given the drift at the policy level and the unfortunate state of DFAIT, it may be time for non-state actors and popular forces to take the lead.[28] A university, think tank, foundation, or several organizations in partnership could champion the construction of a stand-alone national entity dedicated to the exploration of diplomatic alternatives—and alternative diplomacy—that would not suffer from the diffuse objectives, debilitating administrative overheads, or political controls associated with a government department. Such an enterprise could adopt values such as flexibility, adaptability, teamwork, continuous learning, and risk tolerance. The engagement of diasporic communities, the use of new media, and the creation of virtual networks in addressing the globalization suite of scientific and technological challenges would all figure centrally.

The establishment of a crosscutting, public-private, and independent network node for the promotion of diplomacy and international policy would burnish the Canadian brand and serve as a concrete expression of this country's comparative international advantage. [A whole-of-Canada "Institute for Diplomatic Alternatives" could, for example, identify and advocate approaches and solutions to global issues and problems, with an emphasis on those rooted in science and driven by technology; generate creative ideas on crisis remediation and conflict resolution; conduct research and analysis, develop policy, and provide tactical and strategic advice; undertake continuous outreach to journalists, attentive publics, and opinion leaders; reach out to strategic partners on all sides of key issues; organize events (conferences, symposia, round tables); edit and publish an e-journal of alternative diplomacy; and design and deliver training and professional development programs.]

The non-violent management of international relations through dialogue, negotiation, and compromise is a worthy end starved of effective means. When it comes to creativity and innovation, Canada, and Canadians, are well placed to contribute. A determined effort to promote imaginative diplomatic alternatives to threats or use of armed force just might rekindle the once-bright flame of Canadian internationalism for a new generation.

At the very least, it could keep the candle burning.

Key Terms

internationalism	national brand
diplomacy	heteropolarity
public diplomacy	

Study Questions

1. To what extent can the turn away from familiar patterns of Canadian internationalism be attributed to the foreign policy of the Harper government?
2. How does "niche diplomacy" differ from previous Canadian approaches to the pursuit of international policy objectives?
3. In what ways have the role and place of DFAIT and the foreign minister changed during the period under review?
4. To what extent has political leadership been critical in determining international policy outcomes?
5. Are there alternatives to a reliance on the state in the development of international policy?

Notes

1 As illustrated in the editors' introduction, there are many ways to approach and understand the term "internationalism." The simple definition offered above follows from my experience with the use of the word by diplomatic practitioners.

2 Prime Minister St Laurent was entirely comfortable with allowing the foreign minister to get on with the management of his portfolio. In a cable from Ottawa to New York, he advised: "Do as you think best, I will support you here" (cited in Carroll, 2009: 30). In the intervening years, Canadian foreign ministers have rarely been accorded that degree of confidence, trust, or respect. Indeed, the trend has been towards ministerial disempowerment, with command and control assumed increasingly by the Prime Minister's Office (PMO) and the Privy Council Office (PCO).

3 Soft power involves inducing others to want what you want through the power of attraction, rather than coercion. Persuasion and influence are central. See Nye, 2004. Public diplomacy is a model of diplomatic practice that seeks to achieve specified outcomes through direct communication with foreign populations, often in partnership with elements of civil society. See Copeland, 2009a: 143–84.

4 On Axworthy's record and its significance, see Hampson, Hillmer, and Molot, 2001.

5 The Canadian Centre for Foreign Policy Development and the Public Diplomacy Fund, both of which were subsequently abolished, were created early in Axworthy's tenure and proved useful for constituency building.

6 For a first-person account of this period, see Axworthy, 2003.

7 They also illustrate the extent to which leadership can be determinant. The likes of this extraordinary burst of diplomatic energy, flowing in large part from one minister's insistence on focusing resources on those files where Canada "could make a difference," have not been seen since.

8 In 1996–7, for example, the department's Communications Bureau proposed the launch of an ambitious project that would have established for Canada an integrated global presence based on satellite broadcasting, the Internet, public diplomacy, international education, and branding. In the end, however, the Canadian International Information Strategy (CIIS) lost out to the campaign to ban land mines (later christened the "Ottawa Process") at a time of diminishing resources across government.

9 This was not always my view. See Copeland, 2001a.

10 The full story of the decision to intervene in Afghanistan—especially the move in late 2005 from the ISAF (International Security Assistance Force) in Kabul to Afghanistan's Kandahar province in order to join the US-led Operation Enduring Freedom (a subset of the Global War on Terror)—has yet to be told.

11 It might also be argued that the Kandahar deployment accelerated the re-profiling of the Canadian military's force structure away from peacekeeping and in favour of war fighting (Copeland, 2011a). To the extent that large-scale participation in multilateral peacekeeping missions organized under UN auspices qualifies as internationalism, Canada's turn away from activities of that sort in recent years can be interpreted as further evidence of internationalism's decline as a motive force in Canadian foreign policy.

12 A lot of rebuilding will be necessary. Prime Minister Harper hectored Chinese authorities on human rights; the Dalai Lama has been granted honorary Canadian citizenship; and the prime minister was too busy to attend the opening ceremony of the Beijing Olympics.

13 Canada has desperately needed a coherent Asia strategy for years (see Copeland, 1999). The contemporary case is equally compelling (see Woo, 2011; Acharya, 2011).

14 In a similar demonstration of apparent international policy incoherence, at the end of January 2011 and in the midst of popular uprisings against autocracy all over North Africa and the Greater Middle East, Harper visited Morocco to announce with King Hassan II the launching of free trade negotiations. It is difficult to imagine DFAIT supporting the timing of this trip.

15 For the first time ever, Canada's bid for a seat on the UN Security Council generated domestic opposition, based in large part on arguments that current Canadian international performance does not merit our election (see Gavai, 2010; Copeland, 2010a). For its first four years in office, the Conservative government paid almost no attention to the UN, with the prime minister famously preferring to visit a Tim Hortons in Oakville rather than attend the opening of the General Assembly in 2009. The failure to win a seat on the council was a stunning repudiation of both the government and the country. It stands as a severe reminder that international policy decisions—the shift from peacekeeping to aggressive counterinsurgency in Afghanistan, regression on climate change, the almost unconditional support for Israeli policies and actions, the pullback from Africa, and the running-down of DFAIT—have consequences.

16 I prepared a critique of this exercise that was published by the Professional Association of Foreign Service Officers under the title "Bureaucratoxis" (Copeland, 1990). A year later, when asked to describe the current status of the review enterprise, one senior manager looked down and replied, dismally, "We no longer speak of it … ."

17 Some detail is offered here for those with an interest in public administration. In early 2005, amidst much fanfare, then deputy minister Peter Harder and associate deputy Marie-Lucie Morin launched a major organizational change initiative under the banner of "Building a 21st Century Foreign Ministry," or "FAC 21." This included the establishment of a dedicated intranet site on departmental reform; creation of an office of innovation and excellence (DMAX); consolidation of all geographic branches outside North America and launch of a global issues branch; redeployment of positions from headquarters to missions abroad; consideration of a special operating agency to provide common services to missions abroad; and clarification of lines of responsibility for some key elements of public diplomacy. The plan proposed a significant redefinition and sharpening of the department's mandate (*interpreter* of globalization; *articulator* of foreign policy; *integrator* of the international agenda; *advocate* of values and interests; *provider* of services; and *steward* of public resources). It also identified the imperatives for institutional change (strengthen policy capacity, renew core professional skills, increase agility, reduce rigidity, maximize assets in the field, connect with wider networks, and mainstream public diplomacy). Much of this wide-ranging initiative came to a crashing halt in 2006 when the change in government resulted in a decision to reintegrate the departments.

18 This is by no means a uniquely Canadian problem. See, for instance, Van Buren, 2011.

19 On new directions in US e-diplomacy, see Lichtenstein, 2010. DFAIT now uses some social media tools, such as wikis, but only inside the firewall on its intranet site. See Copeland, 2009b.

20 In *Guerrilla Diplomacy* I make the case that because development has in large part become the new security in the age of globalization, diplomacy must displace defence at the centre of international policy. See Copeland, 2009a: 1–16.

21 At DFAIT, this whole-of-government model has been christened the "international platform." One colleague commented recently that it looked more like a formula for becoming a global doormat.

22 On the extent to which Canada's brand equity has become devalued, see Greenhill, 2004.

23 The Canadian brand is from time to time reported to rank number one internationally, but this performance is based usually on the country's image as a tourism destination. According to the United Nations Development Programme's more comprehensive quality of life index (the Human Development Index [HDI]), Canada's position has been slipping steadily since the country lost the top spot in 1997. In 2010 Canada was ranked eighth.

24 I have defined **heteropolarity**, a term coined originally by James Der Derian of Brown University, as "an emerging poly-centric world system in which competing states or groups of states derive their relative power and influence from dissimilar sources—social, economic, political, military, cultural" (http://en.wikipedia.org/wiki/Guerrilla_diplomacy). On the possibilities for Canada, see Canadian International Council, 2010.

25 As part of a more focused attempt to promote the WikiLeaks "Cablegate" disclosures, on 28 April 2011 several hundred cables that had originated at the US Embassy in Ottawa were released to the Canadian media. In one of the more widely reported messages, a former US ambassador lamented Canada's decline from an engaged middle power to an "active observer" on the world stage.

26 During the early stages of the 2011 federal election campaign, Liberal Party leader Michael Ignatieff tried several times to raise issues of international policy, as well as democracy and ethics. They failed to resonate.

27 Variations on this theme are found in Welsh, 2004 and Canada25, 2004.

28 Indeed, this process may already have begun. See *Canada's World*, 2010. Canadians, including several serving and former diplomats, have long been active in the conceptualization and analysis of diplomacy, and especially of public diplomacy, which for countries such as Canada should be the diplomatic business model of choice. See, for instance, Gotlieb, 1991; Smith, 1997; Potter, 2009.

References

Acharya, Amitav. 2011. "Time to Make Up for Lost time in Asia." *Embassy Magazine*, 18 May. At http://www.embassymag.ca/column/author/784.

Armstrong, Matt. 2009. "Hitting Bottom in Foggy Bottom." *Foreign Policy*, 11 September. At http://www.foreignpolicy.com/articles/2009/09/11/hitting_bottom_in_foggy_bottom.

Axworthy, Lloyd. 2003. *Navigating a New World: Canada's Global Future.* Toronto: Knopf Canada.

Berthiaume, Lee. 2010. "Budget Cuts Hurting Embassies: DFAIT Reports." *Embassy Magazine*, 1 September. At http://www.embassymag.ca/page/view/cuts-09-01-2010.

Bourgon, Jocelyne. 2009. "Program Review: The Government of Canada's Experience Eliminating the Deficit, 1994–1999—A Canadian Case Study." *CIGI Papers*, 1 September. At http://www.cigionline.org/publications/2009/9/prorgram-review-government-canadas-experience-eliminating-deficit-1994-99-canadi.

Canada25. 2004. *From Middle to Model Power: Recharging Canada's Role in the World.* At http://www.canada25.com/forum2004.html.

Canada's World. 2010. At http://www.canadasworld.ca/.

Canadian International Council. 2010. *Open Canada: A Global Positioning Strategy for a Networked Age.* At http://www.onlinecic.org/opencanada.

Carroll, Michael. 2009. *Pearson's Peacekeepers: Canada and the United Nations Emergency Force, 1956–67.* Vancouver: University of British Columbia Press.

Clark, Campbell. 2010. "Tories Target Foreign Aid to Tame Deficit." *Globe and Mail*, 4 March. At http://www.theglobeandmail.com/news/national/budget/tories-target-foreign-aid-to-tame-deficit/article1487995/.

Cohen, Andrew. 2003. *While Canada Slept.* Toronto: McClelland & Stewart.

Collins, Michelle. 2009. "Foreign Affairs Hit with $639 Million in Cuts." *Embassy Magazine*, 18 March. At http://www.embassymag.ca/page/view/foreign_affairs_cuts-3-18-2009.

Copeland, Daryl. 1990. "Bureaucratoxis: Thoughts on the Collapse of the Corporate Review." *PAFSO Papers* 1, 2 (November).

———. 1999. "After the Storm: Asia Pacific Prospects and Canadian Foreign Policy." *International Journal* 54, 4: 683–94.

———. 2001. "The Axworthy Years: Canadian Foreign Policy in the Era of Diminished Capacity." In Fen Osler Hampson, Norman Hillmer, and Maureen Appel Molot, eds, *Canada among Nations: The Axworthy Legacy.* Oxford: Oxford University Press, 152–72.

———. 2004. "Guerrilla Diplomacy: Delivering International Policy in a Digital World." *Canadian Foreign Policy/La politique étrangère du Canada* 11: 2: 165–75.

————. 2005. "New Rabbits, Old Hats: International Policy and Canada's Foreign Service in an Era of Reduced Diplomatic Resources." *International Journal* 60, 3: 743–62.

————. 2008. "No Dangling Conversation: Portrait of the Public Diplomat." *Engagement: Public Diplomacy in a Globalised World*. London: Foreign and Commonwealth Office.

————. 2009a. *Guerrilla Diplomacy: Rethinking International Relations*. Boulder, CO: Lynne Rienner Publishers.

————. 2009b. "Virtuality and Foreign Ministries." *Canadian Foreign Policy/La politique étrangère du Canada*, 15, 2: 1–15.

————. 2010a. "What Canada's Security Council Loss Says about Us." *The Mark*, 16 October. At http://www.themarknews.com/articles/2790-what-canadas-security-council-loss-says-about-us.

————. 2010b. "Science, Technology and Global Change." *The Mark*, 7 December. At http://www.themarknews.com/articles/3358-science-technology-and-global-change.

————. 2010c. "How Canada Could Contribute to Science Diplomacy." *The Mark*, 23 December. At http://www.themarknews.com/articles/3622-how-canada-could-contribute-to-science-diplomacy.

————. 2011a. "What's Next for Canada's Armed Forces?" *The Mark*, 18 May. At http://www.themarknews.com/articles/5238-what-s-next-for-canada-s-armed-forces.

————. 2011b. "After Osama: Time to Turn the Page?" *The Mark*, 3 May. At http://www.themarknews.com/articles/4997-after-osama-time-to-turn-the-page.

————. 2011c. "The War That Started While No One Was Watching." *The Mark*, 23 March. At http://www.themarknews.com/articles/4468-the-war-that-started-while-no-one-was-watching.

Copeland, Daryl, and Evan Potter. 2008. "Public Diplomacy in Conflict Zones: Military Information Operations Meet Political Counterinsurgency." *The Hague Journal of Diplomacy* 3, 3: 277–96.

Davis, Jeff. 2010. "Bureaucrats Chafing under 'Unprecedented' PMO/PCO Communications Control." *Embassy Magazine*, 26 April. At http://www.hilltimes.com/page/view/control-04-26-2010.

DFAIT (Department of Foreign Affairs and International Trade). 2010a. *Transformation*. At http://www.international.gc.ca/dfait-transformation-maeci/index.aspx?lang=eng.

————. 2010b. *Policy eDiscussions*. At http://www.international.gc.ca/dfait-transformation-maeci/index.aspx?lang=eng.

————. 2011. *Our Priorities: 2010–11*. At http://www.international.gc.ca/about-a_propos/priorities-priorites.aspx.

Gavai, Avinash. 2010. "Will Domestic Opposition Hurt UN Security Council Bid?" 6 October. At http://www.embassymag.ca/page/view/councilbid-10-06-2010.

Gotlieb, Alan. 1991. *I'll Be with You in a Minute, Mr. Ambassador: The Education of a Canadian Diplomat in Washington*. Toronto: University of Toronto Press.

Government of Canada. 2005. *Canada's International Policy Statement: A Role of Pride and Influence in the World*. Ottawa: Queen's Printer.

Greenhill, Robert. 2004. *Making a Difference? External Views on Canada's International Impact*. Toronto: Canadian Institute of International Affairs. At http://idl-bnc.idrc.ca/dspace/bitstream/10625/33024/1/120694.pdf.

Hampson, Fen, Norman Hillmer, and Maureen Molot, eds. 2001. *Canada among Nations 2001: The Axworthy Legacy*. New York: Oxford University Press.

Hampson, Fen, and Roland Paris. 2010. *Rethinking Canada's International Priorities: 2010*. Ottawa: University of Ottawa, Centre for International Policy Studies. At http://www.sciencessociales.uottawa.ca/cepi-cips/eng/priorities_intro.asp.

Harper, Stephen. 2010. "PM Highlights Canada's Role on the World Stage." Speech to the UN General Assembly. 23 October. At http://pm.gc.ca/eng/media.asp?category=2&pageId=46&id=3672.

Heinbecker, Paul. 2010. *Getting Back in the Game: A Foreign Policy Playbook for Canada*. Toronto: Key Porter Books.

IDRC (International Development Research Centre). 2001. *The Responsibility to Protect: International Commission on Intervention and State Sovereignty*. Ottawa: IDRC. At http://www.idrc.ca/en/ev-9436-201-1-DO_TOPIC.html.

Independent Panel on Canada's Future Role in Afghanistan. 2008. *Independent Panel on Canada's Future Role in Afghanistan.* Ottawa: Queen's Printer. At http://dsp-psd.pwgsc.gc.ca/collection_2008/dfait-maeci/FR5-20-1-2008E.pdf.

Kirton, John. 2009–10. "The Chrétien-Martin Years." At http://www.kirton.nelson.com/student/documents/cfp-11-2009.pdf.

Lang, Eugene, and Eric Morse. 2010. "For Foreign Policy-Making, Don't Look to Foreign Affairs." *Ottawa Citizen*, 30 August. At http://www.ottawacitizen.com/news/foreign+policy+making+look+Foreign+Affairs/3453360/story.html#ixzz0y5lVgbd0.

Lichtenstein, Jesse. 2010. "Digital Diplomacy." *New York Times Magazine*, 16 July. At http://www.nytimes.com/2010/07/18/magazine/18web2-0-t.html?_r=2&hpw.

Lowy Institute. 2009. *Australia's Diplomatic Deficit.* At http://www.lowyinstitute.org/Publication.asp?pid=996.

McRae, Robert, and Don Hubert. 2001. *Human Security and the New Diplomacy: Protecting People, Promoting Peace.* Montreal and Kingston: McGill-Queen's University Press.

Massey, Simon. 1998. "Operation Assurance: The Greatest Operation That Never Happened." 15 February. Coventry University, African Studies Centre. At http://jha.ac/articles/a036.htm.

Nossal, Kim. 1998–9. "Pinchpenny Diplomacy: The Decline of 'Good International Citizenship' in Canadian Foreign Policy." *International Journal* 54, 1: 88–105.

Nye, Joseph. 2004. *Soft Power: The Means to Success in World Politics.* New York: Public Affairs.

Potter, Evan. 1996. "Niche Diplomacy as Canadian Foreign Policy." *International Journal* 52, 1: 25–38.

———. 2009. *Branding Canada: Projecting Canada's Soft Power through Public Diplomacy.* Montreal and Kingston: McGill-Queen's University Press.

Riordan, Shaun. 2003. *The New Diplomacy.* London: Polity Press.

———. 2007. "Reforming Foreign Services for the Twenty-First Century." *The Hague Journal of Diplomacy* 2, 2: 161–73.

Simpson, Jeffrey. 2010. "The Price We Pay for a Government of Fear." *Globe and Mail*, 8 June. At http://www.theglobeandmail.com/news/opinions/the-price-we-pay-for-a-government-of-fear/article1595378/.

Smith, Gordon. 1997. "The Challenge of Virtual Diplomacy." April. New York: United States Institute of Peace. At http://www.usip.org/resources/the-challenge-virtual-diplomacy.

Sneyd, Elizabeth. 2009. "Fighting Over Fish: A Look at the 1995 Canada-Spain Turbot War." At http://www.cda-cdai.ca/cdai/uploads/cdai/2009/04/sneyd05.pdf.

Stein, Janice, and Eugene Lang. 2007. *Unexpected War: Canada in Kandahar.* Toronto: Viking.

Van Buren, Peter. 2011. "The War Lovers." *TomDispatch.com*, 16 May. At http://www.tomdispatch.com/post/175392/tomgram%3A_peter_van_buren%2C_warrior_pundits_and_war_pornographers/#more.

Wallis, William, Andrew England, and Katrina Manson. 2011. "Ripe for Reappraisal." *Financial Times*, 19 May, 9.

Welsh, Jennifer. 2004. *At Home in the World: Canada's Global Vision for the 21st Century.* Toronto: HarperCollins.

Woo, Yuan Pau. 2011. "Pay Attention to Asia, Eh!" *Huffington Post Canada*, 26 May. At http://www.huffingtonpost.ca/yuen-pau-woo/canada-asia-foreign-policy_b_867409.html.

York, Geoffrey. 2009. "Banned Aid." *Globe and Mail*, 29 May. At http://www.theglobeandmail.com/news/opinions/banned-aid/article1160311/.

PART II

Internationalism from the Outside

9 Citizenship, Borders, and Mobility: Managing the Population of Canada and the World

Mark B. Salter

The ideas, agents, and practices of foreign policy have fundamentally changed, and traditional foreign policy analysis relies on an antiquated and obsolete model of the state that assumes that borders are isometric with territorial boundaries.[1] The border is delocalized and disaggregated in the contemporary moment, and an array of domestic and foreign policies are arranged to manage populations both alien and national. These are claims that we can support empirically (Andreas, 2003; Sassen, 2006) or from first principles (Brown, 2010; Rajaram and Grundy-Warr, 2007). Foreign policy analysis, then, must reflect that dislocation and disaggregation of the right to claim rights: Canadian foreign policy analysis must adapt to a fundamentally deterritorialized understanding of *foreign* policy. The distinction between domestic and foreign policy is blurred because controls of (mobile) populations through borders and citizenship are not simply exercised in one place or another. The promotion of human rights abroad, or indeed a wider engagement with "the international," occurs in Canada as well as abroad. In policy terms, the positive rights-promotion norm must be understood in relation to the anti-policy of rights obstruction, the instances in which Canada's foreign policy prevents populations from claiming rights or makes it more difficult for them to do so (Walters, 2008). Canada's refugee policy, in particular the networks of safe third-country agreements and the new category of "designated countries of origin" (formerly safe third countries of origin), makes it increasingly difficult for some populations to claim rights from the Canadian government. A focus on this delocalized and disaggregated border policy, understood as a foreign policy related to populations, demonstrates the degree to which we see an empirical change in what it means to have an "internationalist" foreign policy and also in the ways in which the fundamental division between domestic and foreign policy is analytically misdirected.

Whether understood in traditional realist terms of population as an important national security and economic asset, in constructivist terms of national identity and culture, or in critical terms of **biopolitics**, the management of the citizenship, borders, and mobility (immigration, emigration, and refugee adjudication) is central to any serious consideration of foreign policy (Amoore, 2006; Isin and

Nielsen, 2008; Neal, 2009; Nyers, 2006; Walters, 2002). Determining who counts as Canadian, who may become Canadian, what Canadian citizenship means, who may visit, or who may immigrate are questions that define the population precisely along the domestic/international divide. These boundary and status issues have generally played an important but under-studied role in foreign policy; immigration and identity processes are most often examined from a chiefly domestic point of view. Canada does not occupy a hegemonic or exceptional position in the **global mobility regime**, which we can define as a loose collection of regulations, treaties, and practices that structure and govern international population movement (Koslowski, 2011). However, in this chapter, I want to point to three issues in which Canada is an exemplar of contemporary foreign policy trends: changing dynamics of citizenship, the offshoring of border practices, and the conflation of refugee and immigration regimes.

An increasingly important critical voice at this intersection of foreign and domestic policy analysis, particularly in the field of security studies, is the **International Political Sociology (IPS) School**, named the Paris School by the c.a.s.e. collective because of the location of its patron (c.a.s.e. collective, 2006).[2] Bigo (2001) argues that empirically the distinction between internal and external securities has collapsed; police, border services, and military forces compete for scarce resources and the actual activities of crime fighting, border security, and war fighting are becoming less distinct. While based in the European experience and the clear challenges to the domestic/foreign policy divide that the European Union (EU) might pose, a number of scholars have applied this perspective to non-European examples (Salter, 2008b; Jeandesboz, 2010; Mutlu, 2011; Abrahamsen and Williams, 2011). Work in this vein is inspired by Pierre Bourdieu's notion of **field**, focusing on actual policy practices. From this perspective, analysts should follow the twisted paths that techniques of statecraft follow, crossing the domestic/foreign and private/public divides as need be (Bigo, 2008). The core contention of the IPS School is that in the actual day-to-day work of statecraft, foreign and domestic policy are increasingly intertwined: domestic policies are increasingly enacted and regulated by international bodies, in conjunction with international public and private partners, because of international drivers or technical/commercial codes of practice and for both domestic and international audiences; while foreign policies are performed by domestic agencies and private actors because of domestic drivers and for domestic audiences. This is not policy work that is captured by the usual frame of internationalism, multilateralism, or middlepowermanship, but rather it is policy work that occurs at the sub-state level between various bureaucracies and amongst technocrats because of shared professional beliefs, discourses, and experiences. Border officials or financial fraud investigators share similar challenges, mandates, best practices, and codes of conduct, and have far more in common with their international analogues that they do with their co-national diplomatic corps. In addition to examining elite diplomacy and treaty-making at international and regional forums, we must examine the quotidian cooperation amongst aviation security officials,

money-laundering experts, and profiling agents. In short, we must follow practices
that invoke security—whether they are framed as domestic, international, public,
private, or some combination. When we engage with the field, we are able to understand the multiple and plural ways that citizenship, border, and migration policies
render a strict divide between domestic and foreign policy problematic.

The IPS School methodology, inspired by Bourdieu, if not immediately familiar
to students of foreign policy, is plainly useful. Advocates of this approach insist that
the formulation of foreign policy security practices cannot be limited to one bureaucracy or the diplomatic corps. It is not only the Department of Foreign Affairs
and International Trade (DFAIT) and the Canadian International Development
Agency (CIDA) that *do* policies that have global or international security impacts or
invoke security in order to promote particular practices. Citizenship is increasingly
deployed as a tool of foreign policy; borders are increasingly located offshore on foreign lands and being policed by commercial entities. Passport Canada, Citizenship
and Immigration Canada (CIC), and the Canada Border Services Agency—not to
mention the Canada Security Intelligence Service, the Royal Canadian Mounted
Police, and the Canadian Air Transport Security Authority—all engage with foreign governments and private corporations on matters of security. The intersection
of migration and security has been a particularly productive focus of the IPS School
(Bigo and Guild, 2005; Huysmans, 2006; Neal, 2009). Thus, IPS School advocates
argue that scholars and students must follow the practices of security, however they
bob and weave through different bureaucracies. Finally, it is also important to note
that a "whole of government" approach does not imply internal coherence between
these different bureaucracies. Without engaging in an in-depth prosopography (a
Bourdieusian method in which the careers, education, and social networks of important actors are mapped through a set of biographies), we must recognize that
policies are the result of competition as much as of cooperation between different
agencies and between private actors like corporations, rights groups, non-governmental organizations, and other actors. Similarly, we must look for security
policies that are permissive, that allow for particular mobilities, subjectivities, and
circulations, as much as for policies that prohibit and stop. Citizenship, passports,
and borders represent three important sites of those kinds of domestic/foreign
interfaces.

Citizenship

The substance of Canadian citizenship is demonstrated not only in the major sea
changes in Canadian laws regarding entitlements and status, but also in how the
limits of citizenship are described—the processes of becoming and un-becoming
citizens. There is a robust critical literature on citizenship that I will gesture towards rather than engage directly (Browne, 2005; Isin, Nyers, and Turner, 2008;
Isin and Nielsen, 2008; Nyers, 2009). I want to focus in this chapter on two recent
changes to the Canadian citizenship regime: the practice of becoming a citizen and

the process of un-becoming a citizen—or at least the process of having the rights of citizenship withdrawn.

The 2011 guide to Canadian citizenship, *Discover Canada,* differs from previous versions (CIC, 2011), particularly the 2002 *A Look at Canada* (CIC, 2002), and presents a more cultural notion of citizenship that stresses a conservative understanding of Canadian identity (law-abiding and polite rather than rights-bearing, tolerant, and multicultural). The development of a uniquely Canadian passport is contemporaneous with Canada's separation from the United Kingdom, and the development of the actual form of Canadian citizenship was coincident with the recognition of Canada's independent role in the First World War. Mobility rights are described in the section on "additional rights": "Canadians can live and work anywhere they choose in Canada, and enter and leave the country freely, and apply for a passport" (CIC, 2011: 8). What does it mean for a right to be additional and yet not foundational? This represents a major change from the 2002 document, in which mobility rights are equated with democratic rights, legal rights, equality rights, and the rights of Aboriginal peoples (CIC, 2002: 28). In the remainder of the 2010 document, there is no further mention of passports, mobility, or borders. What the citizenship guide emphasizes are basic human rights that are already guaranteed in the 1948 Universal Declaration of Human Rights, of which Canada is a signatory:

13 (1) Everyone has the right to freedom of movement and residence within the borders of each state.
(2) Everyone has the right to leave any country, including his own, and to return to his country.

However, the guide separates out the human right of entering and leaving and the sovereign prerogative to issue a passport. This royal prerogative has a long history in British common law (Salter, 2003: 12–16), and it demonstrates a fundamental tension identified by Arendt and later Agamben on the paradox of human rights (Arendt, 1973; Agamben, 2000). Though rights adhere to the human, they may only be claimed from a sovereign state (or its proxy, the United Nations High Commission for Refugees, which itself is authorized by the signatory states of its charter). Mobility rights, in this case, do not infringe on the ability and authority of the Canadian sovereign to deny a passport to a citizen, and while this may function to limit the actual ability to be mobile, having the effect of rendering certain Canadian citizens as only mobile in the domestic sphere, it does not limit the right to be mobile. One thinks of post-inquiry Maher Arar: a Canadian citizen with the *right* to move, but one who cannot enjoy those rights because of his presence on the US no-fly list and the absolute inability of the Canadian government to lobby effectively for his removal, despite the clear findings of fact in the Arar inquiry.

Balibar (2002), Walters (2002), Nyers (2006), and others have examined the increasingly prevalent de-citizenship processes. Balibar argues that these processes of *anti*-citizenship are important to study, characterizing them as the repressive supplement to the free movement regime of the Schengen Accord (2002: 78). Walters points to other examples of these proceedings, many of which invoke the discourse of exception and emergency. Citizenship counts as a kind of master signifier in the system of sovereign states; as Arendt argues, it constitutes a right to claim rights (Heuser, 2008). Canadian citizenship represents a right to claim protection of some kind within the context of a society of states from the sovereign government of Canada. In other words, the exercise of Canada's protection of its citizens cannot interfere with the sovereignty of another state. The inscription on the front page of the Canadian passport inscribes precisely this grand dichotomy: the Canadian sovereign asks and requires another foreign sovereign to exercise some duty of care towards the citizen, but the actual services that Canadian passport bearers may invoke from Canada in foreign states are radically limited.[3] Further, the passport does not guarantee the bearer entry into any other country. While there is a right to exit one's own country, there is no right to enter another country.

In the case of Abdurahman Khadr, the rights of mobility for citizens have been radically constrained through the assertion of executive privilege. Having been involved in the Afghani conflict (at a minimum having been arrested by American officials in Kabul and either accused of working with al Qaeda or acting as an informant for the CIA—the story is unclear), Khadr was refused a passport in 2004, which limited the degree to which he could exercise his mobility rights. Passports for everyone remain the possession of the issuing government. The issuance of a passport is a royal prerogative, as is the case in British law. Thus, when Foreign Minister Bill Graham advised the governor general to deny the issuance of a passport for Khadr, despite his legal qualification for one (i.e., he was a citizen, had filled out the appropriate forms, had supporting documentation, and had paid the associated fees), Khadr filed a lawsuit.

In the *Khadr* case, Justice Canada, on behalf of DFAIT, presented two arguments about mobility rights and passports, both of which spoke directly to the issue of the management of population. First, it argued that the issuance of a passport was not a right, but rather a royal prerogative, and that the minister could deny a passport for reasons of national security. The initial judgment found for Khadr, saying that the enabling legislation for Passport Canada did not make this national security exception clear. After an amendment to the legislation, the grounds of national security were available, and Minister Peter MacKay used them to deny Khadr a passport (Passport Canada, 2004). Khadr appealed again to the courts. He argued that the lack of passport restricted his guaranteed mobility rights. Here I think we find the most interesting defence, as it demonstrates the ways in which the management of international population mobility represents a muddying of the inside/outside, domestic/foreign divide. Justice Canada lawyers argued that Khadr's mobility rights were limited to those that could be claimed both in the Canadian constitution, which is internal to Canada, and in the Universal Declaration of Human Rights, which is external. Khadr had a right to leave Canada—for which a passport is not technically necessary—but he had no natural right to enter another country.

There is no corresponding right to enter another country in the Universal Declaration, and so the passport itself could not guarantee his mobility rights. Justice Canada also argued that the national security of Canada was improved by not having Khadr circulate. The issuance and refusal of passports were therefore important tactics in the war on terror. Contemporary reports typify this argument: "It's not only our national security, it's the national security of other countries," a senior government official told the *Globe and Mail*. "And it goes to the integrity and the responsibility that goes with carrying a Canadian passport" (CTV, 2006). Invoking the report of the 9/11 Commission, many believe that terrorist mobility is an important factor in global security, being either facilitated or made more difficult with the issuance or withholding of passports. Thus, the double argument is to assert that the right to mobility is not related to the passport but that the actual practices of global mobility do require a passport. Thus, it is not a right that the individual can claim; rather, it is an effective defence against mobility. Even if this case is, for the moment, exceptional, the selective issuance of passports—regardless of citizenship—for national security reasons indicates a way that the sovereign state is reasserting its ability and capacity to manage global mobility. The issuance of passports, then, is a site for the construction of citizens. The issuance and refusal of passports were therefore important tactics in the war on terror.

This section has argued that citizenship procedures entail more than simply domestic policies, but are derivative of the sovereign state's claim to act on behalf of a population in order to protect that population, and its claim to protect national security by influencing the global mobility regime. Some citizens are safe, productive, and docile and some are dangerous in this reading, and the legal entitlement to citizenship cannot interfere with the state's absolute right to protect itself. Citizenship policies—particularly regarding the extension and withdrawal of citizenship's chief benefits—the right to claim rights—mark a foundational domestic/foreign policy for the securitization of the Canadian and alien population. The right to claim rights does not have a necessary connection to the territory for which those rights are being claimed, because Canadians are subject to a rights-obstruction anti-citizenship policy at home and through passport and refugee policies. We can also substantiate a rights-obstruction culture at the border itself (Salter, 2008a). The border is a crucial site for these inclusionary/exclusionary practices.

Borders

The administration of borders, and the capacity of a state to police its boundaries and its population, is one of the primary political functions. It is a primary marker of sovereignty, and I would argue is the focus of one of the primary foreign policies (Salter, 2009). Border policies face two increasing pressures: volume of border transactions and a heightened sense of threat from individuals. Rather than states, individuals and networks of individuals are currently considered the chief way that border security will be "penetrated." The most important penetration of the

Canadian border is no longer Soviet bombers crossing the Distant Early Warning (DEW) Line in the Arctic, but individuals infiltrating across the quotidian border, as demonstrated by the knee-jerk reaction of the American government to close the US-Canada border immediately after the 9/11 attacks. The creation of the "smart" border policy illustrates the utility of the IPS School approach, which focuses on bureaucratic fields (Kitchen, 2004; Coté-Boucher, 2008; Muller, 2009).

First, the smart border, both in discourse and in practice, was the result of negotiations between the Canadian and US governments. While the idea of applying a risk-management approach (focusing most of the security resources on those who are known to be risky or unknown and facilitating the known to be less risky) had been circulating within the Canadian government, it was the political capital made possible by the 9/11 attacks that provided the opening to convince the United States to engage in these negotiations. Thus, the border is both a domestic and a foreign policy that is framed according to domestic and international drivers for both domestic and international audiences.

Second, the suite of policies that were implemented under the banner of smart borders entailed the enlisting of commercial entities and even individuals to facilitate security border practices. While the NEXUS and FAST ("free and secure trade") programs predated 9/11 and the adoption of the Smart Border Declaration and the Smart Border Accord, they were identified as "best practices" by both the American and Canadian governments. In the FAST program, suppliers and shipping companies apply for partnership with the government and agree to adhere to a set of security regulations—enforcing government regulations on themselves—and are rewarded with facilitated border crossing. Similarly, the NEXUS program, which is an expansion of the INSPASS and CANPASS programs, allows for the facilitation of travellers at the border (shorter queues and fewer questions) who submit to greater security screening and biometric identification. This supports the Foucauldian analyses of power, prevalent in the IPS School, that focus on the kinds of flows that are facilitated as much as on those circuits that are halted or misdirected (O'Connor and de Lint, 2009). **Smart borders** *facilitate* certain kinds of movements by certain kinds of subjects as much as they inhibit or channel other kinds of movements by other kinds of subjects.

There has emerged a bureaucratic consensus that risk management works for border policy as well, although initially risk management was used as a domestic framework for managing the unexpected in terms of industrial accidents, social insurance, or environmental regulation (Amoore, 2006; Salter, 2008b; Muller, 2009). Low-risk, known travellers are expedited; high-risk, unknown travellers are given additional scrutiny. A risk management strategy serves the need for efficient and minimalist government in promoting trade and international exchange, as well as the need to provide national security. One of the specific tactical policies that this chapter will focus on is the Canadian implementation of offshore border controls. This is a wider trend involving the delocalization of the border (Andreas, 2003; Vaughan-Williams, 2008), and indeed one with historical precedents. Canada has participated in the American preclearance program since the 1950s, although its participation has seen a physical change in the past 10 years with the construction of American border posts on Canadian territory. The odd situation of American preclearance areas constructed inside Canadian airports illuminates a real aporia, or gap, in contemporary theories of sovereignty and Canada's attendant foreign policy (Hillier, 2010). Canada has undertaken agreements that allow these spaces, indemnify the agents of the American government from income tax or prosecution, but do not speak about legitimacy, authority, or process. For example, the Canadian-US Preclearance Agreement permits this site but makes no claim about law: the decisions made by American officials on Canadian soil are entirely under American law. There is no way to appeal to a Canadian judge for decisions made by American government actors. With logic similar to the *Khadr* case, the decisions by American officials are representations of sovereign decisions that are entirely deterritorialized—or alienated from American territory—in these preclearance areas. American officials argue that while this preclearance allows for aircraft and their passengers to be treated as "domestic" once within the United States, the US retains the absolute right to re-examine those individuals at the port of entry. In essence, the border decision gets rewritten as a technical issue of the coding of flights. Where is the border in this situation?

As Andreas and others note, we can identify a global trend towards the delocalization of borders. That is to say, the vital decision to allow individuals entry into Canada or to deny them entry (and indeed the right to have rights) is made before they arrive at the physical/legal/geographical frontier. Of course, with the increasing importance of global air travel, we will have anticipated that the border to the world is *in practice* at airports, which are almost never at territorial thresholds. But, more than this, decisions about mobility are made through indirect mechanisms, such as visa, citizenship, or refugee policy.

The focus of the smart border is equally facilitation and security. Operating under a neo-liberal logic of efficiency, a managerial model of best governmental practices, and a security logic of risk management, smart borders promise to focus scarce governmental resources on making good judgments at the border. So, when the vast majority of border crossers are known to be unproblematic and travellers themselves are enlisted to help with this sorting, then the full weight of the border examination should fall on those who are known to be problematic, or unknown. Thus, border security resources are devoted to surveillance and to intelligence, because knowledge production becomes a primary function of the border: the border becomes a machine to create knowledge so that it can function as a filter. As a consequence, pre-emption and precaution become the dominant modes of pre-knowing and preventing (if not deterring) mobility; they are ways of pushing the decision out of the moment of decision, both in time and space (Aradau and van Munster, 2007; Amoore and de Goede, 2008; de Goede, 2012). We can see this in the placement of border intelligence officers in source airports and in the use of carrier sanctions. While I was going through Charles de Gaulle (CDG) Airport in Paris recently, my travel documents were checked more (twice) by subcontractors for Air Canada than they were by the French authorities (once)—at least visibly. The risk scoring that takes place through the Advanced Passenger Information/ Passenger Name Record occurs backstage (Salter, 2010; Hobbing, 2010). It is clear from research by Amoore and de Goede (2008) that the algorithms used in the American and British contexts have been programmed by private actors, but there is little public information about how the Canada Border Services Agency has obtained its risk-scoring software. Why would Air Canada as a commercial enterprise engage in document policing? Canada, like many other countries, has imposed carrier sanctions such that an airline company is fined if it transports illegal migrants to Canada. Thus, over and above its border-policing role, or rather not just through meeting its security obligations under French and Canadian regulation, Air Canada comes to have an economic reason/justification/mode for checking documents. In the case of Air Canada at CDG, the responsibility was subcontracted to a large-scale private security firm. Border policy is consequently intimately domestic and foreign, applicable to both Canadians and foreigners, on Canadian and foreign territories, enacted by private and public actors.

The logic of this foreign policy—according to both neo-liberal and security logic— is for as many decisions as possible to be made, preferably in places where rights cannot be claimed. The refusal of a visa; the "no-go" message to the airline check-in attendant through the no-fly list; the examination by a border guard of identity documents in foreign airports, ports, or railway stations—these are all done without recourse to immediate appeal. Often, the decision-maker is obscured from the appellant. If one is prevented from boarding a Canada-bound flight, for example, by an airline employee, the prohibited traveller is referred to a toll-free telephone number at Transport Canada, not traditionally understood as a security agency. Transport Canada makes decisions based on intelligence and analysis from other agencies, such Citizenship and Immigration Canada, Canadian Security Intelligence Service, Communications Security Establishment Canada, and the Royal Canadian Mounted Police (RCMP). Pushing these decisions away from the border and towards non-governmental actors is more efficient and more secure because the capacity for turbulence (i.e., the claiming of rights) is limited with the latter. To make facilitation and security work—to make the border "smart"—entails the cooperation of travel agents and airline companies, airports and cities, passport agencies and international standards organizations, intelligence agencies and privately run security companies. The field of border practices far exceeds the domestic/foreign or the government/private sector divides.

The next section will look at more indirect ways of controlling, or, in the lexicon of the field, managing global mobility flows.

Mobility

Visas are a similarly productive site for analysis: they represent policies framed in relation to both domestic and international drivers for the consumption of both domestic and international audiences. Unless there is a specific, bilateral visa-waiver agreement, foreign nationals require prima facie approval to journey to and stay in or immigrate to Canada. Visas do not guarantee entry, but they are a kind of meta-claim—they represent preliminary permission by the Canadian government to make a claim. Within this framework of risk management, the visa system requires that the foreign policy bureaucracy can negotiate with local authorities and other Canadian departments to make judgments about identity claims and the requirements or needs of the Canadian population, whether these requirements are framed in terms of tourist dollars, specialist labour, multiculturalism, or security. Canada currently does its visa-processing in-house, but this does not take into consideration the impact of the legal community, both in Canada and in the source countries, and other satellite actors, including immigration consultancies, domestic and foreign chambers of commerce, universities and colleges, professional agencies, and so on. In this section, I want to focus on the imposition of new visa requirements in 2009 and the Balanced Refugee Reform Act of 2010 (CIC, 2010).

In 2009 the Canadian government imposed new visa restrictions on the Czech Republic and Mexico; this was notable because the prevailing trend has been towards visa-free travel. The Czech Republic and Mexico both had their visa-waiver agreement halted. Mexico is a significant trade and tourism partner of Canada's, and the Czech Republic is part of the EU and a signatory of the Schengen Accord, an incredibly important agreement for Canadian business and tourism. The justification for the revocation of the visa waiver was crucial. Minister Kenney argued that because most asylum seekers were coming from these two countries and their numbers were rapidly increasing, it was necessary, in the name of efficiency and fairness, to impose a visa that would provide a prima facie way for the Canadian consular staff to make decisions about the likelihood of an asylum claim. This argument was extraordinary.

What was the logic at the heart of this move? Between the visa-waiver period and the reimposition of visa requirements, there was no change in the *proportion* of asylum claims granted by the Immigration and Refugee Board. Because the proportion of asylum claims had not changed, despite the huge change in the number of claimants from Mexico and the Czech Republic, we can conclude that the issue was a rise in fraud. Whether there were 300 or 3,000 claims by Czech Roma, to make the clear case, 30 per cent were accepted in both 2008 and 2009. The increase in raw numbers did not speak to an increase in the proportion of fraud. This also insulated the Immigration and Refugee Board from any political criticism that they were changing the basic standards by which they judged the claims before them. Thus, the Canadian attempt to manage mobility through the imposition of new visa regimes was not about changes in the sense of substantive justice.

In fact, the appeal by the minister was made on the grounds of procedural justice: asylum seekers from visa-waiver countries were "queue-jumping." With the system being clogged up with a larger number of fraudulent or abandoned claims, making it less efficient, "real" asylum seekers from refugee camps and other clearly abject places were waiting longer for their claims to be heard. Applying for refugee status through the regular procedure, and in particular through the UN High Commission for Refugees, validated the claim of the deserving refugee. Again, we see that it is difficult to disentangle foreign policy and domestic policy. Canada's refugee adjudication system, it was argued, was overwhelmed by the sheer numbers of dropped or fraudulent claims (again, not the proportion, but the numbers), and so it was necessary to decrease the number of raw claims to be adjudicated. We can note that there was a slippage between claims that were not found to be credible and those that were abandoned. While Minister Kenney assumed that a high proportion of the dropped or abandoned claims were due to fraud, it could not be any kind of justice that would retroactively equate a failed asylum claim with fraud.

However, in this way, the appearance of substantive justice reappeared through the back door: the only way that the Canadian government could choose to not hear—to prevent—certain claims from being made, before they were even adjudicated, would be because there was a distinction between "real" and "false" refugees. Refugees from Mexico and the Czech Republic, Kenney argued, were not *real* refugees. The Mexican migrants were often fleeing a combination of drug violence and corruption; Czech Roma had citizenship in a European state. In Paris, the minister said, "I find it hard to believe that the Czech Republic is an island of persecution in Europe" (Canwest, 2009). The new legislation of 2010 introduced a new category— safe country of origin. Claims from these countries would be viewed with scepticism. While there would be a robust appeal process, the assumption was that these claims could be processed more quickly and the failed claimants resettled. This mirrored the EU asylum rule, the so-called Aznar Protocol. Canada has made the argument that there are certain countries whose citizens may claim asylum, but it is unlikely that the claim will be well-founded. Plainly flying in the face of the findings of the Immigration and Refugee Board of Canada in thousands of cases, this policy makes clear a new strategy in global mobility management. Nationals from developed and hence safe countries have a relatively free access to countries around the world (along the circuits of global capital and travel infrastructure); refugees are free to go only if the destination country accepts their claim, but by definition they cannot go home. However, now there is a global middle class of countries that fail to protect their own citizens but do not qualify as failed states whose nationals cannot move with great ease.

The public discourse on the Citizenship and Immigration Canada website reflects this hierarchical moral geopolitics. The good refugees described in the section "Canada Welcomes Refugees" have spent time in camps in protracted refugee situations; they are on the run from their own government, live in fear of the host government (i.e., they cannot integrate into whatever state is there), and are entirely at the disposal of the UN High Commissioner for Refugees (UNHCR). These are deserving refugees—placidly there. They are abject refugees—with bare biological life—who are governed not as political subjects or as rights-bearing individuals. But, crucially, they are not rights-claiming refugees, or rather they only claim rights of procedural justice, not of substantive justice. I want to make the argument that those asylum seekers who come from a country in which there is a rights discourse, who are able to invoke their rights, but who are not protected by that state indict the ability of the state to protect them as individuals, and that is a much more dangerous claim. The claim of rights-bearing asylum seekers is more dangerous to Canada because it marks them as individuals, as being politically-conscience, capable of saying "J'accuse." The abject asylum seekers from the camps, represented as lacking political agency, are described as more reserved, more polite, more patient, and consequently more docile.

It is important to note the history of these tactics of population management—not just in Foucault, but in Malthus. Governments found it useful, at the start of the eighteenth and continuing in the nineteenth century, to constitute national populations—and particularly to understand and consequently govern them through statistics and other kinds of indirect knowledge (Foucault, 2008: 319). The object of governmental rule, in this biopolitical model, is a set of populations, not a set of peoples or communities. The management of populations is determined by statistics that constitute—that create—particular communities, and then make possible communities that take and speak to these aggregates and their data. The target population could be the ill, the perverse, the criminal, the poor, or the mobile. Within a liberal framework, the government feels pressure to not intervene in every moment or action, it wants to govern as little as possible. Malthus produced one of the first and most important historical expressions of this management of populations. In his *Essay on the Principle Population* and indeed in his other work, the poor are defined through statistics and divided even amongst themselves as deserving and undeserving, with differential mobility rights (Malthus, 1973). The deserving poor are described as the sick, the disabled, the old—deserving of state aid; the undeserving poor are simply lazy—undeserving of state support. The creation of these categories renders the subjects able or unable to receive the benefits of local authorities and the state, and indeed, with the Poor Laws, the categories determine whether or not the subjects can move to find work in other parishes. The undeserving are pushed into the market with no state support (workhouses); the deserving are either supported *in situ* (alms houses) or sent to other locales for work. This method of separating the underclass into deserving and undeserving persists in the contemporary refugee regime. Governments argue that deserving refugees are those who are persecuted and entirely without the protection of any persons. And, more importantly, they wait. There. Somewhere else. Deserving refugees follow the policies of the state or the UNHCR, before which they claim rights. Undeserving asylum seekers use false documents and make their claim "here" at the border or at the airport.

In the same way that the bureaucratic process could quantify and thus categorize the deserving and undeserving, Canada is attempting to generate categories of deserving and undeserving populations that would make the asylum-claiming population easier to manage. Canada, in its most recent legislation, the Balanced Refugee Reform Act (2010), argues that it can connect the issue of refugee claims to countries of origin. This, of course, follows the logic of safe third countries of origin, through which states attempt to deter chain migration and "asylum shopping" (i.e., seeking the best destination either in level of development or in ease of claim adjudication). Thus, if an asylum seeker came from France to England, then the bilateral agreement between the countries would dictate that the asylum claim would be heard in the first stop (this could go either way: by foot, it might be French territory first; by boat, the UK). Particularly in the European case, a network of safe third-country agreements has the effect (and the intention) of pushing asylum claims to the periphery of the EU. Canada has a similar agreement with the United States that, again, in the rhetoric, is beneficial to both. This agreement helps manage the mobile populations precisely by limiting the possible routes of circulation. The safe country of origin operates to restrict particular flows, as there is an inherent assumption that asylum seekers are fraudulent. It is perhaps an inversion of the responsibility to protect: a number of countries accept their responsibility to protect and, as such, represent a sovereignty in which Canada would not intervene—even through individual members of the population.

For the Canadian government, this idea of a safe country of origin represents an attempt to manage countries that fail, but are not failed. The governments of these countries, like that of the Czech Republic and Mexico, palpably and clearly cannot protect certain citizens—for example, the Roma, who are subject to violent, racist extremism, often aided and abetted by the authorities; and in Mexico, citizens who are caught up in violent criminal networks and subject to corrupt security forces.

By prioritizing *real* refugees who are understood as coming from long-term displaced refugee situations or from failed states—as evidenced by large Somali and Rwandan refugee communities in Canada—Canada reinscribes its role in an absolute, moral geopolitics: the civilizing mission. Refugees like these can be helped because their sovereign state has collapsed. On the other hand, refugees from states in the EU or from common tourism and trade partners are the ones who challenge the dichotomy between developed Canada and its developing recipients of charity.

Policy of Making Foreign

A tradition of critical foreign policy studies was clearly established by Der Derian (1987), Neumann (1999), and Campbell (1992), who focus on the dynamic creation of national identity through the deployment of "others" in foreign policy. Turenne Sjolander and Smith do the same in this volume by examining what is signified by the invocation of "Canadian" values. In contradistinction to the discursive emphasis in these classic works, this chapter has attempted to examine the same dynamic—the separation of those who might claim Canadian citizenship and those who may not claim rights, even the right to asylum—not through popular or elite discourses, but through on-the-ground policies and practices. We are thus as concerned with the application of law as we are with its abandonment— that is, with those who are subject entirely to the law and with those for whom the law is withdrawn (Nancy, 1993: 44). The ban is the function of the withdrawal of law: the suspension of the right to have rights. This naked expression of fundamental state power can be seen in each of the cases of Canadian foreign policy towards asylum or passport issuance, no matter how masked in administrative or bureaucratic language. The threatened withdrawal of citizenship from dual citizens who do not demonstrate "substantial ties," the offshoring of border decisions into spaces of administrative discretion, and the pre-emptive limiting of refugee claimants through visa policy—these represent a withdrawal of Canadian law, not just from Canada's own citizens or from asylum seekers, but also from the society of states. These abandoned populations are deferred for reasons of security and efficiency but constitute a radical rewriting of Canadian policy that does not engage with the foreign, but rather renders specific populations foreign and consequently denies them access to the right to have rights.

At its root, the division of security policies into domestic and foreign categories is misguided, particularly in the administration of populations through the language of rights. The ideas, practices, and agencies simply do not track cleanly as either national or international: citizenship and mobility policies are not enforced in solely national or foreign spaces by domestic agents, allies, or subcontractors, and mobility is facilitated or prevented by an array of public and private actors. To characterize Canadian foreign policy as internationalist reinforces a state centricism that is not borne out by security practices. Similarly, as much as Canada's foreign policy is "rights promoting," we also identified policies that were "rights obstructing," such as safe third-country agreements and designated countries of origin. In practice, we see that sub-national state agents and their non-state cognates are conceiving and enacting security policies across particular professional fields (such as border security, money-laundering financial tracking, or refugee adjudication). These practices do not reflect an isomorphism between territory, authority, and rights (Sassen, 2006), but reflect common professional fields for the management of security problems. The investigation of actual "international" security practices demonstrates the emptiness of the dichotomy between domestic and foreign policies.

This chapter has demonstrated the utility of the Bourdieusian-inspired IPS School, which focuses on fields. By starting with the practices of the population management done in the name of security, we see that citizenship, passports, visas, and borders all evade the simple dichotomy of domestic/foreign policies or private/ public actors. Further, the management practices indicate that as scholars, we must use a model of power that includes a sensitivity to productive and repressive forms of the conditions of possibility. I express a concern about the securitization of citizenship and the dispersal of sovereign power into spaces that are inhospitable to rights. In particular, I use the cases of the Czech and Mexican visas to demonstrate the importance of these indirect forms of control and the global moral geopolitical order that they inaugurate. The issues of mobility are profoundly political, as they determine the boundaries of the Canadian population and structure the mobility of global populations. They must be integrated into serious discussions of Canadian foreign policy.

Key Terms

biopolitics
field
global mobility regime

International Political Sociology (IPS) School
smart borders

Study Questions

1. What areas of policy transcend the domestic/international boundary, in practice, in theory, or in target?
2. Is citizenship policy a domestic, international, or global issue?
3. How can Canada best balance the need for procedural fairness and its international human rights obligations in the refugee process?
4. What are other examples of Canada's "rights obstructing," rather than "rights promoting," policies?
5. What are the main "thinking tools" of the International Political Sociology School?

Notes

1 This chapter demonstrates that the boundaries of domestic and foreign policy are blurred in terms of the policies themselves, the actors, the objects, and the space of their enactment. I would argue that the rhetoric of "internationalism" plays very little part in the discourse of citizenship, borders, or mobility.

2 "Sociologie politique de l'internationale" is a phrase that resonates in French international relations. It became "International Political Sociology" when translated into English and subsequently institutionalized as an academic journal (although a better translation might be "political sociology of the international").

3 Consular Officials Provide the Following Services: *In emergencies*
   • Assist in arranging an evacuation in the event of war, civil unrest, or a natural disaster, as a last resort ($).
   • Arrange help in a medical emergency by providing you with a list of local doctors and hospitals.
   • Arrange for a medical evacuation if a necessary treatment is not available locally ($).
   • Comfort and assist victims of robbery, sexual assault, or other violence.
   • Provide assistance in cases of missing persons or if a child has been abducted to another country.

When legal issues arise
- Provide you with a list of local lawyers.
- Provide you with sources of information about local laws and regulations.
- Seek to ensure that you are treated fairly under a country's laws if you are arrested or detained (see our publication *A Guide for Canadians Imprisoned Abroad*).
- Notarize documents ($).

(DFAIT, 2010)

References

Abrahamsen, Rita, and Michael C. Williams. 2011. *Security beyond the State: Private Security in International Politics*. Cambridge: Cambridge University Press.

Agamben, Giorgio. 2000. "Beyond Human Rights." In Vincenzo Binetti and Cesare Casarino, trans., *Means without End: Notes on Politics*. Minneapolis: University of Minnesota Press, 15–26.

Amoore, Louise. 2006. "Biometric Borders: Governing Mobilities in the War on Terror." *Political Geography* 25, 3: 336–51.

Amoore, Louise, and Marieke de Goede. 2008. "Transactions after 9/11: The Banal Face of the Preemptive Strike." *Transactions of the Institute of British Geographers* 33, 2: 173–85.

Andreas, Peter. 2003. "Redrawing the Line: Borders and Security in the 21st Century." *International Security* 28, 2: 78–112.

Aradau, Claudia, and Rens van Munster. 2007. "Governing Terrorism through Risk: Taking Precautions, (un)Knowing the Future." *European Journal of International Relations* 13, 1: 89–115.

Arendt, Hannah. 1973. "The Decline of the Nation-State and the End of the Rights of Man." In Hannah Arendt, *The Origins of Totalitarianism*, 267–302. New York: Harvest/HBJ Books.

Balibar, Étienne. 2002. *Politics and the Other Scene*. London: Verso.

Bigo, Didier. 2001. "Internal and External Security(ies): The Möbius Ribbon." In Mathias Albert, David Jacobson, and Yosef Lapid, eds, *Identities, Borders and Orders*. Minneapolis: University of Minnesota Press, 91–117.

———. 2008. "Globalized (In)security: The Field and the Ban-Opticon." In Didier Bigo and Anastassia Tsoukala, eds, *Terror, Insecurity and Liberty: Illiberal Practices of Liberal Regimes after 9/11*. New York: Routledge, 10–49.

Bigo, Didier, and Elspeth Guild, eds. 2005. *Controlling Frontiers: Free Movement into and within Europe*. Aldershot: Ashgate.

Brown, Wendy. 2010. *Walled States, Waning Sovereignty*. New York: Zone Books.

Browne, Simone. 2005. "Getting Carded: Border Control and the Politics of Canada's Permanent Resident Card." *Citizenship Studies* 9, 4: 423–38.

Campbell, David. 1992. *Writing Security: United States Foreign Policy and the Politics of Identity*. Minneapolis: University of Minnesota Press.

CANWEST. 2009. "Canada Flooded with Czech Roma Refugee Claims." 15 April. At http://www.canada.com/news/Canada+flooded+with+Czech+Roma+refugee+claims/1499804/story.html.

c.a.s.e. collective. 2006. "Critical Approaches to Security in Europe: A Networked Manifesto." *Security Dialogue* 37, 4: 443–87.

CIC (Citizenship and Immigration Canada). 2002. *A Look at Canada*. Ottawa: Minister of Public Works and Government Services Canada. At http://dsp-psd.pwgsc.gc.ca/Collection/Ci51-61-2001E.pdf.

———. 2010. Bill C-11: *The Balanced Refugee Reform Act*.

———. 2011. *Discover Canada: The Rights and Responsibility of Citizenship*. Study guide. Ottawa: Minister of Public Works and Government Services Canada. At http://www.cic.gc.ca/english/resources/publications/discover/index.asp#pdf.

Côté-Boucher, Karine. 2008. "The Diffuse Border: Intelligence-Sharing, Control and Confinement along Canada's Smart Border." *Surveillance and Society* 5, 2: 142–65.

CTV. 2006. "Ottawa Again Denies Khadr's Passport Application." 24 August. At http://www.ctv.ca/CTVNews/TopStories/20060830/khadr_application_060830/.

de Goede, Marieke. 2012. *Speculative Security: The Politics of Pursuing Terrorist Monies*. Minneapolis: University of Minnesota Press.

Der Derian, James. 1987. *On Diplomacy: A Genealogy of Western Estrangement*. Oxford: Blackwell.

DFAIT (Department of Foreign Affairs and International Trade). 2010. "Who We Are and What We Do." At http://www.voyage.gc.ca/about_a-propos/role-eng.asp.

Foucault, Michel. 2008. *The Birth of Biopolitics. Lectures at the Collège de France, 1978–79*. Trans. Graham Burchell. New York: Palgrave Macmillan.

Heuser, Stefan. 2008. "Is There a Right to Have Rights? The Case of Asylum." *Ethical Theory and Moral Practice* 11, 1: 3–13.

Hillier, Harry. 2010. "Airports as Borderlands: American Preclearance and Transitional Spaces in Canada." *Journal of Borderlands Studies* 25, 3&4: 19–30.

Hobbing, Peter. 2010. "Tracing Terrorists: The European Union–Canada Agreement on Passenger Name Record (PNR) Matters." In Mark B. Salter, ed., *Mapping Transatlantic Security Relations: The EU, Canada, and the War on Terror*, London: Routledge, 73–97.

Huysmans, Jef. 2006. *Politics of Insecurity: Fear, Migration and Asylum in the EU*. London: Routledge.

Isin, Engin F., and Greg M. Nielsen, eds. 2008. *Acts of Citizenship*. London: Zed Books.

Isin, Engin F., Peter Nyers, and Bryan S. Turner, eds. 2008. *Citizenship between Past and Future*. New York: Routledge.

Jeandesboz, Julien. 2010. "Logiques et pratiques de contrôle et de surveillance des frontières de l'Union européenne. " In Amandine Scherrer, Emmanuel-Pierre Guittet, and Didier Bigo, eds, *Mobilités sous surveillance: Perspectives croisées UE-Canada*. Montreal: Editions Athena, 149–64.

Kitchen, Veronica. 2004. "Smarter Cooperation in Canada-US Relations?" *International Journal* 59, 3: 693–710.

Koslowski, Rey. 2011. "Global Mobility Regimes: A Conceptual Framework." In Rey Koslowski, ed., *Global Mobility Regimes*. New York: Palgrave Macmillan, 1–25.

Malthus, Thomas R. 1973. *An Essay on the Principle of Population*. Toronto: Dent.

Muller, Benjamin J. 2009. "Borders, Risks, Exclusions." *Studies in Social Justice* 3, 1: 67–78.

Mutlu, Can E. 2011. "A De Facto Cooperation? Increasing Role of the EU on Improved Relations between Georgia and Turkey." *Comparative European Politics* 9, 4–5: 543–61.

Nancy, Jean-Luc.1993. *The Birth to Presence*. Trans. Brian Holmes. Stanford, CA: Stanford University Press.

Neal, Andrew. 2009. "Securitization and Risk at the EU Borders: The Origins of FRONTEX." *Journal of Common Market Studies* 47, 2: 333–56.

Neumann, Iver B. 1999. *Uses of the Other: The "East" in European Identity Formation*. Minneapolis: University of Minnesota Press.

Nyers, Peter. 2006. *Rethinking Refugees: Beyond States of Emergency*. London: Routledge.

———, ed. 2009. *Securitizations of Citizenship*. New York: Routledge.

O'Connor, Daniel, and Willem de Lint. 2009. "Frontier Government: The Folding of the Canada-US Border." *Studies in Social Justice* 3, 1: 39–66.

Passport Canada. 2004. "Order Amending the Canadian Passport Order." 22 September. At http://www.passport.gc.ca/publications/pdfs/order_04_113.pdf.

Rajaram, Prem Kumar, and Carl Grundy-Warr, eds. 2007. *Borderscapes: Hidden Geographies and Politics at Territory's Edge*. Minneapolis: University of Minnesota Press.

Salter, Mark B. 2003. *Rights of Passage: The Passport in International Relations*. Boulder, CO: Lynne Rienner.

———. 2008a. "When the Exception Becomes the Rule: Borders, Sovereignty, Citizenship." *Citizenship Studies* 12, 4: 365–80.

———. 2008b. "Securitization and Desecuritization: Dramaturgical Analysis and the Canadian Aviation Transport Security Authority." *Journal of International Relations and Development* 11, 4: 321–49.

———. 2009. "Canadian Border Policy as Foreign Policy: Security, Policing, Management." In J. Marshall Beier and Lana Wylie, eds, *Canadian Foreign Policy in Critical Perspectives.* Don Mills, ON: Oxford University Press, 72–82.

———. 2010. "The North Atlantic Field of Aviation Security." In Mark B. Salter, ed., *Mapping Transatlantic Security Relations: The EU, Canada, and the War on Terror.* London: Routledge, 60–72.

Sassen, Saskia. 2006. *Territory, Authority, Rights: From Medieval to Global Assemblages.* Princeton, NJ: Princeton University Press.

Vaughan-Williams, Nick. 2008. "Borderwork beyond Inside/Outside? Frontex, the Citizen-Detective and the War on Terror." *Space and Polity* 12, 1: 63–79.

Walters, William. 2002. "Deportation, Expulsion, and the International Police of Aliens." *Citizenship Studies* 6, 3: 265–92.

———. 2008. "Anti-Policy and Anti-Politics: Critical Reflections on Certain Schemes to Govern Bad Things." *European Journal of Cultural Studies* 11, 3: 267–88.

10 | Where Is Internationalism? Canada-US Relations in the Context of the Global and the Local

Veronica M. Kitchen

At first glance, it seems odd to look for internationalism in the Canada–United States relationship.* We usually think of the relationship as bilateral, between two sovereign states, and continental, between two political units sharing a geographic space. Internationalism seems to be about looking outward to the world; Canada's relationship with the United States seems fundamentally to be about looking inward to its own interests and to those of its most important ally, trading partner, and neighbour. This is particularly true when it comes to national security. Maintaining security of Canadian borders seems to be most at odds with internationalism's outward focus. If we can show internationalism in the Canadian-American security relationship, then, it would constitute strong evidence for the continued existence of internationalism under Stephen Harper's government. Is it possible to reconcile the seeming incompatibility of internationalism with the bilateral North American security relationship? With some shifts in thinking, it is.

Internationalism, as presented in the Canadian foreign policy literature, comprises two essential elements: first, multilateralism as the preferred form for international action and, second, enlightened self-interest or an awareness of the interests of the international community as the preferred ethical stance towards the world. Neither of these precepts must necessarily inhere to states; there is no reason they cannot apply to the multiple actors who directly engage in foreign policy or foreign policy-like activities in North America. Thus, we should not reject the idea of finding internationalism in the Canadian-American relationship during Stephen Harper's tenure as prime minister. As responsibility for security has shifted to include provinces, cities, and other front-line actors, many new initiatives have been both multilateral and designed to improve the lives of North Americans. However, these were tempered by the **securitization** of everyday space, which is ultimately bad for society, and by the American focus on the war on

* I am grateful to Jessica Russell, Caroline Dunton, and Rhys Machold for research assistance.

terrorism, which constrains Canadian foreign policy options. The mixed record on internationalism in security in North America, then, can be attributed more to the post-9/11 security climate than to Prime Minister Harper's policies.

Deconstructing Internationalism

In a review of the literature on internationalism in Canadian foreign policy, Don Munton and Tom Keating trace the rise of the concept of internationalism to the writing of John Holmes. While Holmes never formally defined the concept, Munton and Keating distill his vision of internationalism to "being aware of the interests of others, being prudent, being pragmatic, seeing realities, avoiding vehemence and hysteria, accepting paradox and contradiction, accepting limitations on sovereignty and independence, and, perhaps above all, being constructive, avoiding absolutes, and, if possible, doing it all multilaterally" (Munton and Keating, 2001: 531). Munton and Keating themselves argue that "active participation, multilateralism, commitment and pursuit of a common good [of the whole]" define internationalism (531). Nossal, Roussel, and Paquin have recently described internationalism as characterized by five elements: the *responsibility* to play a constructive role in international affairs; the pursuit of *multilateralism* as a way of maintaining global order; participation in *international institutions* because they embody multilateralism; the willingness to enter *formal commitments* according to one's abilities (functionalism); and the *reinforcement of, and respect for, international law* (Nossal, Roussel, and Paquin, 2011: 136).

These definitions of internationalism are all state-centric (see Smith, chapter 12). Each author assumes—with some justification—that foreign policy is the purview of states. Similar to other definitions of internationalism, they also define an ethical obligation to others beyond our borders as central to the concept (Rioux and Hay, 1998: 69; Pratt, 1989: 13). In some cases, authors specify the content of this ethical obligation as including altruism, the active promotion of the international community and of the United Nations (Riddell-Dixon, 2006: 152), the provision of aid (Pratt, 1989: 15), the promotion of human security (Bernard, 2006), and a refusal to focus on trade and economics at the expense of other priorities (Rioux and Hay, 1998: 67).

Internationalism in Canadian foreign policy is closely related to the concepts of functionalism, middlepowerdom, and multilateralism. When modified by each of these, internationalism describes a set of foreign policy behaviours as well as a particular ethical stance. Internationalism modified by functionalism holds that states should have responsibility in international affairs (and in the UN in particular) proportionate to their capacity to contribute on any given issue (Riddell-Dixon, 2006). Middle-power internationalism is similarly conscious of the more limited capacity of smaller states in the international system (Bernard, 2006), but it prescribes foreign policy behaviours such as acting as catalysts and facilitators to bring states together to solve global problems (Cooper, 1997), engage in mediation and diplomacy (Painchaud, 1966: 31), and work towards conflict resolution (Chapnick, 2000: 201). Like internationalism, middle-power diplomacy implies a global responsibility. Stephen Lewis called the middle powers "that whole grab bag of countries that verge collectively on angelic perfection" (Lewis and Wurst, 1991: 547). Multilateralism is also inherent in most definitions of internationalism. It refers to agreements made between three or more states, but it also carries John Ruggie's stronger meaning, where such agreements are based on generalized principles of conduct independent of the interests of any of the contributing parties (Ruggie, 1993: 11).

At its most fundamental, then, internationalism requires a structural commitment to multilateralism and an ethical commitment to promoting the good of global society over one's own narrowly defined self-interest. Neither of these tenets must necessarily apply to states. States, provinces, and even cities practise **paradiplomacy** by forging their own foreign policies separate from those of the central government (Aldecoa and Keating, 1999). In Canada, the government of Quebec has long pursued a foreign policy of its own, mostly in areas of provincial jurisdiction. Cities can be part of organizations like the World Mayors Council on Climate Change, and non-central government actors can follow the contents of international treaties when they match their jurisdictions, even if the actors are not party to the treaties (as California did in 2006 when it passed the Global Warming Solutions Act, designed to bring the state into compliance with the Kyoto Protocol, which the United States had not signed). Non-state actors may also independently pursue international affairs in other ways, such as by forming transnational networks with their counterparts in other countries and generating governance that can increase the capacity of national governments (Slaughter, 2005: 52–8). These kinds of transnational relations are important in their own right, not just because of the ways in which they influence foreign policy. If neither structural multilateralism nor altruism and a responsibility beyond borders must, by definition, apply solely to states, it should be theoretically possible to find internationalism in the Canadian-American relationship.

There are two other reasons why internationalism might be fruitfully applied to the Canada-US security relationship. First, Canada's relationship with the United States exists in the context of each state's other global relations, and the continental relationship is influenced by their broader foreign policy interests. The reverse is also true. Patrick Lennox (2009) argues that it is precisely Canada's dual role as the subordinate power in a bilateral relationship and a comparatively small power in the international system that generates the niche-seeking behaviour characteristic of middle-power internationalism. The global war on terrorism, in particular, has profoundly influenced the Canada-US continental relationship.

Second, the study of internationalism and of security in the Canada-US relationship gives us a way of thinking about the **localization of security**. In the post-9/11 era, security has been "rescal[ed], deterritoriali[zed], and reterritoriali[zed]" (Coaffee and Wood, 2006: 503). The rise of international terrorism, combined with the forces of globalization, means that there is little meaningful distinction between domestic and international, or inside and outside (Eriksson and Rhinard, 2009). Threats are portrayed as coming from anywhere, so all spaces must be made secure. Security is increasingly integrated into "everyday" spaces and activities like urban planning, building design, traffic management, and refugee policy (Graham, 2006: 259). Provinces and cities have more responsibility for policy areas that used to look like "foreign" policy, and security policy has infiltrated policy areas that used to be more purely domestic. In the context of a multi-layered relationship where security has been localized, it makes sense to apply concepts like internationalism that have traditionally been applied only to states.

Continentalism and the "Defence against Help" Constraint

Bayless Manning coined the term **intermestic** to describe relations that are "simultaneously, profoundly, and inseparably both domestic and international" (1977: 309), and the word has frequently been applied to the Canadian-American relationship (see, for instance, Hale, 2006). In their book *Power and Interdependence* (1977), Keohane and Nye used Canada and the United States to illustrate a relationship characterized by "complex interdependence"—that is, where relations are connected by multiple interstate, transgovernmental, and transnational channels; where there is no consistent hierarchy among issues; and where military force is not used within the region (1977: 24–5). This interdependence may make achieving internationalism in the field of security difficult because Canadian continental security is so bound up with American security. If American security policy is not internationalist, it makes it more difficult for Canadian security policy to be.

The concept of continentalism lends itself more naturally to the analysis of contemporary Canadian-American relations than internationalism does. Continentalism is the idea that Canada's destiny is inextricably bound up with that of the United States. Nossal, Roussel, and Paquin define continentalism as "a set of ideas about how to advance Canada's interests by shaping the country's relations with the United States and the world" and a concept that acknowledges that "the United States is Canada's most important partner, both economically and geopolitically" (2011: 149). While Canadian foreign and security policy is not dictated by American preferences, it is at least constrained by them (Kitchen and Sasikumar, 2009; Biswas, 2009). Continentalism shows up most often in trade policy, but increasingly in security policy as well (see Massie and Roussel, chapter 3).

The two concepts most often associated with security continentalism are the idea of the Kingston Dispensation and, relatedly, **defence against help**. The Kingston Dispensation, which marks the origin of Canada-US defence cooperation, refers to an informal—but important—agreement struck in 1938, wherein President Roosevelt promised that the United States would "not stand idly by" if Canada were to be attacked and Prime Minister Mackenzie King pledged in return that Canada would do its utmost to protect itself and to protect the United States from an attack originating from Canada (Fortmann and Haglund, 2002). "Defence against help," then, is the idea that Canada must protect itself not to its own standards, but to those of the United States, for fear that otherwise American officials would cross the border and "help" Canada defend itself by enforcing their own standards. After 9/11, the meaning of defence against help shifted as both states became preoccupied with the threat from global terrorism. Now, the nightmare scenario was not Russian nuclear missiles flying over the Arctic, but a terrorist attack on the United States originating in Canada (Fortmann and Haglund, 2002; Charters, 2005).

From the Inside Out: New Actors and Internationalism

While Canada and the United States had long cooperated on matters of national security—most notably through the North American Aerospace Defense Command (NORAD)—this cooperation grew significantly after 9/11, at least partly as a way of managing defence against help by finding ways to maximize both countries' security while preserving Canadian access to the all-important American market. Security cooperation was localized to the front lines as Canada and the United States developed integrated policy initiatives and transnational cooperation between cities and provinces increased. While in some cases these relationships were characterized by internationalism, in others Canadian and American policies undermined internationalism in their attempt to create security.

Post-9/11 policy cooperation in North America has been structured by three major initiatives that attempted to increase security while maintaining the flow of trade. The Smart Border Accords, signed within a few months of the terrorist attacks, contained a series of measures about information sharing, policy coordination, and cooperation between border officials. Many of these initiatives have become mired in politics and bureaucracy over the years. In 2005, the Security and Prosperity Partnership (SPP), a trilateral initiative including Mexico, attempted to extend and reinvigorate the project but was defunct within a few years. In December 2011, President Obama and Prime Minister Harper once against revitalized the project of harmonizing North American security by drafting the Beyond the Border Action Plan, designed to create a continental security perimeter and make "the most ambitious advance in Canada-US relations since the Free Trade Agreement of 1988" (Ibbitson, 2011).

Transnational Actors

Many of the cooperative initiatives undertaken by the Canadian and American governments under the auspices of various cooperative agreements fit neatly into the continentalist paradigm. They clearly prioritize American security, not at the expense of Canadian security, but as an important objective in Canadian foreign policy. However, the initiatives also illustrate how responsibility is shifting to other actors and centres of authority. In many cases, these relationships are transnational, between agencies of the two federal governments. For instance, at the border, Canadians and Americans serve together in Integrated Border Enforcement Teams (IBETs). Originating along the British Columbia–Washington border in the 1990s, the IBET program expanded substantially after 9/11 and now comprises 15 teams in 24 locations along the Canada-US border. Officers from the Canadian Border Services Agency (CBSA) and the Royal Canadian Mounted Police (RCMP) in Canada, and from Customs and Border Protection (CBP), the Coast Guard, and Immigration and Customs Enforcement (ICE) in the United States, work together to "augment the integrity and security of the border by identifying, investigating, and interdicting individuals and organizations that pose a threat to the security of both nations" (IBET Threat Assessment Working Group, 2010).

Since 2009, Canadian and American police officers have participated in the Shiprider program, in which RCMP and US Coast Guard ships are manned by officers from both countries. According to the RCMP, the initiative "removes the international maritime boundary as a barrier to law enforcement" (RCMP, 2010). The RCMP is also operating on American soil in a new "Operational Integration Center" outside Detroit to collect, analyze, and share intelligence data related to border security. A full-time RCMP intelligence analyst has been seconded to the program (RCMP, 2011). The Beyond the Border Action Plan proposes the deployment by summer 2012 of two pilot projects for cross-border law enforcement; these initiatives would expand on the Shiprider program, allowing for integrated law enforcement and intelligence teams in which American and Canadian police officers would work together in the same unit on American and Canadian soil (Government of Canada, 2011: 25).

The Beyond the Border Action Plan also advocates developing a "shared understanding of the threat environment" and extensive information sharing, including tracking and sharing entry and exit data for North American citizens and third-country nationals (Government of Canada, 2011: 11); notifying the American government when someone on their security watch list attempts to enter Canada (10); and "promoting increased informal sharing of law enforcement intelligence, information, and evidence ... consistent with the domestic laws of each country" (4). Most of these programs are in their infancy, and few will grow or survive without a political champion. However, if they are implemented, they will be important despite the fact that we do not usually consider transnational relations to be part of a state's foreign policy. The Smart Border Accords, SPP, and Beyond the Border agreements have all been popularly labelled as creating a "security perimeter." However, this is a misnomer. The goal of the initiatives is not to push the border out to the edges of the continent, but rather to integrate security and policing functions in both countries. As security has been localized, the transnational security initiatives have become more important in and of themselves because they directly shape the governance of security as it is experienced by individual Canadians and Americans.

Sub-national Governments

Responsibility for continental security has also been localized to the governments of provinces and cities. The Ontario Provincial Police (OPP)—operated by the province of Ontario, not the government of Canada—is also seconded to the Michigan Operational Integration Center. Federally, Canada and the United States exchange RCMP and FBI officers through the Liaison Officer and Legal Attaché programs that place officers at embassies and consulates, but the New York City Police Department (NYPD) also has a liaison officer posted in the Toronto Police Service—an example of cooperation not between two states, but between two cities. Canadian provinces and American states have also been cooperating (mostly since before 9/11) in regional emergency preparedness and counter-terrorism organizations, agreements, and exercises. Not all of these include the involvement of federal agencies. In the Great Lakes region, CREMAC (Central Regional Emergency Management Advisory Committee) is in the process of finalizing an agreement that would pool emergency personnel and responders, allowing them to respond to natural disasters, terrorist attacks, or other emergencies on both sides of the border (McCarter, 2011). Similar agreements exist in the Pacific northwest, the Prairies, and the eastern states and provinces. In August of 2011, the US Coast Guard hosted a major exercise involving a terrorist attack on a boat in the Detroit River and the subsequent injuries and oil spill. Approximately 65 Canadian and American actors participated, including the City of Detroit and the Windsor Police, who took on the coordinating role for the Canadian side of the simulation (Pearson, 2011). On a somewhat smaller scale, agreements are often reached between cities along the border (such as Port Huron and Sarnia or Detroit and Windsor, both on the Ontario-Michigan border, or Lacolle and Rouses Point, on the Quebec–New York border), allowing whichever fire or ambulance service is closest to attend to the incident—no matter on which side of the border it occurs (Velasquez III: 2011; CBC News, 2007b).

Continental Internationalism?

If we accept the premise that these transnational and sub-national actors are foreign policy actors in their own right, and not just contributors to the official foreign policy of the state, then we should be able to attribute internationalism to them. The cooperative agreements described above are clearly structurally multilateral. While they only involve representatives from two countries, they involve multiple agencies, provinces, states, and cities, each of which may have competing goals and priorities. These agreements testify to sub-national units' ability to make formal agreements and follow them, and clearly accept limitations on sovereignty and independence—both of which are considered important elements of internationalism (Nossal, Roussel, and Paquin, 2011: 136; Munton and Keating, 2001: 531). The record is mixed, however, when it comes to trying to determine whether these initiatives also value altruism or other values associated with internationalism. We know about the Memorandums of Understanding (MOUs) on emergency services because they make the newspapers when they fail, as happened when a building burned down because the fire crew was delayed at the border or when an ambulance was detained when the border guard asked to see the patient's passport (CBC News, 2007b). In towns like Stanstead, Quebec, and Derby Line, Vermont, where the border runs through homes as well as through a library and theatre that used to be shared, steel gates have been erected across side streets that cross the border and citizens are demoralized over an increased security presence, more interrogations, and the need to carry a passport constantly (Chung, 2011; Associated Press, 2009). While these initiatives were undertaken in the altruistic spirit of improving security while maintaining access, in practice, they have not always done so. If we refer back to the definition Munton and Keating distill from Holmes, some of these so-called cooperative initiatives do not seem to be in the spirit of "being pragmatic, seeing realities, avoiding vehemence and hysteria, accepting paradox and contradiction" (2001, 531).

These examples also illustrate the way in which the spaces of everyday life, notably policing, are increasingly being dominated by security agendas (Murphy, 2007). Circulation itself has become the subject of urban security, with the goal of permitting the circulation of those people deemed "good" and hindering that of those deemed "bad" (Foucault, 2009: 18; see also Salter, chapter 9). Cities and regions are increasingly turning outward to attract mobile global capital, but at the same time, many urban spaces—such as points of entry at airports, land borders, and ports, as well as economically important infrastructure—have been portrayed as places where terrorists could penetrate deep into the centre of a state, and have therefore become the target of policing and surveillance campaigns to increase security (Cowen and Bunce, 2006).

The securitization of everyday space makes it more difficult to judge whether or not security policies conform to the ethical orientation of internationalism. The definitions of internationalism described above all share the ethos that state policies ought at least to work for the betterment of the world community. Some definitions, particularly those from the Canadian foreign policy literature and from international relations literature more broadly, also argue for the promotion of democracy and good governance and "working for the wellbeing of the poorest" (Walzer, 2010: 1).[1] In the context of security, this means that for any given security policy, we should be cognizant not just of how the policy affects society, but also of the citizens whom it might make more insecure in the process.

Because arguments about security are fundamentally arguments about inclusion and exclusion, they are also tools for building the borders of a community, whether the actor implementing security policy is a state or not (Huysmans, 2006: 41, 49). They are also arguments about threat, crisis, and emergency that generate a need for a response from the government (Huysmans, 2006: 60). While the city, province, or federal government may have the intention of reassuring citizens by adopting more security measures, such measures may have the effect of generating "fearfulness, suspicion, paranoia and ultimately insecurity" (Coaffee, O'Hare, and

Hawkesworth, 2009: 507) and hindering the ease of circulation they are meant to promote (Boyle and Haggerty, 2009: 264).[2] Governmental and non-governmental actors may take actions that construct certain people as outsiders and reinforce an us-versus-them view of politics. This can happen within societies as well as between them. During the G20 Summit meeting in 2010, little attempt was made by the police or the media to distinguish between peaceful and violent protesters, or between the destruction of property and violence against people (Yang and McLean, 2010; Dubinsky, 2010; Nguyen, 2010). This boundary construction and the securitization of urban spaces are not just the consequence of a domestic Canadian policy, but are influenced, as we shall see in the next section, by Canadian-American security cooperation. Even in the G20 case, NORAD was involved in air surveillance for the event. Had the Beyond the Border Action Plan been in place during the summit, it is possible that American police officers would have been operating on Canadian soil.[3] The politics of security are complicated by the fact that Canada does not control the rhetoric of North American security. Canadians grapple not only with securitizing arguments generated domestically, but also with those generated in the United States. This conundrum is examined in the next section of this chapter, which considers how global politics, particularly the war on terrorism, influences North American security relations.

Global Politics and Canadian-American Internationalism

Canada's relationship with the United States in North America happens in the context of the relationship between the two countries in the world. Since 9/11, that relationship has been dominated, in the sphere of security, by the war on terrorism. The global focus on terrorism, led by the American focus on terrorism, was well entrenched by the time Prime Minister Harper took office in 2006. Canada had already chosen to be involved in the war in Afghanistan, but not the one in Iraq, and had declined to take part in an American continental ballistic missile defence shield. It was under Harper, however, that Canada decided to extend its mission in Afghanistan to 2011; to launch Passenger Protect, a no-fly list analogous (but not identical) to the one the Americans created; to create the Shiprider program; and to negotiate both the SPP and the Beyond the Border Action Plan. The American focus on security has meant that the defence-against-help dynamic has been particularly acute in the past decade. The global focus on the war on terrorism has arguably made it more difficult to practise internationalism in North America.

Maher Arar

The war on terrorism has particularly influenced information sharing in intelligence and policing, as demonstrated by the cases of Maher Arar, Abousfian Abdelrazik, and Omar Khadr. Maher Arar's case was largely resolved before Prime Minister Harper took office, but it is instructive nonetheless because it illustrates the way in which international and continental relationships are entwined. In 2002,

Arar was deported to Syria—despite being a dual citizen of Canada and Syria and resident in Canada—after being detained by American authorities during a stopover in the United States. This was part of the American practice of "extraordinary rendition," in which the United States sent prisoners abroad for "enhanced interrogation" or torture in jurisdictions with more lax regulations than the United States. While in Syria, Arar was held captive and tortured for more than a year before being returned to Canada. An inquiry into the matter confirmed that there was no evidence linking Arar to terrorist activities. In 2007, the Canadian government formally apologized to Arar and his family, and lodged a request with the American government that he be removed from the terrorist watch list. At time of writing, he had not (despite several requests by the Canadian government and admissions by former Secretary of State Condoleezza Rice that errors were made [Rennie, 2008]), and the Supreme Court of the United States had refused to hear his case against the American Attorney General (Richey, 2010).

The O'Connor Inquiry concluded that the RCMP had failed to follow its own policies for information sharing by failing to confirm the relevance and reliability of the information it passed on to the Americans, and by failing to attach caveats to it (O'Connor, 2006: 13). It has been speculated that these errors were made in the Canadian government's haste to demonstrate its enthusiastic cooperation with the American war on terrorism (Melchers, 2006: 41). Given the "defence against help" paradox described above, this is perhaps not surprising, but suggests a cooperative zeal that ultimately undermined the internationalist value of respecting established rules and norms (Nossal, Roussel, and Paquin, 2011: 136; Ruggie, 1993: 11). When the Canadian government under Prime Minister Harper finally attempted to launch an inquiry, appealing to the United States to remove Arar from the watch list, and beginning an RCMP investigation into the role of Syrian and American officials' role in the matter, several commentators suggested that doing so might undermine relations with the United States (Freeze and Chase, 2010; Ibbitson, 2007; CBC News, 2007a). There was also speculation that new recommendations made in the O'Connor Inquiry might restrict the ability of Canadian officials to share information with the American government.[4] In this case, the Canadian government's attempts to rectify the errors made by the RCMP and perpetuated by other government actors were constrained by a fear of American sanctions.

Abousfian Abdelrazik

Similar cases illustrate the difficulties Canadian governments may face in terms of making policy that conforms to the altruistic ethical orientation of internationalism. Abousfian Abdelrazik, also a Canadian citizen, was arrested without charge in Sudan in 2004 at the request of unknown Canadian officials (Koring, 2009b). While he was there, he was interrogated by the FBI and CSIS, and the United States added him to their no-fly list. That meant that even after he was finally released in 2004, Abdelrazik could not return to Canada, as the airlines feared the revocation of their landing rights in the United States. He was later arrested again and released a second time in 2006. By this time, he had also been added (at the behest of the United States) to the UN terrorist watch list. The Harper government refused to provide the necessary travel documents that would have allowed Abdelrazik to return home. This stalemate persisted until the Supreme Court of Canada ordered his repatriation, finding that the government had violated his right to return. In 2009, secret documents revealed that Canadian security services had been contacted by "a foreign government," probably the United States, requesting that Abdelrazik's return be blocked. It was well known that the CIA had made it known that they wanted to transfer Abdelrazik to the prison at Guantanamo Bay (Koring, 2011a), and a CSIS document obtained by journalists warned that "[s]enior government of Canada officials should be mindful of the potential reaction of our US counterparts to Abdelrazik's return to Canada as he is on the US no-fly list" (Gray and Koring, 2008). Canadian officials in the Liberal government did not know of the request at the time (Koring, 2009a), but documents leaked by Wiki-Leaks and dated just before his release suggest that by the time the Harper government was in power, the Canadian government wished urgently to know whether the United States would "passively or actively obstruct" Abdelrazik's return to Canada (Koring, 2011a). As it turned out, the American government did not block or protest his return.

As recently as the summer of 2011, CSIS documents alleging Abdelrazik's complicity in terrorist acts were leaked to *La Presse*, probably with the design to undermine his attempts to be removed from the UN terrorist watch list (Clark and Freeze, 2011). According to Abdelrazik's lawyer, these same allegations were already determined to be "unproven" by a Federal Court judge in 2007 (Clark and Freeze, 2011). Furthermore, CSIS and the RCMP declared in that same year that Abdelrazik was clear of all activities related to terrorism. Finally, in November 2011, Abdelrazik was removed from the UN terrorist watch list, which had the effect of unfreezing his assets and leaving him free to sue the Canadian government (Koring, 2011b).

In addition to demonstrating the influence of American politics on Canadian policy thinking, this case provides another example of the role of actors other than the central government in making foreign policy. The RCMP and intelligence officials maintain independent and informal relationships with their American counterparts, but their actions ultimately reflect on the Canadian government. Even after the Canadian government had cleared Abdelrazik and the Supreme Court had ordered his repatriation, CSIS, a Canadian transnational actor, seems to have attempted to thwart his efforts to be removed from the UN terrorist watch list.

More importantly, though, Abdelrazik's case shows that at the domestic level, there may be a paradox in the attempt to pursue both continentalism and internationalism. Defence against help means that Canada must take American global security interests into account while making domestic policy. This is simply a reality of Canada's position on the continent as the smaller, less powerful player and as a close ally of the United States. It also means that Canada's foreign policy (like every state's foreign policy) is constrained by decisions made by other states.

Definitions of internationalism allow for this influence by incorporating the concept of functionalism, which accepts the idea that any country will and should only be able to influence international affairs according to its capacity in any given issue area (Riddell-Dixon, 2006; Bernard, 2006; Nossal, Roussel, and Paquin, 2011: 136). In the period after 9/11, American domestic and international policy was consumed by the war on terror. Sweeping new policy initiatives like the Patriot Act, the creation of the Department of Homeland Security, and the crackdown on border security affected Canada as well. With so much of Canadian trade going to the United States and with large sectors of the Canadian economy also dependent on business and personal travel by Americans to Canada, the Canadian government had little choice but to find ways to cooperate with the United States. Canadian policy initiatives like the Smart Border Accords and the Anti-terrorism Act were responses to legitimate fears, not just of terrorist threats against Canada, but also of Canada losing its access to the American market and its privileged status as one of the most important allies of the United States. At a time when the United States was pursuing a foreign policy that was often at odds with the values of internationalism, it was difficult for the Canadian government to pursue a North American policy that did anything other than tweak American priorities. The Liberal governments under prime ministers Chrétien and Martin clearly made errors in the cases of Arar and Abdelrazik, and while the Harper government corrected some of these errors, it was often at the behest of the courts or independent inquiries. The Harper government perpetuated others. The analytical point, though, is that the global policy priorities of Canada and the United States—that is, their priorities in the realm where we usually expect internationalism to apply—affect their bilateral relationship and Canada's ability to pursue an internationalist foreign policy on the North American continent.

Omar Khadr

Omar Khadr's case, too, demonstrates the potentially subversive effects of the need to prioritize continentalist over internationalist thinking. Khadr, the son of one of Osama bin Laden's associates, was taken to Pakistan and trained as a terrorist when he was nine years old. In 2002 (by which time he was 15), he participated in a firefight during which an American soldier was killed. He was captured and transferred to Guantanamo Bay, and in late 2004 he was charged with murder as an enemy combatant. During his detention, CSIS officials (as well as American officials) interrogated him and shared the results of that interrogation with the United States without conditions, which may have been in violation of CSIS policy at the time (Shephard, 2008). According to the Supreme Court, even Khadr's questioning was illegal under international law (Shephard, 2008). Despite the fact that Khadr was widely portrayed in the media and by legal advocates as a child soldier (see Supreme Court of the United States, 2008), neither the Liberal nor the Conservative government asked for his repatriation. While two lower court decisions demanded that the Canadian government bring Khadr back to Canada, a Supreme Court decision in early 2010 overturned those decisions but ruled that the Canadian government had violated Khadr's Charter rights to "life, liberty and security" (Makin, 2010). When Barack Obama became president in 2009, he pledged to close the detention centre at Guantanamo Bay and would thus have to repatriate or otherwise process all the prisoners held there. In late 2010, a plea bargain was reached between the American government and Khadr's lawyers, in which Khadr pled guilty to all charges in exchange for a sentence of eight years, of which one more year was to be served in Guantanamo Bay. At the same time, the United States asked, by diplomatic note, that Canada look favourably on a request to transfer him to a Canadian prison after that year had been served. Canada agreed.[5] As of November 2011, the transfer process had begun, with some officials suggesting it could take up to 18 months, with the final approval of the decision being up to the minister of public safety (Cohen, 2011).

Throughout the case, both the Liberal and Conservative governments supported the American process, even as their other allies demanded the return of their nationals from the Guantanamo Bay prison. One investigation of official documents related to the case found that "the Canadian government has publicly supported [Khadr's] detention and trial despite concerns about his health, his age, and widespread condemnation of the American prison. ... The documents show officials downplayed comparisons between Khadr's case and that of child soldiers and, at times, blindly accepted assurances detention conditions at Guantanamo were humane" (Shephard, 2007). Some commentators have suggested that Canada's refusal to request repatriation was due to the fear that it would negatively affect Canada-US relations (Walkom, 2010). The fact that Canada's allies all repatriated their prisoners gives some credence to this hypothesis. What is clear, though, is that by refusing to treat Khadr as a child soldier, the Canadian government went against both convention and international laws to which it is a signatory. Keeping agreements and obeying international law is a key value of internationalism. While in the cases of Arar and Abdelrazik the Canadian government's attempts to act according to the values of internationalism seem to have been constrained by the need to preserve the relationship with the United States, in this case, the need to maintain the relationship with the United States may have had the perverse effect of leading the Canadian government to pursue a foreign policy at odds with the values of internationalism.

Conclusion

Internationalism is a concept usually applied to Canada's global relations rather than to its relationship with the United States. As a way of thinking about structure, internationalism seems particularly ill-suited to helping us understand many contemporary global problems because of its statist focus. However, the Canada-US relationship is multi-layered and can therefore be conceptualized as structurally multilateral. The middle-power internationalist behaviours of networking, facilitating, and catalyzing cooperation are still possible if we take into account the plethora of actors involved in North American security. Similarly, the primary value of internationalism—pursuing policies that serve the good of global society—and the related values of keeping international agreements, following rules and norms, and helping those less fortunate can also be reflected in the para-foreign policies of non-central governments and in the actions of transnational actors. Moreover, the concept can be analytically useful even if it does not directly apply to the North American relationship, because the continental relationship happens in the context of each country's foreign policy.

The findings of this chapter suggest that internationalism is not consistently present in the North American relationship under Stephen Harper's government. However, this mixed record can be largely explained by the fact that North American relations were set on a particular path by the terrorist attacks of 9/11, and the dominance of the anti-terrorist agenda in the immediate post-9/11 period continues to shape the trajectory of Canada-US security relations. The securitization of everyday spaces has meant that new actors have authority in security policy, which now transcends the distinction between foreign and domestic policy. On the one hand, this means that there has been room for innovative policy initiatives, such as the IBETs or CREMAC, that engage actors at various levels of government. Allowing emergency services to operate on both sides of the border in cases of human-caused or natural disasters seems in keeping with the enlightened self-interest demanded by internationalism. On the other, common initiatives formulated in the service of protecting security have sometimes made life more difficult for Canadians and Americans. Canada's North American policies in the past decade have been shaped, more than usual, by fears of how the United States would react to any given initiative. The cases of Arar, Abdelrazik, and Khadr demonstrate that the Canadian government may, at times, have been overzealous in its eagerness to show the United States that it was being cooperative, with the result that the values of internationalism have not always been well served in the bilateral relationship.

A decade after 9/11, scholars and pundits are finally beginning to question the wisdom of the policy decisions made in the early, fearful days after the terrorist attacks,[6] and the attitude of "either you are with us, or you are with the terrorists" has softened. The constraints on Canadian continental policy imposed by the focus on security may be loosening, and the Beyond the Border Action Plan reflects a mild shift back to focusing on trade rather than security, as was the case in the Smart Border Accords of 2001 (Savage, 2011). However, the logic of defence against help clearly still influences Canadian thinking: during the press conference for the Beyond the Border Action Plan, Prime Minister Harper stated that "Canada has no friends among America's enemies. What threatens the security and well-being of the U.S., threatens the security and well-being of Canada" (Kennedy and Alberts, 2011). The constraints on Canadian foreign policy in North America sometimes overwhelm the impulse to internationalism: the limits of functionalism outweigh the aims of altruism. But the co-existence of North American continentalism with internationalism is not impossible. Under the right global circumstances and with the acknowledgement that the Canada-US relationship contains more actors than the federal governments of each state, both the form and the values of internationalism can be observed in the continental relationship.

Key Terms

intermestic
paradiplomacy
localization of security

defence against help
securitization

Study Questions

1. The record on internationalism in the Canadian-American security relationship is mixed. Is it better or worse in other sectors, such as trade or climate change? Why or why not?
2. What is the effect of international relations undertaken by transnational and sub-national actors on the Canadian central government's ability to pursue a cohesive, coordinated foreign policy in North America?
3. How does the localization of security complicate the pursuit of internationalism in the Canadian-American relationship?
4. Is the defence-against-help effect likely to dissipate the further away we get from the 9/11 terrorist attacks? Why or why not?
5. This chapter examines the effects of global politics (specifically, the war on terrorism) on North American relations. Conversely, how might Canada's relationship with the United States in North America affect its foreign policy more generally?

Notes

1 Beyond the Canadian foreign policy literature, liberal internationalism is closely linked to Kantian peace and the idea that democratic states do not go to war with each other. As such, the concept usually entails democracy promotion as a value. See, for instance, Burley, 1992; Paris, 1997; Hoffmann, 1995.

2 These dynamics are not necessarily intentional and are often the product of particular kinds of training, routines, and practices among security bureaucrats. People trained to think about the world through the lens of security tend to use security to solve problems, even where it may not be warranted. See Bigo, 1996; Bigo, 2002.

3 The Action Plan does not specify the scope of cooperation, nor whether American police would have powers of arrest while operating on Canadian soil. The pilot project is supposed to be operational by summer 2012.

4   Although how much this matters may be in question. On the one hand, the information-sharing relationship may not ever have been as easy as it was made out to be (Ibbitson, 2007). On the other, information sharing also relies on the close intelligence relationships between Canada and the United States, and on informal relationships. Regulations about police intelligence sharing may not matter much.

5   These documents are available at the University of Toronto Faculty of Law, n.d.

6   See, for example, Mueller and Stewart, 2011.

References

Aldecoa, Francisco, and Michael Keating. 1999. *Paradiplomacy in Action: The Foreign Relations of Subnational Governments*. New York: Routledge.

Associated Press. 2009. "New Gates Divide U.S.-Canada Border Towns." MSNBC.com, 2 October. At http://www.msnbc.msn.com/id/33145600/ns/us_news-security/t/new-gates-divide-us-canada-border-towns/#.TsBHLnO0wbl.

Bernard, Prosper. 2006. "Canada and Human Security: From the Axworthy Doctrine to Middle Power Internationalism." *American Review of Canadian Studies* 36, 2: 233–61.

Bigo, Didier. 1996. *Polices en réseaux: L'expérience européenne*. Paris: Presses de Sciences Po.

———. 2002. "Security and Immigration: Toward a Critique of the Governmentality of Unease." *Alternatives* 27 (Special Issue): 63–92.

Biswas, Bidisha. 2009. "Bilateral Cooperation and Bounded Sovereignty in Counter-terrorism Efforts." *Border Policy Research Institute Working Papers*, 5. At http://www.wwu.edu/depts/bpri/files/2009_Nov_WP_No5.pdf.

Boyle, Philip, and Kevin D. Haggerty. 2009. "Spectacular Security: Mega-events and the Security Complex." *International Political Sociology* 3, 3: 257–74.

Burley, Anne-Marie. 1992. "Law among Liberal States: Liberal Internationalism and the Act of State Doctrine." *Columbia Law Review* 92, 8: 1907–96.

CBC News. 2007a. "Ottawa Reaches $10M Settlement with Arar." CBC News, 25 January. At http://www.cbc.ca/news/canada/story/2007/01/25/arar-harper.html.

———. 2007b. "Ambulance Carrying Heart-Attack Patient Delayed at U.S. Border." CBC News, 19 November. At http://www.cbc.ca/news/canada/story/2007/11/19/windsor-hospital.html.

Chapnick, Adam. 2000. "The Canadian Middle Power Myth." *International Journal* 55, 2: 188–206.

Charters, David A. 2005. "'Defence against Help': Canadian-American Cooperation in the War on Terrorism." In David A. Charters and Graham F. Walker, eds, *After 9/11: Terrorism and Crime in a Globalised World*. Halifax: Dalhousie University Press, Centre for Foreign Policy Studies, 288–305.

Chung, Andrew. 2011. "Border Towns Struggle with Post-9/11 Security Measures." *Toronto Star*, 22 September. At http://www.thestar.com/news/article/1048571.

Clark, Campbell, and Colin Freeze. 2011. "CSIS Leak Aimed at Keeping Abdelrazik on No-Fly List, Lawyer Says." *Globe and Mail*, 5 August. At http://www.theglobeandmail.com/news/national/csis-leak-aimed-at-keeping-abdelrazik-on-no-fly-list-lawyer-says/article2121734/.

Coaffee, Jon, Paul O'Hare, and Marian Hawkesworth. 2009. "The Visibility of (In)security: The Aesthetics of Planning Urban Defences against Terrorism." *Security Dialogue* 40, 4–5: 489–511.

Coaffee, Jon, and David Murakami Wood. 2006. "Security Is Coming Home: Rethinking Scale and Constructing Resilience in the Global Urban Response to Terrorist Risk." *International Relations* 20, 4: 503–17.

Cohen, Tobi. 2011. "Khadr's Repatriation Request to Be Handled under Current Transfer Laws." Canada.com, 31 October. At http://www.canada.com/news/canada-in-afghanistan/Khadr+repatriation+request+handled+under+current+transfer+laws/5639739/story.html.

Cooper, Andrew, ed. 1997. *Niche Diplomacy: Middle Powers after the Cold War*. Toronto: Macmillan.

Cowen, Deborah, and Susannah Bunce. 2006. "Debates and Developments: Competitive Cities and Secure Nations: Conflict and Convergence in Urban Waterfront Agendas after 9/11." *International Journal of Urban and Regional Research* 30, 2: 427–39.

Dubinsky, Zach. 2010. "In Wake of G20, Will Police Tactics Change?" CBC News, 5 October. At http://www.cbc.ca/canada/story/2010/10/05/f-october-crisis-policing-g20.html.

Eriksson, Johan, and Mark Rhinard. 2009. "The Internal-External Security Nexus: Notes on an Emerging Research Agenda." *Cooperation and Conflict* 44, 3: 243–67.

Fortmann, Michel, and David Haglund. 2002. "Canada and the Issue of Homeland Security: Does the 'Kingston Dispensation' Still Hold?" *Canadian Military Journal* 3, 1: 17–22.

Foucault, Michel. 2009. *Security, Territory, Population: Lectures at the Collège de France 1977–1978.* New York: Picador.

Freeze, Colin, and Steven Chase. 2010. "Arar Working with RCMP as It Probes His Overseas Torture: Canadian Says Mounties Pursuing Global Investigation." *Globe and Mail*, 15 June. At http://www.theglobeandmail.com/news/national/arar-working-with-rcmp-as-it-probes-his-overseas-torture/article1604235/.

Government of Canada. 2011. *Perimeter Security and Economic Competitiveness Action Plan.* At http://www.borderactionplan-plandactionfrontalier.gc.ca/psec-scep/bap_report-paf_rapport-dec2011.aspx?view=d.

Graham, Stephen. 2006. "Cities and the 'War on Terror.'" *International Journal of Urban and Regional Research* 30, 2: 255–76.

Gray, Jeff, and Paul Koring. 2008. "Ambassador Hints U.S. Won't Fight Canadian's Repatriation." *Globe and Mail*, 28 July. At http://www.theglobeandmail.com/news/national/ambassador-hints-us-wont-fight-canadians-repatriation/article313893/.

Hale, Geoffrey. 2006. *Uneasy Partnership: The Politics of Business and Government in Canada.* Peterborough, ON: Broadview Press.

Hoffmann, Stanley. 1995. "The Crisis of Liberal Internationalism." *Foreign Policy* 98 (April): 159–77.

Huysmans, Jef. 2006. *The Politics of Insecurity: Fear, Migration and Asylum in the EU.* New York: Routledge.

Ibbitson, John. 2007. "Ottawa Sacrificed Arar to Save Face with U.S., Syria." *Globe and Mail*, 10 August. At http://www.theglobeandmail.com/news/national/ottawa-sacrificed-arar-to-save-face-with-us-syria/article775508/.

———. 2011. "U.S., Canada Reach New Security Deal." *Globe and Mail*, 9 September. At http://www.theglobeandmail.com/news/politics/us-canada-reach-new-security-deal/article2160465/.

IBET Threat Assessment Working Group. 2010. "Canada–United States IBET Threat Assessment 2010 (Reporting on Year 2009)." *Royal Canadian Mounted Police.* At http://www.rcmp-grc.gc.ca/ibet-eipf/reports-rapports/2010-threat-menace-eng.htm.

Kennedy, Mark, and Sheldon Alberts. 2011. "Canada-U.S. Border Deal Aims to Strengthen North American Perimeter While Unblocking Trade." *Montreal Gazette*, 7 December. At http://www.montrealgazette.com/travel/Canada+border+deal+aims+strengthen+North+American+perimeter+while/5825937/story.html.

Keohane, Robert O., and Joseph S. Nye. 1977. *Power & Interdependence.* Boston: Little, Brown and Company.

Kitchen, Veronica M., and Karthika Sasikumar. 2009. "Canada (En)Counters Terrorism: US-Canada Relations and Counter-Terrorism Policy." *Terrorism and Political Violence* 21, 1: 155–73.

Koring, Paul. 2009a. "Home at Last, But Not Yet Free." *Globe and Mail*, 28 September, A12.

———. 2009b. "CSIS Asked Sudan to Arrest Canadian, Files Reveal." *Globe and Mail*, 5 March, A1

———. 2011a. "'Secret' Spy Notes and a Canadian in Exile." *Globe and Mail*, 22 September, A10. At http://www.theglobeandmail.com/news/politics/csis-notes-reveal-how-canadian-was-kept-in-exile/article2177157/singlepage/.

————. 2011b. "Canadian Abousfian Abdelrazik Taken Off United Nations Terror List." *Globe and Mail*, 30 November. At http://www.theglobeandmail.com/news/world/africa-mideast/canadian-abousfian-abdelrazik-taken-off-united-nations-terror-list/article2255810/.

Lennox, R. Patrick. 2009. *At Home and Abroad: The Canada-U.S. Relationship and Canada's Place in the World*. Vancouver: University of British Columbia Press.

Lewis, Stephen, and Jim Wurst. 1991. "A Promise Betrayed." *World Policy Journal* 8, 3: 539–49.

McCarter, Mickey. 2011. "Homeland Security Today: Great Lakes States Soon to Strike Emergency Management Agreement with Canadian Provinces." *Homeland Security Today*, 11 October. At http://www.hstoday.us/briefings/today-s-news-analysis/single-article/great-lakes-states-soon-to-strike-emergency-management-agreement-with-canadian-provinces/df34e567463b596874f05610ddbfe7c6.html.

Makin, Kirk. 2010. "Court's Khadr Ruling Throws Down a Challenge: In a 9–0 Decision, Court Denounces Rights Violation, Effectively Daring Harper Government to Ignore Findings." *Globe and Mail*, 30 January, A4.

Manning, Bayless. 1977. "The Congress, the Executive and Intermestic Affairs: Three Proposals." *Foreign Affairs* 55, 2: 306–24.

Melchers, Ronald-Frans. 2006. "The Maher Arar Case: Implications for Canada-US Law Enforcement Cooperation." *Journal of the Institute of Justice and International Studies* 6: 37–46.

Mueller, John, and Mark G. Stewart. 2011. *Terror, Security, and Money: Balancing the Risks, Benefits, and Costs of Homeland Security*. New York: Oxford University Press.

Munton, Don, and Tom Keating. 2001. "Internationalism and the Canadian Public." *Canadian Journal of Political Science* 34, 3: 517–49.

Murphy, Christopher. 2007. "'Securitizing' Canadian Policing: A New Policing Paradigm for the Post 9/11 Security State?" *Canadian Journal of Sociology/Cahiers canadiens de sociologie* 32, 4: 449–75.

Nguyen, Linda. 2010. "Police Sound Off on G20 Security Tools." Canada.com, 3 June. At http://www.canada.com/business/Police+sound+security+tools/3108265/story.html.

Nossal, Kim Richard, Stéphane Roussel, and Stéphane Paquin. 2011. *International Policy in Canada*. Toronto: Pearson Education Canada.

O'Connor, Dennis. 2006. *Report of the Events Relating to Maher Arar: Analysis and Recommendations (Part I: Factual Inquiry)*. Ottawa: Commission of Inquiry into the Actions of Canadian Officials in Relation to Maher Arar. At http://www.pch.gc.ca/cs-kc/arar/Arar_e.pdf.

Painchaud, Paul. 1966. "Middlepowermanship as an Ideology." In J. King Gordon, ed., *Canada's Role as a Middle Power*, 29–35. Toronto: Canadian Institute of International Affairs.

Paris, Roland. 1997. "Peacebuilding and the Limits of Liberal Internationalism." *International Security* 22, 2: 54–89.

Pearson, Craig. 2011. "Exercise Stirs Drama on Detroit River." *Windsor Star*, 24 August, A5. At http://www.windsorstar.com/Exercise+stirs+drama+Detroit+River/5296911/story.html.

Pratt, Cranford. 1989. *Internationalism under Strain: The North-South Policies of Canada, the Netherlands, Norway, and Sweden*. Toronto: University of Toronto Press.

RCMP (Royal Canadian Mounted Police). 2010. "Canada-U.S. Shiprider." *Government of Canada*, 25 June. At http://205.193.86.86/ibet-eipf/shiprider-eng.htm.

————. 2011. "RCMP to Join New Operational Integration Centre in Detroit." *Royal Canadian Mounted Police/Gendarmerie Royale du Canada*, 24 April. At http://www.rcmp-grc.gc.ca/on/news-nouvelles/2011/11-03-24-windsor-eng.htm.

Rennie, Steve. 2008. "Day Tried Four Times to Get Arar off U.S. No-Fly List: Sources Say Case 'Just a Blip on the Screen' for American Officials Who Have More Than 100,000 Names on Their Watch List." *Globe and Mail*, 4 February, A8.

Richey, Warren. 2010. "Supreme Court Refuses Maher Arar Torture Case: The US Supreme Court Declined to Take the Case of Canadian Citizen Maher Arar, Who Alleged that US Officials Deported Him to Syria in 2002 Knowing He Would Be Tortured during Terrorism Interrogations." *Christian Science Monitor*, 14 June.

Riddell-Dixon, Elizabeth. 2006. "Canada at the United Nations 1945–1989." *International Journal* 62, 1: 145–60.

Rioux, Jean-François, and Robin Hay. 1998. "Canadian Foreign Policy—From Internationalism to Isolationism." *International Journal* 54, 1: 57–75.

Ruggie, John Gerard, ed. 1993. *Multilateralism Matters: The Theory and Praxis of an Institutional Form.* New York: Columbia University Press.

Savage, Luiza Ch. 2011. "About That Border Deal." *The Bilateralist*, 8 December. At http://www.bilateralist.com/2011/12/08/border-deal/.

Shephard, Michelle. 2007. "Ottawa Played Down Khadr Concerns." *Toronto Star*, 20 August, AA1. At http://www.thestar.com/article/247900.

———. 2008. "Judges Question Khadr Secrecy." *Toronto Star*, 27 March. At http://www.thestar.com/News/Canada/article/357020.

Slaughter, Anne-Marie. 2005. *A New World Order.* Princeton, NJ: Princeton University Press.

Supreme Court of the United States. 2008. "Brief for International Law Scholars as Amici Curiae Supporting Respondent Omar Khadr, Al Odah v. United States." 553 U.S. 723, 128 S. Ct. 2229, no. 06-1196. At http://www.law.utoronto.ca/documents/Mackin/khadr_AmicusChildSoldier.pdf.

University of Toronto Faculty of Law. n.d. "The Omar Khadr Case." At http://www.law.utoronto.ca/faculty_content.asp?itemPath=1/3/4/0/0&contentId=1617.

Velasquez, Andrew. 2011. Written Statement of Region V Administrator Andrew Velasquez III, Federal Emergency Management Agency before the U.S. House Committee on Homeland Security's Subcommittee on Emergency Preparedness, Response, and Communications: "The State of the Northern Border Preparedness: A Review of Federal, State and Local Coordination." *Department of Homeland Security*, 28 October. At http://www.dhs.gov/ynews/testimony/20111028-velasquez-northern-border-preparedness.shtm.

Walkom, Thomas. 2010. "Khadr's Only Hope Is U.S. Embarrassment." *Toronto Star*, 20 October. At http://www.thestar.com/article/878122--walkom-khadr-s-only-hope-is-u-s-embarrassment.

Walzer, Michael. 2010. "Internationalism." *Dissent* 57, 1: 1.

Yang, Jennifer, and Jesse McLean. 2010. "Anatomy of the G20: What Went Wrong; Reflections from Both Sides of the Fence—The People, The Police—On How a Gathering of World Leaders and Thousands of Peaceful Citizen Protesters Was Sidelined by a Small Band of Anarchists." *Toronto Star*, 21 August, IN1.

11 Women and Children First: Maternal Health and the Silencing of Gender in Canadian Foreign Policy

Krystel Carrier and Rebecca Tiessen

The expression "women and children first" originated as a seafaring practice with the sinking of the HMS *Birkenhead* off the coast of South Africa in 1852. As the ship quickly took on water, Lieutenant-Colonel Alexander Seton ordered his men to "Stand fast!" (Friedman Ross and Coffey, 2003: 14) so that the 26 women and children on board could safely evacuate on the few serviceable lifeboats. The command was obeyed, and all the women and children were saved, while 445 of the estimated 612 men onboard drowned or were taken by sharks (Turner, 1988). The saying, also known as the Birkenhead Drill, is most famously associated with the sinking of the RMS *Titanic* in 1912, where 74 per cent of the female and 52 per cent of the child passengers were saved and 80 per cent of the men perished (Stevans and Gleicher, 2004: 34). Even though the Birkenhead Drill never formally became part of international maritime law, the phrase has been widely used and is part of the modern folklore of chivalrous men and caregiving mothers.

Yet the "reality is that women and children are not first in our world; indeed, they are often last" (Chervenak and McCullough, 2009: 351). A study on sex discrimination in disasters concluded that women and children usually come last; for example, female children are the most likely cohort to face nutritional vulnerability during famines (Rivers, 1982: 265). A closer examination of the Birkenhead Drill during the sinking of the *Titanic* further illustrates that not *all* women and children have come first. Based on a regression analysis of the *Titanic* casualties, we can see that the rescue effort was imbued with a "complex class determination of survival rates" amongst women and children (Stevans and Gleicher, 2004: 28), as a female passenger in first class was nine times more likely to survive than a female passenger in second or third class (Stevans and Gleicher, 2004: 10).

The veiled gender inequalities and discriminatory nature of the Birkenhead Drill are replicated in Canadian foreign policy and are especially apparent in the Harper government's recent attempt at internationalism through the **Muskoka Initiative** on maternal, newborn, and child health. In this chapter, we will consider how the Muskoka Initiative and the Harper government's policy of "equality between men and women" have effectively "othered" (Smith, 2003: 25; Turenne

Sjolander, chapter 14) the Third World woman by victimizing her and silencing gender. Like the Birkenhead Drill, Canadian internationalism under the Harper government is predicated on a view of women as mothers and caregivers in need of rescuing, as opposed to individuals with agency who are defined by much more than their reproductive capacity. As such, Canada's internationalism obfuscates gender and class distinctions. Smith (chapter 12) extends this analysis to the exclusion of the human dimension, the silencing of specific voices, and the assumed race neutrality of internationalism. The face of Canada that is presented to the world (see Gecelovsky, chapter 7 and Smith, chapter 12) under the Harper government is not an Africa-friendly one (Black, chapter 13) and is not one that promotes an internationalism based on **gender equality**.

This chapter underscores the problem with focusing on women and children as helpless victims in foreign policy on **maternal health**. To do this, we examine Canadian foreign policy initiatives on maternal health in the context of gender inequality. To document the underlying causes of maternal health problems, we examine community-wide gender inequality issues with examples from South Sudan.

Canada and Gender Equality—A Leader No More

In June 2010, the Group of Eight (G8) leaders convened in Huntsville, Ontario, for their thirty-sixth annual summit. Preparing to host the summit for his first time, Prime Minister Stephen Harper announced that Canada would champion a "major initiative" (2010) to improve child and maternal health in developing countries. Canada's leadership in advancing maternal health as an issue worthy of the G8's attention was initially praised by the international medical community and development experts (Lancet, 2010; Webster, 2010: 399). Improving maternal health (MDG 5) is the fifth of eight Millennium Development Goals (MDGs) introduced by the United Nations in 2000, its target being to reduce maternal mortality by 75 per cent by the year 2015. MDG 5 also seeks to achieve universal access to reproductive health in areas of contraceptive use, a reduction of birth rates among adolescents, and an increase in antenatal-care coverage, as well as meet broader needs relating to family planning.

The reaction to Harper's child and maternal health initiative was particularly enthusiastic given that progress towards the achievement of MDG 5 on improving maternal health has been slow (Bhutta et al., 2010: 2037) and that the MDG 5 target was not expected to be achieved by 2015 (Walsh and Jones, 2009: 17), particularly in Sudan, where women face one of the highest rates of maternal mortality in the world. The United Nations raised the alarm in 2009, claiming that MDG 5 was "the goal towards which there has been least progress so far" (UN, 2009: 4). The risk of a woman dying as a result of pregnancy or childbirth is about 1 in 6 in the poorest parts of the world compared with about 1 in 30,000 in Northern Europe. Such a discrepancy poses a huge challenge to meeting the MDG 5 goal of reducing maternal mortality by 75 per cent between 1990 and 2015 (Ronsmans and Graham, 2006: 1189).

The UN has attributed the slow progress towards achieving MDG 5 to a lack of political will to reduce maternal mortality, particularly in sub-Saharan Africa and Southern Asia, and to a drastic reduction from mid-1990s levels in donor funding for family planning services (UN, 2009: 4, 11–13). The eponymous Muskoka Initiative was therefore touted as "putting women and children first" on the G8 agenda. G8 leaders committed US$5 billion towards the initiative, with Canada pledging $1.1 billion in new funding over five years (Guebert, 2010).

The enthusiasm that surrounded the Muskoka Initiative, however, soon gave way to criticism. When Prime Minister Harper announced in January 2010 that Canada would champion the issue of woman and child health at the G8 Summit, very little information was provided. The maternal health program envisioned by Harper and his Conservative Party came under intense scrutiny for lack of concrete action and commitment of funds and resources. Former UN special envoy for HIV/AIDS Stephen Lewis rebuked the women and children's initiative's lack of detail, arguing that the failure to attach a dollar figure to the initiative was cause for scepticism (Berthiaume, 2010). Minister of Foreign Affairs Lawrence Cannon then announced in March 2010 that the G8 funds would be directed towards prenatal, childbirth, and postpartum care; health education; treatment and prevention of diseases; prevention of mother-to-child transmission of HIV; immunization; basic nutrition; and water and sanitation (Cannon, 2010). Notably absent from the list were funding for family planning, for abortion, and for the treatment of victims of sexual and gender-based violence. When pressed on the issue of contraception in Parliament, Cannon categorically emphasized that the initiative "does not deal in any way, shape or form with family planning. ... Indeed, the purpose of this is to be able to save lives" (Cannon, 2010). A day later, Minister of International Cooperation Bev Oda added that "we [the Conservative government] have chosen to focus the world's lens on saving the lives of mothers and children" (Craine, 2010). Days after his minister of foreign affairs and minister for international cooperation firmly refused to allow for funding of family planning in the Muskoka Initiative, Prime Minister Harper reversed the government's decision. Canada agreed that funds for family planning would be part of the Muskoka Initiative and even permitted other donor countries to finance abortions as part of the initiative.

The maternal health strategy proposed by the Conservative government immediately became a topic of great controversy, both in Canada and internationally. The debate focused around the Canadian government's initial refusal to allow the funding of organizations involved in family planning efforts, particularly those that supported abortions. American secretary of state Hillary Clinton lambasted the Canadian proposal, stating that "you cannot have maternal health without reproductive health. And reproductive health includes contraception and family planning and access to legal, safe abortion" (CBC News, 2010b). British foreign secretary David Miliband made it clear that the British government would oppose any initiative that did not include family planning, asserting that the British position on this issue "is very much as stated by Secretary Clinton" (CBC News, 2010a). Clinton's and Miliband's comments contradicted a widely held perception of Canada's international leadership in the area of gender equality (Rathgeber, 1990; Rathgeber, 1995; Swiss, forthcoming) and "gender mainstreaming in international policy and practice" (Turenne Sjolander, 2005: 19). The criticisms of Canada's maternal health initiative reflect a growing body of literature that has challenged Canada's contributions to gender equality and gender mainstreaming in the area of foreign policy (Turenne Sjolander, 2005; Smith, Stienstra, and Turenne Sjolander, 2003; Turenne Sjolander, Smith, and Stienstra, 2003; Denholm Crosby, 2003; Tiessen, 2003; Baines, 2003; Tiessen and Tuckey, forthcoming; Gecelovsky, chapter 7).

G8 Muskoka Initiative—A Program for "Mothers and Whores"[1]

The Muskoka Initiative announcement focused primarily on women in their role of mothers and on the necessity of "saving" them. The prominence accorded to the identity of women as mothers and caregivers, however, hides the fact that efforts to improve maternal health in developing countries often "have been the result not of a concern for women but rather a concern that is primarily about protecting the health of men and children" (Carovano, 1992: 2). For example, the majority of AIDS prevention programs for women funded by the international community have targeted women in the sex industry (Carovano, 1992: 2; Heise and Elias, 1995; Hearst and Chen, 2004), even though sex workers constitute only a small percentage of the women in developing countries who are infected with the virus (Heise and Elias, 1995: 932; Pettifor, Rosenberg, and Behets, 2011), or have been designed to prevent mother-to-child HIV transmission (Potts et al., 2008).

Instead of focusing on the sexual health needs of all women in developing countries, the Muskoka Initiative followed in the donor-health-initiative tradition of targeting "mothers and whores" (Carovano, 1992). For example, funds could have been allocated towards governance reforms to increase and enforce legal sanctions against sexually violent crimes or against soliciting prostitution, which have proven to be more efficient and cost-effective tools to reduce HIV transmission in developing countries (Jha et al., 2001) than targeting sex industry workers. Prevention services that target all women, regardless of their childbearing intentions, tend to be more effective in preventing the spread of infection than services that only target pregnant women, particularly in countries characterized by a generalized HIV epidemic, where "sexual networking in the general population is sufficient to sustain an epidemic independent of sub-populations at higher risk of infection" (UNAIDS, 2005: 18). Yet empirical evidence shows that resource allocations for HIV/AIDS prevention programs in Africa are rarely optimized and resource-allocation decisions are rarely evidence-based (Bautista-Arredondo et al., 2008: 69).

Funds could also have been invested in improving the physical and psychological health of victims of sexual violence. "Sexual violence during war and other conflict situations is increasingly recognized as a severely traumatic event," yet we don't know much about the "health strategies women develop in an attempt to overcome their health problems or live with them" (Tankink and Richters, 2007: 191). Moreover, because women have important cultural motivations to stay quiet about their experiences, there is a lack of good information about the nature, extent, and consequences of sexual violence during and after armed conflict. As we will discuss later, victims of sexual violence may face a lifetime of stigmatization if they admit to it. Gender-based violence hence poses many challenges for maternal health. In Sudan, women have reported being gang-raped and bayoneted in the vagina, and young girls especially have reported having their external genitalia cut out (Isis-WICCE, 2007: 87–8). As a result of injuries to sexual organs inflicted on women during the years of war, Sudanese women report experiencing a high rate of complications during birth. In a study conducted by Isis-WICCE (Isis-Women's International Cross-Cultural Exchange, which links women internationally) in 2007, researchers found that 30.9 per cent of women have one or more gynaecological problems, including abnormal vaginal discharge, vaginal and perineal tear, leaking urine or feces, infertility, chronic lower abdominal pain, abnormal vaginal bleeding, swelling, genital sores, unwanted pregnancy, and sexual dysfunction. These health problems were often caused by sexual abuse (such as rape or exposure to sexually transmitted infections [STIs], including HIV/AIDS) and/or physical abuse. The gendered physical, sexual, and psychological violence that women experience in situations of armed conflict is directly related to maternal health issues and must therefore be considered in maternal health initiatives.

Unsafe abortions are the second leading cause of maternal mortality in the world (Okonofua, 2008), with an estimated 68,000 women dying every year as a result of complications (Grimes et al., 2006: 1913). Ninety-eight per cent of these deaths occur in developing countries (Cornwall, Standing, and Lynch, 2009: 3). By failing to see women as more than "mothers and whores," the Canadian foreign policy on maternal health in its current form entrenches women's inability to exercise control over their body through sexual health education, protection from gender-based violence, or access to safe abortions. The Muskoka Initiative reflects the indisposition and absolute failure of the Harper government to address both the strategic and practical needs of women in Canadian foreign policy.

Furthermore, the Muskoka Initiative, largely targeted at women, is void of any reference to gender equality. The Harper government's failure to take gender inequality seriously and to treat it as a cornerstone of maternal health needs is made clear in the proposed maternal health strategy. The goals of "saving lives" (Craine, 2010; Cannon, 2010; Harper, 2010) and meeting the needs of women have been pitched in practical terms with little attention to the underlying challenges that women face as a result of gender inequality in their communities and societies. The silencing of gender in the Muskoka Initiative reflects broader trends in Canadian policy; this omission points towards the "progressive disappearance of the gendered subject, both in discourse and practice" (Brodie and Bakker, 2008), in Canadian domestic and foreign policy. Gender equality has essentially been edited out of Canadian foreign policy; diplomats working in the Department of Foreign Affairs and International Trade have been under instructions since 2009 to replace the term "gender equality" with "equality of men and women" and to avoid references to gender-based violence (Collins, 2009).

Brodie and Bakker attribute the **erasure of gender** in domestic Canadian policy "to the priority given to market accountability and sound macroeconomics. Questions of social cohesion, poverty reduction, social and gender justice have taken on a secondary import; any attention to these issues is seen as conditional to the realization of a sound fiscal picture" (2008: 8). We argue that the **degendering process** (Brodie and Bakker, 2008: 9) is also evident in Canadian foreign policy and underscores the abating humane internationalism that Black (chapter 13) argues is also evidenced in Canada's diminished interest in Africa in both the Chrétien and Harper governments. The Muskoka Initiative is but one example that illustrates how gender issues in Canadian foreign policy have been "delegitimized, dismantled," and even "disappeared" (Brodie and Bakker, 2008: 9). Spending related to and senior management support for gender equality at the Canadian International Development Agency (CIDA) have decreased under the Conservative government to such an extent that non-governmental organizations have been reportedly encouraged to "remove the words 'gender equality' from their proposal" and have been told by a Conservative senator to "shut the f*** up" about it to increase their chances of receiving funding (Plewes and Kerr, 2010). The directive issued by Minister of Foreign Affairs Cannon demonstrates that neither transformative feminism nor gender mainstreaming is a feature of Canadian foreign policy under the Harper regime; in fact, Canada's foreign policy does not include "gender" at all. By removing "gender equality" from the foreign policy discourse, Harper's Conservative government effectively denies that socially constructed roles tend to result in women bearing the brunt of the suffering associated with inequalities between men and women and to experience gender-based violence disproportionately: for example, 25 per cent of American women report experiencing partner violence, as compared to 8 per cent of men, and these women are twice as likely to be injured during an assault than men are (Tjaden and Thoennes, 1998: 2); UNICEF reports that early marriage disproportionately affects girls, with up to 100 million girls marrying before the age of 18, and that "girls may be married young to ensure obedience and subservience within their husband's household and to maximise their childbearing" (UNICEF, 2010); and a study of 1,366 women presenting for antenatal care in South Africa concluded that intimate-partner violence and high levels of male control in a woman's life are associated with HIV seropositivity (Dunkle et al., 2004; see also Maman et al., 2000; Garcia-Moreno and Watts, 2000; Zierler and Krieger, 1997; Maman et al., 2002). The Muskoka Initiative ignores the fact that the health status of women and girls is compounded by societal norms and expectations for women and girls that limit their participation in decision-making and negatively impact their health and well-being.

The Hypocrisy of Harper's Foreign Policy—A Hypocritical Internationalism

The renowned medical journal *The Lancet* criticized the Canadian position on abortion as "hypocritical and unjust" (*Lancet,* 2010). This was not the first time that Canadian foreign policy was characterized as hypocritical. For example, Shelagh Day, an expert on human rights activism, argues that Canada's international commitments are "not reflected in an equivalent political commitment to fulfill women's human rights at home" (2003: 135). Kim Nossal, on the other hand, contends that while accusing Canadian officials of hypocrisy in the foreign policy decision-making process is "both easy and comforting," it provides "an unsatisfactory explanation" for the large gap between rhetoric and reality (1988: 49). Nossal instead puts forth that the divergence between commitments and disbursements is a consequence of Canada's quest for prestige on the international stage, of the bureaucratic interest of civil servants at CIDA in continuing to maintain a large official development assistance bureaucracy, and of the imperative of limiting real expenditures. We argue, however, that seeking to acquire prestige through the promotion of values and moral standards—such as the imperative of "saving mothers and children"—is hypocritical when the behaviour of the state is not in conformity with the discourse it proclaims on international platforms. We adopt Angus's definition of hypocrisy in this context, which he sees as occurring "only if Canadians defend, on grounds of high morality, a policy of drift which is dictated by political necessity. ... A line which is fine but clear can be drawn between hypocrisy and reluctance to abandon ideals the moment one realizes that it is impossible to live up to them" (Angus, 1934: 268). Hypocrisy is a valid lens through which to assess Canadian internationalism, as well as the Canadian position on maternal health and gender at the G8. In this section, we will discuss the multiple layers of hypocrisy of Harper's foreign policy as evidenced by the Muskoka Initiative.

First, removing the words "gender equality" from the diplomatic vocabulary "stands in stark contrast to the international and national commitments of Canadian governments to undertake gender-based analysis and promote gender equality across the broad spectrum of public policy" (Brodie and Bakker, 2008: 9). Diplomats have described the removal of the term "gender equality" as "a substantial change in philosophy" (Collins, 2009) away from Canada's traditional pursuit of "humane internationalism" (Black, chapter 13), particularly given that Canada pioneered the establishment of the term and practice of "gender equality" in international forums. This change in the discourse disengages Canada from the globally established tradition of gender and development. Yet the Harper government continues to exploit women in developing countries for the sake of political gain (Turenne Sjolander, chapter 14)—for example, by justifying the mission in Afghanistan in terms of Canada's "crucial responsibility" to ensure "that the advances made by Afghan women over the last 9 years are not lost" (Oda, 2010).

The silencing of gender in Canadian foreign policy is a calculated and deliberate strategy to appeal to a conservative domestic constituency that perceives "gender equality" as an objectionable policy. Gecelovsky (chapter 7) expands on this argument with examples of conservative values–based lobby groups (e.g., REAL Women for Canada) that have taken a strong stand on issues such as abortion. Brown and Hessini argue that we must "focus on power dynamics . . . to understand the continued marginalisation of abortion by drawing attention to those whose interests are at stake, those who benefit and those who suffer as a result" (2004: 44). The calculated silencing of gender in Canadian foreign policy is part of the "principled decisiveness" that characterizes the Conservative government's foreign policy "flowing from Harper's penchant for rational policy analysis, the constraint of minority government, and his concern with the next election campaign" (Kirton, 2009). Harper had much to gain from not allocating Canadian funds to abortion in developing countries. The Conservative government appeased the traditional conservative political base in Canada through a modest maternal health proposal, while enabling Harper to avoid committing political suicide by reopening the abortion debate in Canada. Harper instead pleased his traditional domestic constituency by presenting himself as "pro-life" in his foreign policy (Gecelovsky, chapter 7). The hypocrisy in the Conservative government's foreign policy is clear: the Harper government exports a policy that negates the right of women living in developing countries to access safe abortions, but it makes it clear that women's right to access abortion services in Canada will not be revisited (Chase, 2011).

The duplicity of Canada's foreign policy is also evident in the fact that Harper emphasized that Canada would respect the health policies of developing countries in instituting the Muskoka Initiative. Even though Canada conceded that family planning would be funded as part of its contribution to the strategy, the "countries of focus" (consistent with a broader trend at CIDA towards "less and bigger projects" and increased geographic concentration, the majority of funds will be disbursed in the 10 countries of focus) selected by the Harper government for the Muskoka Initiative are countries where the rights of women are marginalized, such as Afghanistan and Sudan, and where decision-making on matters of maternal and reproductive health remains a male prerogative. Indeed, in all of the countries of focus, abortion is illegal (except, in certain instances, where the life of the mother is at risk), and in most, access to contraception is limited. As a result, of the eight projects announced by Canada in May 2011 as part of the Muskoka Initiative, only one, "Accelerating the reduction of maternal and newborn mortality in Nigeria," deals to some extent with enhancing access to family planning resources (Government of Canada, 2011).

Second, the hypocrisy of the Conservatives' foreign policy is evident in that Harper preaches about the moral imperative of reducing maternal mortality even while not all Canadian women have equal access to quality health care. Canada has one of the world's lowest rates of maternal mortality. However, the rate of infant, post-neonatal, and maternal deaths in Nunavut is more than three times the national average (Health Canada, 2004). Inuit women are "evacuated" from their communities to give birth in southern Canada owing to a shortage of doctors, nurses, and skilled midwives in the North. Evacuated women face emotional, social, cultural, and financial costs related to their evacuation. Indeed, a connection with the land bears significant importance in Inuit culture, and thus many communities do not view children born outside Nunavut as "real Inuit." What's more, if complications arise prior to the scheduled medical evacuation, such as an ectopic pregnancy (the leading cause of maternal death in Canada), the health of Inuit women is further compromised. If Harper's motives for championing maternal and newborn health at the G8 were truly motivated by a desire to "save lives" and achieve MDG 5, why has this desire for action not been translated into improved health services for Inuit women in Canada's North?

Lastly, the Harper government was late in jumping on the maternal health bandwagon. Several other donors, such as the British Department for International Development (DFID), the Nordic countries, the Bill & Melinda Gates Foundation, and the Clinton Foundation, have been leaders in improving maternal health in developing countries for much longer, and have dedicated far more resources, than Canada. International attention and policy commitments to reproductive health issues were reaffirmed in 1994 in Cairo, where delegates formally recognized that reproductive and sexual health, as well as the promotion of gender equality, are important for improvement of quality of life for women, children, and communities (International Conference on Population and Development, 1994). G8 countries have also been active on this issue since the alarm was raised by the UN about the danger of not reaching MDG 5, with the United Kingdom, the United States, and Nordic countries leading the charge (Berthiaume, 2010). Harper's and Oda's announcements that Canada is a world leader in catapulting maternal health onto the international stage are disingenuous and serve to reinforce the fictitious notion of Canada as a functionalist power, a moral compass on the international stage, an honest broker, a humane internationalist (Pratt, 1989), and a valiant supporter of multilateral organizations. The reality, however, is much different, and Stephen Lewis accuses the Conservative government of "pretending" to lead the world: it "stumbled on it [the maternal health issue] and finds it politically advantageous to pursue it at the G8" (Berthiaume, 2010). By championing maternal health at the G8, the Conservative government was able to Canadianize an international program of action already in progress. This resulted in positive media reports on the Harper government both in Canada and abroad; gender health was thus used as a tool of Canadian foreign policy rather than as an end in itself. The hypocrisy of the Harper government's Muskoka Initiative demonstrates that Canadian foreign policy—and official development assistance in particular—has been instrumentalized to advance Canada's national interests, leaving little room for values and humane internationalism in the policy process.

The consequence of Harper's **hypocritical internationalism** is that those who have the most to lose from the Muskoka Initiative—namely the 68,000 women who die each year from unsafe abortions in Africa and Asia—are silenced in the policy process. The fact that 98 per cent of women who die from an unsafe abortion are in developing countries and that most of maternal deaths in Canada are from the Inuit population is reminiscent of the class discrimination of the Birkinhead Drill aboard the *Titanic*. Canada's foreign policy demonstrates a clear division between the rights of Canadian women and the rights of women in developing countries. Even though Harper would never dare reopen the abortion debate in Canada for fear of the political repercussions, the health of women in poor countries has been put on the line for the sake of the political gain of the Conservative government, which, since having taken power, has blatantly rejected gender equality as a fundamental principle of Canadian foreign policy. In the next section, we present the case of maternal health in Sudan, one of Canada's 10 countries of focus for the Muskoka Initiative, to demonstrate how gender considerations cannot be divorced from maternal health, and we discuss the consequences of the silencing of gender in Canadian foreign policy.

Why Maternal Health Is a Gender Equality Issue. Examples from South Sudan

In order for the international donor community to be effective in addressing maternal health problems, it is essential that the causes of poor maternal health be understood. In this section, we examine the societal, cultural, and gender-related issues that contribute to maternal health complications and high rates of maternal mortality. Examples from South Sudan are used to highlight the range and depth of issues to be considered in foreign policy initiatives aimed at improving maternal health and to decrease maternal mortality dramatically.

South Sudan has one of the highest rates of maternal mortality in the world, with more than 2,000 maternal deaths for every 100,000 live births (UNDP Sudan, 2008) and with maternal mortality increasing since the end of the civil war in Sudan (*Sudan Tribune*, 2001). Thus, the target of reducing maternal mortality by 75 per cent by 2015 is "seriously off track" (Cross and Graham, 2010: 147). The maternal deaths have direct causes, such as haemorrhage and sepsis, as well as indirect causes, such as HIV/AIDS and malaria (Cross, Bell, and Graham, 2010: 147). To understand the causes of high maternal mortality rates in South Sudan, however, one must understand the broader historical, societal, cultural, and gender-specific challenges faced by these communities.

Women in South Sudan face numerous health challenges as a result of Sudan's 21-year war, which ended in 2005. The enduring effects of the conflict—particularly violence, torture, rape, and the spread of sexually transmitted infections—and the ongoing humanitarian disasters in the region—the consequence of small-scale violence and food insecurity—contribute to ongoing health issues. In addition, the lack of a health infrastructure, insufficient health-care facilities, and few practitioners for women of child-bearing age result in numerous maternal health and gynaecological problems.

Some of the maternal health practices that were identified by women in South Sudan can also help us make sense of the broader issues in the communities. A common childbirth practice for women in South Sudan is to give birth under a tree with the assistance of another woman from the village, as health clinics are often too far away to reach in time. The traditional birth attendants have little training and few supplies, and thus the birth is carried out in unsanitary conditions. Maternal deaths are most commonly attributed to occur during labour, delivery, and the immediate postpartum period. While obstetric haemorrhage is the main medical cause of death, other causes of maternal death include unsafe abortions and the spread of STIs, including HIV/AIDS (Ronsmans and Graham, 2006). The decades-long civil war, the ongoing resettlement of returning refugees, and polygamous marriage customs have led to very high rates of STIs such as syphilis.

Cultural practices in South Sudan can also contribute to maternal health complications. Early marriage poses an additional maternal health risk, as girls may not have achieved the required physical maturity necessary for childbirth, putting them at greater risk of maternal complications and death. Early marriage also reflects gender inequality and human rights abuses in the region, as girls are more likely than boys to be married at an early age (UNICEF, 2010). Research by USAID (2007) indicated that women have inhibitions about using services when experiencing complications in labour. An obstruction in labour—or, more generally, a difficult labour—is culturally considered as a sign that the woman has been unfaithful to her husband. In cases of obstructed labour, the mother is frequently denied help unless she admits to infidelity (Pearson and Shoo, 2005; USAID, 2007). An obstructed labour resulting in maternal death in these instances is frequently blamed on the mother for "hiding the truth" (Pearson and Shoo, 2005). In other cultural practices, labour is considered a test of courage—a woman who complains or cries is considered a coward or weak. Women are therefore less likely to complain about pain, report potential labour problems, or seek assistance, wishing to appear as brave as possible (USAID, 2007: 21). Finally, a culture of violence against women, particularly domestic violence, makes it difficult for women to demand better maternal health services.

The challenges faced by women in South Sudan need to be understood in the context of institutionalized gender inequality and gender norms in society. Women are treated as second-class citizens in many parts of Sudan. Girls are generally treated as commodities and exchanged for cows once they are of marriageable age. The subordinate position of women in South Sudanese society means that women suffer from immense gender inequality. Their societal position needs to be understood in relation to inequitable gender roles, unequal access to resources, and few decision-making rights. Gender inequality, then, manifests itself in other issues and challenges experienced by women, such as in the areas of health, sanitation, water, education, participation, security, and violence. The enduring effects of the war in South Sudan have exacerbated the community-level challenges and contributed to greater gender inequality; women and children are even more insecure because of the "disruption of community and family structures, breakdown in conflict resolution mechanisms, presence of arms and vigilantes, prevalent trauma, increased alcohol consumption, weak security institutions, poor law and order and tensions between those who have been displaced and those who have stayed put" (Elia, 2007: 39). Furthermore, there is limited understanding of the link between these health challenges and broader societal issues, including sexually transmitted infections, malnutrition, violence, and lack of education.

Customary laws continue to be used to justify discriminatory actions towards women. Customs and traditions such as forced and early marriages perpetuate gender discrimination and contribute to challenges in maternal health. Furthermore, the "low status of women in society and their dependency on others, financially and in decision-making, undermine their autonomy and negatively affect their ability to access essential maternal health services. There is a direct link between harmful traditional practices and the spread of HIV/AIDS, which is a major cause of indirect maternal mortality" (Ratsma and Malongo, 2009: 51). While there is international recognition of the challenges of gender inequality for improved maternal health, challenges still exist in the implementation of gender-sensitive health policies. One such challenge stems from foreign aid programs that target women and children in maternal health programs but fail to consider the broader societal, cultural, and gender-inequitable communities in which maternal health remains such a large problem. To address maternal health, we must begin by recognizing that there are gendered obstacles that prevent men and, especially, women from realizing their potential for health (Doyal, 2000: 931). We must also recognize that international programs and foreign aid packages do not do enough to ensure that the underlying causes of maternal health are addressed. In fact, international assistance is temporary and most likely ineffective and unsustainable. Thus, the slow advances—and even setbacks—in female well-being and gender equality point to a lack of political will, as well as to insufficient and ineffective resource allocation to the priority areas (Billson and Fluehr-Lobban, 2005).

Conclusion

In 2010, Prime Minister Harper announced that maternal health would be addressed as a key issue at the G8 meeting held in Canada, and in 2011, he backed the UN's commitment to address maternal health around the world in an effort to save the lives of millions of women and children. However, Harper's Muskoka Initiative fails to acknowledge that poor maternal health is a symptom of broader societal, cultural, and gender issues. Policy-makers addressing maternal health must move beyond the chivalrous facade of rescuing "women and children first" and instead seek to understand why the ship is sinking in the first place and how to prevent it from sinking in the future.

Focusing on maternal health from a gender-based starting point allows us to understand women's health in relation to women's access to resources and facilities and to their participation in community-level decision-making, as well as to gender norms and societal practices that have a disproportionately negative impact on women and girls. Exposing the multi-layered nature of health and human rights issues in South Sudan reveals the myriad challenges facing communities in this region, but especially the challenges of gender-based violations of rights and the gendered human insecurity linked to maternal health issues. This example is used to illustrate the importance of a broader and deeper programmatic focus on gender in maternal health and to expose the silencing of gender in Canadian foreign policy. Indeed, programming areas that could strengthen gender equality are for the most part absent from the first eight projects announced by the government of Canada in May 2011, prior to the Deauville G8 meeting. The outlook for a gender-sensitive maternal health initiative under the current Conservative regime is bleak given the silencing of gender in Canadian foreign policy; the instrumentalization of Canadian official development assistance, which serves to advance Canada's national interest; the gradual demise of humane internationalism (Black, chapter 13); and the hypocrisy that surrounds Canada's pursuit of "equality of men and women" on the international stage. Harper's internationalism, as embodied by his maternal health initiative, meets the hypocrisy criteria established by Angus in the 1930s: while the Canadian government has sought to justify its action on the moral grounds of "saving women and children first," the maternal health policy was propelled by the political need to appeal to a conservative political base that thinks that gender equality is an objectionable policy objective, and to appease a constituency that resents Harper's refusal to revisit abortion rights in Canada. Again, the gendered needs of women and children in developing countries come last.

Key Terms

gender equality
erasure of gender/degendering process
Muskoka Initiative

hypocritical internationalism
maternal health

Study Questions

1. Carrier and Tiessen put forth that "hypocrisy" is a valid lens through which to assess Canadian foreign policy. What makes hypocritical internationalism a contested concept?
2. Are there any specific connections between domestic and foreign Canadian policy-making?
3. In what ways do traditional constructions of femininity constrain maternal health?

4. Should foreign policies be gender-neutral or recognize gender difference? In both cases, what would be the impact? And in the latter case, should this apply to both biological factors and social constructions?
5. Is the erasure of gender in Canadian foreign policy a recent phenomenon?

Note

1   "Mothers and Whores" is the title of Kathryn Carovano's 1992 article on AIDS prevention campaigns targeting women in developing countries.

References

Angus, H.F. 1934. "Canada and a Foreign Policy." *Dalhousie Review*, October.

Baines, Erin K. 2003. "The Contradictions of Canadian Commitments to Refugee Women." In Claire Turenne Sjolander, Heather Smith, and Deborah Stienstra, eds, *Feminist Perspectives on Canadian Foreign Policy*. Don Mills, ON: Oxford University Press, 155–71.

Bautista-Arredondo, Sergio, et al. 2008. "Optimizing Resource Allocation for HIV/AIDS Prevention Programmes: An Analytical Framework." *AIDS* 22, 1: 67–74.

Berthiaume, Lee. 2010. "Harper's Maternal, Child Health Speech 'Political Opportunism': Stephen Lewis." *Embassy Magazine*, 3 February. At http://www.embassymag.ca/page/printpage/maternal-02-03-2010.

Bhutta, Zulfiqar A., et al. 2010. "Countdown to 2015 Decade Report (2000–10): Taking Stock of Maternal, Newborn, and Child Survival." *The Lancet* 375, 9730: 2032–44.

Billson, Janet Mancini, and Carolyn Fluehr-Lobban. 2005. "Toward Global Female Well-Being." In Billson and Fluehr-Lobban, eds, *Female Well-Being: Toward a Global Theory of Social Change*. London and New York: Zed Books, 392–411.

Brodie, Janine, and Isabelle Bakker. 2008. "Where Are the Women? Gender Equity, Budgets and Canadian Public Policy." *Canadian Centre for Policy Alternatives*. At http://www.policyalternatives. ca/sites/default/files/uploads/publications/National_Office_Pubs/2008/Where_Are_the_Women-en_Contents_Intro.pdf.

Brown, Tamara, and Leslie Hessini. 2004. "The Power Dynamics Perpetuating Unsafe Abortion in Africa: A Feminist Perspective." *African Journal of Reproductive Health* 8, 1: 43–51.

Cannon, Lawrence. 2010. "Maternal Health Plan about Saving Lives, Not 'Family Planning': Canadian Foreign Affairs Minister." *LifeSiteNews*, 17 March. At http://www.lifesitenews.com/news/archive/ldn/2010/mar/10031710.

Carovano, Kathryn. 1992. "More Than Mothers and Whores: Redefining the AIDS Prevention Needs of Women." *International Journal of Health Services* 21: 131–42.

CBC News. 2010a. "G8 Maternal Health Initiative Draws Flak." 23 June. At http://www.cbc.ca/news/world/story/2010/06/23/g8-maternal-health-initiative.html.

CBC News. 2010b. "Clinton Backs Contraception for Maternal Health." 31 March. At http://www.cbc.ca/news/canada/story/2010/03/30/clinton-contraception.html.

Chase, Steven. 2011. "Majority Won't Spur Change on Abortion or Same-Sex Marriage, Harper Says." *Globe and Mail*, 4 April. At http://www.theglobeandmail.com/news/politics/ottawa-notebook/majority-wont-spur-change-on-abortion-or-same-sex-marriage-harper-says/article1970073/.

Chervenak, Frank A., and Laurence B. McCullough. 2009. "Women and Children First: Transforming a Historic Moment into a Contemporary Ethical Imperative." *American Journal of Obstetrics & Gynaecology* 201, 4: 351.

Collins, Michelle. 2009. "'Gender Equality,' 'Child Soldiers' and 'Humanitarian Law' Are Axed from Foreign Policy Language." *Embassy Magazine*, 29 July. At http://www.embassymag.ca/page/view/foreignpolicy-7-29-2009.

Cornwall, Andrea, Hilary Standing, and Andrea Lynch. 2009. "Introduction: Putting Unsafe Abortion on the Development Agenda." *IDS Bulletin* 39, 3: 1–9.

Craine, Patrick B. 2010. "PM Harper 'Caves': 'Not Closing the Door' on Contraception in G8 Maternal Health Push." *Lifesitenews*, 19 March. At http://www.lifesitenews.com/news/archive/ldn/2010/mar/10031911.

Cross, Suzanne, Jacqueline Bell, and Wendy J. Graham. 2010. "What You Count Is What You Target: The Implications of Maternal Death Classification for Tracking Progress towards Reducing Maternal Mortality in Developing Countries." *Bulletin of the World Health Organization* 88, 2: 147–53.

Day, Shelagh. 2003. "Women's Human Rights: Canada at Home and Abroad." In Claire Turenne Sjolander, Heather Smith, and Deborah Stienstra, eds, *Feminist Perspectives on Canadian Foreign Policy*. Don Mills, ON: Oxford University Press, 126–36.

Denholm Crosby, Ann. 2003. "Myths of Canada's Human Security Pursuits: Tales of Tool Boxes, Toy Chests, and Tickle Trunks." In Claire Turenne Sjolander, Heather Smith, and Deborah Stienstra, eds, *Feminist Perspectives on Canadian Foreign Policy*. Don Mills, ON: Oxford University Press, 90–108.

Doyal, Lesley. 2000. "Gender Equity in Health: Debates and Dilemmas." *Social Science and Medicine* 51, 6: 931–9.

Dunkle, Kristin L., et al. 2004. "Gender-Based Violence, Relationship Power, and Risk of HIV Infection in Women Attending Antenatal Clinics in South Africa." *The Lancet* 363, 9419: 1414–21.

Elia, Lona. 2007. "Fighting Gender-Based Violence in South Sudan." *Forced Migration Review* 27: 39–40. At http://www.fmreview.org/FMRpdfs/FMR27/25.pdf.

Friedman Ross, Lainie, and Justin M. Coffey. 2003. "Women and Children First: Applicable to Lifeboats—Applicable to Human Experimentation." *Journal of Health Care Law and Policy* 6, 1: 14–33.

Garcia-Moreno, Claudia, and Charlotte Watts. 2000. "Violence against Women: Its Importance for HIV/AIDS." *AIDS* 14, 3: S253–65.

Government of Canada. 2011. "Backgrounder—New Maternal, Newborn and Child Health Initiatives." 27 May. At http://news.gc.ca/web/article-eng.do?nid=603569.

Grimes, David A., Janie Benson, Susheela Singh, Mariana Romero, Bela Ganatra, Friday E. Okonofua, and Iqbal H. Shah. 2006. "Unsafe Abortion: The Preventable Pandemic." *The Lancet* 368, 9550: 1908–19.

Guebert, Jenilee. 2010. "What Happened to the Maternal and Child Health Initiative at the 2010 G8 Muskoka Summit?" *G8 Information Centre*, 29 June. At http://www.g8.utoronto.ca/evaluations/2010muskoka/guebert-mcnh.html.

Harper, Stephen. 2010. "G8 Agenda: Focus on Human Welfare." *Toronto Star*, 26 January. At http://www.thestar.com/opinion/article/755721--g8-agenda-focus-on-human-welfare.

Health Canada. 2004. "Special Report on Maternal Mortality and Severe Morbidity in Canada—Enhanced Surveillance: The Path to Prevention." Ottawa: Minister of Public Works and Government Services Canada. At http://www.phac-aspc.gc.ca/rhs-ssg/srmm-rsmm/pdf/mat_mortality_e.pdf.

Hearst, Norman, and Sanny Chen. 2004. "Condom Promotion for AIDS Prevention in the Developing World: Is It Working?" *Studies in Family Planning* 35, 1: 39–47.

Heise, Lori L., and Christopher Elias. 1995. "Transforming AIDS Prevention to Meet Women's Needs: A Focus on Developing Countries." *Social Science & Medicine* 40, 7: 931–43.

International Conference on Population and Development. 1994. Summary of the Programme of Action. At http://www.un.org/ecosocdev/geninfo/populatin/icpd.htm#chapter4.

Isis-WICCE. 2007. "Women's Experiences during Armed Conflict in Southern Sudan, 1983–2005: The Case of Juba County, Central Equatorial State." At http://www.isis.or.ug/component/docman/

doc_view/115-womens-experiences-during-armed-conflict-in-southern-sudan-1983--2005-the-case-of-juba-county--?tmpl=component&format=raw.

Jha, Prabhat., J.D. Nagelkerke, E.N. Ngugi, J.V. Prasada Rao, B. Willbond, S. Moses, F.A. Plummer et al. 2001. "Reducing HIV Transmission in Developing Countries." *Science* 292, 5515: 224–5.

Kirton, John. 2009. "The Harper Years: Lecture on Canadian Foreign Policy." 24 November, University of Toronto, Lecture Notes. At http://www.g8.utoronto.ca/teaching/312/cfp-12-2009.pdf.

Lancet, The. 2010. "Canada's G8 Health Leadership." *The Lancet* 375, 9726: 1580.

Maman, Suzanne, Jacquelyn Campbell, Michael D. Sweat, and Andrea C. Gielen. 2000. "The Intersections of HIV and Violence: Directions for Future Research and Interventions. *Social Science & Medicine* 50, 4: 459–78.

Maman, Suzanne, Jessie K. Mbwambo, Nora M. Hogan, Gad P. Kilonzo, Jacquelyn C. Campbell, Ellen Weiss, and Michael D. Sweat. 2002. "HIV-Positive Women Report More Lifetime Partner Violence: Findings from a Voluntary Counselling and Testing Clinic in Dar es Salaam, Tanzania." *American Journal of Public Health* 92, 8: 1331–7.

Nossal, Kim. 1988. "Mixed Motives Revisited: Canada's Interest in Development Assistance." *Canadian Journal of Political Science* 21, 1: 35–56.

Oda, Beverley J. 2010. "Minister Oda Talking Points on Canada's New Role in Afghanistan." 16 November. At http://www.afghanistan.gc.ca/canada-afghanistan/speeches-discours/2010/2010_11_16a.aspx.

Okonofua, Friday E. 2008. "Contribution of Anti-abortion Laws to Maternal Mortality in Developing Countries." *Expert Review of Obstetrics & Gynecology* 3, 2: 147–9.

Pearson, L., and R. Shoo. 2005. "Availability and Use of Emergency Obstetric Services: Kenya, Rwanda, Southern Sudan and Uganda." *International Journal of Gynecology & Obstetrics* 88, 2: 208–15.

Pettifor, Audrey, Nora Rosenberg, and Frieda Behets. 2011. "The Need to Focus on Sex Workers in Generalized Epidemic Settings." *Journal of the American Sexually Transmitted Diseases Association* 38, 4: 324–5.

Plewes, Betty, and Joanna Kerr. 2010 "Politicizing, Undermining Gender Equality." *Embassy Magazine,* 22 September 22. At http://www.embassymag.ca/page/email_story/equality-05-05-2010.

Potts, Malcolm, Daniel T. Halperin, Douglas Kirby, Ann Swidler, Elliot Marseille, Jeffrey D. Klausner, Norman Hearst, Richard G. Wamai, James G. Kahn, Julia Walsh et al. 2008. "Reassessing HIV Prevention." *Science* 320: 749–50.

Pratt, Cranford. 1989. "Humane Internationalism: Its Significance and Variants." In Cranford Pratt, ed., *Internationalism under Strain*. Toronto: University of Toronto Press.

Rathgeber, Eva M. 1990. "WID, WAD, GAD: Trends in Research and Practice." *Journal of Developing Areas* 24, 4: 489–502.

———. 1995. "Gender and Development in Action." In M.H. Marchand and J.L. Parpart, eds, *Feminism/Postmodernism/Development*. International Studies of Women and Place series. London: Routledge, 204–20.

Ratsma, Ymkje, and Joyce Malongo. 2009. "Maternal Health and Human Rights." *Malawi Medical Journal* 21, 2: 51–3.

Rivers, J.P.W. 1982. "Women and Children Last: An Essay on Sex Discrimination in Disasters." *Disasters* 6, 4: 256–67.

Ronsmans, Carine, and Wendy J. Graham. 2006. "Maternal Mortality: Who, When, Where and Why." *The Lancet* 368, 9542: 1189–200.

Smith, Heather A. 2003. "Disrupting Internationalism and Finding the Other." In Claire Turenne Sjolander, Heather Smith, and Deborah Stienstra, eds, *Feminist Perspectives on Canadian Foreign Policy*. Don Mills, ON: Oxford University Press, 24–39.

Smith, Heather A., Deborah Stienstra, and Claire Turenne Sjolander. 2003. "Taking Up and Throwing Down the Gauntlet: Feminists, Gender, and Canadian Foreign Policy." In Claire Turenne Sjolander, Heather Smith, and Deborah Stienstra, eds, *Feminist Perspectives on Canadian Foreign Policy*. Don Mills, ON: Oxford University Press, 1–12.

Stevans, Lonnie K., and David Gleicher. 2004. "Who Survived the *Titanic*? A Logistic Regression Analysis." *International Review of Maritime History* 16, 2: 61–94.

Sudan Tribune. 2010. "Maternal Mortality Continues to Increase in Southern Sudan." 15 September. At http://www.sudantribune.com/spip.php?article36271.

Swiss, Liam. Forthcoming. "Gender, Security, and Instrumentalism: Canada's Foreign Aid in Support of National Interest?" In Stephen Brown, ed., *Struggling for Effectiveness: CIDA and Canadian Aid Policy*. Montreal and Kingston: McGill-Queen's University Press.

Tankink, Marian, and Annemiek Richters. 2007. "Silence as a Coping Strategy: The Case of Refugee Women in the Netherlands from South-Sudan Who Experienced Sexual Violence in the Context of War." In Boris Drozdek and John P. Wilson, eds, *Voices of Trauma Treating Psychological Trauma across Cultures*. Springer, 191–210.

Tiessen, Rebecca, 2003. "Masculinities, Femininities, and Sustainable Development: A Gender Analysis of DFAIT's Sustainable Development Strategy." In Claire Turenne Sjolander, Heather Smith, and Deborah Stienstra, eds, *Feminist Perspectives on Canadian Foreign Policy*. Don Mills, ON: Oxford University Press, 108–26.

Tiessen, Rebecca, and Sarah Tuckey. Forthcoming. "Losing Gender along the Way: CIDA, Gender Mainstreaming and the Securitization of Development." In Rosalind Warner, ed., *Ethics and Security in Canadian Foreign Policy*. Vancouver: University of British Columbia Press.

Tjaden, Patricia, and Nancy Thoennes. 1998. "Prevalence, Incidence and Consequences of Violence against Women: Findings from the National Violence against Women Survey." National Institute of Justice/Centers for Disease Control and Prevention. At http://www.ncjrs.gov/pdffiles/172837.pdf.

Turenne Sjolander, Claire. 2005. "Canadian Foreign Policy: Does Gender Matter?" *Canadian Foreign Policy Journal/La politique étrangère du Canada* 12, 1: 19–31.

Turenne Sjolander, Claire, Heather Smith, and Deborah Stienstra, eds. 2003. *Feminist Perspectives on Canadian Foreign Policy*, 1–12. Don Mills, ON: Oxford University Press.

Turner, Malcolm. 1988. *Shipwrecks & Salvage in South Africa—1505 to the Present*. Cape Town: Struik.

UN (United Nations). 2009. "The Millennium Development Goals Report." At http://www.un.org/millenniumgoals/pdf/MDG_Report_2009_ENG.pdf.

UNAIDS. 2005. "Intensifying HIV Prevention: A UNAIDS Policy Position Paper." Geneva.

UNDP Sudan. 2008. "Status of MDGs in Sudan in 2008." *United Nations Development Program*. At http://www.sd.undp.org/mdg_fact.htm.

UNICEF. 2010. "Child Protection from Violence, Exploitation and Abuse." At http://www.unicef.org/protection/index_earlymarriage.html.

USAID. 2007. "Southern Sudan Maternal and Reproductive Health Rapid Assessment." 8–21 September. At http://pdf.usaid.gov/pdf_docs/PNADN752.pdf.

Walsh, C., and N. Jones. 2009. "Maternal and Child Health: The Social Protection Dividend." UNICEF, February. At http://www.unicef.org/wcaro/wcaro_UNICEF_ODI_4_Health_Social_Protection_Dividends.pdf.

Webster, P.C. 2010. "International Experts Laud Canadian Child and Maternal Health Plan." *Canadian Medical Association Journal* 182, 9: 399–400.

Zierler, Sally, and Nancy Krieger. 1997. "Reframing Women's Risk: Social Inequalities and HIV Infection." *Annual Review of Public Health* 18: 401–36.

12 Forget the Fine Tuning: Internationalism, the Arctic, and Climate Change

Heather A. Smith

→ multilateral approach

In the introduction to their volume *Canadian Foreign Policy in Critical Perspective*, J. Marshall Beier and Lana Wylie write: "[T]he imaginable possibilities at play in discussions and debates about Canadian foreign policy have largely been confined to that which sits well with at least the broad strokes of the status quo. ... [T]hese discussions and debates have been more hospitable to those whose project is in some way to fine-tune the status quo and to make it function better than to those who see it as something to be transformed or transcended altogether" (2010: xiv).

This observation has had a profound impact on my thinking about internationalism as a theme or organizing framework in my own research. Why do I keep going back to internationalism? Am I using internationalism as my foil or framework because it legitimizes my work as somehow "Canadian foreign policy" (CFP)? If I use the language of internationalism, good international citizenship, multilateralism, and volunteerism, does that give my work credibility and provide greater access to a larger number of readers? Does it mark it as worthy of inclusion in volumes on Canada in the world? By adopting the traditional lexicon of CFP, do I seek a stamp of approval, a nod, a place on a reading list? Does using internationalism as a central theme in a number of my published works (Smith, 2003, 2008–9, 2009) undermine the critical project that also informs my work?

I have used internationalism largely as a foil. Typically, I've tried to turn internationalism on its head, to show the places where motifs associated with internationalism—and the model of Canada that is articulated in government discourse—are used as a means by which to obfuscate the realities of those who are silenced. But there is still a feeling that my sense of imaginable possibilities is limited by the terms of reference, regardless of my rather disruptive intentions. Part of my project, of course, is to speak to a particular audience with the intent of showing them the value of a critical approach. There is value to this path because it provides alternatives to mainstream approaches, challenges scholars to consider the insights offered by critical approaches, and provides students with a glimpse of other ways of seeing the world. At the same time, it is I—the critical scholar—coming to the core, coming to work within the parameters defined by the core, using the language of the core. By doing this, I feel as though I've come to the dinner table to find that my meal has already been ordered for me, by someone else. I can put as much hot sauce as I want on that meal, but it is still not the meal I would have ordered. In the meantime, I'm checking out what is going on at other tables.

At those other tables are authors such as Marysia Zalewski (2006), Roxanne Doty (2001), Steve Smith (1995), and Cynthia Enloe (1996, 2004). Marysia Zalewski is writing about feminist methodology in a way that has me returning time and time again to her work, inspired by her "distracted" reflections that reject being a "mainstream clone" (2006: 46). She disrupts mainstream "methodological security" and encourages her readers to "refuse the rush to decidability" (60).

In the dinner discussion at another table, Roxanne Doty may make the following observation:

> Theories have become commodities, adorning us, dangling like gaudy jewels from our intellectual egos. They often say more about the academic community that trades in them than the issues they are ostensibly addressing and the people whose lives are at the center of these issues. Too often they fail to do justice to what is happening in the world to flesh-and-blood people. They almost always fail to recognize and take responsibility for the violence of their own representations. (2001: 525)

Steve Smith, similar to Doty, joins in by reminding us that "silences are the loudest voices" (1995: 2). In the world of international relations, the voices are those of political leaders and diplomats—if we are lucky. Too often the voices are abstractions buried in an authoritative tone and a methodological rigor that renders people silent. The state, power, and war are privileged, and "thus, in the name of enlightenment and knowledge, international theory has tended to be a discourse accepting of, and complicit in, the creation and re-creation of international practices that threaten, discipline and do violence to others" (1995: 3).

Cynthia Enloe's (1996) work describes the Jackson Pollock nature of the world as she seeks to paint for us the wonderful chaos that is a Pollock piece of work. She colours our world with the voices of women who are sex workers, flight attendants, chambermaids, secretaries, and Mayan nannies. And in the midst of her feminist investigations, she calls on us to remain curious. Enloe argues that status quo power structures rely on our lack of curiosity and that "*uncuriosity* is dangerously comfortable if it can be dressed up in the sophisticated attire of reasonableness and intellectual efficiency: 'We can't be investigating everything'" (2004: 3).

And, of course, sitting at one of those tables is Robert Cox. Cox's observation that "theory is always for someone and for some purpose" (1986: 207) is a mainstay in my work—a constant presence and reminder of the need to reflect on what a theory brings to the table. We—I—need to remember that "there is ... no such thing as theory in itself, divorced from a standpoint in time and space. When a theory so represents itself, it is more important to examine it as an ideology, and to lay bare its concealed perspective" (207).

None of this is to suggest that my own assessments of internationalism have lacked feminist or **critical theory** influences. Those influences have indeed shaped almost all my previous analyses, and yet I feel that by focusing on internationalism, even disrupting internationalism, I've still allowed the **concealed perspective** that informs internationalism to shape my thinking. And I am uncomfortable with this situation. I wonder if I have been sufficiently curious.

My aim here, then, is to "lay bare" the concealed perspective embedded in internationalism and show the limitations of the components of that perspective when examined in the case of climate change and the Arctic. This is not an analysis of whether or not the Canadian government discourse related to the Arctic and climate change is informed by internationalism or whether Canadian Arctic policy is internationalist or continentalist. For this chapter I want to try to stand outside internationalism.

Standing outside internationalism, consistent with a Coxian framework, means standing "apart from the prevailing order of the world" and assessing the "social and political context as a whole" (Cox, 1986: 208). In this instance, my intent is to consider the ways in which our academic and intellectual world order is constructed by mainstream interpretations of internationalism. Questions from the outside ask about the theoretical project itself and the embedded epistemological and ontological assumptions that mainstream interpretations of internationalism share. These assumptions function as parameters for what is acceptable for investigation or privileges particular vantage points. In the case here, it will be seen that internationalism constructs a theoretical world that privileges the state, excludes a human dimension and abstracts from the everyday, and assumes race neutrality.

When we start with these epistemological and methodological assumptions, our analyses are inevitably circumscribed and limited. These assumptions shape our analysis and have implications for how we see the world. The limits of the concealed perspective can be seen when we consider the Conservative government discourse and mainstream political science analyses of the Arctic and climate change. In that world, the state is supreme, humans are routinely absent, and race is rarely considered.

Internationalism: A Starting Point

As this volume shows, internationalism has been defined in a variety of ways and has been subject to multiple interpretations. In an analysis of internationalism during the Chrétien era, Kim Richard Nossal identifies four characteristics of internationalism: multilateralism, "creation, maintenance and managing community" (1998/9: 98), good international citizenship, and voluntarism. In *International Policy and Politics in Canada*, Kim Richard Nossal, Stéphane Roussel, and Stéphane Paquin consider internationalism under the umbrella of "dominant ideas" and argue that internationalism has five elements. The first element is responsibility, understood to be that "each state with an interest in avoiding war must take a con- structive part in the management of conflicts that will inevitably arise in global politics" (Nossal, Roussel, and Paquin, 2011: 136). The second element is multi- lateralism, and the third is "participation in international institutions" (136). The fourth element they identify is "a willingness to enter into formal commitments to use national resources for the system as a whole," and the fifth element is "the reinforcement of, and respect for international law" (136).

John Kirton argues that there are variants of internationalism over time. According to Kirton, "thematic variations are dominant ideas, or orienting themes and rhetorical symbols" (2007: 39). These variants were created by policy-makers over time and often overlap, and the variations are "the sequential answers pro- vided by Canadian foreign policy practitioners in turn to the dilemmas and cen- tral questions of what Canada's international activity, association and approach to world order would be" (39). The four thematic variations identified by Kirton are as follows. Functionalism, the first variant, arose during the Second World War. Mediatory middlepowermanship, the second thematic variant, arguably arose through incremental practice and informed Canadian foreign policy until the late 1960s. With the arrival of Pierre Trudeau in office, we witnessed the emergence of what Kirton calls "distributive internationalism," which "aimed to reduce inequal- ities between rich and poor countries." Distributive internationalism has, accord- ing to Kirton, risen and fallen in importance over the last 40 years but has grown "in strength in the 21st century" (2007: 43). The final thematic variant identified by Kirton is niche diplomacy, which he associates with the Chrétien era. Niche diplomacy was designed as a response to the fiscal constraints facing the Liberal government and justified the contraction of Canadian participation abroad and Canadian spending on foreign and defence policy as well as on development assis- tance (Kirton, 2007: 43; see also Cooper, 1995; Potter, 1996/7; Smith, 2000).

Whether or not internationalism is still a dominant idea shaping Canadian for- eign policy or a tool used by the Conservative government to serve particular ends is a question subject to debate. Nossal, Roussel, and Paquin, for example, argue that even "if the governments of Jean Chrétien, Paul Martin, and Stephen Harper no longer use the word 'internationalist' to describe their foreign policies, there is lit- tle doubt that basic internationalist principles ... undergird Canada's international policies" (2011: 141). In contrast, I've argued that the Conservative government has manipulated the internationalist lexicon to serve its own purpose and to deflect attention away from policies that are contrary to internationalist principles (Smith, 2009). Claire Turenne Sjolander and Kathryn Trevenen (2010) have assessed the way in which the narrative of the good international citizen has been used in Con- servative government discourses related to Afghanistan in ways that limit dissent (see also Turenne Sjolander, chapter 14).

Identifying competing definitions of internationalism is valuable because it shows us the degree to which the idea is contested. Asking questions about the continued relevance of internationalism is useful because, as so many of the chapters in this volume show, the resulting analyses help us to understand the ways in which the Conservative government presents itself to the world. However, to consider internationalism from the outside, we need to step back from these debates and ask, what kind of theoretical world order is embedded in the debates and the competing interpretations? While my critique examines both mainstream and critical scholars' work from different epistemological assumptions, it is focused largely on the mainstream literature. Although, as will be seen, critical scholars who address mainstream questions are not immune from critique. It is now to the concealed perspective that I turn.

What Is Concealed in Internationalism?

When we consider the concept of internationalism, one of the elements that is glaringly obvious is that it is state-centric. Internationalism is about state behaviour, statecraft, diplomacy, and Canada in the world. And in spite of different theoretical projects, mainstream scholars and some critical scholars have focused on the actions of the state or the discourses of the state. Too often our analyses become about "Canada" and "Canada in the world." This is not to suggest that the state is entirely black-boxed because within analyses of internationalism, or of components of internationalism, there is typically reference to domestic actors such as provinces or ministers or prime ministers. However, our common starting point is the state, and the state is typically treated as unproblematic. The discourses of internationalism may be problematized and challenged, the policy actions may be questioned, but rarely does one find interrogations of the concepts of the state, state sovereignty, territory, and diplomacy that can be found in work of scholars such as Mark Salter (see Salter, chapter 9 and Salter, 2010), Roxanne Doty (2001), and Ravi de Costa (2009).

Scholars such as Salter, Doty, and de Costa remind us to think critically about the creation and recreation of sovereignty and borders. Salter, for example, argues that "the performance of the national border is fundamental to the appearance of security, the territorial limit of the state, and the integrity of the population" (2010: 75). Doty, too, reminds us that the "project of statecraft [is] ... a project that requires unambiguous boundaries that evoke a secure sense of knowing just who 'we' are" (2001: 527). De Costa focuses on indigenous diplomacies and argues that "the very notion of diplomacy is a European convention, a way of denoting formal practices of encounter across sovereign boundaries. Orthodox accounts of diplomacy thus reinscribe modernity's desire for boundaries and categorization, privileging separation and distinctiveness rather than connection and relation" (2009: 62).

However, these are not the questions that inform analyses of internationalism. The implications of the unproblematized state and unquestioned sovereignty are profound. The lack of reflection on our constructions of the state limits our debate, reinforces and legitimizes state-based or imagined boundaries, and supports (even if it is not our intent) government discourses that curtail our own imaginations.

The mainstream internationalism literature also abstracts from the everyday and lacks a human dimension. This is not a new argument, but it is one that bears repeating—and one that is worthy of reflection. As noted above, I am influenced by the insights of Christine Sylvester (1996) and Cynthia Enloe (1996, 2004), and I believe that we need to consider incorporating **everyday practice** into our understanding of Canada and the world. We need to look beyond statements and speeches by diplomats and prime ministers. We need to step away from the abstractions that we create in our constructions of Canada where we anthropomorphize the state but simultaneously neuter our analysis of emotional content. Who are the people affected by our policies and our actions? What are the voices that we don't hear when we spend all of our time dissecting the speeches of the prime minister or minister of foreign affairs? How do questions of Canada in the world translate "on the street"? Analyses of public opinion and internationalism as done by Don Munton (2002–3) do not count as "on the street" because they are yet again examples of abstracted human voices being categorized and quantified to serve the academic project. As Doty asks, where are the "flesh-and-blood people"? (2001: 525).

Following directly from the absence of flesh-and-blood people is the absence of any sense that race has any relevance to internationalism. In the discussions of multilateralism or the rule of law or good international citizenship in the mainstream literature, we are not encouraged to ask about race (just as we are not encouraged to inquire about gender). Interestingly, we have no systematic assessment of race and internationalism or race and Canadian foreign policy. Yet there are authors who have raised questions about race and internationalism, or about components of internationalism. For example, I have argued previously (Smith, 2003) that in assessments of internationalism we find no acknowledgement that the so-called golden era of Canadian foreign policy—an era that seems to have some mythological hold on some authors—was also an era of forced relocation of Inuit in the Eastern Arctic. Claire Turenne Sjolander and Kathryn Trevenen have questioned "the racial logic that informs narratives depicting peacekeepers as subduing unruly and savage Third World people" (2010: 49). Colleen Bell, in an analysis of Afghanistan, has shown us that the Canadian discourse around the humanitarian response to Afghanistan is rife with assumptions about the white man's burden (2010: 65). The work of these critical scholars is encouraging, but the fact remains that internationalism from the mainstream perspective is informed by a worldview according to which race doesn't seem to matter or is irrelevant. Starting with a vision of the world where race is rendered irrelevant, where colonial pasts and presents are not interrogated, is problematic.

This section has focused on laying bare the concealed perspective that informs internationalism. As I argued above, we need to look beyond debates about whether or not internationalism is still relevant to the current government or which is the preferred definition of internationalism. We need to remove ourselves from the details of definitions and debates and assess the kind of theoretical worldview that is modelled by scholars of internationalism. Doing this, we see that internationalism is state-centric and privileges the state, and that it lacks any human dimension and disregards everyday practice and assumes race neutrality. This concealed perspective is not unique to internationalism. It is shared. It cuts across much of our theorizing about Canadian foreign policy. The ways in which the elements of the concealed perspective work to limit our imaginations can be seen in the case of Canada, climate change, and the Arctic.

Reinforcing or Challenging Concealed Perspectives: The Case of Canada, the Arctic, and Climate Change

If we want to see a point of view of the Arctic that focuses on the state, is state-centric, and is focused on state sovereignty and territory in ways that reinforce the state and create or seek to secure unambiguous borders, all we need to do is turn to the Conservative government discourse around the Arctic. Securing "Canadian" sovereignty in the Arctic is of paramount importance to the Conservative government. In the words of our prime minister, "As I've said before, use it or lose it is the first principle of Arctic sovereignty. To develop the North, we must know the North. To protect the North, we must control the North. To accomplish all our goals for the North, we must be in the North" (Office of the Prime Minister, 2008). The priority placed on state sovereignty is reinforced in the 2009 *Northern Strategy* (Government of Canada, 2009), which tells us that "international interest in the North has intensified because of the potential for resource development, the opening of new transportation routes, and the growing impacts of climate change" (Government of Canada, 2009: 5). In response to these opportunities and challenges, the federal government is crafting policy with four priorities or pillars in mind: "exercising our Arctic Sovereignty; promoting social and economic development; protecting our environmental heritage; improving and devolving northern governance" (Government of Canada, 2009: 2). And while the four pillars may be presented as equally important in the 2009 *Northern Strategy*, the 2010 "Statement on Canada's Arctic Foreign Policy" leaves little doubt that sovereignty is the most significant priority. It states that "in our Arctic foreign policy, the first and most important pillar toward recognizing the potential of Canada's Arctic is the exercise of our sovereignty over the Far North" (DFAIT, 2010: 4). Ultimately, we are told that "protecting national sovereignty, and the integrity of our borders, is the first and foremost responsibility of a national government. We are resolved to protect Canadian sovereignty throughout our Arctic" (DFAIT, 2010: 9).

The Conservative discourse about the Arctic emphasizes sovereignty as control and ownership. Control translates into a militarized presence and a securitization of the North that ultimately requires, indeed justifies, protection of the North through military means. And while the federal government does not suggest we will be facing a traditional war in the North, it does point to a number of nefarious threats that Canadians may be facing as a result of the melting sea ice, such as drug trafficking, illegal migrants, and other threats to our national security.

If we want to see the dominance of the state in academic analyses and the limits imposed on debate by that kind of thinking, all we need to do is turn to the "debate" on the future of the Arctic, which focuses on conflict or cooperation. The work of Rob Huebert epitomizes scholarly contributions that focus on "conflict." Huebert (2008) has publicly speculated about a return to the Cold War era and routinely writes about the potential of the Russian threat (2010), thus conjuring up images again of the Cold War era. His work is rife with references to Canada's national interest that—like the Conservative discourse—homogenize "Canada." In a 2005–6 piece written for the *Canadian Military Journal* (2005–6: 29), he adopts the same rhetorical device of verbal flag planting as the Conservatives when he states: "It appears likely that the government will remain—and *needs* to remain—committed to improving Canada's ability to truly be the 'True North *Strong* and Free.'"

In contrast, there are a host of authors who privilege the "cooperation" dimension. Scholars such as Michael Byers (2010), Andrea Charron (2005), and Donald McRae (2007) tend to focus on the international legal dimension of the issues facing Canada. Byers, for example, emphasizes cooperation in the Arctic and has argued that "thanks to international law, there is no race for Arctic resources. Nor is there any appetite for military confrontation. The Arctic, instead, has become a zone of quiet cooperation, as countries work together to map the seabed, protect the environment, and guard against new, non-state security threats" (2010: 911–12). Byers has also been publicly critical of those advocating the conflict perspective and has suggested that "if you talk about conflict you can actually create conflict" (2009: 17).

And while there is a debate over priorities, over whether Canada should be "strong" or should focus on something more "soft" like international law, it is important to note the shared qualities of these two positions. In both instances the analyses are state-centric and the state is black-boxed. There is a random line or paragraph that acknowledges the existence of Inuit, but for the most part the analyses are about states competing in the Arctic or diplomats and scientists drawing lines around ocean seabeds. The state and different constructions of power and peace become the centrepiece of the so-called debate, which is ultimately about what kind of state Canada should be in the context of the changing Arctic. Canada is homogenized and Western diplomacies are celebrated. The context in which they are working is largely the same. There is a debate, a debate between people starting to work from within the same framework, thus limiting our range of choices. But what is left out of this picture? What does the state-centric focus exclude?

The state-centric focus of both the Canadian Conservative government and mainstream political science scholars leaves out those who contradict the image of the state as prescribed by the government and reinforced by the scholars—those who challenge the "project of statecraft," to return to Doty (2001: 527). Mary Simon, president of the Inuit Tapiriit Kanatami, directly challenges the prime minister's construction of sovereignty when she states: "The prime minister has promoted, in his words, a 'use it or lose it' strategy with respect to Canada's sovereignty in the Arctic. Inuit view these comments with a certain level of irony. Inuit have been living in … and using … the Arctic for millennia, and have no intention of 'losing it'" (2009: 252). The state-centric focus denies the sites of resistance.

The state-centric focus also privileges a view of the prevailing world order that separates the state from the broader environmental context. Environmental impacts are acknowledged, but there is no acknowledgement that the environment knows no borders. The government constructions of sovereignty as control and academic debates about securing the Arctic or practising cooperation in the Arctic as means by which we can protect our sovereignty seem to assume that the environment is somehow external to all of these processes. These constructions marginalize nature and the environment and are a reflection of "a fundamentally masculinist perception of the natural world as seen from a position of detachment and power" (Fogel, 2004: 106). We externalize the environment while we simultaneously consume it. And in the Arctic discourse crafted by the state and by mainstream academics, the state is bent on consumption. As I have argued previously (Smith, 2010), in the government discourse, the issue of climate change is largely treated as a matter of thinning ice, and climate change in general is treated as a catalyst for enhanced economic opportunity. Academic analyses of the future of the Arctic also downplay climate change. There is recognition that climate change is taking place and that the sea ice is thinning. However, this passing reference then becomes the rather shaky foundation upon which to build their analysis. Adam Lajeunesse (2008: 1039), as the entry point to his discussion of the Northwest Passage, mentions the thinning of sea ice. Huebert (2005–6: 27) identifies climate change as a factor in the renaissance in Canadian Arctic security, and while Byers (2010: 900–1) provides almost three paragraphs on climate change, they are all about sea ice.

On the matter of climate change resulting in economic opportunities, the Arctic is referred to as a "region [that] contains a treasure trove of resource wealth" (Huebert, 2008: 18) and described as "rich in hydrocarbons" (Byers, 2010: 901). Similar to the government pronouncements, the possibility of great resource wealth is identified regularly as the source of the elevated interest in the Arctic (Huebert, 2010: 1).

The problem with this construction, as argued elsewhere (Smith, 2010), is that climate change is not just about thinning and melting sea ice. The Arctic Climate Impact Assessment (ACIA), one of the most substantive regional impact assessments to date, details the range and depth of climate change impacts. First and foremost, central to the ACIA is the observation that the Arctic is one of the regions most vulnerable to the effects of climate change. As a result of annual temperature increases, tree lines are expected to shift northwards, fires are expected to be more common, and new species can be expected in the Arctic. The melting sea ice will have—and is having—a devastating impact on habitat for polar bears, seals, and seabirds, "pushing some species toward extinction" (ACIA, 2004: 10). Coastal communities will be faced with coastal erosion, and rising sea levels. The relocation of communities is expected (and indeed planned and underway in some cases). Thawing permafrost will disrupt current transportation routes, and as "frozen ground thaws, many existing buildings, roads, pipelines, airports, and industrial facilities are likely to be destabilized, requiring substantial rebuilding, maintenance and investment" (ACIA, 2004: 11). As well, indigenous peoples are facing devastating cultural and economic impacts Finally, the impacts being felt in the Arctic and the future predictions are not isolated events; they are caused by global emissions and themselves will have broader impacts. The focus on sea ice effectively denies the significance of all the other impacts taking place in the Arctic and denies that the impacts are global and unpredictable.

Ultimately, a state-centric focus denies sites of resistance because they challenge the unambiguous "we," separates the state from the environment, and resists the very troubling vision of humanity as parasitic. In the world of states, what counts is "conflict or cooperation," securing the place of the state and constructing images of state control over space and territory that defy the borders that state leaders imagine.

The second component of the concealed perspective, identified in internationalism and shared by interpretations of and mainstream approaches to the Arctic and climate change, is the lack of a human dimension. With regard to government speeches and statements, you will find references to the human dimension, but what is meant is unclear. There are certainly no human voices beyond those of the authoritative speech acts engaged in by Canadian political leaders. There are also no discussions of the human dimensions of climate change, such as the loss of traditional ways of knowing or the loss of traditional ways of living—as noted above. The government also includes no mention of the long list of health impacts that have been associated with climate change. In 2008 Health Canada (Sequin and Berry, 2008) produced a document that identified the varied health-related impacts arising from climate change. Temperature extremes are linked to more heat waves, which are then linked to more heat-related deaths. The changing climate is also expected to change the transmission range for a variety of disease-carrying insects, and consequently we can expect a rise in the rate of infectious diseases and the introduction of new diseases to Canada (Sequin and Berry, 2008: 7). Human health, human voices—neither are privileged in the speeches and statements of Canada's political leaders.

To a large extent, there are no, or few, humans in the scholarly discourse as well. The fixation with debates over line drawings and seabeds privileges Western science and Western understandings of sovereignty. The discussion about the militarization of the Arctic securitizes state boundaries, black-boxes the state, and views the national interest as a homogenized whole. If we consider Rob Huebert's 2005–6 article, we would get the sense that no one lives in the Arctic and that there are no cultural or social impacts associated with climate change. Byers (2010: 910–11) does offer us two paragraphs of information about Inuit and the Arctic, but Inuit are discussed in the context of their association with the Arctic Council. There is a brief reference to the important work done by the Inuit Circumpolar Council on climate change and persistent organic pollutants. There is also reference to the Circumpolar Inuit Declaration on Sovereignty in the Arctic, but nowhere in the discussion is there any effort to include Inuit voices, let alone indigenous knowledge. The focus on the state, and thus the abstract that is so integral to these analyses, functions to deny the voices of those who live in the Arctic, limits our sense of the impacts of climate change on humans, and excludes alternative visions of the world in which we live.

The absence of the human dimension works in ways that deny that climate change can have life-and-death consequences. If we think too carefully about climate change, we become aware of the ethical issues it raises, the profound consequences it has for our environment and for us. As argued by Donald Brown, "global warming ... raises the question directly of whether some people will be allowed to gain at other peoples' expense, including their very life. Global warming will force us to think more deeply about human duties to plants and animals than any other environmental crisis, because the decision on atmospheric greenhouse gas stabilization levels will make us decide which plants and animals survive" (2003: 233). Climate change should also make us think about our duties to others and the impact of our consumptive behaviours. We are the makers of this environmental tragedy.

The absence of a human dimension in the internationalism literature, in the government discourse on the Arctic, and in the scholarly literature on the Arctic reinforces denial about climate change—denial about its impact on the Inuit, on our health, and on our sense of duty to each other, to plants, and to animals. The absence of a human dimension serves the strategic forgetting of how we are complicit in the making of climate change and silences the voices of those who would remind us of such.

The third component of the concealed perspective identified in internationalism is the absence of any consideration of race. Race, colonialism, imperial discursive moves, and the construction of foreign others are all present in the literature, but these practices are not interrogated. Given that the Canadian government discourse and the mainstream political science literature is so state-centric, it should come as no surprise that there is neither recognition of the state as a colonial creation nor recognition of the impact of the state on indigenous peoples. Recognizing the diverse experiences of indigenous peoples, Taiaiake Alfred and Jeff Corntassel nonetheless observe that "their existence is in large part lived as determined acts of survival against colonizing states' efforts to eradicate them culturally, politically and physically" (2005: 597). The 2009 *Northern Strategy* does celebrate the North and acknowledges the long-standing presence of the Inuit—a presence that preceded the arrival of Europeans. However, the distinct sense of Inuit as a people, with transnational connections beyond the state, is contained by and shaped to become part of "our nation" and "Canada's North" (Government of Canada, 2009: 3). Colonial pasts are erased by colonial linguistic turns in contemporary government visions of the North.

The securitization of the Arctic by the Canadian government and scholars such as Rob Huebert limits discussion about priorities, as they impose their views of the Arctic on those who live in the Arctic. However, these imposed views have not gone unchallenged. Consider, for example, the words of Sheila Watt-Cloutier, former chair of the Inuit Circumpolar Council, speaking at the time of the meeting of the 15th Conference of the Parties to the Framework Convention on Climate Change, in Copenhagen in 2009: "[T]he people whose lives depend upon the ice and snow for cultural survival must be a central component of all our plans. We must not permit the discussion of northern development to be conducted only in terms of sovereignty, resources, and economics. The focus must be on the human dimension, human communities and protection of human cultural rights" (2009). Watt-Cloutier reminds us that those Western configurations of security, identity, and citizenship created by the government and like-minded academics are not representative of all the peoples of Canada.

Not only do the securitizing moves circumscribe debate and dissent, they impose particular views of security that are Western and state-based. Similarly, assumptions about the Arctic as a treasure trove and the state as distinct from nature are reflections of Western thought. And language matters. As argued by Marie Battiste and James Youngblood Henderson, there are "subtle effects [in] the cognitive and linguistic frameworks created and legitimized by imperialism [that] have displaced the systemic discrimination against Indigenous peoples during colonial times, and pose the most crucial cultural challenges facing humanity today" (2000: 12). The imposition of these linguistically imperial frameworks can be seen in the 2009 *Northern Strategy*, where it is stated that "the North is ... home to vast renewable and cultural resources that make important contributions to its economy and society" (Government of Canada, 2009: 16). In one line of text, nature and Inuit ways of knowing and being are made consumable and subject to the "acquisitive ideals" (Turner and Clifton, 2009: 186) of the West. Nature and culture are represented as distinct "resources," thus reflecting a Western way of knowing that seeks to separate, contain, and compartmentalize. Traditional knowledges, in contrast, are typically understood to be "unique and situated, holistic and processual" (Martello, 2001: 116).

In both the Conservative government discourse and the mainstream, race is invoked, or at least imagined, in ways not dissimilar to those observed by Bell (2010), Turenne Sjolander and Trevenen (2010), and Turenne Sjolander (chapter 14). What is imagined is the "other," the threat to our well-being—the terrorist or the illegal migrant. This is seen in the government discourse, for example, when the government tells us that "this increased Canadian capacity demonstrates Canada's presence in the region and will also ensure that we are better prepared to respond to unforeseen events" (DFAIT, 2010: 6). And the government further suggests that future potential problems could include criminals, and illegal migrants accessing Canada through the Arctic and during environmental emergencies (DFAIT, 2010: 9).

Moreover, Byers and Huebert both argue that we need to worry about non-state threats. Huebert, for example, warns us that melting in the Arctic would enhance access to Canada by "foreigners" (2005–6: 27; see also Purdy and Smythe, 2010). These foreigners seem to translate into "terrorists" when Huebert writes: "[W]hile no one is expecting an immediate attack on Inuvik by al Qaeda, potential dangers do exist in the long term. If southern borders are made more secure and northern ones are not, it stands to reason that the latter will constitute vulnerability. Terrorists will be willing to exploit such shortcomings" (2005–6: 28). In a similar vein, Byers states of the Arctic that "no one is envisioning a military conflict. The concern is with policing non-state actors. This might be shipping companies or international criminal syndicates that see the Arctic as a way of smuggling drugs or illegal immigrants to places further south, or terrorist elements that seek to utilize the Arctic in some way" (2009: 17).

Much like the federal government, leading Arctic scholars such as Huebert and Byers create an image of a future wild zone full of "foreigners" intent on threatening our future well-being. The Conservative government builds on our fear and argues that this future can only be countered by policing, surveillance, and more boots on the ground. Lost in the creation of this dark side of the Arctic is any sense that these issues need to be problematized and unpacked and that feeding on the fears of Canadians can, in some ways, result—and has resulted—in a garrison state mentality. Moreover, the construction of "foreigners" as a threat is loaded with racial implications—especially when linked to "terrorists."

In the Canadian government discourse and mainstream literature on the Arctic, race is concealed or manipulated to serve particular ends. It is not interrogated, not problematized, but either ignored or used as a tool to set priorities and to justify a future of consumptive behavior and continued disregard for competing ways of knowing. When the concealed perspective is revealed, the limits imposed on our imaginations are exposed.

Concluding Reflections

This chapter has taken an unusual path. The standard approach would be to apply some concept of internationalism to the case of the Arctic and then reflect on the findings. My approach has been to expose the underlying assumptions of internationalism and to see how they are operationalized in the Conservative government discourse and mainstream political science literature on the Arctic. Some may claim that I am comparing apples and oranges. I can't possibly leap from internationalism to the Arctic and climate change without somehow making this a paper about whether or not internationalism helps us to understand Canadian policy on the Arctic. But I don't think I am comparing apples and oranges. You can only make that argument if you regard the intellectual project that informs internationalism as separate and distinct from the government discourse on climate change and the academic analyses of the Arctic. It is typical to compartmentalize subjects into "issue areas," but too often that leads us to the fine-tuning of the status quo, because we don't see the concealed perspective that is shared by mainstream Canadian foreign policy theorists. We need to see the way in which that concealed perspective shapes not just internationalism, but also Arctic discourses and assessments of climate change, not to mention the host of other issue areas that fall under the umbrella of CFP.

Taking this rather unconventional path, regardless of the twists and turns, prompts several valuable observations. First, it is striking that to problematize the concealed perspective in the Arctic literature, I turned not only to critical scholars in both international relations and international studies, but also to scholars working in other disciplines, such as environmental studies and First Nations studies. While this observation merits a more systematic analysis, it does speak to the ways in which the mainstream literature reinforces disciplinary boundaries and raises questions about the implications of this scholarly isolation. Our analyses would be so much richer if we were to include other disciplinary insights into Canadian foreign policy. Second, the absence of a more substantive body of literature on race and Canadian foreign policy is troubling. There is one volume—Beier's *Indigenous Diplomacies* (2009)—that includes some Canadian content, and there are scholarly contributions that draw on post-colonial influences, but a systematic analysis of race and Canadian foreign policy is strikingly absent. There is an article by Debra Thompson (2008) on race and Canadian political science, but oddly Canadian foreign policy does not seem to be included (which also speaks to the divisions between Canadian politics and Canadian foreign policy). There is so much work to be done in this area. Even the brief analysis here shows that images of empire, constructions of the "other," and denial of other ways of knowing are part of the mainstream project. Third, practically speaking, I have to wonder what all of this says about the state of Canadian democracy and the role of citizens in Canadian foreign policy. The concealed perspective prizes analytical abstraction and as such creates worlds that are far away and distant. But climate change continues apace and the impacts are being felt. The general standard of living for Canada's indigenous people is horrid, and our everyday behaviour has impacts on others. Is the government's discourse about future terrorists in the Arctic so compelling that we don't see that its constructions of control and security in the Arctic are built on naive assumptions about the environment?

I began this chapter by reflecting on my use of internationalism as a central theme in my work. I pondered on whether or not my use of internationalism meant that I was coming to the core and thus limiting my own critical project. My inclusion of internationalism here, in this volume, feels less like coming to the core and allowing the core to define the parameters of my research. I am happier, now, sitting at the interdisciplinary critical table, ordering from a menu that is rich with all sorts of still-undiscovered menu items.

Key Terms

concealed perspective   everyday practice

critical theory

Study Questions

1. What does it mean to ask questions "from the outside"?
2. What are the elements of the concealed perspective, and why does the concealed perspective matter to our understanding of Canadian foreign policy?
3. What are the key elements of the Conservative government's Arctic foreign policy, and how do those elements shape our understanding of the Arctic?
4. Smith shows that the voices of the Inuit are marginalized in the Arctic discourse as crafted by both the federal government and mainstream academics. Do you think there are other issue areas in Canadian foreign policy where Inuit, Metis, and First Nations voices are marginalized?

References

ACIA (Arctic Climate Impact Assessment). 2004. *Impacts of Warming in the Arctic: Arctic Climate Impact Assessment, Executive Summary*. Cambridge: Cambridge University Press. At http://amap. no/acia/.

Alfred, Taiaiake, and Jeff Corntassel. 2005. "Being Indigenous: Resurgences against Contemporary Colonialism." *Government and Opposition* 40, 4: 597–614.

Battiste, Marie, and James Youngblood Henderson. 2000. *Protecting Indigenous Knowledge and Heritage: A Global Challenge*. Saskatoon: Purich Publishing.

Beier, J. Marshall, ed. 2009. *Indigenous Diplomacies*. New York: Palgrave.

Beier, J. Marshall, and Lana Wylie. 2010. "Introduction: What's So Critical about Canadian Foreign Policy?" In J. Marshall Beier and Lana Wylie, eds, *Canadian Foreign Policy in Critical Perspective*. Don Mills, ON: Oxford University Press, xi–xix.

Bell, Colleen. 2010. "Fighting the War and Winning the Peace: Three Critiques of the War in Afghanistan." In J. Marshall Beier and Lana Wylie, eds, *Canadian Foreign Policy in Critical Perspective*. Don Mills, ON: Oxford University Press, 58–71.

Brown, Donald A. 2003. "The Importance of Expressly Examining Global Warming Policy Issues through an Ethnical Prism." *Global Environmental Change* 13, 4: 229–34.

Byers, Michael. 2009. "Who Owns the Arctic: Interview with Jess Worth." *New Internationalist Magazine*, 1 July. At http://www.newint.org/features/2009/07/01/sovereignty/.

———. 2010. "Cold Peace: Arctic Cooperation and Canadian Foreign Policy." *International Journal* 65, 4: 899–912.

Charron, Andrea. 2005. "The Northwest Passage: Is Canada's Sovereignty Floating Away?" *International Journal* 60, 3: 831–48.

Cooper, Andrew F. 1995. "In Search of Niches: Saying 'Yes' and Saying 'No' in Canada's International Relations." *Canadian Foreign Policy/La politique étrangère du Canada* 3, 3: 1–13.

Cox, Robert W. 1986. "Social Forces, States and World Orders: Beyond International Relations Theory." In Robert O. Keohane, ed., *Neorealism and Its Critics*. New York: Columbia University Press, 204–54.

de Costa, Ravi. 2009. "Indigenous Diplomacies before the Nation-State." In J. Marshall Beier, ed., *Indigenous Diplomacies*. New York: Palgrave, 61–77.

DFAIT. 2010. "Statement on Canada's Arctic Foreign Policy: Exercising Sovereignty and Promoting Canada's Northern Strategy Abroad." *Government of Canada*. At http://www.international.gc.ca/polar-polaire/canada_arctic_foreign_policy-la_politique_etrangere_du_canada_pour_arctique.aspx?lang=eng.

Doty, Roxanne. 2001. "Desert Tracts: Statecraft in Remote Places." *Alternatives* 26, 4: 523–43.

Enloe, Cynthia. 1996. "Margins, Silences and Bottom Rungs: How to Overcome the Underestimation of Power in the Study of International Relations." In Steve Smith, Ken Booth, and Marysia Zalewski, eds, *International Theory: Positivism and Beyond*. Cambridge: Cambridge University Press, 186–203.

———. 2004. *The Curious Feminist: Searching for Women in a New Age of Empire*. Berkeley: University of California Press.

Fogel, Cathleen. 2004. "The Local, the Global and the Kyoto Protocol." In Sheila Jasanoff and Marybeth Long Martello, eds, *Earthly Politics: Local and Global in Environmental Governance*. Cambridge, MA: MIT Press, 103–27.

Government of Canada. 2009. "Canada's Northern Strategy: Our North, Our Heritage, Our Future," p. 5. At http://www.northernstrategy.gc.ca/cns/cns.pdf.

Huebert, Rob. 2005–6. "Renaissance in Canadian Arctic Security?" *Canadian Forces Journal* 6, 4. At http://www.journal.forces.gc.ca/vo6/no4/north-nord-eng.asp.

———. 2008. "Canadian Arctic Security: Preparing for a Changing Future," in Roundtable on "Canada's Arctic Interests and Responsibilities." *Behind the Headlines* 65, 4: 14–26.

———. 2010. *The Newly Emerging Arctic Security Environment*. Calgary: Canadian Defence and Foreign Affairs Institute. At http://www.cdfai.org/PDF/The%20Newly%20Emerging%20Arctic%20Security%20Environment.pdf.

Kirton, John. 2007. *Canadian Foreign Policy in a Changing World*. Toronto: Thomson-Nelson.

Lajeunesse, Adam. 2008. "The Northwest Passage in Canadian Policy: An Approach for the 21st Century." *International Journal* 63, 4: 1037–52.

McRae, Donald. 2007. "Arctic Sovereignty? What Is a Stake?" *Behind the Headlines* 64, 1. At http://www.opencanada.org/wp-content/uploads/2011/05/BTH_vol64_no11.pdf.

Martello, Mary Beth. 2001. "The Paradox of Virtue? 'Other' Knowledges and Environment-Development Politics." *Global Environmental Politics* 1, 3: 114–41.

Munton, Don. 2003. "Whither Internationalism?" *International Journal* 58, 1: 155–80.

Nossal, Kim Richard. 1998–9. "Pinchpenny Diplomacy: The Decline of 'Good International Citizenship' in Canadian Foreign Policy." *International Journal* 54, 1: 88–105.

Nossal, Kim Richard, Stéphane Roussel, and Stéphane Paquin. 2011. *International Policy and Politics in Canada*. Toronto: Pearson Education Canada.

Office of the Prime Minister. 2008. "Prime Minister Harper Announces the Geo-mapping for Northern Energy and Minerals Program." 26 August. At http://pm.gc.ca/eng/media.asp?category=2&featureId=6&pageId=46&id=2256.

Potter, Evan H. 1996–7. "Niche Diplomacy as Canadian Foreign Policy." *International Journal* 52, 1: 25–38.

Purdy, Margaret, and Leanne Smythe. 2010. "From Obscurity to Action: Why Canada Must Tackle the Security Dimension of Climate Change." *International Journal* 65, 2: 411–33.

Salter, Mark B. 2010. "Canadian Border Policy as Foreign Policy." In J. Marshall Beier and Lana Wylie, eds, *Canadian Foreign Policy in Critical Perspective*. Don Mills, ON: Oxford University Press, 72–82.

Sequin, Jacinthe, and Peter Berry. 2008. *Human Health in a Changing Climate: A Canadian Assessment of Vulnerabilities and Adaptive Capacity*. Ottawa: Health Canada.

Simon, Mary. 2009. "Inuit and the Canadian Arctic: Sovereignty Begins at Home." *Journal of Canadian Studies* 43, 2: 250–61.

Smith, Heather A. 2000. "Niche Diplomacy and Mission-Oriented Diplomatic Behaviour: A Critical Assessment." In Andrew F. Cooper and Geoffrey Hayes, eds, *Worthwhile Initiatives? Canadian Mission-Oriented Diplomacy.* Toronto: Irwin, 12–22.

———. 2003. "Disrupting Internationalism and Finding the Other." In Claire Turenne Sjolander, Heather A. Smith, and Deborah Stienstra, eds, *Feminist Perspectives on Canadian Foreign Policy.* Don Mills, ON: Oxford University Press, 24–39.

———. 2008–9. "Political Parties and Climate Change." *International Journal* 64, 1: 47–66.

———. 2009, "Unwilling Internationalism or Strategic Internationalism? Canadian Climate Change Policy under the Conservative Government." *Canadian Foreign Policy/La politique étrangère du Canada* 15, 2: 57–77.

———. 2010. "Choosing Not to See: Canada, Climate Change and the Arctic." *International Journal* 65, 4: 901–12.

Smith, Steve. 1995. "The Self Images of a Discipline: A Genealogy of International Relations." In Ken Booth and Steve Smith, eds, *International Relations Today.* University Park, PA: Penn State Press, 1–37.

Sylvester, Christine. 1996. "The Contributions of Feminist Theory to International Relations." In Steve Smith, Ken Booth, and Marysia Zalewski, eds, *International Theory: Positivism and Beyond.* Cambridge: Cambridge University Press, 254–79.

Thompson, Debra. 2008. "Is Race Political?" *Canadian Journal of Political Science* 41, 3: 525–47.

Turenne Sjolander, Claire, and Kathyrn Trevenen. 2010. "Constructing Canadian Foreign Policy: Myths of Good International Citizens, Protectors, and the War in Afghanistan." In J. Marshall Beier and Lana Wylie, eds, *Canadian Foreign Policy in Critical Perspective.* Don Mills, ON: Oxford University Press, 44–57.

Turner, Nancy, and Helen Clifton. 2009. "'It's So Different Today': Climate Change and Indigenous Lifestyles in British Columbia." *Global Environmental Change* 19, 2: 180–90.

Watt Cloutier, Sheila. 2009. "Reclaiming the Moral High Ground: Indigenous Peoples, Climate Change and Human Rights." *Nunatsiaq Online,* 21 December. At http://www.nunatsiaqonline.ca/stories/article/4567_reclaiming_the_moral_high_ground/.

Zalewski, Marysia. 2006. "Distracted Reflections on the Production, Narration, and Refusal of Feminist Knowledge in International Relations." In Brooke Ackerly, Maria Stern, and Jacqui True, eds, *Feminist Methodologies for International Relations.* Cambridge: Cambridge University Press, 42–61.

13 | The Harper Government, Africa Policy, and the Relative Decline of Humane Internationalism

David Black

Much press, political, and civil society commentary has noted the Harper government's apparent retreat from Africa in its foreign policy. Two other trends are often linked to this one: a new emphasis on Latin America and an erosion of Canada's commitment to development assistance.

These trends must be kept in perspective. Less has changed *in practice*, with regard to both Africa and Latin America, than many accounts have suggested. Similarly, changes in foreign aid policy were very slow to be articulated, let alone implemented. As a result, much of Canada's approach in these key dimensions of its foreign policy towards the global "South" was guided for the first several years of the Harper era by inertia, or a foreign policy of drift. Nevertheless, some real changes of interest, emphasis, and engagement have emerged, with potentially far-reaching ramifications. These ramifications are likely to be reinforced by the government's 2011 electoral majority. In short, there are signs of a clear shift not only from the high-profile emphasis on Africa articulated in the latter years of the Chrétien government, but also from 50 years of broad bipartisanship in policies towards the continent.

There are both more proximate and more foundational explanations for this apparent shift.[1] In this chapter, I will briefly review and assess the former, which have received more attention and focused mainly on the role of Prime Minister Harper and the "new" Conservative Party in government. However, these influences cannot be properly understood without taking account of longer-term and more foundational dynamics within Canadian political culture—namely, the relative decline and changing character of what Cranford Pratt, two decades ago, had already characterized as "An Eroding and Limited (Humane) Internationalism" (1989a). In other words, I will focus on the longer-term trajectory of the more cosmopolitan tradition of Canadian internationalism, emphasizing global poverty, inequality, and justice.[2] Four specific factors will be proposed as explanations for the declining influence of this tradition: the corrosive effects of attacks on the utility of foreign aid; the changing face of organized religion in Canada; the decline of radical solidarity politics; and the shift in the dominant ethical frame of Canadian foreign policy from humane internationalism to global citizenship. Broadly speaking then, this chapter is consistent with the emphasis in the introduction to this volume on the salience of changing dynamics in the domestic sources of Canadian foreign policy.

In order to establish what it is that needs to be explained, I will begin with a brief assessment of what has, and has not, changed in Canada's approach to Africa and to the related policy domains of Latin America and development assistance. I will then briefly review the more immediate explanations for the trends in these policy domains before exploring the longer-term decline in humane internationalist influence on Canadian policies towards the global South.

A New Foreign Policy Direction towards the "South"?

Characteristically, the Harper government was slow and sketchy in articulating specific policy directions concerning Africa, Latin America, and **development assistance**. Bold new policies were promised on both Latin America and development assistance, but for more than three years after the government was first elected, nothing was elaborated in either area. On Africa, the perceived "shift" was more a product of omission than of commission: what was *not* said and done rather than what *was*.

This began to change with several documents, speeches, and announcements in 2009. A policy document on "Canada and the Americas" (Government of Canada, 2009), a brief policy pronouncement on aid concentration (CIDA, 2009), and a May 2009 speech by Minister for International Cooperation Bev Oda setting out the Canadian International Development Agency's (CIDA's) thematic priorities (Oda, 2009) supplemented broad statements of intent (or lack thereof) and relatively small policy openings and departures to provide observers with at least a limited basis upon which to assess government intentions.

On Latin America there was, broadly speaking, both less in terms of the *content* of this "new course for Canada's foreign policy" (Gee, 2007) and more in terms of continuity with past Liberal and Progressive Conservative policy approaches than the rhetoric of change implied. Canada's three "interconnected and mutually reinforcing objectives" towards the region, as articulated in "Canada and the Americas," are the promotion of democratic governance, prosperity, and security (Government of Canada, 2009: 6). Even as elaborated upon in the remainder of the document, these objectives are hard to distinguish from those of their predecessors. As Randall and Dowding summarize, "there is little in the Harper government's overtures to Latin America or in the concrete policies which are being pursued toward Colombia [and, one could add, other specific cases] that depart in any significant way from either the general premises of Canadian foreign and defence policy or the Canadian policies which have been pursued since the late 1980s" (2008: 42). Moreover, because of the pattern of inconstancy in Canada's professions of intent regarding its "vocation" as a "country of the Americas," veteran policy-watchers greeted this latest round of professions with both scepticism and caution (Daudelin and Dawson, 2008: 7).

Nevertheless, there have been signs of a harder edge in the Harper government's approach to the region, with more concrete and focused steps towards promoting free trade and establishing defence linkages in hemispheric affairs as well as a discernible closeness to American perspectives and objectives.[3] "What Prime Minister Harper has done," write Randall and Dowding, "is to wed the softer power dimensions of the former Liberal government's approach to human security to a more practical economic and defence-oriented understanding of Canada's security agenda in Latin America" (2008: 39). The most concrete manifestation of this was the precipitous decision to negotiate free trade agreements with Peru and, more controversially, Colombia, despite widespread "disbelief and anger" on the part of labour movements, human rights organizations, opposition parties, and solidarity groups in Canada, Colombia, and elsewhere. This move to institutionalize a privileged economic relationship with a country "known for having the worst human rights record in the hemisphere" (Healy and Katz, 2008: 35) reflected several noteworthy tendencies: a disdain for the critics; an ideological conviction concerning the beneficent effects of economic liberalization; and, on the analysis of Healy and Katz, a particular sensitivity to, and effective coordination with, the policy objectives of the previous Bush administration in the United States. Similarly, Kirk and McKenna (2009) identify a clear convergence between the Harper government's policy approach towards Cuba and that of the Bush administration.

On development assistance, the prime minister's September 2007 address to the Council on Foreign Relations in New York was taken to signal that major changes in foreign aid policy were imminent ("An Interview with Stephen Harper," 2007; Freeman, 2007a). Among the changes that were speculated upon was a significant concentration of bilateral aid, with Canada's professed intent to be among the five largest donors in each of the "core countries" of CIDA. Despite these and other intermittent professions of intent, however, there was no clear leadership or direction on aid programming for several years after the government took office. At the Heiligendamm G8 Summit in 2007, the government restated its commitment to double aid to Africa between 2003–4 and 2008–9, while at the same time stressing that it would emphasize Latin America going forward (Freeman, 2007b). Through an extraordinary accounting adjustment, however, it effectively reduced the value of the commitment to double aid to Africa from C\$2.8 billion to C\$2.1 billion. In the meantime, CIDA officials, even in core countries like Tanzania or Ethiopia, were left to disburse still large and growing bilateral funds with no clear marching orders.[4]

In late February 2009, Minister for International Cooperation Bev Oda finally revealed a new list of 20 countries in which the government committed to concentrate 80 per cent of its bilateral funding.[5] If fully implemented, this will indeed represent a significant degree of concentration compared to that in the previous list of 25 core development partners, announced in the context of the Martin government's 2005 *International Policy Statement* (IPS), in which "at least two thirds"

of bilateral assistance was to be concentrated.[6] The 2009 announcement therefore represented one of the clearest signals to date of shifting government priorities. Several features of the new list stand out (see Tomlinson, 2009). First, the
government formally erased the distinction drawn in the IPS between the 25 "core
development partners" and a separate funding category for "Failed and Fragile
States." Of the 20 new core countries, 5 (Afghanistan, Haiti, Colombia, West Bank/
Gaza, and Sudan) had previously been designated recipients through the "Failed
and Fragile State" window. This suggests a more strategic, security-oriented
approach to aid policy. Second, Africa was the big loser in terms of the new countries of concentration, with 8 of 14 African states on the previous list dropped from
the new one.[7] Similarly, several strategic priorities in the Americas—specifically
Colombia, Haiti, Peru, and the Caribbean Region—as well as the West Bank/Gaza
were added. Finally, the net effect of these shifts was to reduce the concentration
of bilateral aid resources in countries with the highest levels of poverty. Whereas
in the 2005 list 55 per cent of designated core development partners were specified
as "low" Human Development Index (HDI) countries in the 2008 UNDP Human
Development Report, in the 2009 list only 37 per cent of core recipients fell into this
category (Tomlinson, 2009).[8]

In terms of new directions in practice, the most striking developments were
the rapid emergence of Afghanistan as CIDA's largest bilateral program and the
bureaucratic reorganization of the agency's large Afghanistan Task Force, with a
CIDA vice-president at its head—unprecedented for a bilateral country program. As
Canada reduces both its military and aid commitments in that country, it is unclear
what sort of lasting impact this massive reorientation will have for the agency's
more "routine" programming. On a far smaller scale, but of symbolic importance,
was the decision in October 2006 to create a new Office for Democratic Governance
as a focal point for "developing and promoting innovative and effective democratic
governance programming across the Canadian International Development Agency" as well as to be "of service to the whole of government and to Canadians involved in democratic governance programming" (CIDA website). This office was
subsequently dismantled, with the plan being to inaugurate a new Democracy Promotion Agency to reflect a broader governmental foreign policy emphasis on this
theme, but this agency, too, has not been initiated (as of November 2011). Taken
together, these departures reflect a tendency towards the instrumentalization of
the aid program in support of the government's primary political objectives, as
well as the ongoing trend towards the "securitization" of aid (Simpson, 2007).[9] The
mooting of a new emphasis on democracy promotion reflects a certain ideological
orientation on the part of the government, but the failure to act on this emphasis
indicates relative indifference towards the more normative dimensions of aid and
foreign policy.

Finally, concerning Africa and notwithstanding the streamlined February 2009
list of core aid recipients, it could be argued that much remained unchanged. As
noted above, for example, the government reiterated Canada's commitment to

double its aid to Africa and maintained a relatively large and (until 2009) growing aid presence there, even if its "recalculation" of this commitment meant a net loss of $700 million to projected programming for the continent.[10] With regard to its security engagements, Canada continued to be an active participant in, and the largest donor to, the peace process in Northern Uganda, and a relatively major contributor to the parallel humanitarian relief effort there (Bradbury, McDonough, and Dewar, 2007; Wijeyaratne, 2008). Canada also sustained and reiterated its relatively large (among Western donor states) commitment to Sudan's north-south peace process and its contribution to the international effort to ameliorate human suffering in Darfur. Indeed, Canada became the co-chair (with the US) of the "friends of UNAMID" (African Union/United Nations Hybrid Operation in Darfur) donor group supporting the hybrid UN-AU peacekeeping force launched in January 2008 with the stated objective of ending the violence in the Darfur region (Black and Williams, 2008). Canada continued to deploy peacekeepers in small numbers to these operations, as well as to the critical United Nations Organization Mission in the Democratic Republic of the Congo (MONUC).

Nevertheless, these efforts of Canada's seemed more a product of inertia than intent—simply carrying forward the commitments already made, particularly to its preferred international peers in the G8. As former Progressive Conservative prime minister and foreign minister Joe Clark writes, "The major Africa-related decision of the Harper government was not to abandon the commitments Canada had made before. That tells us more about a prudent regard for keeping Canada's word in the G-8 than it does about an attitude towards Africa" (2007: 3).[11] The important Ugandan engagement became almost invisible publicly. The Darfur commitment continued to serve as an exemplar for the "whole of government" approach, but again this simply sustained a policy direction set by the Harper government's predecessor, in a context of extensive public and Western governmental interest.[12] More broadly, Clark usefully applied three tests to the Harper government's approach to Africa: "What does the government say? Where does it spend? Where does it travel?" (2007: 6). He demonstrated that, at least up to the end of 2007, the Harper government had had almost nothing to say about Africa; that its foreign policy spending increases have been heavily concentrated in the Department of National Defence, where Africa is of least interest and priority as compared with Foreign Affairs and CIDA; and that its ministers' foreign visits have been heavily concentrated in Afghanistan and Pakistan, with only three short visits to Africa for conferences and, prior to Stephen Harper's trip to the Commonwealth Heads of Government Meeting (CHOGM) at the end of November 2007, none by either the prime minister or the foreign minister. This pattern was in sharp contrast to the ministerial travel of the Martin government. While there was a small flurry of visits in the first part of 2010—by Governor General Michaëlle Jean as well as by Foreign Minister Lawrence Cannon and International Trade Minister Peter Van Loan— these can be seen as motivated primarily by a late push to promote Canada's failed bid for a non-permanent seat on the UN Security Council.[13]

In terms of economic interests and relations, the fact that Africa has become a major focus of Canadian extractive industry investment and activity seemed to have negligible policy impact. At least in part, this is likely because Canadian extractive industry activity has been even more substantial in Latin America. An apparent change of tone in this regard was signalled by International Trade Minister Peter Van Loan, who, in opening the Africa Rising[14] conference in Toronto in March 2011, asserted that "our businesses are well positioned to take on a leadership role in Africa's economic development in the years ahead." Nevertheless, of the nearly 50 countries the government had begun discussing bilateral free trade with by this time, only one—Morocco—was African (DFAIT, 2011). This provides a clear indication of the relative priority Canada has placed on economic ties with the African continent.

On the diplomatic front, the government has closed at least four missions in Africa, further reducing what is already the smallest number of African embassies among all G8 countries save Japan (CCA, 2009; see also York, 2009). More specifically, whereas in the past Canadian governments have been moved by Commonwealth and trans-societal links to play active and significant roles in the challenges facing Zimbabwe, the current government has evinced little interest in becoming engaged in efforts to mitigate that country's ongoing travails.

In short, while there has been considerable continuity in Canada's practice regarding Latin America, foreign aid, and Africa, the pattern of attention, interest, and initiative seems clearly to indicate a turn away from Africa as compared not only with previous Liberal governments, but also with the Progressive Conservative governments of Brian Mulroney and John Diefenbaker (see Clark, 2007). This impression is reinforced by the changes to CIDA and aid policy. How do we explain this pattern—and how durable is it likely to be? The answer to the second question depends, of course, on how one answers the first. In the remainder of this chapter, I will argue that more proximate explanations, though clearly important, need to be situated in the context of longer-term trends in the influence of humane internationalism.

Idiosyncratic and Party-Political Explanations

One compelling explanation for this emergent shift emphasizes the influence of Prime Minister Harper. As Kim Nossal noted some years ago (1994: 91), the influence of individuals—the "idiosyncratic variable"—is typically given relatively little weight in foreign policy analysis. Nossal argues, however, that in certain situations an individual's influence on policy change can be decisive. Such an idiosyncratic explanation might carry more weight in relation to the current Conservative government than most others, because the government and caucus have been so thoroughly dominated and disciplined by the prime minister and his inner circle (see also Kirk and McKenna, 2009: 31–3; Martin, 2010; Gecelovsky, chapter 7).

That Harper has little personal background on, or interest in, Africa is well established. In addition, however, as an economist and economic conservative,

Harper has displayed an abiding antipathy towards "big government" and socially redistributive transfers (see Johnson, 2009). These convictions are sharply at odds with the "logic of solidarity" that Noël and Thérien (1995: 552) have shown underpins relatively generous foreign aid programs. In short, Harper's intellectual views would incline him to be deeply sceptical about the usefulness of aid. Lacking any real conviction concerning the potential value of stable aid relationships in fostering poverty alleviation, Harper could be expected to see the *real* value of foreign aid, beyond humanitarian and charitable impulses, as lying in the leverage it provides to the promotion of Canadian security and economic interests. This would explain both the lack of interest in the more routine aid programs that predominate in Africa and the tendency towards the deployment of more Canadian aid for instrumental purposes in Afghanistan, Haiti, Colombia, and Peru, for example.

Accompanying this intellectual understanding is a strongly pro-Western, pro-NATO, and pro-American worldview (see also Salutin, 2008; Lui, chapter 6). There are various examples of this, including Canada's strong pro-Israel stance in the Middle East and its decision to concentrate scarce security resources in the high-cost, high-risk, NATO-led Afghan operation at the expense of UN-led African peacekeeping operations such as MONUC. Similarly, as noted above, the decision to pursue a free trade agreement with Colombia has been linked with a particular sensitivity to, and *de facto* coordination with, the Bush administration's hemispheric policy objectives (Healy and Katz, 2008). This vigorously pro-Western worldview could be understood as reflecting the "rational utility maximizing" framework of the economic conservative, insofar as Canada's core economic and security interests are seen as indissolubly linked to those of the United States in particular and the West in general. Similarly, a tilt towards Latin America versus Africa could be partly motivated by the prospects of a bigger potential "up side" to investment and trade promotion activities there (Government of Canada, 2009: 4–5, 11–12).

A third influence is Harper's disdain for the special interest groups and celebrity diplomats that have been so prevalent in the social mobilization surrounding Africa and that were regular fixtures at G8 Summits in the 2000s (see Cooper, 2008; CBC.ca, 2007).

Finally, a distinguishing feature of Harper's politics has been its intense partisanship. In this context, the Harper government was at pains to distance itself from prominent policies that it construed as linked to the Liberal "brand."[15] Moreover, "it is no secret that the current government sees Africa as a Liberal idea" (Owen and Eaves, 2007)—a function of the political mileage Prime Minister Chrétien got out of his orchestration of the Africa Action Plan (AAP) at the 2002 G8 Summit in Kananaskis. Hence, Harper's emphasis on Latin America, whatever its substance and merits, may be seen at least partly as an exercise in partisan rebranding. Here, prime ministerial leadership shades into party politics. How much is this intense partisanship a function of Harper's leadership, and how much a function of the dynamics within the "new" Conservative Party? The conventional academic wisdom on political parties and Canadian foreign policy is that the impact of partisanship on policy outcomes is marginal and that there has been a high level of continuity in practice (see Bow and Black, 2008–9). Indeed, historically, the Canadian approach to Africa and the global South has featured a high level of bipartisan continuity between Liberal and Progressive Conservative governments (Clark, 2007; Owen and Eaves, 2007).

The new Conservatives seemed intent on breaking this historic pattern, although as noted above, the practical repercussions of this shift are less clear. What is particularly striking about the current government's cabinet and caucus is how little evidence one finds of the humane internationalist tendencies and the concomitant interest in Africa that were always vitally represented in previous Tory governments—a theme to which I will return in the next section.[16] In short, if the new direction in Canadian foreign policy towards the developing world reflects prime ministerial preference, there has been little to no resistance to this preference from within Harper's cabinet and caucus. In this respect among others, the new Conservative government is clearly distinct from its Progressive Conservative predecessors, having gained a more economically and socially conservative cast through the incorporation of the Reform/Alliance tradition and having shed most of its traditional Red Tory element.

The implications of this more unadulterated conservatism for aid policy preferences specifically and humane internationalist tendencies generally can be extrapolated from the work of Noël, Thérien, and Dallaire (2004). They found that "[t]he rhetoric of the left about aid typically evokes social justice, solidarity, and public commitments, whereas discourses on the right refer instead to dependency, inefficiency, and waste" (38). Their survey of polling data from the late 1990s and early 2000s shows a robust correlation between party preference and level of support for foreign aid, with Reform Party supporters being least favourably disposed towards official development assistance (ODA), followed by then Progressive Conservative supporters, and NDP supporters being most favourable. The reborn Conservative Party has, of course, (re)incorporated the most conservative party-political element on the Canadian landscape from the old Reform Party, often in positions of leadership, and has shed its more socially progressive faction. It should come as no surprise, therefore, that the party has supported a tilt away from an activist policy towards the world's poorest continent and, more broadly, the politics of global poverty.

A second salient change in the policy approach of the new Conservatives is the weakening of their collective attachment to the Commonwealth. Historically, Progressive Conservative governments and their supporters in English Canada were strongly attached to the British Crown and, through it, to the "modern" post-colonial Commonwealth. This attachment, in turn, predisposed these governments (and, more hesitantly, their Liberal counterparts) towards active engagement with Africa, since the single largest regional grouping of Commonwealth member states was African (see Matthews, 1976; Black, 2010). The new Conservative leadership is clearly enthusiastic about Canada's historic link to the Crown, but evinces little of the traditional Conservative attachment to the post-imperial Commonwealth. One key marker of this is that among the eight African countries dropped as core bilateral aid recipients in February 2009, half were long-standing Commonwealth partners. In this regard, the new Conservatives' variant of conservatism has grown steadily closer to the main currents of American conservative politics and increasingly indifferent to its more cosmopolitan Commonwealth roots. Similarly, the Conservatives' earlier efforts to court Quebecois voters (now largely abandoned) did not lead the government to show any special sensitivity towards the member states of *la francophonie,* since the other African countries dropped as core recipients were founding members of that organization.

In short, and consistent with the predominant ideological predisposition of the right globally (Noël and Thérien, 2008), the new Conservative Party has demonstrated little interest in global social justice. Nor has it shown any real commitment to a generous foreign aid program or to African renewal – priorities that have characteristically been bundled with it. While this party-political shift should not be seen to have caused the emerging reorientations that this chapter focuses on, it has certainly enabled and reinforced them. Yet the new Conservatives did not attain power—or consolidate it—in a socio-political vacuum. Broader trends have created an enabling environment for the transitions they are engineering.

The Declining Influence of Humane Internationalism

The Conservatives' apparent lack of interest in engaging with Africa's challenges, juxtaposed with the high-profile initiatives on Africa that marked the final years of the Chrétien era and the Martin interregnum, could be portrayed as a sharp departure from the more ethically oriented internationalist tradition in Canadian foreign policy. To attribute this shift exclusively to the role of Stephen Harper and/ or the Conservative Party, however, is both to overestimate the degree of change that has taken place and to underestimate the more persistent weakness of the public culture of humane internationalism as an influence on Canadian foreign policy.

As discussed above, the degree of change in Canada's foreign policy towards the global South has been smaller in practice than the government's rhetorical framing implies. Here, however, the point I wish to emphasize is that this reframing has taken place in a highly permissive domestic political environment, in which the influence of humane internationalism has been limited and arguably weakening for several decades (see Pratt, 1989a).

The essence of **humane internationalism** as an element of rich countries' political culture, as it pertains to their relations with the "Third World," is defined by Pratt as "an acceptance of an obligation to alleviate global poverty and to promote development in the LDCs [least developed countries]; a conviction that a more equitable world would be in their (developed countries') real long-term interests; and an assumption that the meeting of these international responsibilities is compatible with the maintenance of socially responsible national economic and social welfare policies"

(1989: 16). Writing two decades ago, Pratt argued that humane internationalism constituted a vital tradition in Canadian political culture, manifested not only in the hundreds of organizations that took up these issues in communities across the country (which he characterized as the **counter-consensus**), but in the all-party support they enjoyed in Parliament. Even then, however, he argued that this tradition had little influence on Canadian policies beyond development assistance—an influence that his subsequent writing argued was steadily waning (see Pratt, 2003). Given the influence of the "dominant class" embedded within the state and in the capital-owning sectors of society, as well as the eroding concern with the fortunes of other Canadians reflected in the decline of welfare state policies, Pratt argued that it was only in particular moments, or "strategic conjunctures," that humane internationalism will significantly influence policy—and then only in ways that are difficult to sustain (2003; see also Freeman, 1997: 297).

In this light, while the Conservatives' emergent reforms in foreign aid policies and their diminished interest in Africa underscore the limited policy influence of humane internationalism, this broader trend is neither new nor confined to the Conservatives and their supporters. Noël, Thérien, and Dallaire, writing about public support for foreign aid in the latter years of the Chrétien era, note that despite considerable support for foreign aid among the electorate, this support was "a mile wide and an inch deep," and that "collectively Canadians appear profoundly ambivalent, if not incoherent, about foreign aid" (Noël, Thérien, and Dallaire, 2004: 37). Kim Nossal, writing in the late 1990s, noted the marked decline in "good international citizenship" and "voluntarism" in Canadian foreign policy under the Chrétien government. He argued that these more genuinely internationalist tendencies had been effectively displaced by "pinchpenny diplomacy"—"seeing how low Canadian expenditures in foreign affairs can be kept without forfeiting Canada's position in international forums like the G-8" (1998–9: 104). Mark Neufeld, writing from a neo-Gramscian perspective, highlighted both the essentially contested character of "middlepowermanship" (or Pearsonian internationalism) and the rise to the fore of a "limitationist" variant of it amongst policy elites from the Mulroney era onwards (1995).

It was, after all, a combination of Progressive Conservative and especially Liberal governments that undertook the most severe cuts to foreign aid in the history of Canadian development assistance during the 1990s. As reported by David Morrison (1998: 413), ODA was the hardest hit of all government programs in these years of austerity, declining by 33 per cent in real terms between 1988–9 and 1997–8, as compared with a 22 per cent decline in defence spending and an average 5 per cent decline in spending on all other programs. Africa was most affected by these cuts, with a decline in bilateral aid of 7.2 per cent between 1990 and 2000 compared with 3.5 per cent for the Americas and 5.3 per cent for Asia (de Masellis, 2003: 78). This sustained budgetary bloodletting occurred with minimal reaction, let alone opposition, from the Canadian electorate. Similarly, it was the Chrétien government that, after the mid-1990s, demonstrated a clear reluctance to deploy significant troop numbers to UN-led peacekeeping operations in the context of the disastrous conflicts that ravaged a number of African countries (see, for example, Smillie, 2006). And it was the government of Prime Minister Paul Martin, said to be "even more committed to Africa" than Chrétien's (Brown and Jackson, 2009: 19), that, despite the strongest fiscal position of any G8 government, firmly resisted pressure to commit to a timetable for increasing aid to 0.7 per cent of GDP in the context of the 2005 Gleneagles Summit and the Live 8 process (Leblanc et al.: 2005).[17]

From this vantage, the Chrétien government's late surge of interest in Africa, leading to the entrenchment of African issues on the G8 agenda (see Fowler, 2003; Black, 2004), can be seen not only as the very personal campaign of a legacy-minded prime minister but as an effort to deploy a humane internationalist "cover," in an expansive budgetary environment, for the far less impressive record of the government through most of its tenure. It was also consistent with an emerging transnational hegemonic consensus on a "new deal" for Africa, linking G8 member states with a select group of Africa's "new leaders" behind the New Partnership for Africa's Development (NEPAD). This African activism can be seen, in short, as the product of a propitious strategic conjuncture. In this broader context, the Conservatives' turn away from Africa appears considerably less idiosyncratic and extraordinary. Rather, it both reflects and is enabled by the much longer-term weakness of humane internationalism as a vital influence on public policy.

The degree to which humane internationalism has been in a state of long-term erosion or decline is less clear. For one thing, it is doubtful how much force it has ever held beyond the sphere of a relatively elite minority of the "attentive public." Don Munton (2002–3), in his influential assessment of the internationalist tradition in Canadian foreign policy, argued in the early years of the new millennium that internationalist proclivities in Canadian public opinion have waxed and waned, but have remained relatively consistent and robust over time. Certainly, humane internationalist flourishes, like the government's rapid and generous response to the Haitian earthquake of early 2010, remain conspicuously popular. However, it is widely agreed in the literature on Canadian foreign policy that public opinion has only a limited "parameter setting" impact on the content and conduct of Canada's international relations. More telling is the possibility that the influence of humane internationalism has weakened at the level of political and social elites. Canadians have thrice (re-)elected a Conservative government—now with a parliamentary majority—that has no discernible humane internationalist tradition in the terms elucidated by Pratt.[18] And whereas, historically, parliamentary opinion across party lines was firmly ahead of government policy in championing a more generous approach on international development issues (Pratt, 2003), it can be persuasively argued that there is less depth of knowledge or interest in development and African issues in recent Parliaments than there was a generation ago. Even this assessment must be qualified, however, by the fact that in 2008 a minority Parliament unanimously adopted Bill C-293, the Better Aid Bill, legislating that poverty reduction must be the central focus of Canadian development assistance (Freeman, 2008: 1).

More broadly, the vitality of a variant of humane internationalism in Canadian society is manifested in the rapid growth of international development and global studies programs in Canadian universities,[19] as well as in the continued numbers of non-governmental groups and coalitions concerned with issues of global social justice and in the countries and peoples of the developing world.

Despite these ambiguities, three specific points can be made in support of an argument that the humane internationalist tradition is in a state of relative decline and has thus enabled the policy transitions described above. First, public and political support for development assistance as *a*, if not *the*, key marker of humane internationalism in Canadian foreign policy has now repeatedly shown itself to be the softest of soft targets politically. As noted above, aid was disproportionately targeted in the austerity cuts of the 1990s. More recently, in the 2010 federal budget that began to come to grips with the fiscal implications of the global financial crisis of the late 2000s, aid was once again targeted disproportionately as the only major portfolio to be "flatlined" and therefore effectively cut in real terms.[20] Second, the development constituency in Canadian civil society, which Pratt famously characterized in the mid-1980s as a part of a substantial and deeply rooted counter-consensus concerning Canadian foreign policy (Pratt, 1983–4), has similarly proven itself to be a soft political target, with the church-based KAIROS coalition being summarily defunded in late 2009 after 35 years of support by CIDA and the umbrella grouping the Canadian Council for International Cooperation (CCIC) being similarly defunded in 2010. Third, the more idealistic and activist youth constituency that has gravitated towards international development and global studies programs in universities and towards civil society groups engaged with global social justice issues has only limited concern with, and involvement in, formal political debates in Canada on these or other issues, as manifested in its low rates of electoral and party-political participation.[21]

How might we explain the evident decline in the influence of humane internationalism over the past generation? At least four elements seem to have contributed and would benefit from further research. The first relates to the weakness of support for foreign aid. Since its "invention" in the early years of the post–Second World War era, development assistance has served as a key marker of a government's commitment to global poverty alleviation and hence humane internationalism (see Lumsdaine, 1993). Yet throughout its history, aid has been subject to critiques from both the left and the right concerning the mixed motives it has served (security, commercial, and class-based as well as ethical), and has faced persistent accusations that it is ineffectual or even counterproductive. These critiques have waxed and waned in popularity, but over time their impact on support for this modest form of global redistribution has arguably been highly corrosive. Certainly they have been deployed to undercut the arguments of proponents of more generous foreign aid policies in Canada, especially under a Conservative government that is predisposed towards scepticism. High-profile critics such as Dambisa Moyo (2009) have achieved minor celebrity status, and the broad thrust of these critiques has been echoed within this country by a parliamentary senate committee (Senate of Canada, 2007) that, in the past, might have been expected to beat the drum for more and better aid, as previous parliamentary committees have done.

It is not possible to engage in the complex debate over whether, and how, aid "works" in this paper. Certainly, there is much to critique in the aid practices of Canada and other donor states and agencies. At the same time, however, much of the criticism has been ahistorical and decontextualized (see, for example, Moorsom, 2010, on Moyo). In particular, the notion that CIDA has wasted vast sums of money in Africa is contradicted both by the programs that *have* worked and by the limited and highly inconstant pattern of aid spending and priorities that has undermined the potential to achieve better results. For example, the 2007 Senate report *Overcoming Forty Years of Failure* noted that CIDA has spent C$12.8 billion in Africa since the agency's inception in 1968. Spread over 30 years and across a continent that now numbers a billion people, expenditures of this modest level can hardly be expected to have had a clearly discernible impact. The point here, however, is that oft-repeated attacks on the utility of Canadian aid and aid organizations, reinforced by the still-entrenched neo-liberal common sense that markets are the answer, has undercut the political foundation for one of the principal expressions of post-war humane internationalism.

Second, the foundations of humane internationalism have arguably been undermined by the changing place and face of organized religion in Canadian society. This is a strikingly understudied dynamic within post-war Canadian foreign policy. In short, many of the most prominent scholarly and organizational proponents of the humane internationalist tradition had roots in the then-dominant mainstream Christian churches—Anglican, Mennonite, Presbyterian, United, Roman Catholic, etc.—with their strong (though not uncontested) **social gospel** traditions reflecting an emphasis on compassion towards those in need (see Gecelovsky, chapter 7). These included, for example, scholars like Cranford Pratt, Robert Matthews, and Douglas Anglin, and organizations like Project Ploughshares, the Taskforce on the Churches and Corporate Responsibility, and Ten Days for World Development. Similarly, a number of the leading architects of the internationalist tradition in the practice of post-war Canadian foreign policy had strong religious influences in their upbringing. To cite only two prominent examples, both Lester Pearson and Escott Reid were the sons of ministers.

These religious traditions and organizations have been in a steady, long-term decline since the 1960s (see Valpy and Friesen, 2010). Insofar as there has been growth in organized religion in Canada, it has come in more conservative faith traditions. These include evangelical Christianity, emphasizing a theology of personal responsibility versus social compassion (a particularly strong influence within the Conservative caucus—see McDonald, 2010, and Gecelovsky, chapter 7), Roman Catholicism,[22] Islam, Hinduism, Sikhism, and Buddhism. These are obviously rich, complex, and diverse faiths. For the most part, however, they lack the social gospel orientation (or its equivalent) that was so instrumental in the rising salience of a solidaristic and humane internationalist tradition in the post–Second World War era. Whether this mission-oriented impulse was, on balance, normatively positive or negative is beside the broader point that its decline has reshaped the social foundations of Canada's role in the world.

Third, the tradition of radical solidarity politics, or "radical internationalism" in Pratt's terms (1989b: 13–22), has declined markedly in the post–Cold War era. This tradition never had a significant *direct* influence on policy, nor did it seek to have. Rather, as an anti-capitalist *cum* socialist orientation, it sought to champion and support more far-reaching, transformative change, and typically viewed the Canadian government as being "on the wrong side."[23] Still, the tradition can be argued to have had a significant *indirect* influence on policy, through its research, advocacy, and coalition-building efforts. Collectives like the Toronto Committee for the Liberation of Southern Africa (TCLSAC) and the Centre d'information et de documentation sur le Mozambique et l'Afrique australe (CIDMAA) were substantial influences in academic centres and labour and civil society politics, within and beyond Canada.[24] They were particularly active in support of liberation movements in Southern Africa and had substantial analogues in Latin American solidarity work. These collectives were led by intellectually compelling scholar-activists who had a very substantial influence on a generation of students and social movements.[25]

How might we think about the influence of this sub-tradition on the trajectory of humane internationalism? Through their critical analysis and advocacy, as well as their role in graduate training and media engagement, the supporters of this tradition tended to push the centre of debate in more radical directions. While it was never realistic to imagine that Canadian government policy would be brought into line with the positions they championed, their positions provided an incentive for relatively reformist and progressive political and policy elites to move official approaches some distance towards more generous and solidaristic positions vis-à-vis developing countries—notably the frontline states of Southern Africa.[26]

With the demise of apartheid, however, as well as the end of the Cold War, this radical internationalist tradition lost much of its impetus. While radical solidarity politics have not disappeared, they have become more diffuse and unfocused as the causes for which they struggled have ended, mostly in various degrees of disillusionment. This, too, can be said to have contributed to the declining salience of the broader humane internationalist tradition.

Finally, as noted above, there remains significant evidence of something akin to humane internationalism in Canadian society. This can be seen, for example, in the popularity of international development, global studies, and environmental studies programs in Canadian universities, with their cosmopolitan sensibility; in the many non-governmental organizations that continue to proliferate despite an uncertain financial climate; and in the periodic upsurges of mass street-level social movement activism, seen most recently in the dramatic protests that accompanied the 2010 G20 Summit in Toronto and the "Occupy" movements beginning in late 2011.

Many, though not all, of the protagonists of these forms of engagement and activism are relatively youthful. However, rather than framing their engagement in terms of a humane internationalist orientation that sees the Canadian state and Canadian foreign policy as principal targets and vehicles of their normative agenda, those who engage in these forms of activism increasingly do so under a rubric of global citizenship. This flexible and fluid frame has become increasingly popular in both public and academic discussion; Rebecca Tiessen (2011) notes, for example, that it was advanced in the Martin government's 2005 *International Policy Statement*. Tiessen defines **global citizenship** as "a way of understanding the world in which an individual's *attitudes and behaviours* reflect a compassion and concern for the marginalized and/or poor and for the relationship between poverty and wealth—within and between communities, countries and regions" (2011: 573). This is very close, in conceptual and normative terms, to the definition of humane internationalism offered by Pratt a generation ago, with one key difference. Whereas humane internationalism had as the focus of its advocacy *state* obligations and policies, global citizenship reflects an ethic of global cosmopolitanism, disarticulated from national states and oriented towards transnational mobilization and direct action by engaged *individuals*. The domestic political analogue of this orientation is the tendency of young Canadians, both politicized and depoliticized, to disengage from the formal political process and policy debates, and to see state action as comparatively ineffectual and/or irrelevant.

The point here is less that the humane internationalist tradition has declined than that it has taken on a more cosmopolitan and deterritorialized orientation. The result as it relates to Canadian foreign policy would, however, be similar: a Canadian state relatively unbound from the requirement to answer to those who think its policies towards developing countries should be more generous, responsive, and self-critical.

Conclusion

The purpose of this analysis is not to discount the importance of the Harper government's efforts to reorient Canadian priorities and policies towards the developing world, and Africa in particular; neither is it to engage in a critical analysis of humane internationalism as an orientation for foreign policy.[27] Rather, it is to suggest that for one to properly understand the changes that have been unfolding under the Harper government, these changes need to be situated in relation to both the persistent weaknesses and the changing foundations and nature of the humane internationalist tradition. In short, there are important reasons to believe that this vital tradition has become significantly less important politically and that where its normative impulse persists, it has been redirected away from a focus on the policies of the Canadian state and towards "direct" or non-governmental action. The result is a much more permissive context for changes of government policy— including some quite important ones—in relation to what is sometimes called the "two-thirds world." This, I think, is regrettable and worth resisting. In this regard, there is a case to be made for more firmly reconnecting the motif of global citizenship to one of responsible, indeed humane, international citizenship.

Key Terms

counter-consensus
development assistance
global citizenship

humane internationalism
social gospel

Study Questions

1. How has Canadian foreign policy towards the "developing world," and in particular towards Africa, Latin America, and development assistance, changed under the Harper Conservative government from previous post-war Canadian governments?
2. To what extent, and in what ways, has humane internationalism influenced Canadian foreign policy? To what extent *should it* influence foreign policy?
3. Are ethical considerations becoming less prominent in the formulation of Canadian foreign policy?
4. How do you explain the apparent shift in emphasis from Africa to Latin America under the Harper Conservatives?
5. Is humane internationalism, in effect, a cloak for paternalism and neo-colonialism, as Anita Singh suggests in chapter 5?

Notes

1 For an earlier effort to explain the shift on which this chapter builds, see Black, 2009.
2 My focus on humane internationalism is important because of the pivotal role of this tradition in both motivations for and critiques of Canadian policy towards the developing world in the post–Second World War era. Humane internationalism is related to, but extends beyond, liberal internationalism. In fact, in Pratt's fullest conceptualization of the term, he distinguishes a modest "liberal internationalist" variant of humane internationalism from a "reform internationalist" variant, broadly defined as "social democracy applied internationally," and a "radical internationalist" variant emphasizing "an obligation to show solidarity with the poor of other lands." See Pratt, 1989b: 19–20.
3 This was particularly clear during the latter years of the George W. Bush administration but has persisted under the Obama administration, at least to some degree. For example, Canadian naval vessels are now regularly engaged in drug interdiction patrols in the Caribbean, with US law enforcement personnel embarked for enforcement purposes.
4 On the reduced value of Canada's commitment to Africa, the Harper government recalculated this commitment from the original target, based on the *projected* value of aid spending in 2003–4, to the smaller amount derived from *actual* bilateral expenditures that year.

Despite this reduced target, bilateral programs in core African partners continued to grow significantly.

5 Bilateral funding currently accounts for 53 per cent of the total Canadian aid budget.

6 In fact, Denis Stairs (2005) has shown that as an exercise in concentration, the IPS process was largely illusory.

7 Benin, Burkina Faso, Cameroon, Kenya, Malawi, Niger, Rwanda, and Zambia.

8 In May 2009, Minister for International Cooperation Oda followed the announcement of new countries of concentration with the articulation of a new and ostensibly more focused set of thematic priorities, on food security, sustainable economic growth, and securing the future of children and youth (Oda, 2009). In addition, however, she cited democracy promotion and ensuring security and stability as crosscutting foreign policy themes, and governance, the environment, and equality between men and women as "critical considerations." Indeed, by the end of her speech it was not clear which of CIDA'S previous priorities could not find a home somewhere in this new list.

9 This brief summary draws heavily on Brown, 2008.

10 What happens to Africa's share of Canadian aid beyond 2008–9, especially in light of the reduction in the number of African states among core bilateral aid recipients, is still unclear at the time of writing.

11 Indeed, much of the Harper government's emphasis in the context of the 2009 G8 Summit in l'Aquila and again at the 2010 summit it hosted was on persuading other governments to follow its example in fulfilling their commitments.

12 As a thought experiment, imagine how the government would justify its "abandonment" of the people of Darfur.

13 Compare this with the 19 ministerial-level visits made to India in the 2007–9 period; see Singh, chapter 5.

14 The full title of the conference was "Africa Rising: Entrepreneurship and Innovation Frontiers."

15 In fairness, Kim Nossal has noted the same tendency in his analysis of the Chrétien government's "Pinchpenny Diplomacy": "Both the Liberal party and its leader discovered that there was considerable electoral mileage in distancing themselves from Mulroney's foreign policies" (1998–9: 94). In this regard the "new" Conservative approach is merely an intensification of this tendency. This larger trend could be seen to reflect the increasing substitution of partisan posturing aimed at domestic audiences for genuine engagement with the hard dilemmas of world affairs.

16 One looks in vain among the current crop of Conservative MPs for voices comparable to those of, for example, Howard Green, Flora MacDonald, David MacDonald, William Winegard, Walter McLean, Douglas Roche, Joe Clark, or indeed Brian Mulroney in their advocacy of Canadian activism on humane internationalist issues.

17 According to the Development Assistance Committee of the Organisation for Economic Co-operation and Development (OECD), Canadian aid continued to languish at 0.29 per cent of gross national income (GNI) in 2007.

18 Albeit with less than 40 per cent of the 2011 popular vote.

19 As a rough guide, there are now 18 member institutions of the Canadian Consortium on University Programs in International Development Studies (CCUPIDS), and these programs are among the fastest growing at leading research-oriented universities such as Dalhousie, Guelph, Ottawa, Queen's, and York.

20 A trend that has continued in the most recent (2012) federal budget, with aid funding absorbing a disproportionate share of budget cuts.

21 Young voters are much more likely to support parties on the political left and centre, according to opinion polling, but only 37 per cent of them voted in the 2008 federal election, compared with an overall voter turnout of 59 per cent and 68 per cent participation rates among

those aged 65 and older. Early evidence suggests that this pattern has held in 2011, despite unprecedented efforts to encourage youth voting. See Grenier, 2010.

22 The Roman Catholic tradition obviously contains both progressive and conservative elements. However, it is evident that the more progressive element, associated in foreign affairs with liberation theology, has declined in influence in Canada as elsewhere, while the conservative orientation has been reinforced by the principal sources of growth in Canadian Roman Catholicism, associated with recent immigrants. See Bibby, 2009.

23 The words are those of one of Canada's leading "radical internationalists," John S. Saul, articulated during the 2010 conference of the Canadian Association of African Studies.

24 TCLSAC produced *Southern Africa Report,* a prominent source of critical analysis and commentary that was widely read among Africanists in Canada and internationally.

25 Key examples include John Saul, Dan O'Meara, Linda Freeman, and Otto Roesch.

26 Those states that bordered on the white minority regimes in the region (South Africa, Rhodesia, and colonial Angola and Mozambique) and that bore the brunt of their destabilization efforts.

27 Though it is likely clear to readers that I think there is much of value in this tradition. For an alternative, more critical view of the paternalistic and neo-colonial potentialities of Canadian internationalism, see Singh, chapter 5.

References

Bibby, R. 2009. "Restless Gods and Restless Youth: An Update on the Religious Situation in Canada." Paper presented at the annual meeting of the Canadian Sociological Association, Ottawa, May.

Black, David. 2004. "Canada and Africa: Activist Aspirations in Straitened Circumstances." In Ian Taylor and Paul Williams, eds, *Africa in International* Politics. London: Routledge, 136–54.

———. 2010. "Canada and the Commonwealth: The Multilateral Politics of a 'Wasting Asset.'" *Canadian Foreign Policy/La politique étrangère du Canada* 16, 2: 61–77.

Black, David, and Paul Williams. 2008. "Darfur's Challenge to International Society." *Behind the Headlines* 65, 6: 1–23.

Bow, Brian, and David Black. 2008–9. "Does Politics Stop at the Water's Edge in Canada? Party and Partisanship in Canadian Foreign Policy." *International Journal* 64, 1: 7–27.

Bradbury, Adrian, Alexa McDonough, and Paul Dewar. 2007. "Quiet Diplomacy or Lost Opportunity?" *Chronicle-Herald* (Halifax), 18 November.

Brown, Chris, and Ted Jackson. 2009. "Could the Senate Be Right? Should CIDA be Abolished?" Paper presented to the annual meeting of the Canadian Association for the Study of International Development (CASID). Carleton University, Ottawa, 27–29 May.

Brown, Stephen. 2008. "CIDA under the Gun." In Jean Daudelin and Daniel Schwanen, eds, *Canada among Nations 2007: What Room for Manoeuvre?* Montreal and Kingston: McGill-Queen's University Press, 91–107.

CBC.ca. 2002. "Harper Plans to Battle 'Culture of Defeatism' in Atlantic Canada." 30 May. At http://www.cbc.ca/news/story/2002/05/29/harper_atlntc020529.html.

CBC.ca. 2007. "Harper Says Meeting Bono Isn't His 'Shtick.'" 7 June. At http://www.cbc.ca/world/story/2007/06/07/harper-bono.html.

CCA (Canadian Council on Africa). 2009. "Presentation to the Standing Committee of Foreign Affairs and International Development of the Parliament of Canada by the Canadian Council on Africa." Ottawa, 3 June.

CIDA (Canadian International Development Agency). 2009. "Canada Moves on Another Element of Its Aid Effectiveness Agenda." *CIDA,* 23 February. At http://www.acdi-cida.gc.ca/CIDAWEB/acdicida.nsf/EN/NAT-223132931-PPH.

Clark, Joe. 2007. "Is Africa Falling off Canada's Map? Remarks to the National Capital Branch of the Canadian Institute of International Affairs." Ottawa, 6 November.

Cooper, Andrew. 2008. *Celebrity Diplomacy.* Boulder, CO: Paradigm Publishers.

Daudelin, Jean, and Laura Dawson. 2008. "A New Chapter?" *Canadian Foreign Policy/La politique étrangère du Canada* 14, 3: 5–10.

de Masellis, L. 2003. "Statistics." *Canadian Development Report 2003: From Doha to Cancun, Development and the WTO.* Ottawa: North-South Institute.

DFAIT (Foreign Affairs and International Trade Canada). 2011. "Harper Government Committed to Opening New Markets in Africa / International Trade Minister Peter Van Loan Highlights New Opportunities for Canadian Business in Africa's Emerging Markets." Press release, 16 March.

Fowler, Robert. 2003. "Canadian Leadership and the Kananaskis G8 Summit: Towards a Less Self-Centred Canadian Foreign Policy." In David Carment, Fen Osler Hampson, and Norman Hillmer, eds, *Canada among Nations 2003: Coping with the American Colossus.* Don Mills, ON: Oxford University Press, 219–41.

Freeman, Aaron. 2008. "Official Development Assistance Accountability Act—Plain Language Overview." *Canadian Council for International Cooperation*, October.

Freeman, Alan. 2007a. "Ottawa to Re-evaluate Foreign Aid Priorities." *Globe and Mail*, 6 October, A21. At http://www.theglobeandmail.com/news/world/article125343.ece.

———. 2007b. "Harper Signals Shift from Africa to Americas." *Globe and Mail*, 8 June, A19. At http://v1. theglobeandmail.com/servlet/story/RTGAM.20070608.wg8africa08/business/Business/Business/.

Freeman, Linda. 1997. *The Ambiguous Champion.* Toronto: University of Toronto Press.

Gee, Marcus. 2007. "Setting a New Course for Canada's Foreign Policy – South." *Globe and Mail*, 20 July.

Government of Canada. 2009. "Canada and the Americas." Department of Foreign Affairs and International Trade, 13 August. At http://www.international.gc.ca/americas-ameriques/priorities_progress-priorites_progres.aspx.

Grenier, Eric. 2010. "How Parliament Would Look If Only Youth Voted." *Globe and Mail*, 7 October. At http://www.theglobeandmail.com/news/politics/how-parliament-would-look-if-only-youth-voted/article1747999/.

Healy, Teresa, and Sheila Katz. 2008. "Big and Little Brother Bilateralism: Security, Prosperity, and Canada's Deal with Colombia." *Studies in Political Economy* 82: 35–60.

"Interview with Stephen Harper, An." 2007. *Americas Quarterly* 1, 2.

Johnson, William. 2009. "The Outsider: How Stephen Harper Brought Canada to Conservatism, and the Conservatives to Crisis." *The Walrus*, March. At http://www.walrusmagazine.com/articles/2009.03-stephen-harper-outsider-william-johnson?ref=2009.04-stephen-harper-outsider-william-johnson&page=.

Kirk, John, and Peter McKenna. 2009. "Stephen Harper's Cuba Policy: From Autonomy to Americanization?" *Canadian Foreign Policy/La politique étrangère du Canada* 15, 1: 21–39.

LeBlanc, Daniel, Campbell Clark, and Jan Wong. 2005. "Leaders Deaf to Live 8 Call." *Globe and Mail*, 4 July, A1.

Lumsdaine, David H. 1993. *Moral Vision in International Politics: The Foreign Aid Regime 1949–89.* Princeton, NJ: Princeton University Press.

McDonald, Marci. 2010. *The Armageddon Factor: The Rise of Christian Nationalism in Canada.* Toronto: Random House.

Martin, Lawrence. 2010. *Harperland: The Politics of Control.* Toronto: Viking Canada.

Matthews, Robert. 1976. "Canada and Anglophone Africa." In Peyton V. Lyon and Tareq Y. Ismael, eds, *Canada and the Third World.* Toronto: Macmillan of Canada, 60–132.

Moorsom, Toby. 2010. "The Zombies of Development Economics: Dambisa Moyo's Dead Aid and Fictional African Entrepreneurs." Paper presented to the annual meeting of the Canadian Association of African Studies, Carleton University.

Morrison, David R. 1998. *Aid and Ebb Tide: A History of CIDA and Canadian Development Assistance.* Waterloo, ON: Wilfrid Laurier University Press.

Moyo, Dambisa. 2009. *Dead Aid: Why Aid Is Not Working and How There Is a Better Way for Africa.* New York: Farrar, Straus and Giroux.

Munton, Don. 2002–3. "Whither Internationalism?" *International Journal* 58, 1: 155–80.

Neufeld, Mark. 1995. "Hegemony and Foreign Policy Analysis: The Case of Canada as a Middle Power." *Studies in Political Economy* 48 (Autumn): 7–29.

Noel, Alain, and Jean-Philippe Thérien. 1995. "From Domestic to International Justice: The Welfare State and Foreign Aid." *International Organization* 49, 3: 523–53.

————. 2008. *Left and Right in Global Politics.* Cambridge: Cambridge University Press.

Noel, Alain, Jean-Philippe Thérien, and Sebastien Dallaire. 2004. "Divided over Internationalism: The Canadian Public and Development Assistance." *Canadian Public Policy* 30, 1: 29–46.

Nossal, Kim. 1994. *Rain Dancing: Sanctions in Canadian and Australian Foreign Policy.* Toronto: University of Toronto Press.

————. 1998–9. "Pinchpenny Diplomacy: The Decline of 'Good International Citizenship' in Canadian Foreign Policy." *International Journal* 54, 1: 88–105.

Oda, Beverley J. 2009. "A New Effective Approach to Canadian Aid: Speaking Notes for the Honourable Beverley J. Oda, Minister of International Cooperation, at the Munk Centre for International Studies." Toronto, 20 May.

Owen, T., and D. Eaves. 2007. "Africa Is Not a Liberal Idea." *Embassy Magazine*, 3 October. At http://embassymag.ca/page/view/.2007.october.3.africa.

Pratt, Cranford. 1983–4. "Dominant Class Theory and Canadian Foreign Policy: The Case of the Counter-Consensus." *International Journal* 39, 1: 99–135.

————. 1989a. "Canada: An Eroding and Limited Internationalism." In Cranford Pratt, ed., *Internationalism under Strain: The North-South Policies of Canada, the Netherlands, Norway, and Sweden.* Toronto: University of Toronto Press, 24–69.

————. 1989b. "Humane Internationalism: Its Significance and Variants." In Cranford Pratt, ed., *Internationalism under Strain: The North-South Policies of Canada, the Netherlands, Norway, and Sweden.* Toronto: University of Toronto Press, 3–23.

————. 2003. "Ethical Values and Canadian Foreign Aid Policies." *Canadian Journal of African Studies* 37, 1: 84–101.

Randall, Stephen, and Jillian Dowding. 2008. "Canada, Latin America, Colombia and the Evolving Policy Agenda." *Canadian Foreign Policy/La politique étrangère du Canada* 14, 3: 29–46.

Salutin, Rick. 2008. "Harper Sahib at the G8." *Globe and Mail*, 11 July, A15.

Senate of Canada. 2007. *Overcoming 40 Years of Failure: A New Road Map for Sub-Saharan Africa.* Standing Committee on Foreign Affairs and International Trade. Senate of Canada. At http://www.parl.gc.ca/Content/SEN/Committee/391/fore/rep/repafrifeb07-e.pdf.

Simpson, Erin. 2007. "From Inter-dependence to Conflation: Security and Development in the Post-9/11 Era." *Canadian Journal of Development Studies* 28, 2: 263–75.

Smillie, Ian. 2006. "Whose Security? Innovation and Responsibility, Perception and Reality." In Sandra MacLean, David Black, and Timonthy Shaw, eds, *A Decade of Human Security*, 19–31. Aldershot, UK: Ashgate.

Stairs, Denis. 2005. "Confusing the Innocent with Numbers and Categories: The International Policy Statement and the Concentration of Development Assistance." *Canadian Defence and Foreign Affairs Institute Research Paper Series*, December. At http://www.cdfai.org/PDF/Confusing%20the%20Innocent.pdf.

Tiessen, Rebecca. 2011. "Global Subjects or Objects of Globalisation? The Promotion of Global Citizenship in Organisations Offering Sport for Development and Peace Programmes." *Third World Quarterly* 32, 3: 571–87.

Tomlinson, Brian. 2009. "A Review of CIDA's Countries of Priority: A CCIC Briefing Note." *Canadian Council for International Co-operation*, February. At http://www.ccic.ca/_files/en/what_we_do/002_aid_2009-02_cida_priority_country_review.pdf.

Valpy, Michael, and Joe Friesen. 2010. "A Twist of Faith." *Globe and Mail*, 11 December, A16.

Wijeyaratne, Surendrini. 2008. "Promoting an Inclusive Peace: A Call to Strengthen Canada's Peace-making Capacity. Part Four: Country Study: Peace and Justice in Northern Uganda." Discussion Paper, Canadian Council for International Cooperation, November.

York, Geoffrey. 2009. "Banned Aid." *Globe and Mail*, 30 May, F1.

14 Canada and the Afghan "Other": Identity, Difference, and Foreign Policy

Claire Turenne Sjolander

> Fellow Canadians, as the combat mission here in Kandahar draws to a close and Canadian boots no longer tread this dusty ground, always remember that we Canadians are not here for ourselves. We do not dream of empire. We do not covet what other nations possess, and we do not make war to advance selfish or cynical aims.
>
> Canadians will strive for justice and stand for what is right, and Canada has young men and women like you who will march to the ends of the Earth ... to defend what makes Canada the best country in the world.
>
> Let no one forget it. My friends, you have done exceptionally well. You came into the toughest part of this country, and you held it, and now it is being developed.

With these words, Prime Minister Stephen Harper capped off a surprise visit to Kandahar, in the southern region of Afghanistan. In a speech delivered before an audience of Canadian soldiers preparing for the July 2011 end to their combat mission, Harper expressed the thanks of his government and that of all Canadians. At the conclusion of his remarks, he reflected that the selflessness revealed by Canada's soldiers in conducting their mission in Afghanistan was simply the expression of "a great truth about Canada": "... we Canadians are not here for ourselves" (Harper, 2011).

This chapter uses the case of Afghanistan and more specifically the representations of Canada's mission in Afghanistan since 2006 as found in the speeches of Canadian political leaders, particularly in those of the prime minister, in order to unpack the ideas (and ideals) embedded in the use of internationalist rhetoric in contemporary Canadian foreign policy. Treating internationalism as a discursive frame, this chapter examines the ways in which its use establishes some of the markers of a "Canadian" identity—an identity that is both projected in and defined by Canada's foreign policy ventures, and most specifically by the representations of these. As is the case with any discourse that contributes to the establishment of identity, however, internationalism also participates in the definition of Canadians through constructions of the "**other**." In defining Canadian virtuousness abroad, as Harper's comments cited above attempt to do, the **discourse** of internationalism shapes the understanding of the "others" upon whom Canada acts or with whom Canada can be compared. The "great truth" about Canada is notable because it is not a truth shared by others, at least not by others in the same way. "Others" are not like "us"; "others" are not like Canadians. Used in this way, internationalism is an inherently relational idea; it defines Canada's difference with respect to the rest of the world, and as such, its theoretical edifice depends upon an unspoken and often unseen "other."

As Smith has suggested, however, Canadian internationalism understood in this way is hardly neutral. This use of internationalism embeds within it forms of "**othering**" that manipulate, marginalize, and silence the objects of our foreign policy (2003: 25; see also Smith, chapter 12). The construction of the "other" rests upon a series of assumptions about Canadian superiority, assumptions that are often gendered, racialized, and colonial. Nowhere is this clearer than in the case of Canada's mission in Afghanistan, where the discourse of internationalism has served as a prism reinforcing the construction of a laudable identity for Canada, all the while leaving Afghanistan and all the actors within largely silent and without agency—the vessel of the "other" into which Canadian virtuousness has been poured. Despite being silent throughout the Afghan mission, the "other" is omnipresent. The mobilization of the discourse of internationalism in prime ministerial and ministerial speeches about Canada's mission in Afghanistan not only provides a powerful illustration of the constructions that flow from internationalist rhetoric, but also offers a critical examination of the limits and contradictions of internationalism, particularly as expressed in the Harper era.

The Substance of Canadian Internationalism

In order to assess the nature of Canadian internationalism, it is useful to return to the disciplinary narratives of Canada's role and place in world affairs, at least as they have been represented since the end of the Second World War. Neither a great nor a small power, Canada was constructed as the best exemplar of the **middle power**. John W. Holmes is often credited with lending the necessary intellectual weight to the concept of middle power as a lens through which Canadian foreign policy might best be understood and assessed. As Holmes argued, the concept of middle power had a very specific meaning in the Canadian context:

[The concept of middle power] had been conceived in the first place as a way of explaining to the world that Canadians were of greater consequence than the Panamanians but could not take on the obligations of the Americans, or even the French. It was useful in encouraging a wallflower people to get responsibly involved in keeping the peace and unleashing the world economy while warning them at the same time that they should not expect to wield the influence of a "great" power. (1984: 366–7)

The middle power had to be engaged in the affairs of the world and could not seek refuge in an isolationist foreign policy, according to Holmes, even if its capacity to influence world affairs was not equivalent to that of its southern neighbour.

Following from this activist conception of (and prescription for) Canada as a middle power, the characteristics of internationalism as a policy orientation began to take shape. Nossal, Roussel, and Paquin (2011) have provided a useful summary of the characteristic elements of a foreign policy defined by a commitment to internationalism—elements that are the antithesis of isolationism:

1. States accept and willingly take on the *responsibility* of playing a constructive role in the management of international conflict.
2. States do not act unilaterally in global affairs, but rather see *multilateral* support as essential for defusing conflicts.
3. States support *international institutions* (because such institutions contribute to multilateralism and thus reduce the tendency to unilateralism).
4. The support for international organizations must be robust, defined by a willingness to enter into *formal commitments* to use national resources for the support of the system as a whole.
5. Finally, states support *international law* as a vehicle to ensure the stability of the interstate system. (135–6; see also Nossal, chapter 2)

Defined as in the five points above, the characteristics of internationalism are closely linked to the capabilities of a middle power; the emphasis on international organizations, multilateralism, and international law ensures that the non-great power has the potential to affect the international system through international collaboration and "team player" policies and behaviours. In this sense, internationalism is an "influence multiplier" for the middle power; international institutions, multilateral processes, and international law enable it to identify allies within the context of established and accepted international structures in the promotion of particular policies. These opportunities create the potential to influence great powers—and possibly to constrain great power unilateralism—within multilateral structures. For the Canada that emerged from the Second World War, the concept of middle power and its associated internationalist orientation became in many ways the *raison d'être* of Canadian foreign policy; as Black and Turenne Sjolander have argued, at many times it appeared as if the processes of multilateral cooperation within international organizations had become more important than the content of the resulting policy itself (1996).

Nossal, Roussel, and Paquin also acknowledge that internationalism is more than simply a series of characteristic elements of foreign policy. In addition, they suggest that internationalism also "promoted a sense of Canadian identity at the national and international levels" (2011: 136). Defending the view that the basis of internationalism is liberalism (both in partisan terms, reflecting the role of post-war Liberal governments in formulating its approach, and in terms of liberal political philosophy and values), they argue that "[s]ince the liberal values on which internationalist ideas are based reflect an idealistic vision of international relations, it is possible for Canada to distinguish itself from the great powers that prefer a more 'realistic' approach to global politics. Canadians can thus more easily claim to be following a policy that is distinct from the United States, and to assume roles that Americans cannot or do not want to play, such as mediator or peacekeeper" (2011: 136). As such, and as Holmes argues, the middle-power role and its attendant internationalist orientation differentiated Canada from the United States, all the while supporting an engaged foreign policy. From the outset, the construction of a Canadian identity through internationalism necessarily defined Canada by reference to an "other"—in the first instance, the United States.

The way in which internationalism facilitated the construction of a Canadian identity, distinct from the United States, was not without moral content or consequence. The construction of this identity was lent support through the perception of a unique "fit" between internationalism (as the foreign policy orientation of the middle power) and Canada as its best exemplar, a fit that appeared to be confirmed in Lester B. Pearson's leadership during the 1956 Suez Crisis. Pearson worked through the United Nations (UN) to find a multilateral solution to the escalating crisis, and his promotion of a UN peacekeeping force had both short- and longer-term consequences. Beyond his evident contribution to the resolution of the crisis itself, his advocacy of the creation of the first UN peacekeeping mission and the international recognition that stemmed from this seemed almost destined, at least within Canada, to transform internationalism from being simply the necessary policy orientation of the prudent middle power to being an article of faith and virtue. In effect, the subsequent awarding of Pearson's Nobel Peace Prize appeared to confirm the uniqueness and merits of Canadian internationalism, as well as to define a unique place for Canada on the world stage and solidify Canada's potential for international influence. While peacekeeping was strongly rooted within the five characteristic elements of internationalism, the Nobel Peace Prize associated it (as a concrete manifestation of internationalism) with a particular ideal of virtue. Peacekeeping was laudable—as was the internationalism it represented—because it harkened back to liberal values such as peace, freedom, justice, and democracy (Nossal, Roussel, and Paquin, 2011: 136). The Nobel Peace Prize suggested that Canadian internationalism was superior to the internationalism practised by others, if indeed others were even able to practise it. Internationalism was no longer just the foreign policy orientation of the prudent middle power, but rather an ideal that constructed a virtuous Canadian identity on the world stage. The Peace Prize cemented the translation of internationalism from a set of policy orientations to a particular moral posture associated with liberal values that defined Canada's identity—one that was played out in response to world events.

Prime Minister Harper was hardly the first to have invoked the "great truth about Canada" (the selflessness of Canadians as one of the cornerstones of Canada's internationalist identity) when he did so in his May 2011 address to the soldiers stationed in Kandahar, although not all have felt equally inspired by it. Holmes raised warnings about what he perceived to be the glorification of the internationalist ideal in Canadian foreign policy (most notably in its close association with a particular form of moral virtue)—and thus the glorification of Canada's (virtuous) international role. "[A] certain moral arrogance has crept into the concept of middle power," Holmes lamented. "That might is not right all would agree—but neither is weakness. Middle powers are middle powers because they are weaker, not because they are more virtuous" (1976: 36). For his part, Denis Stairs refers to the expression of this "truth" as a component of Canada's "self-deluded" approach to international affairs. Canadians, Stairs has argued, "have come to think of themselves not as others are, but as morally superior. They believe, in particular, that they subscribe to a distinctive set of values—'*Canadian*' values—and that those values are special in the sense of being unusually virtuous" (Stairs, 2003: 239). The prime minister was nonetheless unabashed in naming the elements of this "truth." Canadians at war in Kandahar are not there for themselves; unlike others, the prime minister implies, Canadians do not dream of empire and do not covet what others possess. Rather, Canadians have been engaged in combat in Afghanistan and will remain to train the Afghan National Army for reasons that speak to a higher moral purpose.

Samantha Arnold extends this argument in her analysis of the functions of public diplomacy and of foreign policy more generally. She contends that "foreign policy works in important ways to *create* the sphere of 'the foreign'—and thus also 'the domestic'—that is generally presumed by foreign policy analysis." She goes on to argue that, as a consequence, foreign policy is "implicated in the process of creating the very national identity that it is otherwise seen as projecting" (2010: 16). If we describe Canada's mission in Afghanistan as part of Canada's virtuous international role, reflective of the great selfless "truth" about Canadians, these representations of Canada's mission become a constitutive element shaping the very Canadian identity that Canada's foreign policy seeks to project abroad.

Understood as part of the process of constructing and reinforcing a specific Canadian identity, internationalist tropes are not without their consequences. If Canada is unusually virtuous and moral on the world stage, this necessarily implies that others are not quite as virtuous or possessing of the same moral superiority. This has two immediate effects. First, it **depoliticizes** the policies and initiatives that are framed discursively as internationalist—that is, those policies and interventions that are constructed as noble and laudable. On what ground— moral or otherwise—is it possible to argue against a military intervention that is framed, or whose protagonists are framed, as virtuous and morally superior? The second effect is both a cause and a consequence of the first: if Canada is constructed as noble and laudable in its intervention in Afghanistan, others are thereby constructed as less noble and laudable.

In her study of Canada's intervention in Afghanistan, Colleen Bell underscores the need to recall Edward Said's observations about the ways in which **Orientalism** plays itself out in relations between the West and the developing world. Referring to the West in general, she notes that the representations of Afghanistan in political speeches "can be made sense of as undeniably Orientalist not only because they privilege Western interests, but also because they treat the West as though it is beyond the troubled precincts of global order. In other words, these representations depict the West in ahistorical terms and as morally superior" (2010: 66). Canada's inherent virtue and its moral authority are unquestioned in the representations of the noble middle power; we see echoes of Bell's caution in Harper's evocation of the selflessness of Canadian soldiers who "strive for justice and stand for what is right." What is important here is not the truth of this characterization of Canada's soldiers, but the fact that the characterization implicitly suggests that Canada's armed forces are particularly well suited, and perhaps unique, in their capacity to seek justice and to stand for what is right, and that they therefore have an unquestionable responsibility—and moral duty—to bring this capacity to Afghanistan's "dusty" (unpaved, underdeveloped) ground. In order to fully appreciate the ways in which this construction of the "other" participates in the shaping of Canada's internationalist identity, we now to turn to the dimensions of the images that define it: first, in the construction of the moral superiority of Canada's internationalism, and then, in the ways in which the "other" is defined in support, and as a consequence, of that very internationalism.

Representations of Canada's Internationalism

As Canada's combat mission was drawing to a close, Prime Minister Harper reflected on its origins—the need to respond to the events of September 11, 2001. Commenting on the challenge confronting the global order as a result of the attacks of that day, he made the following observation: "We all remember the choice that confronted us: how should a country like ours respond? Canada, the good and peaceful citizen of the world that makes tolerance a national trait; what should we do when everything we uphold is assaulted by those whose only goal is violence and who will tolerate nothing but their own intolerance?" (Harper, 2011). Canada's peaceful pedigree is held up as a national trait in another speech delivered by the prime minister. Speaking before the House of Commons in support of his government's motion to extend the Canadian mission in Afghanistan until 2011, Stephen Harper summarized the roots of this peaceful Canadian nature:

> The dominion of Canada was not born of conflict. We have never displayed a taste for imperialism. We have largely escaped foreign aggression, and we are a nation of immigrants who came here seeking to leave behind us the violent histories of many of our ancestral lands. To a greater extent than most countries, we have also learned how to resolve our domestic disputes through democratic debate, honourable compromise and peaceful evolution. From all of this history, stems our reluctance to take up arms. Our reluctance to take up arms is a virtue. (Harper, 2008)

Here, the "good and peaceful citizen" is contextualized: the Canadian reluctance to take up arms is born of the lessons of history and the maturity of a people who have learned compromise and democratic debate. The insistence on Canada's historical (and, one might argue from this perspective, almost genetic) peacefulness allows Harper to draw implicit links with Canada's peacekeeping tradition—a particularly important link in the case of the nature of Canada's participation in the conflict in Afghanistan, which, despite the efforts of successive governments, could never convincingly be sold to the public as a peacekeeping mission (see Turenne Sjolander, 2009). Canada's peaceful history is painted as unique in the world—we "were not born of conflict" (unlike others, the prime minister might have added); we do not have "a taste for imperialism," our people sought to escape the "violent histories" of their homelands, and as a result, "to a greater extent than most," we have learned the art of "peaceful evolution."[1] Canada's history has made us different from the others.

For such a peaceful country, the decision to take up arms is always a considered one. "We have always demonstrated a willingness to take up arms in defence of our values and our interests, *when it has been necessary to do so*" (Harper, 2008; emphasis added). Here, Harper continues his speech before the House of Commons by juxtaposing his construction of Canada's supposed peaceful history with the responsible and engaged nature of its international commitment. Of course, it is important to remember that this peaceful history—this Canada's peacefulness— is in itself a powerful overstatement; as Justin Massie argues, Canadian history demonstrates that Canada is hardly a peaceable kingdom (2007: A31). Despite this, Harper's evocation of Canada's willingness to take up arms when necessary is perfectly consistent with the internationalist demands of responsibility and a willingness—indeed, an obligation—to commit resources for the maintenance of the system as a whole. A similar idea is put forward in the 2007 Speech from the Throne, this time adding emphasis to the multilateral nature of the mission: "Canada has joined the United Nations–sanctioned mission in Afghanistan because it is noble and necessary" (Canada, 2007).

Underscoring Canada's commitment to multilateralism is a recurrent theme in the prime minister's speeches. During a speech to the troops in Kandahar in May 2009, Harper emphasized the mission's legitimacy by referring to the United Nations. "But as you carry on this work," he told the soldiers, "we must never lose sight of the mission that brought us. Canada came here as part of a United Nations– sanctioned international rescue effort. We did not come as permanent occupiers— and we do not measure our success by the length of our stay. We came here to help the Afghan people secure the country" (Harper, 2009). Of course, in this speech, the conflict in Afghanistan is not a war, but a rescue effort—a framing that paints Canadian troops leading the mission as noble rescuers rather than as combatants. If a peaceful Canada has participated in the Afghanistan "international rescue effort," then this is both because the mission is inherently laudable (as a rescue mission must inherently be) and because Canada is unquestionably committed to multilateral processes and to the international institutions that animate them. Canada is not only different from other countries, it is morally unimpeachable. Peaceful by nature, yet committed to the international system, it only takes up arms when necessary to protect the common good.

Despite Harper's recalling of the events of 9/11 as the defining factor in the Canadian decision to participate in the Afghan mission, he is quick to underscore that Canada is different from the United States. Consistent with the idea that middle-power internationalism was constructed around Canada's distinctiveness from the United States, Harper makes the point that our "noble international efforts reflect a fundamental characteristic of Canadian society. Unlike our friends to the south, this country has never been isolationist and we have always harboured a strong desire to contribute to a better and safer world" (Harper, 2008). Canada has always accepted its place *in* the world, Harper seems to tell us, and has always willingly shouldered its responsibilities. The United States is effectively constructed as a more self-interested and less virtuous country than is Canada. Sherene Razack returns to Roméo Dallaire's experiences to explore this construction. She notes that, upon Dallaire's return from Rwanda, "he spoke passionately of Canada's noble calling. As he put it in an interview, 'To be that intermediary between the superpowers—who don't give a s*** anyways [*sic*]—and the Third World Countries who know they need the presence of our capabilities ... you've got a hard time to find a more noble concept'" (2004: 24). For Canada, middle-power internationalism constitutes the international realm as an "'affective space,' a place where middle-power nations can experience belonging" (24). Canada is different from—and implicitly better (more noble, more virtuous) than—the United States. Nowhere is this imagery more clearly expressed than in the 2007 Speech from the Throne: "Like the North Star, Canada has been a guide to other nations; through difficult times, Canada has shone as an example of what a people joined in common purpose can achieve" (Canada, 2007). Canada is an exemplar, not only to its neighbours to the south, but to the entire world.

As Nossal, Roussel, and Paquin have reminded us, internationalism also contributes to the construction of a Canadian identity through its reference to the liberal values of peace, freedom, justice, and democracy. These values are often repeated in prime ministerial speeches, both as justification for and legitimation of Canada's presence in Afghanistan. Speaking in Kandahar in 2009, Stephen Harper explained to troops that Canada had to participate in the international effort against the Taliban: "As part of the family of civilized nations, we have a national obligation to do our part to contribute to our peace and security. As a prosperous and free country, we have the moral duty to share our good fortune, our freedoms and our opportunities with the citizens of the world who have too long had to endure violence, oppression and privation" (Harper, 2009). Canada, as an engaged internationalist, has an obligation to share in the international burden.[2] More than that, however, Canada's peacefulness, security, prosperity, and freedom translate into a duty that it do so—particularly in the case of Afghanistan, where its favoured position stands in stark contrast to the violence, oppression, and privation experienced by Afghan citizens. This, of course, is not to dispute the considerable advantages that accrue to citizens of Canada when compared with the lot of Afghanis, but it does not justify why Canada should be militarily involved in Afghanistan more than in other devastated, violent, or oppressed countries in the world, nor does it explain how Canada brings about freedom or peace through the deployment of combat troops and engagement in a military mission. Evoking a "moral duty," however, shifts the political ground and, within the context of Canadian internationalism, makes it difficult to question the reasons for, or merits of, the mission. To raise such questions, Harper's words implicitly suggest, is to revoke one's moral duty—to stake out an amoral position.

Despite—and more likely because of—their depoliticizing consequences, the liberal values evoked by Harper as an explanation for Canada's role in Afghanistan have been used on numerous occasions. In the same 2009 speech, Harper celebrated that "[i]n the seven years since our work here began, incredible progress has been made—progress that continues each and every day. The foundations of democracy have been laid; basic human rights and freedoms are being restored; private enterprise is growing; millions of children are going to school; basic medical care has improved; and the infrastructure of a viable economy is emerging" (Harper, 2009). In 2007, the prime minister told Canadian troops in Afghanistan: "We are not daunted by shadows because we carry the light that defines them—the light of freedom and democracy, of human rights and the rule of law.... Our role in Afghanistan is Canada at its best and the Canadian people are proud to stand with you" (Blanchfield, 2007: A3). In these instances, Canada is portrayed as a champion of liberal values, playing a critical role in bringing and implanting those (unquestionable) values in Afghanistan. The Orientalist nature of this discourse is clear. Bell reminds us that "[a]s Edward Said recounted, the 'Oriental' is regarded as irrational, depraved, conflictual/violent, illiberal, childlike, animal-like, different, while the European is none of these but is rational, virtuous, peaceful, liberal, logical, mature, normal" (2010: 66). From this perspective, as part of the West, Canada has an obligation to bring its values to Afghanistan—and this obligation is not open to debate. Canadian internationalism contains within it a profoundly Orientalist streak; Canadian (Western) values are unquestionably superior and it is Canada's responsibility to bring them to the less advantaged corners of the world.

The celebration of Canada's unique role in Afghanistan is reinforced when the prime minister focuses his comments more specifically on Canadian troops. Addressing Canada's military contingent in Afghanistan in 2009, Stephen Harper noted:

> You came here to defend our national interests, our freedoms and our values. You are here to protect your country and the entire world against terrorism and barbarism; you are here to help the Afghan people rebuild this country too long ravaged by war; your challenges are legion; your work is extremely

dangerous; you are making enormous sacrifices; and I am here to say thank you and to tell you that all Canadians are proud of you. (Harper, 2009)

Canada's internationalist engagement is here tempered by its national interests—but this is not as far from internationalism as it might seem at first glance. After all, as Holmes reminded us earlier, the overwhelming motivation of internationalism as a policy orientation was to avoid isolationism. Nossal, Roussel, and Paquin explain this as follows: "[I]nternationalism rested on a simple strategic premise: the idea that peace is indivisible.... [T]he fate of any one state and the peace of the international system as a whole are deeply interconnected.... In short, the concept of the 'fireproof house' was obsolete" (2011: 135–6). The national interest invoked by Harper includes protecting Canadian freedoms from terrorism and barbarism. He strikes the same note later in the same speech: "Your compassion for the long-suffering people of Afghanistan, your resolve in the face of a savage enemy, your skill and professionalism, are credits to Canada. Your work here is the highest form of public service. It is undertaken neither for fortune, nor fame. It is not easy, nor is it safe. But it truly is a noble path; one that displays character; one that defines a life" (Harper, 2009).

The competence and compassion of the members of the Canadian Armed Forces are framed in stark contrast to the savages, terrorists, and barbarians who have ruled Afghanistan. This portrayal of Canada, and of Canadians, has several layers. First, as Bell notes, there is more than an element of the "white man's burden" in these depictions. As she argues, the challenges and sacrifices of the Canadian troops evoked by Harper speak of the "burden" assumed by the West in Afghanistan. More specifically, though, "the acclaimed moral character of the West's burden today is derived not merely from an imperative to 'improve' the conditions of Southern populations, but derives from Western values themselves, which are taken to offer the requisite capabilities to achieve success" (Bell, 2010: 65–6). The discourse of Canadian values, particularly when combined with the professionalism of Canada's soldiers, defines Canadian identity as both laudatory and selfless. Stephen Harper makes the point even more strikingly when he noted that "behind every girl now in a classroom, behind every healthy baby in its mother's arms, behind every farmer who can feed his family without taking up arms, behind all of this progress are innumerable acts of heroism, of selfless duty by you, the men and women of the Canadian Armed Forces, our diplomats and our aid workers" (Harper, 2011).

The nature of Canadian internationalism, therefore, is defined by Canada's support for multilateralism, its international engagements and responsibilities, its Western values, and its moral superiority, as well as its professional and compassionate military. As Turenne Sjolander and Trevenen have argued, "The narrative of Canada as good citizen depends on the assumption that Canadians are better equipped than Afghans—equipped not only with material resources like military hardware and development dollars but also with *moral* resources such as courage and professionalism" (2010: 51). Canadian soldiers in Afghanistan are the physical embodiment of Canadian (Western) values. Their hard work and selflessness is unquestionable. Again, without doubting the legitimacy of this assertion, such a construction erases the reality of the work that combat soldiers must do. Maja Zehfuss makes a similar point in her examination of the obituaries of UK armed forces killed in Iraq and Afghanistan. She argues that "[t]he violence that is an inevitable part of the military profession is erased from these obituaries." This draws our attention to a powerful construct: "the understanding of the lives that Western forces end as lives that cannot be grieved, as lives that are not really lives. This differentiation makes it appear as though Western armed forces do not kill, but are killed" (Zehfuss, 2009: 437). Framed as such, the Canadian mission is effectively depoliticized, for the grounds for questioning and opposition have been occulted. In each of Harper's speeches to Canadian troops in Afghanistan, he pays his respect to the fallen soldiers—as one would expect. In his final speech to Canadian soldiers preparing to leave Kandahar, however, he draws the full circle. The proof of Canadian selflessness is to be found in the deaths of its soldiers. He tells the story of a stone maple leaf flag made up of painted rocks in a clearing in Ma'sum Ghar, Afghanistan. "And if you know that flag," he tells the soldiers, "you also know that when a Canadian soldier is killed, a white stone is placed at its base, placed there by comrades, a simple gesture of friendship, of solidarity and of remembrance." It is that flag of stones, Harper goes on to explain, "placed in such a far-flung corner of the world, to the memory of friends," that "reminds us of a great truth about Canada" (Harper, 2011).

Constructions of the "Other"

As the representations of Canadian internationalism illustrate, however, Canada's uniqueness is necessarily defined with respect to an "other." This, of course, is obvious—no country, indeed, no one or nothing, can be unique unto itself. If Canada is an exemplar of middle-power internationalism, it is exemplary as compared to others who are not exemplars, or who are less exemplary. Just as the construction of Canadian internationalism acts to depoliticize the Afghanistan mission, however, so too does it construct the "other" upon which Canadian internationalism has been called to act.

Much has been said by political leaders about the situation confronting Afghan women and children and their need for Canadian rescue. Prime Minister Harper used the situation facing women as a reason to seek the extension of the Canadian mission from 2007 to 2009. He argued that Canadian troops had to stay in Afghanistan so as to "ensure that the rights of the Afghan people are protected. The right of women to be treated as human beings. The right to look at, read and say whatever they want" (Harper, 2006a). Two months earlier, during his first visit to Afghanistan, Harper had noted the progress for women and children made possible by the presence of Canada's troops: "Reconstruction is reducing poverty;

millions of people are now able to vote; women are enjoying greater rights and economic opportunities ... [than] could have been imagined under the Taliban regime; and ... Afghan children... are now in school studying the same things Canadian kids are learning back home" (Harper, 2006b).[3] Canadian soldiers are implicitly constructed as saviours here, riding in on white stallions to restore rights to women and children—and remaining to protect them from any backsliding under Taliban rule.

In 2007, Harper's minister of national defence struck the same chord:

> We are supporting women who, under the Taliban regime, were forbid-
> den to go to school, to work or to vote. Their voices were silenced, and to
> drive home that point, they were beaten for unimaginable things, such as
> for wearing shoes that made noise on the pavement as they walked. We are
> building a future for children, so that they can all be educated, have access to
> medical care, and have the freedom to grow up in a climate of security and
> hope rather than in fear. (MacKay, 2007)

At the same time, Canada's minister of international cooperation was underscoring the point even further: "Women in Afghanistan suffered terribly under the Taliban regime. Previously, they were teachers, doctors, journalists, and homemakers. Then, overnight, they lost the right, not only to practise their profession, but also to leave their homes. Girls did not go to school. Now, things are gradually changing" (Verner, 2007). As Turenne Sjolander and Trevenen have argued with respect to such representations, they are ahistorical (in their claim that rights for women disappeared "overnight" as a consequence of Taliban rule, showing no understanding of the history of women's struggles in Afghanistan over centuries) and blind to the complexity of women's contemporary experiences in Afghanistan. Women are constructed as objects of rescue (2010: 53). Even in his final speech to troops in Kandahar, Harper returned to women and children: "Before [the arrival of Canadian forces], Afghan children remained in ignorance. Now there are more than 150,000 teachers in this country, more than seven times as many as a decade ago. Of them, almost one third are women, providing education to hundreds of thousands of girls to whom it was once cruelly denied" (Harper, 2011).

Through these portrayals, Afghan women and children have no agency; they are constructed as backward and subjugated, in need of rescue from Canadian (Western) men. As Chandra Mohanty has noted, such portrayals conceal a number of colonizing and ethnocentric assumptions: they "construct a uniform representation of an average Third World woman who 'leads an essentially truncated life based on her feminine gender (read: sexually constrained) and her being "Third World" (read: ignorant, poor, uneducated, tradition-bound, domestic, family-oriented, victimized, etc.).' They also constitute the counter-image of the independent, educated, and empowered Western woman" (quoted in Turenne Sjolander and Trevenen, 2010: 54). All the complexity, flexibility, contradictions, and agency found in Afghan women's experiences are erased, while the superiority of Canadian women and of Canadian (egalitarian) society is unquestioningly both constructed and celebrated through these portrayals. Canada's moral superiority is thereby reinforced.

While the plight of women and children is defined as among the most compelling reasons legitimating Canada's intervention in Afghanistan, perhaps the most striking construction of the Afghan "other" is found in the portrayal of the Taliban. They are consistently painted as devoid of humanity and, as a result, as somehow subhuman, or even non-human. They stand as the antithesis of progress and development (at least, as these are defined in Canada and the West). Reflective of Zehfuss's discussion of British soldiers, the Taliban represent the lives that are not really lives, unworthy of respect beyond that dictated by Canadians' own moral sensibilities and the codes of military combat. Speaking before the House of Commons to the motion proposing the extension of Canada's mission to 2009, Harper began to paint the image of the Taliban as evil incarnate, a particularly vile species of subhuman. "Al Qaeda and the Taliban are not interested in peace, Harper argued. "They target civilians, including women and children, in a quest to once again impose their will, and their dark and backward vision of life on the Afghan people. They promise their followers Heaven in the afterlife, they deliver hell on earth" (Harper, 2006a). Harper's minister of defence, Peter MacKay, further elaborated upon the menace of the Taliban: "[T]he Taliban are targeting doctors, they are targeting progress. They are burning schools. They are working to destroy any sign of developmental progress" (MacKay, 2007).

Two years later, the prime minister raised the same theme in his speech to the troops in Afghanistan, further defining the Taliban's inherently evil nature: "Before you came here, the Taliban ran Afghanistan like a mediaeval gulag. They kept ordinary Afghans poor, unhealthy and uneducated; they treated women and girls as sub-human; they subjected people to barbaric punishments; they trampled all freedoms; and they conspired with Al Qaeda to export terrorism around the world" (Harper, 2009). In his final visit to the troops in Kandahar, Harper again portrayed the Taliban regime as the very incarnation of evil; the contrast with the morally superior Canada could not have been made more starkly: "These 9/11 attacks were conceived, planned and prepared here in Afghanistan, here where there were plenty of training camps but very few schools. Here where there were enough places for terrorists to plot to murder and maim, but hardly any hospitals. Here where the vicious Taliban regime bludgeoned its own citizens, but welcomed the world's worst killers; men so immersed in their own evil that they believed their appalling ambitions to be nothing less than the will of God" (Harper, 2011).[4] The Taliban are antithetical to the virtues embodied in Canadian internationalism. They are painted in stark moral terms, constructed as barbaric and inhuman, cruel and backward, amoral (rather than morally inferior) and without any virtue. This moralism would have distressed no less a figure than Hans Morgenthau; as he noted with respect to the US intervention in Vietnam, determining or justifying foreign policy on ideological (or one might add, civilizational) grounds does not lead to sound foreign policy (Cozette, 2008: 17).

The unquestionable justification for Canada's mission in Afghanistan is strengthened in this portrayal of the Taliban, for it re-emphasizes the internationalist discourse of moral superiority and virtue in the face of absolute evil. In defining the Taliban as the very incarnation of evil, however, these political speeches further entrench the notion that the Taliban are a homogeneous and horrific group. These representations, however, mask the complexity of those who identify with the Taliban; as Larry Goodson has described them, "the Taliban are internally divided between various Pashtun tribes and subtribes, ideological moderates and Islamist hard-liners, and native Afghans and Pakistani 'volunteers'" (2001: 125). There is no "one" figure of the Taliban. The difficulty, of course, is that the caricatures of the Taliban constructed in the prime minister's speeches conceal this fact and, at a minimum, are unhelpful in promoting the very orientations that are supposed to be celebrated in Canadian internationalism: a recognition "that civil wars are much more likely to be settled at the negotiating table than on the battlefield" (Regehr, 2010). It was easy, given these constructions of the Taliban, for the Harper government to argue against negotiating with the Taliban—after all, how could it even be conceivable to negotiate with those who are barely human? In 2007, as Regehr reports, Maxime Bernier, then Canada's minister of foreign affairs, put it very succinctly: "Canada does not negotiate with terrorists, for any reason" (Regehr, 2010). One cannot negotiate with those who, in the representations made of them, represent the antithesis of Canadian internationalism and, at the same time, celebrate the inherent virtue of Canada's internationalist identity.

Conclusion

In the end, one needs to ask: what does this all mean? Internationalism is more than a set of foreign policy orientations or strategies for the middle power; it participates in the construction of Canada's national identity. In itself, this is neither a contentious nor a unique observation. Internationalism shapes Canadians' perception and understanding of their role in the world and the reasons for the importance of that role, and in its construction of Canada's foreign policy, it acts as a mirror reflecting the best of Canadians back to themselves, even if the image in the mirror is only aspirational.

The construction of Canadian internationalism has its consequences. Democratic debate is impoverished if Canada is painted as uniquely moral and virtuous. The framing of the Afghanistan mission in internationalist terms constructed an understanding of the motivations and reasons for Canada's intervention that could not be easily contested—Afghanistan was the moral duty of an engaged and responsible middle power, rather than a political choice. Perhaps more importantly, however, the Harper government insisted on portraying the "other" in homogenizing and dehumanizing terms. Ironically, even after claiming that "it has always been our position that [talks with the insurgents] are part of an eventual solution, and that it's not simply military action alone" (Regehr, 2010), Harper continued to paint the Taliban as evil incarnate, as his 2011 speech to Canada's troops reveals. His description of Afghanistan as the place "where the vicious Taliban regime bludgeoned its own citizens, but welcomed the world's worst killers; men so immersed in their own evil that they believed their appalling ambitions to be nothing less than the will of God" (Harper, 2011) hardly constructs the Taliban as worthy negotiating partners.

In this construction, though, the contradiction between the demonization of the "other" and the representation of a virtuous Canada is clear. In the deployment of internationalist rhetoric, founded on the construction of Canada as morally superior and inherently virtuous, the "other" is constructed as less than fully human—as amoral and incapable of virtue. Clearly, then, the deployment of this form of internationalist discourse hardly establishes the basis for the multilateral and deliberative efforts that would lead to the sustainable peace to which Canadian internationalism is both rhetorically and materially committed.

Key Terms

Orientalism
"other"/"othering"
discourse

middle power
depoliticize

Study Questions

1. What is the "great truth" about Canada? Do you accept its validity? Why or why not?
2. How does the discourse of internationalism construct Canadian identity? What are the elements of this identity?
3. Why was the awarding of the Nobel Peace Prize to Lester B. Pearson an important element in shaping Canada's internationalist identity?
4. What are the consequences of the use of internationalist discourse when the government speaks about Canada's military presence in Afghanistan?
5. How and why does the use of internationalist discourse in explaining Canada's intervention in Afghanistan construct Canada as different—and from which countries?

Notes

1   See chapter 5 by Anita Singh for a discussion of how imperialistic and colonial echoes have been present in Canada's foreign policy towards India.

2   As David Black notes (chapter 13) Afghanistan has become an important recipient of Canadian aid since Canada undertook its mission in the country, suggesting a more "strategic, security-oriented approach to aid policy."

3   Carrier and Tiessen make the case in chapter 11 that using women to legitimate Canada's presence in Afghanistan is another example of Canada's "hypocritical internationalism."

4   Harper's references to God, Heaven, and Hell in his description of the Taliban have one other effect: they underscore that the Taliban are part of the "Islamic other," who do not share in the Christian values Harper espouses. For the importance of religion in Canadian foreign policy under Stephen Harper, see chapter 7 by Gecelovsky.

References

Arnold, Samantha. 2010. "Home and Away: Public Diplomacy and the Canadian Self." In J. Marshall Beier and Lana Wylie, eds, *Canadian Foreign Policy in Critical Perspective*. Don Mills, ON: Oxford University Press, 15–26.

Bell, Colleen. 2010. "Fighting the War and Winning the Peace: Three Critiques of the War in Afghanistan." In J. Marshall Beier and Lana Wylie, eds, *Canadian Foreign Policy in Critical Perspective*. Don Mills, ON: Oxford University Press, 58–71.

Black, David, and Claire Turenne Sjolander. 1996. "Multilateralism Re-constituted and the Discourse of Canadian Foreign Policy." *Studies in Political Economy* 49 (Spring): 7–36.

Blanchfield, Mike. 2007. "PM Shines Light on 'Canada at Its Best': Harper Touts Rebuilding of Afghanistan." *Calgary Herald*, 23 May, 23.

Canada. 2007. *Speech from the Throne*. 17 October. At http://www.sft-ddt.gc.ca/eng/media.asp?id=1364.

Cozette, Murielle. 2008. "Reclaiming the Critical Dimension of Realism: Hans J. Morgenthau on the Ethics of Scholarship." *Review of International Studies* 34, 1: 5–27.

Goodson, Larry P. 2001. *Afghanistan's Endless War: State Failure, Regional Politics, and the Rise of the Taliban*. Seattle: University of Washington Press.

Harper, Stephen. 2006a. "Prime Minister Stands by Canada's Commitment to Afghanistan." Ottawa, 17 May. At http://pm.gc.ca/eng/media.asp?category=2&featureId=6&pageId=46&id=1165.

———. 2006b. "Address by the Prime Minister to the Canadian Armed forces in Afghanistan." Ottawa, 13 March. At http://pm.gc.ca/eng/media.asp?category=2&featureId=6&pageId=46&id=1056.

———. 2008. "PM Unveils Revised Motion on the Future of Canada's Mission in Afghanistan." Ottawa, 21 February. At http://pm.gc.ca/eng/media.asp?category=2&featureId=6&pageId=46&id=1995.

———. 2009. "Prime Minister's Address in Kandahar." Kandahar, Afghanistan, 7 May. At http://pm.gc.ca/eng/media.asp?category=2&featureId=6&pageId=46&id=2569.

———. 2011. "Statement by the Prime Minister of Canada." Kandahar, Afghanistan, 31 May. At http://pm.gc.ca/eng/media.asp?id=4150.

Holmes, John W. 1976. *Canada: A Middle-Aged Power*. Toronto: McClelland & Stewart.

———. 1984. "Most Safely in the Middle." *International Journal* 39, 2: 366–88.

MacKay, Gordon. 2007. "Address to the Chateauguay Chamber of Commerce—'The Hard Questions.'" Châteauguay, QC, 17 October. At http://www.forces.gc.ca/site/news-nouvelles/news-nouvelles-eng.asp?id=2485.

Massie, Justin. 2007. "Des mythes tenaces: En matière de politique étrangère, le Canada a réussi à bâtir une série de mythes qui ont contribué au maintien de l'unité nationale." *La Presse—Forum*, 27 March, A31.

Nossal, Kim Richard, Stéphane Roussel, and Stéphane Paquin. 2011. *International Policy and Politics in Canada*. Toronto: Pearson Education Canada.

Razack, Sherene. 2004. *Dark Threats and White Knights: The Somalia Affair, Peacekeeping, and the New Imperialism*. Toronto: University of Toronto Press.

Regehr, Ernie. 2010. "Finally, We're All Talking about Talking to the Taliban." *Embassy Magazine*, 10 November. At http://www.embassymag.ca/page/view/regehr-11-10-2010.

Smith, Heather. 2003. "Disrupting Internationalism and Finding the Others." In Claire Turenne Sjolander, Heather A. Smith, and Deborah Stienstra, eds, *Feminist Perspectives on Canadian Foreign Policy*. Don Mills, ON: Oxford University Press, 24–39.

Stairs, Denis. 2003. "Myths, Morals, and Reality in Canadian Foreign Policy." *International Journal* 58, 2: 239–56.

Turenne Sjolander, Claire. 2009. "A Funny Thing Happened on the Road to Kandahar: The Competing Faces of Canadian Internationalism?" *Canadian Foreign Policy/La politique étrangère du Canada* 15, 2: 78–98.

Turenne Sjolander, Claire, and Kathryn Trevenen. 2010. "Constructing Canadian Foreign Policy: Myths of Good International Citizens, Protectors, and the War in Afghanistan." In J. Marshall Beier and Lana Wylie, eds, *Canadian Foreign Policy in Critical Perspective*. Don Mills, ON: Oxford University Press, 44–57.

Verner, Josée. 2007. "Notes for a Speech by the Honourable Josée Verner, Minister of International Cooperation, at the Breakfast at the Board of Trade of Metropolitan Montreal." Montreal, 2 February. At http://www.acdi-cida.gc.ca/acdi-cida/ACDI-CIDA.nsf/eng/RAC-2511126-LSX.

Zehfuss, Maja. 2009. "Hierarchies of Grief and the Possibility of War: Remembering UK Fatalities in Iraq." *Millennium—Journal of International Studies* 38, 2: 419–40.

CONCLUSION

Canada, the World, and the Inside/ Outside of Internationalism

Claire Turenne Sjolander and Heather A. Smith

A t the end of September 2011, Minister of Foreign Affairs John Baird addressed the United Nations General Assembly and used the occasion to express the principles guiding Canada's foreign policy—the foreign policy of a majority Harper administration.

> Canada does not just "go along" in order to "get along."
> We will "go along," only if we "go" in a direction that advances Canada's values: freedom, democracy, human rights and the rule of law.
> ... The Second World War taught us all the tragic price of "going along" just to "get along."
> It was accommodation and appeasement that allowed fascism to gather strength. As Winston Churchill said: "An appeaser is one who feeds a crocodile, hoping it will eat him last." (Baird, 2011)

The Harper government's Canada would not be an appeaser, trying to avoid conflict or the tough decisions. Whether in the case of North Korea, Libya, the Palestinian Authority, Iran, China, Iraq, Burma, Syria, or Sri Lanka, Canada would not sit idly and wait—potentially in vain—for consensus to emerge from the United Nations.

> While multilateral action should be preferred, failure to achieve consensus must not prevent the willing from acting to uphold human rights and the Founding Principles of the United Nations. [Rather,] [m]ultilateral institutions and multilateral action result from a collection of sovereign decisions based on individual states' own interests: Not narrow self-interest in sovereignty's name, but an expanded view of mutual interest in which there is room for all to grow and to prosper.
> Canada calls this "enlightened sovereignty."
> It is the natural extension of enlightened self-interest. (Baird 2011)

The principles outlined in Baird's speech and the place of the United Nations in Canadian foreign policy might seem to constitute a repudiation of Canada's internationalist tradition. With its clear emphasis on national self-interest and its questioning of UN consensus as the criterion by which Canadian foreign policy action is engaged, Baird's speech appeared to suggest that a majority Harper government was breaking with Canada's foreign policy past.

The lessons of this volume, however, lead us to be far more cautious in determining whether or not the Harper government meets the internationalism litmus test—or indeed, far more cautious in determining whether or not such a litmus test can even be said to exist. Rather, as Heather Smith's review of her experience in teaching the internationalism literature demonstrates, the concept of internationalism has always been constructed, although the meanings associated with internationalism have never been the object of consensus. Our students' nostalgic image of Canada—the helpful fixer, the peacekeeper, the altruistic good international citizen—corresponds to an almost mythical Canada: a country that might have existed in public discourse framed to meet political ends, but a country whose altruism rarely, if ever, lived up to that discourse. Instead, we must see internationalism as a set of discourses and practices, both in the "real world out there" and in the disciplinary world of Canadian foreign policy. How internationalism is understood, interpreted, and deployed in thought and practice mirrors the divides between "inside" and "outside"—inside the boundaries of Canada and outside; inside the state, as bureaucratic or political actors, and outside, as scholars and academics; inside the traditions of the discipline and outside. The meanings associated with internationalism reflect these inside/outside divisions, divisions that are crosscutting and that transcend easy compartmentalization. These inside/outside divisions are reflected in the boundaries that exist in international practice (boundaries that demarcate sovereign states, boundaries that define who is inside and who is outside the state apparatus) and in the discursive boundaries that define academic disciplines (boundaries that attempt to delimit the subject matter of the academic discipline from other disciplines and that seek to prescribe the legitimate field of inquiry for each discipline—whether the field is Canadian foreign policy or any other area of study). Just as these boundaries are constructed, at least to some extent, so too is the concept of internationalism in Canadian foreign policy.

Internationalism: Inside/Outside of Canadian Foreign Policy

One of the central ways in which internationalism is framed throughout this collection is as political practice and policy orientation. Here, the clearest and most often cited reference is that to the five elements of *liberal* internationalism as outlined by Nossal, Roussel, and Paquin (2011: 135–41), which include the responsibility to play a constructive role in international conflict, engagement with multilateral processes rather than unilateral action, involvement in international institutions, a willingness to support these institutions through the deployment of national resources, and a commitment to international law. This understanding of internationalism posits that internationalism guides the practice of Canadian state-craft and implies particular political orientations and the privileging of specific policy choices. When internationalism is understood in such a way, it is possible to speak of the decline of, or the move away from, liberal internationalism under the Harper government, as do Nossal, Massie and Roussel, Boucher, Copeland, Lui, and Singh. Each of these chapters emphasizes the policy orientations or jus-tifications that have been advanced by the Harper government, and evaluates them in terms of the statecraft prescribed by liberal internationalism. Measured against the elements of liberal internationalism outlined by Nossal, Roussel, and Paquin (2011), Canadian foreign policy under the Harper government is found wanting—or at least, found to have changed. In chapter 2 of this volume, Nossal argues that both a Manichaean and an instrumental view of world affairs guide the Harper government, where foreign policy is at once a struggle between good and evil and an instrument that can be used to advance a domestic partisan agenda. Even where Canada's foreign policy can be perceived as responding to the multi-lateral commitments inherent in an internationalist policy (Canada's mission in Afghanistan is, after all, under UN auspices), Nossal reminds us that the Harper government has not chosen to explain or justify these policies by reference to the Canadian tradition of liberal internationalism—in part, to distinguish itself from everything "Liberal."

For their part, Massie and Roussel argue in chapter 3 that liberal interna-tionalism is giving way to a neocontinentalist orientation in Canadian foreign policy, where the expression of hard power and the commitment to maintaining a privileged relationship with the United States (for whom the expression of hard power matters) trump liberal internationalist orientations supporting multilateral processes and international organizations. In chapter 4, Boucher argues that while the Harper government has not completely alienated itself from broad internationalist principles, the internationalism that motivates this government is not that most closely identified with liberal internationalism; rather, Boucher contends, the Harper government's foreign policy represents another strand of internationalism—realist internationalism—as manifested in the government's decision to reject R2P and, through that rejection, in its insistence on the primacy of national interests in foreign policy-making. According to both chapters 3 and 4, liberal internationalism as a handbook for Canadian statecraft is being replaced by another set of guiding principles. Whether or not these new principles—be they neocontinentalist or realist internationalist—produce better or worse policy outcomes is not the issue; rather, the point is that liberal internationalism is no longer the overarching political practice defining Ottawa's foreign policy orienta-tion under the Harper government.

In chapter 8, writing from the perspective of an insider charged with carry-ing out Canada's foreign policy, Copeland points to a dismantling of Canada's internationalist legacy. This dismantling is not only reflected in Canada's lack of meaningful engagement in the pursuit of collaborative international solutions, elements that Copeland argues are the very hallmarks of internationalism, but also in the "radical downsizing" of the Canadian state, with the foreign policy bureaucracy (in its largest sense) bearing a disproportionate weight of the cuts. Assessing a specific example of foreign policy disengagement, Lui argues in chapter 6 that the pullback from liberal internationalism as a guide to Canadian statecraft has had real consequences for the management of Canada's relationship with China. A move away from the meaningful international engagement highlighted by Copeland, a retrenchment in foreign policy priorities towards a focus on Canada's traditional relationships (most notably with the United States and the European Union) and select new ones (in the Americas), and a disengagement with the international community more broadly have left Canada with few, if any, levers to influence China's human rights record meaningfully or even to manage the Canada-China relationship successfully. For Copeland and Lui, the decline (or disappearance) of liberal internationalism as the defining trademark of Canadian foreign policy has had clear and negative consequences.

While still seeing a shift in Canada's foreign policy away from liberal internationalism under the Harper government, Anita Singh argues in chapter 5 that in the development of the Canada-India relationship, such a change has been positive. The guide to Canadian statecraft offered by liberal internationalism, Singh tells us, qualified the nature of Canada's engagement with India—and that qualifier was paternalistic. The Canadian "father knows best" attitude, particularly evident in the imposition of sanctions by Canada against India after the latter's nuclear weapons tests, was part of the liberal internationalist project. For Singh, liberal internationalism is not only a commitment to a particular form of international engagement that privileges multilateral processes, it is also a guide to statecraft that advances a specific (Western) normative agenda—a values-based and, in Singh's words, an imperialist internationalist agenda. Moving away from liberal internationalism to a less normatively (or at least, to a differently) based mutually beneficial economic relationship has put the management of the Canada-India bilateral agenda on an entirely different footing.

As argued above, all of these chapters "read" liberal internationalism as political practice and policy orientation. Liberal internationalism, therefore, is something the state "does" or practices. It implies that the Canadian state privileges certain actions and particular fora (notably the United Nations) in the pursuit of its international political agenda. Liberal internationalism is evaluated on the basis of what the Canadian state does and the orientations it brings to the formulation and implementation of foreign policy. While Copeland's chapter is perhaps the clearest expression of a critique of the demise of liberal internationalism from the "inside" (inside the state and the machinery of government), each of these chapters—alongside others in this volume—locates internationalism within and produced by the state.

Other chapters in this volume locate internationalism more broadly, finding important societal referents for the emerging form of Canada's foreign policy. Here, internationalism ceases to be exclusively state practice and becomes a discourse to be problematized. As discourse, the meanings given to internationalism (and, therefore, the political practices that might or might not be consistent with internationalism) begin to evolve and change. Gecelovsky in chapter 7, for example, traces the impact of evangelical Christianity on the expression of foreign policy under the Harper government. In part through the influence of growing and increasingly vocal (and, at times, politically active) evangelical Christian movements in Canada, traditional liberal internationalism has been modified and stretched into an ethos of "personal responsibility" internationalism. This "stretching" is a discursive one—it is not about political practice in the first instance, but rather about the ways in which internationalism is reframed over time. Predicated on the notion that people need to act in a responsible manner and be a benefit to society in order to be rewarded, Gecelovsky argues that personal responsibility has crept into Canada's foreign policy under the Harper government. The shift to unquestioned support for Israel, for example, has been encouraged and endorsed by a number of conservative Christian organizations, as have the policies developed around women's rights (notably access to abortion and the definition of the family and of marriage). For Gecelovsky, Harper's personal religious values are mirrored by those of conservative Christian movements, and these groups contribute to the construction of a new form of Canadian internationalism.

We see a similar example of "stretching" internationalism through an examination of the changes in societal attitudes and values. In chapter 11, Carrier and Tiessen elaborate the case of maternal health in more detail and point to the phenomenon of conservative groups applying pressure to push forward an agenda that limits women's access to family planning. This leads them to critique Harper's policies as being an example of hypocritical internationalism. Black, in chapter 13, also points to the importance of societal changes in identifying declining popular support for foreign aid as a conditioning factor enabling the decline—if not the demise—of Cranford Pratt's humane internationalism. Foreign policy practice cannot be thought of as only residing "inside" the narrow boundaries of the state or as being "led" by only those state actors.

In chapter 10, Kitchen goes beyond thinking of actors "outside the state" in terms of societal groups. Examining the post-9/11 security environment, she identifies a number of sub-national and transnational actors that now have key foreign policy roles in the management of continental security. While she finds that, in the main, the Harper government has not been promoting a foreign policy that can be clearly labelled as internationalist (at least according to the definition provided by Nossal, Roussel, and Paquin), she notes that other actors have been engaging in internationalist foreign policy—certainly in terms of facilitating cooperation and promoting a more just world, as well as a discourse consistent with values of respect for international norms and rules. Kitchen's chapter points to the need to unpack the state and to think outside or beyond its institutional boundaries in order to find compelling instances of the practice of internationalism.

Derived from her teaching experience, Smith's insights into internationalism as a foreign policy concept both fundamentally embedded in state practice and in disciplinary emphasis on the primacy of state-centric analyses (discussed in chapter 1) allow us to understand how the parameters of the traditional discipline of Canadian foreign policy have been constructed. Interrogations into internationalism as political practice clearly lead to an analysis of state policy. While the *political practice* of internationalism leads some authors to evaluate and to critique the state's foreign policy (clearly a central analytical task), problematizing the concept of internationalism allows others to unpack the ways in which it is used as both political and disciplinary discourse framing constructions of Canada and the world.

Internationalism: Inside/Outside Canada and the World

As noted in the introduction and in Smith's chapter, the organization of this volume loosely adopts a Coxian framework based on the divide between problem-solving and critical theory. This does not mean that, for us, some of the authors in this volume are critical and others are not—far from it. All the chapters engage in an important critique, whether from the inside or the outside, however those boundaries are defined. In this volume, however, we do see a divide between those who understand internationalism as a series of foreign policy choices or orientations, privileging the state, and those who evaluate internationalism as a discursive practice, used to stake out political ground. Internationalism is thus a set of conceptual markers as much as a set of policy choices, and the disciplinary divide (the inside and the outside of the traditional or mainstream discipline) is not as clear as one might think. Nossal, for example, while clearly evaluating state practice under the government, also sees internationalism as a discourse that frames a particular understanding of Canadian identity. If we move beyond internationalism as state practice, however, the extent to which internationalism is a slippery concept for which there are no real markers is revealed—many things can be evaluated discursively as "internationalist" just as easily as not.

Smith's examination of internationalism as a concept leads her to question the effects of its use in the discipline of Canadian foreign policy. She argues that accepting internationalism as state practice (whether or not this acceptance is ever articulated or acknowledged clearly) blinds us to sites of resistance. Unpacking the case of climate change and the Arctic, she finds voices outside the state (the Inuit Tapiriit Kanatami, for example) that fundamentally contradict the Harper government's policy choices with respect to the range of issues (from climate change through sovereignty claims) touching the Arctic. In locating these possibilities for resistance, Smith problematizes internationalism as fundamentally state-centric, race neutral, and a concept that pushes both state and academic critics to a level of analysis that abstracts from the real experience of humans on the ground. Internationalism as state practice blinds us—whether practitioners or scholars—to people and the way in which they live in the world.

Salter's dismissal of internationalism, multilateralism, or middlepowermanship (in chapter 9) leads us to another insight about the consequences of using internationalism as a lens through which we see political practice. Similar to Kitchen's unpacking of internationalism and the state, Salter's dismissal of internationalism allows him to see places and spaces—around the awarding of passports and visas or the creation of preclearance facilities in Canadian airports for US-bound travellers—where the construction of citizens, the identification of the deserving (and not), and the location of borders lose the meanings that internationalism as state practice would attribute to them. Salter's analysis allows us to see that internationalism is predicated on an inside (territorial boundaries) and an outside. The cases he explores confuse the location of the inside and the outside (is someone waiting in a Canadian airport departure lounge, having passed through US immigration control, inside Canada or outside?) and, in so doing, stretch the conceptual limits of internationalism—potentially beyond the breaking point.

In chapter 14, Turenne Sjolander examines internationalism as political discourse, and in ways similar to Smith, she seeks to unpack what its deployment constructs (in terms of Canada's identity in the world) and what it conceals. Using Harper's speeches on Canada's intervention in Afghanistan, she finds that while the tropes of internationalism construct Canada as a benevolent and altruistic saviour of the Afghan people, they rest on gendered, racialized, and colonial assumptions. Much more than simply political practice, the language of internationalism both constructs Canada as laudable and constructs others in the world as far less so. The inside and outside of internationalism as state practice that Salter and Smith (among others) effectively challenge are complemented with a new inside and outside inherent to internationalism—inside Canada and outside in the world. If internationalism serves to construct a laudable Canada for those who live within its traditional (and unproblematized) borders, it can *only* do so through the construction of a violent and backward (or uncivilized) world upon which Canada's benevolence can act.

Black's analysis also uses internationalism as a descriptor of Canadian identity. Focusing on Pratt's elaboration of the concept of humane internationalism, he traces the evolution of the markers of internationalism within Canadian society. Internationalism is not merely state practice, for as we have seen in Gecelovsky above, foreign policy (internationalist or not) is defined within parameters that stem from the social context in which policy is made. For Black, (humane) internationalism needs to be thought of as an ethical frame that conditions foreign policy, and this ethical frame has been eroding for at least two decades—since well before the arrival of the Harper government to office. Without this erosion, however, there would be no possibility of a Harper foreign policy that would be seen as a betrayal of Canada's internationalist traditions.

We see a similar critique of the erosion of the ethical frame of humane internationalism in the chapter by Carrier and Tiessen. Using a gender lens to unpack

Harper's maternal health initiative, the authors demonstrate the extent to which the Harper government's efforts to project concern for the lives of women and children are at best window dressing designed to make a segment of the Canadian population feel good about the actions of its government "in the world." Maternal health initiatives disconnected from gendered realities (as seen in South Sudan) have no hope of addressing any serious concerns with respect to maternal health. In refusing to take gender seriously (and more than that, in refusing to acknowledge gender—rather than men and women—as a serious issue of concern), the government's initiatives cannot assist the very women they pretend to help.

The chapters of this volume ask what Canada is doing, of course, but they also ask what "Canada" and its multiple voices are saying (or not). Internationalism is not only about political practices or policy orientations; it is about constructing Canadian identity in the world. Internationalism as discursive practice conceals within it a set of values that contribute to the construction of a Canadian identity. These chapters suggest that what we say about ourselves, what we say about how we understand the world, and thus how we understand our identity to be constructed are critical in evaluating the importance of internationalism not only for the field of Canadian foreign policy, but for Canada.

Concluding Comments

In the end, then, what and where is Canadian internationalism under a Harper government? At one level, the chapters in this volume suggest that this is not necessarily the right question. Internationalism is both political practice *and* discourse, and as discourse, internationalism embodies values that have—at least historically—contributed to a definition of Canadian identity as benign, helpful, and altruistic. It is the conflation between the political practices and policy orientations of internationalism (as elaborated in the Nossal, Roussel, and Paquin definition of the term) and the discourses of internationalism that makes the concept both so malleable and in such need of unpacking. Once we take internationalism seriously as a set of ideas, always evolving, knowing what internationalism *is* becomes more problematic, for context—both the narrow context of the Canadian state and the broad context of Canadians' understanding of themselves, the world, and the relationship between the two—begins to matter.

While the Harper government might represent a new chapter in the evolution of Canadian internationalism, this volume points to the extent to which it is impossible to state categorically what that new chapter might conclude or where the subsequent chapters might lead. The authors of this volume have invited us on a journey that explores the different ways in which we might understand internationalism—as practice, as discourse, or as largely irrelevant. The answers are as different as are the authors and the different theoretical perspectives they have adopted. In being taken on this journey, though, we are challenged to confront the theoretical lenses we all bring to bear in understanding Canada in the world.

References

Baird, John. 2011. "Address by the Honourable John Baird, Minister of Foreign Affairs, to the United Nations General Assembly," New York City, 26 September. At http://www.international.gc.ca/media/aff/speeches-discours/2011/2011-030.aspx?lang=eng&view=d.

Nossal, Kim Richard, Stéphane Roussel, and Stéphane Paquin. 2011. *International Policy and Politics in Canada*. Toronto: Pearson Education Canada.

Glossary of Key Terms

agent-structure debate At the heart of this debate, in the context of Canadian foreign policy, is the question of how much manoeuvrability and room for "independent" action the Canadian state has relative to the influence of the international system and external determinants.

Arctic card In the context of Canadian politics, "playing the Arctic card" refers to the attempt by Canadian political leaders to appeal to the unique place that the Arctic plays in the nationalist imagination, particularly in English-speaking Canada, by pursuing policies that stress defending Canada's North against the predations, real or constructed, of other powers in the international system.

biopolitics Governance of populations (rather than individuals or groups) such as the ill, the perverse, the criminal, the poor, or the mobile through statistical means, inspired by the work of Foucault.

Chrétien doctrine on human rights The principle that trade and commercial interests will be pursued parallel to, rather than being contingent upon, differences and concerns over human rights in the conduct of Canadian foreign policy.

Comprehensive Economic Partnership Agreement (CEPA) Essentially a free trade agreement. However, the term "free trade" suggests open or unrestricted access between markets. A CEPA allows countries to control which industries and sectors are open to free trade.

concealed perspective Epistemological and ontological assumptions that underpin and shape the study of Canadian foreign policy.

conservatism A political attitude standing on the right side of the political spectrum, notably based on scepticism towards the ability of the state to correct, by social engineering measures, socio-economic disparities.

continentalism A Canadian foreign policy approach based on the assumption that the destiny of Canada (both the society and the state) is inextricably tied to that of the United States, and that it is in Canada's national interest to align itself openly with its southern neighbour to guarantee its access to the American market and keep a functional and friendly relationship with Washington.

cosmopolitanism The belief that states can pursue altruistic ends based on their membership in an international community and on cosmopolitan values such as "the satisfaction of global or human needs; . . . the respect of universal human rights; and the importance of moderation, communication, generosity, and cooperation in international affairs" (Melakopides, 1998: 4–5; see chapter 4 of this volume).

counter-consensus A term originally coined by Cranford Pratt (1983–4; see chapter 13 of this volume) to refer to the "substantial number of internationally minded public interest groups which are in serious opposition to many components of the present consensus which underlies Canadian foreign policy" on broadly humanitarian grounds. These groups became an increasingly prominent influence in debates about Canadian foreign policy beginning in the late 1960s. They included church-based groups, labour groups, solidarity groups, and many development non-governmental organizations.

critical theory Associated with the neo-Gramscian approach of Canadian scholar Robert Cox, who argued that international relations are marked by a division between problem-solving theory and critical theory. Critical theory critiques the existing world order, challenges the status quo, uncovers hidden manifestations of hegemony, and is informed by an emancipatory project.

defence against help The idea that in order to preserve its own security while maintaining its sovereignty, Canada (or any small country) must meet the security standards of the United States (or its larger neighbour).

depoliticize To remove something from its political context or to remove its political content. Something that is depoliticized is no longer debatable; it simply exists as reality or truth.

development assistance Also known as foreign aid or ODA (official development assistance). A post-WWII innovation, these are transfers of financial and technical assistance to "less developed countries" with the formal aim of promoting their "development" and alleviating poverty. In practice, these objectives have virtually always been combined with more self-interested diplomatic, security, and economic motivations.

diplomacy A non-violent approach to the management of international relations characterized by dialogue, negotiation, and compromise.

discourse A way of thinking that is revealed through language. Discourses affect our views on all things; they frame or define the ways we speak about issues. Discourses are seen to define the reality of the way things are.

dominant idea In the context of foreign policy, the broad currents of ideas, values, and concepts that dominate debates and discussions about a country's proper place in global politics at any particular time.

erasure of gender/degendering process A concept introduced by Janine Brodie and Isabelle Bakker to characterize the delegitimization, dismantling, and disappearance of gender issues in Canadian domestic (and, as Carrier and Tiessen argue in chapter 11, foreign) policy. The degendering process can be associated with "the priority given to market accountability and sound macroeconomics. Questions of social cohesion, poverty reduction, social and gender justice have taken on a secondary import; any attention to these issues is seen as conditional to the realization of a sound fiscal picture" (Brodie and Bakker, 2008: 8; see chapter 11 of this volume).

ethnopolitics Most commonly a reference to the role ethnic identity plays in domestic politics. It can be used as a critical term describing the politicization of ethnic differences for political/electoral gain.

everyday practice An international relations feminist perspective that encourages us to challenge dominant ideas about how we study and whom we study in international relations. Everyday practice reminds us that international politics, and thus Canadian foreign policy, takes place in everyday locations often hidden in the abstractions of the state.

field Bourdieusian "thinking tool" that focuses analytic attention on a set of practices and everyday beliefs that is not limited by formal institutions.

gender equality Understood as the equitable impact of society on the rights, freedoms, and interests of women. Gender equality is a goal endorsed by the 1995 Development Assistance Committee High Level Meeting, which defined it as "an overall strategic objective for promoting the role of women and therefore sustainable, people-centred development." Gender equality was also referred to in the 1995 Beijing Declaration as "women's empowerment and their full participation on the basis of equality in all spheres of society, including participation in the decision-making process and access to power."

global citizenship Defined by Rebecca Tiessen (2011; see chapter 13 of this volume) as "a way of understanding the world in which an individual's *attitudes and behaviours* reflect a compassion and concern for the marginalized and/ or poor and for the relationship between poverty and wealth—within and between communities, countries and regions."

global mobility regime A loose connection of regulations, treaties, and practices that structure and govern international population movement.

Harper doctrine on human rights The principle that Canada's international human rights policies will be contingent on a geopolitical emphasis away from China and the Asia Pacific in favour of closer ties with the US, strengthening old bonds with Britain and the EU, and the possibility of forging new ones with emerging markets in Latin America and India.

heteropolarity An emerging poly-centric world system in which competing states or groups of states derive their relative power and influence from dissimilar sources—social, economic, political, military, cultural.

humane internationalism An element of Canada's (and some other countries') political culture(s) defined by "an acceptance of an obligation to alleviate global poverty and to promote development in the Less Developed Countries; a conviction that a more equitable world would be in [developed countries'] real long-term interests; and an assumption that the meeting of these international responsibilities is compatible with the maintenance of socially responsible national economic and social welfare policies" (Pratt, 1989: 16; see chapter 1 and elsewhere in this volume).

human rights Those rights to which a person is entitled simply because he or she is a human being. Human rights can also be described as equal (the same for all human beings), inalienable (they cannot be transferred or repudiated, as one does not stop being human), and universal (applicable to everyone).

hypocritical internationalism Hypocritical internationalism characterizes the conduct of a state that seeks to acquire international prestige through the vociferous promotion of values and humanitarian moral standards, when the behaviour of the state is not in conformity with the discourse it proclaims on international platforms.

ideology A system of political thought arising out of, and reflecting, the economic, political, and cultural experience of particular social groups.

intermestic An issue that is at once domestic and international.

internationalism As shown by this volume, this concept has no one definition and is subject to multiple, competing definitions. Copeland, in chapter 8, uses internationalism to mean a predisposition towards meaningful engagement with peoples, organizations, and states abroad in the pursuit of collaborative international solutions to identified problems and challenges. Nossal, in chapter 2, in contrast, links internationalism to liberal political values that underpin the concept and focuses on characteristics such as multilateralism, involvement with and support of international institutions, respect for international law, a willingness to use national resources to support the international system, and a willingness to play a constructive role in international politics.

internationalism lite A somewhat pejorative characterization of the policy of the government of Jean Chrétien, which embraced the rhetoric of internationalism but actually reduced significantly Canada's contributions to the international system, primarily through budget cuts.

International Political Sociology (IPS) School Group of scholars in critical security studies who investigate actual policy practices and whose work is inspired by Bourdieu and his notions of *field*.

Khalistan "Land of the Pure"—the projected territory envisioned by a separatist movement to create an independent state for Sikhs. Geographically, this may include sections of "Greater Punjab," including Punjabi-speaking regions of current-day Pakistan.

localization of security The process by which local actors, such as police officers or cities, gain more responsibility over security policy.

Manichaeanism A religion named for the prophet Mani that spread from Persia to Europe in the third century AD. Because Manichaean teachings focused on a struggle between the spiritual world of goodness and light and the material world of evil and darkness, the term is used today figuratively to describe a worldview that simplistically reduces world politics to a dualistic struggle between good and evil.

maternal health The World Health Organization defines maternal health as the "health of women during pregnancy, childbirth and the postpartum period." Improving maternal health is one of the eight Millennium Development Goals (MDGs) adopted by the international community in 2000. Under MDG 5, countries made the commitment to reduce maternal mortality by three-quarters between 1990 and 2015. The high number of maternal deaths in some areas of the world reflects gender inequities in access to health services and highlights the gap between rich and poor. Almost all maternal deaths (99 per cent) occur in developing countries. More than half of these deaths occur in sub-Saharan Africa, and one-third in South Asia.

Message Event Proposal Prior to speaking in public, any member of the Harper government or civil service is required to submit a plan outlining the speaking objective, desired newspaper headline and sound bite, speaking backdrop, and speaker's wardrobe, as well as the ideal event photograph.

middle power The idea of middle power was initially promoted after the Second World War as a way to convince Canadians that they had a responsibility to remain engaged in the international arena. Larger than a small power, a middle power possesses the resources and skills that make it a valuable player on the world stage.

multilateralism As a practice, multilateralism is an instrument through which foreign policy pursues different ends. It is a support and preference for multilateral dealings where more than two states engage in a collaborative relationship to define or diffuse political issues.

Muskoka Initiative The Muskoka Initiative is the program of action announced by the Harper government to address the Millennium Development Goal on maternal health (MDG 5) at the Huntsville G8 Summit. Through the Muskoka Initiative, Canada is providing $1.1 billion in new funding between 2010 and 2015 towards maternal health. It is also providing $1.75 billion in ongoing spending on maternal and child health programming, the total contribution being $2.85 billion. The focus of the initiative is on three paths: strengthening health systems, reducing the burden of diseases, and improving nutrition. CIDA's investments in maternal health are concentrated in 10 countries: Afghanistan, Bangladesh, Ethiopia, Haiti, Malawi, Mali, Mozambique, Nigeria, Sudan, and Tanzania.

national brand A generalized but widely shared sense of the essential elements of a country's image, reputation, identity, and performance.

neocontinentalism The geographical and functional expansion of "continentalism," outside North America and across a larger spectrum of activities (including diplomacy, trade, environment, and forward security), driven by a neoconservative ideology.

non-aligned movement/bloc An alliance created by developing states in the early Cold War years that chose not to be aligned with either the Eastern or the Western bloc.

Orientalism A concept associated with Edward Said's work *Orientalism*, in which he argues that Western scholars (among others in the West) defined the Oriental non-West as being the opposite of the West. As Colleen Bell summarizes, "the 'Oriental' is regarded as irrational, depraved, conflictual/violent, illiberal, childlike, animal-like, different, while the European [or Westerner] is none of these but is rational, virtuous, peaceful, liberal, logical, mature, normal" (Bell, 2010: 66; see chapter 14 of this volume).

"other"/"othering" The process by which societies and groups define themselves. Societies and groups that are deemed to be "others" are excluded, for they are seen as not fit within a particular society or group. Identity depends in part on the presence of "others," and this is arguably particularly important in the case of national identities. "Othering" allows national societies to define those who are part of "us" and those who are not; those who are worthy of the rights and advantages "we" share and those who are not. In so doing, "othering" or the identification of "others" helps to define the differences between one society and another.

Parable of the Good Samaritan A hypothetical story found in the Bible (Luke 10) that stresses the responsibility of each person to ensure the well-being and health of other members of the community.

Parable of the Talents A hypothetical story found in the Bible (Matthew 25) that centres on the notion that individuals are personally responsible for their own position in society.

paradiplomacy Diplomacy practised by governments other than the central government, such as provinces, states, or cities.

Pearsonian internationalism The tendency to identify the internationalist approach to foreign policy with Lester B. Pearson, Canada's foreign minister from 1948 to 1957. For his diplomacy during the Suez Crisis of 1956, he was awarded the Nobel Peace Prize the following year.

personal responsibility internationalism States that make proper choices and use their resources (talents) in a responsible manner are rewarded and deemed a benefit to the international community.

positivism A set of assumptions about how one engages in research that privileges the "scientific" method. An emphasis is placed on scholarly objectivity and neutrality, the separation of subjects and objects, and the identification of universal laws and patterns. In contrast to post-positivism, which regards reality as socially constructed, positivism assumes scholars are not separate from what and whom they study and eschews assumptions about universally applicable laws, patterns, and truth claims.

public diplomacy A model of diplomatic practice that seeks to achieve specified outcomes through direct communication with foreign populations, often in partnership with elements of civil society.

public internationalism Used differently depending on the author, public internationalism is typically associated with attitudes held by the Canadian public and/or activities engaged in by members of the Canadian public that reflect central tenets of internationalism.

quiet diplomacy Confidential, closed-door discussions between ministerial officials, often concerning contentious issue areas that government parties would prefer to discuss in private with minimal public scrutiny.

realist internationalism The dominant idea that argues that Canadian foreign policy should be aligned to the country's national interests. Considering the evolving nature of such interests, such a foreign policy should be conducted on a case-by-case basis. That being said, its internationalist foundation asserts forcefully that such interest, however egoistical in nature, can best be met through a commitment to multilateralist cooperation (in an instrumental sense), a sense of responsibility, and a support for international law.

Responsibility to Protect "The idea that sovereign states have a responsibility to protect their own citizens from avoidable catastrophe, but that when they are unwilling or unable to do so, that responsibility must be borne by the broader community of states" (ICISS, 2001: 8; see chapter 4 of this volume).

securitization The process by which an issue previously not seen as a security issue comes to be seen as one.

smart borders Border policies structured by a risk management framework that facilitate certain kinds of movements by certain kinds of subjects as much as they incarcerate or channel other kinds of movements by other kinds of subjects.

social gospel A movement and tradition originating in some North American Protestant churches in the early twentieth century that sought to apply the principles of the Gospel to society's most pressing problems and thereby promote social justice and progressivism. The social gospel was a significant influence in Canadian politics, most directly within the Co-operative Commonwealth Federation that later became the New Democratic Party, but in other party-political traditions as well.

strategic culture A distinctive, dominant, and persistent system of ideas and practices regarding international security held by a socio-political community.

strategic partnership A general term used to describe an exclusive arrangement between two or more state parties for the purposes of achieving specific outcomes on high-level issues of mutual concern such as, but not limited to, security, trade, investment, energy, human rights, and the environment.

the three Fs of faith, family, and freedom These traditional values comprise the core of Prime Minister Stephen Harper's ethical calculus and are at the heart of personal responsibility internationalism.

two-nation thesis Founding ideology of Pakistan that argues that Hindus and Muslims constitute two separate nations and could not peacefully co-exist within a unified, independent India.

Index

gender equality, 184, 266; hypocrisy and, 195; lack of in Muskoka Initiative, 187–8; removing reference to, 189–90
genocide, 65
Gilley, Bruce, 93
globalization, 135, 138
global mobility regime, 147, 266
global studies programs, in universities, 228, 230
Global Warming Solutions Act, 166
Golden Temple in Amritsar, 79–80
Goodson, Larry, 251
Gotlieb, Allan, 56
Graham, Bill, 132, 150
Gray Lecture, 4–5, 53
greenhouse gas (GHG) emissions, 27–8
Group of Eight (G8), 60; meeting in Huntsville, 132, 184; meeting in Heiligendamm, 219
Group of 20 (G20), 60; Summit in Toronto, 132, 172, 230
Guantanamo Bay, 175, 176
Gwyn, Sandra, 21

Hagee, John, 119
hard power: neocontinentalism and, 48
Harper, Stephen, 46, 168; on abortion, 29; Africa policy and, 222–4; on aid, 223; cabinet and caucus and, 110, 224; on Canada's peaceful nature, 243–4; on Canada's pursuit of middle-power diplomacy, 29; on Canada–US relations, 47–8, 177; on Canadian foreign policy, 22, 53; on Canadian troops, 246–7; Colombia and, 96; faith and politics of, 108, 109–11, 111–17; family and, 114; freedom and, 114; on marriage, 114; message control, 110; on multilateralism, 244–5; partisanship and, 223–4; Preston Manning and, 114–15; on progress of Afghan women and children, 248–9; pro-Western worldview, 223; special interest groups and celebrity diplomats and, 223; value system of, 46, 112–14, 117; visit to China, 101; visit to India, 79–80; visit to Kandahar, 238, 241–2
Harper doctrine on human rights, 94, 266
Hart, Michael: *From Pride to Influence*, 44
Health Canada, 209
Healy, Teresa and Sheila Katz, 219
Heinbecker, Paul, 53, 56, 57

Here for Canada (2011 Conservative election platform), 62
heteropolar/heteropolarity, 137, 141n24, 266
Heubert, Robert, 207
Hillier, Rick, 111
HMS *Birkenhead*, 183
Holding the Bully's Coat (McQuaig), xiii–xiv, 21–2
Holmes, John, 29, 43, 97–8, 171, 242; on internationalism, 57, 72, 97, 165; on middle power, 239, 241; "Most Safety in the Middle", 5–6
Howard, John, 27
Huebert, Robert, 209, 212
Hu Jintao, 94, 101
Human Development Report (UNDP), 220
humane internationalism, 7, 59, 109, 121, 225–6, 230, 232n2, 259, 261, 266; decline of, xvi–xvii, xxv, 225–31; opinion of political and social elites, 227–8; organized religion and, 229–30; public opinion and, 227
human rights, 91, 267; China and, 90, 91–2, 100
Human Security Agenda, 130
hypocrisy, 189, 195; gender equality and, 195; Harper's stand on abortion and, 189–90

identity, Canadian, 138, 238; Canadian Armed Forces and, 249; defined by reference to "other", 241; internationalism and, 31, 241–2, 245–6, 251, 260, 261, 262; mission in Afghanistan and, 242, 246–7; nostalgic, xiv, 256; as peaceful, 243–4; as virtuous, 252
ideology, 37–8, 267; neocontinentalism and, 49
Ignatieff, Michael, 66–7, 142n26
immigrants: support for Conservatives, 116
immigration, 79, 137
Immigration and Customs Enforcement (ICE) (US), 169
Immigration and Refugee Board, 155, 156
Immigration and Refugee Protection Act, 79
imperialism, British Canadian, 39–40, 41
Implementing the Responsibility to Protect (Ban Ki-moon), 63–4
India, 131; in Afghanistan, 85; immigrants to Canada, 79; independence of, 71, 74;

Universal Declaration of Human Rights,
149, 151
US Coast Guard, 169, 170
US Council on Foreign Relations, 99

values, 55; Canadian, 242, 245–6, 248;
Canadian identity and, 245–6;
cosmopolitan, 55–6, 58, 59, 64, 66, 217;
international, 74; neocontinentalism
and, 46; projection of, 74–6, 84;
Western, 74–5, 247, 248
Van Loan, Peter, 221, 222
violence: gender-based, 188; sexual, 186–7
visas, 154–6
voluntarism, 202

Walters, William, 149, 150
Watt-Cloutier, Sheila, 211
Weber, Max: *Objectivity in Social Science
and Social Policy*, 55

Wells, Paul and John Geddes, 26
Welsh, Jennifer, 56
Wen Jiabao, 101
Western alienation, 40
"white man's burden", 205, 247; nuclear, 76
"Whither Internationalism" (Munton), 7, 8
Wolfe, Robert, 96
women: in Afghanistan, 248–50;
representations of Third World,
249–50; reproductive rights, 119–21;
violence against, 186–7, 188
Woodsworth, J.S., 113

youth: global citizenship and, 231; voters,
233–4n21

Zalewski, Marysia, 12, 201
Zehfuss, Maja, 248
Zhu Rongji, 94
Zimbabwe, 222